Religious Culture in Modern Mexico

Celebration of the Patroness of Nochixtlan, Oaxaca, Our Lady of the Assumption, 1955. Over the course of a long career as a small-town photographer, Zanabria produced a remarkable photographic record of twentieth-century rural life in Oaxaca. Note the men carrying large, heavy candle offerings. Photographed by Ignacio Zanabria. (Source: Centro Fotográfico Álvarez Bravo, Fondo Ignacio Zanabria)

Religious Culture in Modern Mexico

Edited by Martin Austin Nesvig

ROWMAN & LITTLEFIELD PUBLISHERS, INC.
Lanham • Boulder • New York • Plymouth, UK

ROWMAN & LITTLEFIELD PUBLISHERS, INC.

Published in the United States of America
by Rowman & Littlefield Publishers, Inc.
A wholly owned subsidiary of The Rowman & Littlefield Publishing Group, Inc.
4501 Forbes Boulevard, Suite 200, Lanham, Maryland 20706
www.rowmanlittlefield.com

Estover Road, Plymouth PL6 7PY, United Kingdom

British Library Cataloguing in Publication Information Available

Library of Congress Cataloging-in-Publication Data
Religious culture in modern Mexico / edited by Martin Austin Nesvig.
    p. cm. — (Jaguar books on Latin America)
  Includes bibliographical references and index.
  ISBN-13: 978-0-7425-3746-0 (cloth : alk. paper)
  ISBN-10: 0-7425-3746-3 (cloth : alk. paper)
  ISBN-13: 978-0-7425-3747-7 (pbk. : alk. paper)
  ISBN-10: 0-7425-3747-1 (pbk. : alk. paper)
  1. Mexico—Religious life and customs. I. Nesvig, Martin Austin, 1968-
  BL2530.M4R45 2007
  200.972—dc22
                                        2006028057

Printed in the United States of America

∞™ The paper used in this publication meets the minimum requirements of
American National Standard for Information Sciences—Permanence of Paper
for Printed Library Materials, ANSI/NISO Z39.48-1992.

Contents

Acknowledgments

In any project, one accumulates a large number of debts and benefits from the input of several different people. This project is no exception. This book was the result of collaboration and collective enterprise, and the contributors of the individual chapters helped to bring the project to fruition. I offer my heartiest thanks and appreciation to all the contributors for their unflagging patience, tremendous collegiality, and dedication to this collaboration. Pamela Voekel and Silvia Arrom, in particular, offered their feedback on numerous levels during this project, and I wish to thank them for their advice and support. The contributors as a whole offered enthusiasm for a project that will, we hope, provoke further discussion, debate, and investigation.

The series editors, Colin MacLachlan and William Beezley, offered crucial support for the project as well as excellent close readings of the material; any success the book may have owes much to their input. One would be hard pressed to find editors who read as carefully and thoughtfully as they have. Susan McEachern has offered her timely advice and shepherded the project to completion. The staff of Rowman & Littlefield, especially Jessica Gribble and Alden Perkins, gave the final stages of the project their closest attention, endured my numerous (and tedious) questions, and tackled numerous technical dilemmas on all fronts.

The College of Arts and Sciences at the University of Miami offered financial support to pay for a professional indexer and thus facilitated the final stages of production. Thanks in particular go to Dean Michael Halleran and Senior Associate Dean Daniel Pals.

On the technological front, Edward Wright-Rios has provided images for this collection that he obtained while conducting research in Oaxaca. He also wrote the helpful captions that adorn the various images interspersed throughout the text; many thanks for his help on this front. The Archivo Histórico de la Aquidiócesis de Oaxaca and the Centro Fotográfico Álvarez Bravo were kind enough to allow us to reproduce several images from their collections.

Paul Vanderwood allowed us to use a photo from his personal collection on Juan Soldado. Finally, David Rumsey of Cartography Associates generously permitted us to reproduce images from Antonio García Cubas's nineteenth-century atlas of Mexico that he has made available to the scholarly community through the David Rumsey Map Collection at www.davidrumsey.com. His munificence offers a fine example for all scholars engaged in collaborative work who share a love for Mexico and its history.

1
Introduction
Martin Austin Nesvig

Townspeople and Bicycle Pilgrims at the Feast of Our Lady of the Assumption, Nochixtlan, Oaxaca, 1971. Photographed by Ignacio Zanabria.

Some one hundred evangelicals in the town of San Nicolás of Hidalgo protested on October 9, 2005, in the state capital, Pachuca, over what they felt were burdensome informal taxes. At stake were community expectations that all members of the small town help with the fiestas of San Nicolás (the patron saint of the town) as well as with celebrations for the Virgin of Guadalupe. Furthermore, all town members were expected to join in a communal cemetery cleaning during the last week of October preceding the Days of the Dead (or All Saints) on November 1 and 2, or pay a fine to the municipality.[1] The evangelicals protested that such expectations violated their constitutional freedom of religion, since such demands effectively made all community members Catholic or punished them monetarily if they chose to be evangelical or Protestant.

More than constitutionality was at stake. Much deeper lies a sense that to be Mexican is to be Catholic; that the Virgin of Guadalupe is the special patroness of Mexico; that she gives favor to its people, nation, and society. It is no accident that in the seventeenth century the phrase *non fecit taliter omni natione* (which is a reference to Psalms 147:20: "God has not done this for every nation," but which can be read also as "He [or She] has not done this for every nation" since the Latin does not specify the subject [or the gender of the subject] of the sentence, and which also implies that Mexico is a new Israel, privileged above other nations) began to appear on Guadalupe images. Religion and communal obligations, responsibilities, and rights have always been deeply embedded in Mexican cultural consciousness. The protests in Pachuca in October last year simply highlight just how deeply entrenched these traditions remain.

1

2   *Martin Austin Nesvig*

This collection—*Religious Culture in Modern Mexico*—examines the cultural, social, and political importance of both church and religiosity in Mexico. No one can study or visit Mexico without being besieged by the religiosity of the culture. This centrality remains despite efforts by various political groups to separate religion from the state and to strip away much of the political power of the church. Indeed, when Pope John Paul II visited in July 2002 to canonize Juan Diego, a massive outpouring of popular devotion literally flooded the streets of Mexico City.

Despite this clear religiosity, North American scholars are sometimes reluctant to discuss religion as a category of analysis for modern Mexico. This country fought two wars over the church and its proper role in society and political affairs in the last two centuries. Even before these wars, in the eighteenth century, reform efforts were under way. Inspired by Enlightenment ideology and Bourbon reforms of the church, there were concerted efforts to strip away the ostentatious and public nature of Catholicism and redirect religion toward inner reflective practices. As Pamela Voekel shows in her study, *Alone before God*, there was a move in this direction in Mexico, symbolized fittingly in attempts to reform burial practices and establish public cemeteries, thus shifting the emphasis of death and burial customs from church control to the public and the secular.[2]

In the 1850s liberals, led by Benito Juárez, strove to disentail the physical property of the church, remove it from the political sphere, nationalize a good deal of its property, and move many previous church-led functions, like marriage, under the auspices of the state. Conservatives opposed these secular innovations—known broadly as the Reform—and the result was a bitter war, ultimately won by the liberals. One of the principal issues was that of *fueros*, or privileges, that protected the clergy and the church from most civil and criminal legal proceedings. Liberals wanted to scrub society free of what they considered religious superstitions like saint propitiation and elaborate pilgrimages, to secularize politics, and to create a modern nation based on constitutional principles. The conservatives called the liberals atheists, socialists, and heretics who would bring the wrath of God down on the nation. The majority of people fell somewhere in between and continue to do so today.

The schism, and the debate that surrounded it, did not die out in the nineteenth century. After the Revolution of 1910–20, under the leadership of President (or—if you were a religious Catholic—dictator) Plutarco Elías Calles, the government strove to enforce a variety of radical anti-church articles of the 1917 Constitution. These articles promoted what was called a Jacobin view of the relationship between church and state—that is, they stripped the church of any political identity and rights, banned religious education, forbade clerics from wearing the collar in public, and gave the state the power to decide how many priests could exist in the population. While Calles may not necessarily have shared the radical Jacobinism of some authors of these constitutional articles (e.g., self-described Jacobins like Francisco Mújica), he did see the church as competing with the state and as such viewed it as a rival for power. In many ways this reconstituted the classical liberal vision of the 1857 generation. This did not, however, stop many from calling him an atheist and antichrist. Militant political Catholics, especially in the center west in Jalisco, Aguascalientes, and Michoacán, ultimately rose in rebellion in a kind of counterrevolution called the Cristiada (or Cristero Revolt) from 1926 to 1929.

Yet even after the much-lauded Reform, the radical Jacobinism of many revolutionaries, like Mújica, and the official program of removing the church from public politics, Mexico City—that emblem of Latin American modernity—remains the home to one of the Catholic world's most visited pilgrimage sites: Tepeyac, home of the Virgin via Mexica goddess, holy site atop a metro stop, modern-day six-lane thoroughfare superimposed on ancient Tenochtitlan's grand *calzada*. The presence of these multifaceted religious, ethnic, and political layers could not be more appropriate, since, despite the assertions of liberal historiography, the Virgin of Guadalupe is the symbolic patroness of a deeply religious society.

One might note that there tends to be a division between the study of religion and the study of politics in this field. One theory for this is posited by Silvia Arrom here in this volume: a Manichean vision of political history in which conservatives were evil and liberals good. There also may be a tacit Jacobinism to North American scholarship of modern Mexico in which religion is viewed not as a valuable analytical category but as a political liability, a vestige of colonial superstition, or an impediment to the goals of social progress. Whether or not Jacobinism is the root of this tendency, religion has not occupied the same level of importance in the broad historiography of modern Mexico by North Americans, who have, in general, been more interested in political ideology, labor, foreign relations, and lately, gender and sexuality.

Another important factor is that historical discussions have often taken a linear view of historical development. Many have (perhaps unwittingly) assumed the conclusions posited by Max Weber quite some time ago—that modernization and secularization of the state fit hand and glove. In other words, to become modern requires the separation of the church from the state. This analytical scheme holds tremendous allure for the trajectory of political history, since the liberals of the 1850s and the revolutionaries of the 1910s and 1920s held to this view. In examining the available scholarly discussions one often finds that this process of secularization is assumed to be an inextricable part of the linear and forward-moving progress of social and political history.

This trajectory, however, was not always so simple nor was it always so linear or ineluctable. Rather, as Mexico became more modern and even as it moved toward a one-party revolutionary state after 1920, religion and religiosity remained deeply embedded in the culture. But even before the Revolution this was the case. The triumph of the liberals did not mean the end of the church. As recent studies have begun to show, there was a Catholic resurgence in the late nineteenth century, countervailing against the dominant trends of liberal politics and secularization campaigns.[3]

The reexamination of religion within the context of modern Mexico is not entirely new, though it remains a discrete, if growing, area of interest for historians. Beginning in 1973 Jean Meyer revolutionized the study of religion in modern Mexico with his broad analysis of the Cristiada.[4] At the time Meyer was one of a few historians to demonstrate deep connections between religiosity and political culture (though the Jesuit Mariano Cuevas promoted a similar, if politically motivated, view in the 1920s).[5] Since the appearance of Meyer's study, the analysis of religion has seen steady growth among historians and sociologists.[6]

This collection adds to this growing scholarship by offering distinct analytical conclusions. First, specific essays in this volume challenge the dichotomous opposition of nineteenth-century liberals and religion. The collection shows that rather than erasure of religiosity from national culture, the late nineteenth century witnessed resurgence of spirituality and Catholic activities.[7] The twentieth century, by comparison, saw the emergence of militant Catholic groups that strove to reassert the political role of Catholicism in light of liberal and revolutionary political victories (and would famously emerge in the Cristiada).

Second, specific essays in this volume reassess the nature of the liberals themselves. While previous works have tended to focus on liberals' anticlerical politics, there tends to be little attention given to the actual religiosity of liberals, many of whom, despite their anticlerical politics, considered themselves to be devout Catholics. Their version of Catholicism, while anticlerical, was utopian and promoted a kind of socially conscious religion in place of a hierarchic and political Catholicism.

Third, religion can be analyzed in relation to political and national processes as well as in specifically spiritual terms. Thus the book argues that religion is so deeply imbricated in everyday life that it cannot be separated from politics and society more generally. In this way it rejects the exclusive distinction between religion and politics. Instead, we show that religion continued to play a vibrant role in society and politics despite the efforts of liberal reforms and revolutionary constitutional changes.

Fourth, in addition to paying attention to the intersection of the political with the religious, this collection examines popular religious phenomena. The problem is how to avoid the hard dichotomy between popular and official religion while still capturing the dynamic relationship between these two ostensible poles of religious thought and practice. The historian of early modern Spain, Carlos Eire, has argued that this distinction is too rigid for effective use as a methodological key. Yet even Eire recognizes that breaking down such a dichotomy involves no small measure of potential confusion, both linguistically and theoretically. In an introductory essay to the collection *Local Religion in Colonial Mexico*—a project with considerable methodological overlap with this present volume—Eire argues that the conceptualization of opposites in Western religious culture is as old as the church itself. The result is a long inheritance for historians of a model that assumes that popular and official are ever in opposition.[8]

This collection also reflects the growing sense among historians of religion in Mexico that while we know a fair amount about the dramatic and formal aspects of religious culture and expression—the cult of Guadalupe, the debate between liberals and conservatives, the Reform and disentailments, the bishops, cardinals, and papacy—we know considerably less about more prosaic expressions of religious culture. This collection does not pretend to resolve once and for all the debate on the role of religion in the culture. By their nature—vignette instead of broad narrative, local rather than national, cultural instead of political—these essays suggest, spur, or evoke future debate, research, and analysis.

Finally, directly or indirectly, this collection draws on conceptions of Catholicism as popular and springing not from papal centrality but rather from the local instead of the universal, of the *consuetudinario* (or customary) rather than the proscriptive.[9] This local character implies further what historian William Christian Jr. calls the "decentralizing entropy" inherent to Catholicism as opposed to its ostensible universalism. Indeed, this volume reiterates one of Christian's principal theses concerning Hispanic Catholicism—that it is "a decentralized, collective, articulated process that serves the spiritual needs of Catholics and perpetuates itself, a community of memory with a particular purpose."[10] Consider the following example. The church and its diocesan authorities, especially after the tenure of the theological conservatism of John Paul II, have insisted time and again that birth control is a sin and that those who engage in it must be excluded from the rites and sacraments of the church. Yet one can purchase birth control pills in virtually any pharmacy in Mexico without a prescription, and this does not seem to be considered particularly offensive or inconsistent.

The contents of this volume range in geographic and epochal scope from the U.S.-Mexico border to the indigenous peoples of Oaxaca in the southern mountains, from the transition from a royal viceregal system to a republic to the era of a one-party national government. The essays have been arranged in largely chronological sequence out of convenience and not for any sense of inherent progression.

SOME NEW SUGGESTIONS FOR STUDY

Matthew O'Hara's essay begins the collection, chronologically at the beginning of independence in 1821. With the abolition of the colonial government and the institution of an independent Mexico, racial categories were abolished by law. O'Hara outlines this tenuous process by examining the locally specific concerns of parish priests in the Valley of Mexico, showing that legally abolishing such categories did not eradicate their use. The major distinction here is methodological. O'Hara analyzes this process, in which racial categories continued to be used, through the lens of parish registries and the attitudes inherent in the still criollo priesthood that administered to largely Indian and mestizo areas. A "confluence of legal, social, and cultural forces thus reproduced the category of *indio* while it was otherwise being eclipsed in civil law." Two republics exist in this assessment: that of the civil world and that of the still strong religious world that until the 1850s remained in much the same form as it had before independence.

The persistence of local religious identities and racial categorization highlights how the colonial-modern, preliberal Catholic, and modern secular dichotomies are challenged. Daniela Traffano's essay analyzes the ways that rural Indian communities in Oaxaca responded to the Reform. Rather than religion and religiosity disappearing, ancient associations of religion with land, community, and property continued despite the efforts of liberals. Traffano examines what she calls the deep history of cultural forms in which the intimate connection between communal property and communal religiosity is difficult to break. When the Reform strove to disentail much church property, many indigenous communities balked at these reforms, since various church institutions, like confraternities, community religious ceremonies, and *mayordomías*, lent Indians a sense of identity and purpose in their communities. Ultimately, communal religious identity in Oaxaca was maintained in a much-altered form. Consequently, newer Catholic associations became the principal organs and overseers of collective religiosity in Oaxaca, with an increasing emphasis on doctrinal instruction and a move away from elaborate public ritual, festival, and confluence of community and church property. But communal religious expression remained strong despite the efforts of the liberals to convince Indians that they should eschew the very forms of religion they insisted on retaining.

Similarly, Silvia Arrom's essay shows that even though liberal reforms sought to curtail and even shut down Catholic political associations, women continued to lead a Catholic revival through lay associations like the Ladies of Charity, associated with the Congregation of the Mission of St. Vincent de Paul. Arrom offers convincing evidence that far from disappearing from the public and civic stage, Catholics played an important role in that same public life. Despite the efforts of the liberal Reform, Catholic organizations remained active and robust in the later nineteenth century. This analysis undermines the narrative stressing the political continuity of liberal secularization and challenges the Weberian vision of modernization being linked inexorably to secular society.

In addition to a reassessment of this linear progressive analysis, two essays in particular reevaluate the liberals themselves. Alejandro Cortazar and Pamela Voekel examine the ways that the liberal reforms were either pushed by deeply religious reformers or were met with resistance at the local level. For example, anticlericalism has been a staple of analysis of the Reform. But can this anticlericalism also be considered antireligion and antispirituality? Cortazar offers an analysis of novels written by liberals like Ignacio Manuel Altamirano that belies the anticlerical/proclerical division. In many cases liberals, and liberal novelists, considered themselves to be deeply committed Catholics *and* liberals. Their goal was to strip away the supposedly superstitious and impractical elements of Catholicism. Authors like Altamirano blamed the elite clergy and the church hierarchy for having impoverished rural communities and abused their power. In their place liberal Catholic authors promoted a utopian and yet still highly religious social reform. They wanted to reform the church on an Erasmian, early primitive church model, in which the priesthood looked to simplicity, charity, and humility as models. This church would be almost Lutheran in its lack of physical structure and its insistence that the true religion comes from within, from faith, and from charitable action and social reform rather than from public pomp and ceremony.

In another vein, Voekel examines the development of a constitutional clergy in the fallout from the 1857 Constitution. She shows through extensive research in contemporaneous press discussions that the easy distinction of anticlerical liberals lined up against pious diocesan officials aligned with conservatives tends to oversimplify the situation. Rather, there was no small faction of liberal priests who supported the Reform for political reasons. These constitutional clergy saw nothing inconsistent with scaling away the physical property of the church, eliminating *fueros*, or moving certain activities into the civil realm. In their assessment, the church ought to administer only to the spiritual needs of the people and let the national government concern itself with questions of community property, the administration of law, and the regulation of republican values.

If the essays mentioned above examine the ways that secularization remained incomplete or that liberals as a group were not as uniformly anticlerical as supposed, other essays in the volume contribute more explicitly to an understanding of the relationships between religion and politics. Mark Overmyer-Velázquez examines diocesan policies toward unions and work, combining labor and religious history in Porfirian Oaxaca. The Oaxacan diocese made considerable efforts to blunt the success and efforts of nascent unions and workers' groups. Blending a concern with the ways that workers organized in the Porfiriato with an analysis of the ways that religion was mixed into this process, Overmyer-Velázquez challenges assumptions about the mutual exclusivity of labor and religion as analytical categories, insisting that in a place like Oaxaca religion was never far from the immediate political concern and activity of workers, the church, and rival unionization efforts.

Where Overmyer-Velázquez shows how on a local level there frequently occurred opposition to or failure to enforce much of the liberal reform agenda, Jason Dormady shows that even leaders of the revolutionary party were willing to ignore certain elements of their own anticlerical agenda when it fit their economic goals. His essay offers an examination of a much understudied and less understood phenomenon: the presence of Protestants and, in particular, of Mennonites in northern Mexico in the twentieth century. This essay offers one of the more intricate analyses of the close connections between national policies toward religion and their effect on regional circumstances. Dormady shows that beginning with the presidency of Álvaro Obregón the ostensibly antireligious revolutionary regime began to allow a variety of exemptions to the 1917 Constitution and the prohibitions on foreign clergy. Obregón, in particular, made exemptions for the Mennonites, whom he saw as potential engines of capitalist agricultural development in the somewhat barren north. In addition to showing how the government did not always follow its own policies, Dormady's essay also gives the lie to the presumption that to study Mexican religion is to study Catholicism by including in this volume an essay on religious minorities.

In both cases the essays by Overmyer-Velázquez and Dormady show that even the liberal or revolutionary state did not always uniformly enforce its own anticlerical directives. Likewise, Arrom and Traffano show that forms of popular religious expression remained robust despite efforts to curtain them. Two further essays exemplify in more locally specific ways how popular religious expressions and devotions developed in the face of centralizing efforts.

Edward Wright-Rios examines the development of a cult of the Virgin of Juquila. It was developed as a highly specific phenomenon in the mountains of southern Oaxaca but also importantly was promoted by a woman mystic, which argues that anticlerical measures of the Reform did not eliminate popular religious sensibilities in the Porfiriato or even in the aftermath of the Mexican Revolution. Moreover, women played a vital role in the development and propagation of local Catholic practices. Like the Ladies of Charity who counted substantial support among the laity, laywomen in Oaxaca played an important role as confidantes to parish priests. While the parish priest held no small measure of social power, the laywomen who fulfilled the role of interlocutor between priest and community shared a good deal of social prestige and even local political power. Wright-Rios assesses the conceptualization of women as the defenders of the faith among the laity. This vision is the result of a much-honored view of *marianismo* that sees women as "the primary protectors of the faith from male malevolence and folly." In this discourse the anticlericalism of Calles and the ethos of the radical revolutionaries, manifested in a one-party hegemony that aimed to eliminate the competition of the church, was described as the outgrowth of "impious" men bent on power, contrasted with the image of the "long-suffering" and pious woman, defender of the faith against the Jacobins and atheists.

Paul Vanderwood's essay demonstrates the "decentralizing entropy" of Catholicism described by William Christian and the profoundly local nature of much Mexican religiosity. Cities like Nuevo Laredo and Tijuana, border towns in the far north, have often been seen as not quite Mexican by other Mexicans, intricately local and noncentral, and consequently popular as opposed to official. In Tijuana in 1938, a young Oaxacan soldier, Juan Castillo Morales, reputedly raped and killed a young girl. He confessed to the crime and was executed under the *ley fuga* by his military superiors.[11] Yet Juan Soldado, as he came to be known, began to be revered as a folk saint by people in Tijuana. How did a confessed rapist-murderer come to be venerated as if he were a saint? In Vanderwood's assessment, much like those of scholars of early modern Europe, such as Carolyn Walker Bynam, the factual details are less important than the fact that people revere him.[12] Did miracles really happen? Were people truly cured via intercession from Juan Soldado? Vanderwood suggests, indirectly, that we leave such questions to the phenomenologists and theologians. Historians, on the other hand, can wonder about the cultural implications of the devotion to Juan Soldado.

As noted above, Vanderwood's essay follows in line with Christian's view of Hispanic Catholicism as local and particular. The concerns of people who venerate Juan Soldado are specific and practical: a job, a love affair, a work visa, a student's exam. At the same time, the church has made no formal recognition of Juan Soldado. The same can be said for Jesús Malverde, of Culiacán, who is the folk saint of drug dealers and smugglers. Yet the people who revere these folk saints see themselves as good Catholics, not as heretics or fringe members of society.

This collection concludes with a broad historiographic essay by Adrian Bantjes. His goal is to provide readers, students, and historians with a thematic apparatus to conceptualize the religious history of modern Mexico. He sees the field of popular religion as ripe and wide-open to future research. To that end he suggests a future agenda for investigation, especially of popular religion. Bantjes argues that the lack of studies of religion within the broad context of the Mexican Revolution can be addressed through a variety of theoretical tools. Primarily, he suggests Christian's view of religion as local and nonuniversal. Additionally, he looks to William Taylor's vision of what we might call religious parallelism, in which "people may operate comfortably in more than one religious tradition at a time, enlarging their cosmovision and repertoire of world renewing."[13] In short, his essay is suggestive, giving impetus for further research, study, and debate on religion as an analytical category.

This collection of essays is intended to spur future debate and research on a growing field. Numerous areas of future research remain open and ready for analysis and discussion. It is our hope that we can offer one further piece to this growing literature and its unexplored realms.

One final vignette highlights the complexity and tenacity of religiosity in Mexico nearly five centuries after the arrival of Catholicism. To the south of Mexico City lies a mountainous and rugged terrain just west of Cuernavaca. If one leaves the main highway from Mexico City to Cuernavaca and travels west, one drives through Huitzilac. One can still buy fresh pulque there along with quesadillas. The roads rise and wind through pine forests and then fall to subtropical zones with spectacular, steep valleys. Along this road lies the shrine to the Christ of Chalma, a popular pilgrimage site. The Christ of Chalma, located in a hermitage built originally by Augustinians in the 1680s, is revered by many as providing miracles and guidance.[14] Not far from Chalma, along the same route, lies Ahuehuete, where pilgrims stop to gather water from a stream believed to have curative properties. On Sundays, enormous crowds come to Chalma and Ahuehuete for spiritual reflection, for succor, and, importantly, for community outings, reflecting an old conception of religion as communal and public. Neighborhoods in Mexico City rent out *peseros* (minibuses) for the day to take them on this important pilgrimage. The liberals of the 1857 generation had said that spending time and money on pilgrimages and church supplies ruined society and the nation. Altamirano once asked: "What use are so many churches in a country which can barely afford to maintain one? Of harmfully multiplying the number of festivals? . . . Unhappy Indians whose wealth goes up in the smoke of the candles, the censers and the fireworks!"[15] A century and a half later these words continue to fall on deaf ears.

Only a few miles west from Chalma (as the crow flies but separated by valley walls) lies Malinalco. The Augustinians built a church there in the 1550s, recognizing the area as an important locus of missionary activities among the Nahua.[16] On the hills above the valley where Malinalco lies remains a temple of a Mexica military order. The Augustinian church is often seen full of corn stalks in a direct propitiation for a good harvest. Maize is an ancient Mesoamerican symbol of life and fecundity, of the grain that was and continues to be central to Mexican life and society. That centuries after the arrival of Catholic missionaries maize remains deeply embedded in religious consciousness; that propitiation of saints remains a central concern; and that religion remains a practical tool for people—all this reminds us that religion, in addition to theology and dogma, is also a deeply personal and quotidian affair. That personal and local character is the subject of this book.

NOTES

Chapter opening image source: Centro Fotográfico Álvarez Bravo, Fondo Ignacio Zanabria.

1. *Los Angeles Times*, December 15, 2005.

2. Pamela Voekel, *Alone before God: The Religious Origins of Modernity in Mexico* (Durham, NC: Duke University Press, 2002).

3. The literature has become more extensive of late. Classics of the genre remain: Jorge Adame Goddard, *El pensamiento político y social de los católicos mexicanos, 1867–1914* (Mexico City: UNAM, 1981); Manuel Ceballos Ramírez, *El catolicismo social: Un tercero en discordia: Rerum Novarum, la "cuestión social" y la movilización de los católicos mexicanos (1891–1911)* (Mexico City: El Colegio de México, 1991). Good examples of more recent work include Laura O'Dogherty Madrazo, *De urnas y sotanas: El Partido Católico Nacional en Jalisco* (Mexico City: CONACULTA, 2001); and William Fowler and Humberto Morales Moreno, eds., *El conservadurismo mexicano en el siglo XIX* (Puebla: Benemérita Universidad Autónoma de Puebla, 1999).

4. Jean Meyer, *La cristiada*, 3 vols. (Mexico City: Siglo Veintiuno Editores, 1973–1976). Others at this time were also investigating the Cristiada. See, e.g., David C. Bailey, *¡Viva Cristo Rey! The Cristero Rebellion and the Church-State Conflict in Mexico* (Austin: University of Texas Press, 1974); Robert E. Quirk, *Mexican Revolution and the Catholic Church, 1910–1929* (Bloomington: Indiana University Press, 1973); José Díaz and Román Rodríguez, *El movimiento cristero: Sociedad y conflicto en los Altos de Jalisco* (Mexico City: Editorial Nueva Imagen, 1979); Ramón Jrade, "Counterrevolution in Mexico: The Cristero Movement in Sociological and Historical Perspective"

(Ph.D. diss., Brown University, 1980); and Jim Tuck, *The Holy War in Los Altos. A Regional Analysis of Mexico's Cristero Rebellion* (Tucson: University of Arizona Press, 1982). Additionally, there was substantial (mostly partisan) discussion of the Cristiada before the 1970s.

5. Mariano Cuevas, *Historia de la iglesia en México*, 5 vols. (El Paso: Editorial "Revista católica," 1928).

6. This literature is reviewed more extensively in the essay in this collection by Adrian Bantjes. For examples, see Luis González y González, *Pueblo en vilo: Microhistoria de San José de Gracia* (Mexico City: Fondo de Cultura Económica; SEP, 1984); Yolanda Padilla Rangel, *El Catolicismo social y el movimiento Cristero en Aguascalientes* (Aguascalientes: Instituto Cultural de Aguascalientes, 1992); Roberto Blancarte, ed., *Cultura e identidad nacional* (Mexico City: Fondo de Cultura Económica; Consejo Nacional para la Cultura y las Artes, 1994), esp. the essay by Blancarte, "Aspectos internacionales del conflicto religioso mexicano en la década de los treinta"; Paul J. Vanderwood, *Power of God against the Guns of Government: Religious Upheaval in Mexico at the Turn of the Nineteenth Century* (Stanford, CA: Stanford University Press, 1998) and his recent *Juan Soldado: Rapist, Murderer, Martyr, Saint* (Durham, NC: Duke University Press, 2004); Jennie Purnell, *Popular Movements and State Formation in Revolutionary Mexico. The Agraristas and Cristeros of Michoacán* (Durham, NC: Duke University Press, 1999); Édgar González Ruiz, *La última cruzada. De los cristeros a Fox* (Mexico City: Grijalbo, 2000); and Fernando M. González, *Matar y morir por Cristo Rey: Aspectos de la cristiada* (Mexico City: Plaza y Valdés; Universidad Nacional Autónoma de México; Instituto de Investigaciones Sociales, 2001). For a recent study of religion in Mexico across a wide time frame, see David Brading, *Mexican Phoenix: Our Lady of Guadalupe: Image and Tradition across Five Centuries* (Cambridge: Cambridge University Press, 2001).

7. On the resurgence of religion in the late nineteenth century and the context of the papal bull *Rerum Novarum*, see, for example, Mark Overmyer-Velázquez, *Visions of the Emerald City: Modernity, Tradition, and the Formation of Porfirian Oaxaca, Mexico* (Durham, NC: Duke University Press, 2006); Manuel Ceballos Ramírez, *Historia de Rerum Novarum en México, 1867–1931*, 2 vols. (Mexico City: Instituto Mexicano de Doctrina Social Cristiana, 1991); Manuel Ceballos Ramírez, *El catolicismo social: Un tercero en discordia* (Mexico City: Colegio de México, 1991); and Manuel Esparza, *Gillow durante el Porfiriato y la revolución en Oaxaca, 1887–1922* (Tlaxcala: Talleres Gráficos de Tlaxcala, 1985).

8. Carlos M. N. Eire, "The Concept of Popular Religion," in *Local Religion in Colonial Mexico*, ed. Martin Austin Nesvig (Albuquerque: University of New Mexico Press, 2006).

9. William A. Christian Jr., "Catholicisms," in *Local Religion in Colonial Mexico*.

10. William A. Christian Jr., *Visionaries, the Spanish Republic and the Reign of Christ* (Berkeley: University of California Press, 1996), 400.

11. The *ley fuga*, or law of flight, was a method by which the military executed a person arrested for a crime by shooting him dead when he attempted to escape. In the case of Juan Soldado, his escape was staged since his military captors compelled him to flee so that they could execute him.

12. Carolyn Walker Bynam, *Holy Feast, Holy Fast: The Religious Significance of Food to Medieval Women* (Berkeley: University of California Press, 1987), esp. 6, 8.

13. William B. Taylor, *Magistrates of the Sacred: Priests and Parishioners in Eighteenth-Century Mexico* (Stanford, CA: Stanford University Press, 1996), 73.

14. Peter Gerhard, *Geografía histórica de la Nueva España, 1519–1821*, trans. Stella Mastrangelo (Mexico City: UNAM, 2000), 175.

15. Quoted in Enrique Krauze, *Mexico: Biography of Power. A History of Modern Mexico, 1810–1996*, trans. Hank Heifetz (New York: HarperPerennial, 1997), 153.

16. Gerhard, *Geografía histórica*, 175.

2
Miserables and Citizens: Indians, Legal Pluralism, and Religious Practice in Early Republican Mexico

Matthew D. O'Hara

Front Page Parish Vow/Rogation to the Virgin of Guadalupe, San Juan Yaeé, Oaxaca, 1910. Concerned by the outbreak of the Mexican Revolution, the archbishop of Oaxaca, Eulogio Gillow, directed that all Catholics in Oaxaca take the oath and sign their names, and thus affirm their fealty to the Virgin Mary and the Catholic Church, and beg for forgiveness as a nation. Many priests sent back bound stacks of paper listing hundreds of names, although they acknowledged that in many cases individuals could not write but were nonetheless eager to verify their devotion for the Virgin.

> If there is a people in the world who can truly be called *miserable*, it is the Indians of America: so great are their sorrows that even the most brazen hearts will pity them.
>
> —Alonso de la Peña Montenegro,
> *Itinerario para párrocos de indios*, Quito, 1668.[1]

Indian identity in nineteenth-century Mexico presents a conundrum. Prior to Mexican independence, both the colonial state and the Catholic Church recognized the existence of social groups based on racial and ethnic criteria, in a formal and informal system of social control known as the *sistema de castas*. The category of *indio* (Indian) comprised the juridical bedrock of the *sis-*

tema de castas. Colonial law considered Indians *miserables*, wretched people who were to receive special care from state and society.[2] Citing Isidore of Seville, Alonso de la Peña Montenegro, the author of one of the most widely used pastoral manuals for parish priests during the colonial era, defined a *miserable* as one who has lost an earlier state of happiness and therefore deserves the pity of his fellow man. In the years following Mexico's separation from Spain in 1821, however, new civil laws eroded the legal foundations of the colonial social order. Most importantly, civil edicts issued on the cusp of Mexican independence eliminated the category of *indio*. Subsequent constitutions and legislation would reinforce these early decrees. Such legal changes notwithstanding, social divisions inherited from the colonial era, including the distinction between Indians and non-Indians, continued to inform political thought, economic policy, local religious practices, and many other aspects of daily life. Simply put, the colonial term "Indian" lived on despite its abolition under civil law.

An examination of religious practice reveals and partly explains this paradox. Throughout the nineteenth century, religious administration and practices relied on social and legal categories inherited from the colonial era, which helped to maintain a particular kind of *indio* identity in Republican Mexico. Parish priests, for example, referred to sixteenth-century canon law, colonial pastoral manuals, and eighteenth-century fee schedules to inform their work. In all such sources, Indians comprised a distinct social category with its own religious obligations and privileges, and parish priests tailored their ministry, or pastoral care, to their Indian parishioners. In the parishes of Republican Mexico, Indians remained *miserables*.

This story, however, cannot be reduced to a simple narrative of colonial vestiges or the anachronistic work of parish priests, for parishioners themselves also kept alive *indio* identity by exploiting colonial legal categories. Well after Mexico's independence from Spain, self-ascribed Indians manipulated forms of colonial religious administration to their own benefit. Parishioners took advantage of religious dispensations and privileges, including lower fee schedules for the sacraments and more lenient restrictions on marriage partners, which were only available to Indians. So while much of this narrative is told from the perspective of non-Indians, such as parish priests, republican politicians, and others who were grappling with colonial knowledge about race and good governance, ultimately it is about the ways such knowledge became embedded in local religious practices and how those deemed to be Indians or non-Indians acted upon it. A confluence of legal, social, and cultural forces thus reproduced the category of *indio* while it was otherwise being eclipsed in civil law. By examining the transition of religious administration into the republican era, this story reveals one of the many ways that religious culture and practices mediated imported political theories such as classical liberalism and helped shape the political community of modern Mexico.

In 1821 Indians ceased to exist in Mexican civil law. The famous Plan de Iguala—the political program that eventually led to Mexico's independence from Spain—pronounced an end to caste distinctions inherited from the colonial period. Article 12 of the plan confidently decreed, "All the inhabitants of New Spain, without any distinction of Europeans, Africans, or Indians, are citizens of this monarchy with the option to pursue all professions, according to their merits and virtues."[3] In the following decade, subsequent edicts and legislation confirmed the intent of Article 12 and further eroded the legal status of caste. On 17 September 1822, Agustín de Iturbide, the first leader of independent Mexico, decreed that parish priests could no longer use caste categories such as *indio*, *mestizo*, or *español* in parish documents.[4] Given that registers of baptisms, marriages, burials, and other religious practices provided some of the most detailed and intimate records of colonial life, Iturbide's seemingly mundane decree was in fact a radical departure from the status quo.[5] The use of caste labels in parish registers was one of the basic ways colonial subjects and officials created, fixed, or manipulated individual identities. If one takes edicts such as Iturbide's at face value, it seems that early republican leaders aimed to repudiate the colonial past and chart a new course toward a society comprised of citizens equal before the law.

Despite these changes, colonial categories continued to structure Mexican society in fundamental ways. The elite, in particular, linked race and social status and often showed disdain toward nonwhites. Foreign travelers to nineteenth-century Mexico described the racial logic often employed by the upper class. In 1841 Fanny Calderón de la Barca, the Scottish-born wife of the Spanish ambassador to Mexico, relayed the attitude of one of her Mexican counterparts toward Afro-Mexicans. "We saw a horribly ugly man today," Calderón wrote, "and were told he was a *lobo*, the name given here to the *Zambos*; who are the most frightful human beings that can be seen. La Güera Rodríguez told us that on an estate of hers, one woman of that race was in the habit of attending church, and that she was so fearfully hideous, the priest had been obliged to desire her to remain at home, because she distracted the attention of the congregation!"[6] The very terms used by Calderón and "la Güera" (Blondie) Rodríguez—*lobo* and *zambo*—were products of the colonial period and described supposed admixtures of Indian and African descent. Similar descriptions of racial difference were widespread during this time, and while some colonial racial labels fell out of use over the course of the nineteenth century, the category of Indian remained central to social commentary.

Whether rendered by upper-crust Mexicans or foreigners, nineteenth-century descriptions of Indians were often caricatures that emphasized their supposed melancholy and "craftiness." Jean Louis Berlandier, a Swiss naturalist traveling about Mexico in the 1820s and 1830s, remarked that Indians "are not generally handsome, although their physiognomy is not disagreeable. Their eyes are black and very expressive. . . . With respect to their character, the pure indigenes are gentle but a little distrustful."[7] Calderón made a similar diagnosis of Indians, noting that "under an appearance of stupid apathy they veil a great depth of cunning."[8] While such accounts betrayed the attitudes of the Europeans who recorded them, their descriptions suggest that colonial racial categories, especially "Indian," still formed part of Mexico's social vocabulary. Indeed, the "problem of the Indian" was a hotly debated issue in national politics throughout the nineteenth century.[9]

Fundamentally the issue was one of political community. The Spanish monarch had perched on top of a body politic that, in theory, was ordered hierarchically and divided into a variety of corporations, each with its own set of privileges and responsibilities. Clerics and members of the military, for example, both enjoyed legal rights known as *fueros* that protected them from prosecution in civil courts; merchants and artisans belonged to guilds that regulated production and trade; religious brotherhoods and devotional groups, which often limited their membership based on caste, segmented the faithful into a plethora of discrete devotional communities. The corporate culture of the colonial era also permeated institutional practices related to Indians, such as tribute collection and religious administration, which were codified in law. Though many such directives were more forceful on paper than in practice, legal changes that followed independence nonetheless eliminated or weakened many of these hallmarks of Spanish colonialism. If colonial categories no longer ordered society, then what political structure would support the new nation? How would colonial corporatism translate into the republican era?

The answers seemed obvious to some liberals.[10] If Mexico could be freed from the burden of its colonial past, including the juridical distinctions that created a chasm between Indians and other Mexicans, the unfettered individual would lead the country toward a bright future of progress and prosperity. Even the most doctrinaire liberals, however, found Mexico's diverse and heavily Indian population to be a potential obstacle. José María Luis Mora described Indians as "backward and degraded remains of the ancient Mexican population," who "in their present state and until they have undergone considerable changes, can never reach the degree of enlightenment, civilization, and culture of Europeans nor maintain themselves as equals in a society formed by both."[11] For Mora and others, Mexico's Indians required transformation before a new social fabric could be woven. Liberal ideologues railed against many of the "traditional" features of Indian villages, including communal landholding, which seemed to block the flow of the free market. Many

liberals concluded that the instincts associated with *Homo economicus* (e.g., a desire to exchange and accumulate and timely responses to market cues) did not
come naturally to Mexico's Indians. Instead, if Mexico was to advance economically and socially, the state would need to inculcate such "natural" traits.
The famous Ley Lerdo, first promulgated in 1856 and then codified in the
Mexican Constitution of 1857, represented one such attempt. The decree
outlawed corporate landholdings and opened the way for the breakup of Indian village lands during the second half of the nineteenth century. According to liberal theory, Indian communities were to be atomized into rational
economic actors—a Mesoamerican variant of the yeoman farmer.[12]

Conservatives, on the other hand, feared social instability in the new republic. They fought to maintain or reinstate many of the corporate orderings
of colonial society, which, as they understood them, served as vital levees
against an imminent flood of social disorder. As one warned, "in Mexico there
is no commonality between whites and Indians; everything is different: physical aspects, language, customs, [and] state of civilization. In Mexico there are
two different nations on the same land, and worse still, two nations that are to
a point enemies."[13] To some conservatives, religion or "moral force" seemed
the only recourse. An 1848 article in the Mexico City newspaper *El Universal*
praised the "religious sentiment" of the colonial era, which "tempered the
fierce passions of the savage, softening his customs and making him useful to
society. Costing the government nothing, it was an insuperable barrier against
the furious torrent that is now overflowing to lay waste to the republic."[14] So
while conservatives and liberals could not find a common answer to the "Indian question," they did agree that Mexico's indigenous population constituted
a problem in need of a solution.[15]

Later in the nineteenth century, amidst the ongoing attacks against Indian
communal lands, Mexico's modernizers would put the nation's "Indian heritage" to the service of economic development. In a variety of contexts, including exhibits at international expositions, the governing elite during the dictatorship of Porfirio Díaz (1876–1910) revised Mexico's Indian past to offer to
the world an image of a unique, but modernizing, nation. Such exoticizing
may seem at odds with contemporaneous attempts to assimilate Indians into national life, but it also was an attempt to harness and transform Indian Mexico,
for it suggested that "Indianness" might be put to the service of liberal notions
of progress. Mexico's pavilion at the 1889 World's Fair in Paris offered one of
the more fully conceived versions of this project. In a stunning attempt to present a marketable image of Mexico—one that would attract foreign investment
and northern European immigration—Porfirian cognoscenti represented the
indigenous past in a classical, Greco-Roman style. The Parisian "Aztec Palace"
presented an exalted but sanitized version of Indians, sufficiently distant in time

and unusual in appearance to attract the curiosity of foreign observers, but not so palpable and raw that the international gaze and pocketbook would be scared away.[16] Just as the legal category of *miserable* assumed some prior state of grace from which Indians had fallen to arrive at their current position, the visual representation of "classical Aztecs" also reflected back to an idealized Indian who formed part of a well-ordered polity. Such projects were inherently contradictory as they both embraced and rejected Mexico's colonial past. On the one hand, by omitting the Spanish presence in the visual narrative they treated the colonial era as a kind of unhappy interregnum in the march of Mexican history. On the other hand, the attempt to present an idealized Indian—adorned with ancient European styles to suit contemporary European tastes—reified the very categories created by colonialism and emphasized the supposed cultural distance that separated Indians and non-Indians.

In a similar vein, nineteenth-century geographers and statisticians endeavored to catalog the nation's productive resources, which included social and cultural assets. In the visually exquisite national atlas produced in 1858, for example, Antonio García Cubas composed an "ethnographic map" to

Antonio García Cubas, Atlas geográfico, estadístico e histórico de la República Mexicana. *(Mexico: Imprenta de José Mariano Fernández de Lara, 1858)*

Antonio García Cubas, Atlas geográfico, estadístico e histórico de la República
Mexicana. (Mexico: Imprenta de José Mariano Fernández de Lara, 1858)

communicate the diversity of Mexico's inhabitants.[17] At the center of the
document, García Cubas placed a map of Mexico that listed the locations
and population figures for different "families" of Indians. The total population for each state was also provided, including the numbers of "white
race," "mixed race," and "indigenous race" found in each. García Cubas surrounded the map with a series of vignettes that cataloged different peoples
of Mexico. Most of these scenes captured Indian groups in supposedly typical dress and activities. In the upper left-hand corner of the image, the
"white race" is enjoying itself at an elegant gathering. Juxtaposed against
this opulent scene of leisure, in an adjacent frame, "Mexicanos," or Nahuatl-
speaking Indians, travel peacefully across one of the canals south of Mexico

City. These Indians from Santa Anita, a hamlet attached to the parish of San Matías Ixtacalco, carry vegetables, flowers, and other products produced on the famous *chinampas*, or floating gardens, that were common in the lakebeds and canals near the capital. Elsewhere in the atlas, García Cubas described each region's indigenous peoples and products in great detail. By cataloging indigenous peoples along with the nation's productive capacity, the García Cubas atlas suggested that a transformed Indian could form a part of Mexico's economic future. Like the Plan de Iguala, the García Cubas atlas can thus be read as an optimistic statement on the potential of Mexico's diverse peoples and, by extension, on the abstract entity of the Mexican nation.[18] But the atlas also demonstrates the persistence of a racialized framework for interpreting Mexican society.

Viewing the nineteenth century as a whole suggests that we should reevaluate any simple equation of Indian identity in Mexico. Though politicians rewrote civil law in ways that undermined the corporate culture of the colonial era, colonial social categories continued to shape opinions and institutions. The category of Indian, moreover, was contested. Some policies, such as the attacks on corporate landholding, rejected traditional institutions and attempted to assimilate Indians into an emerging liberal, mestizo nation. At the same time, the image makers behind the "classical Aztecs" created idyllic visions of the Indian past as they gestured toward a Mexican national identity. Others, such as García Cubas, suggested that the Indian present might be harnessed as a part of national economic development. Politicians and intellectuals, it seems, both revered and reviled an imagined Indian identity.

PRIEST AND PARISHIONER IN SAN MATÍAS IXTACALCO

Pastoral care in the postrepublican era offers an ideal vista onto the legacy of colonial social categories, since parish administration continued to be predicated on the very caste labels that were formally abolished by Iturbide's decrees. During the colonial era both royal and canon law governed the Catholic Church and its parishes. The role of the parish in the Americas was defined in canon law through local synods, papal decrees, and universal church councils, of which the Council of Trent was the most famous example. For colonial New Spain, the Third Mexican Provincial Council (1585) laid the legal foundation that governed the Mexican church throughout the colonial period and most of the nineteenth century.[19] Royal law could come in the form of an edict or a decision by the king's administrative body responsible for the American colonies, the Council of the Indies. Because two sets of jurisprudence governed the church, the legal environment was rife with potential conflict, but the tight linkage between church and state as a result of the *real patronato* (royal patronage) tended to mitigate legal discrepancies in practice.[20]

To examine this juridical slippage and its effect upon local practices historians must negotiate a difficult methodological obstacle. Much of the excellent work on caste in the colonial era relies on detailed civil census records and parish registers, which among other data recorded individual caste identities.[21] The absence of caste identification in censuses and parish registers after independence complicates similar studies for the postrepublican era. Instead, evidence of the relationship between religion and race during the national period is found in qualitative descriptions of religious life. A unique body of documents from the parish of San Matías Ixtacalco offers such an entry point for studying the socioreligious dynamics of race in the early nineteenth century. Among these records is a pastoral manual and diary written by the parish priest of Ixtacalco during the early 1830s, which provides a detailed account of religious administration for Indians during the pivotal years following independence.[22] In such sources, one finds that church law and traditional practices often trumped emerging civil law, causing religious practice to retain a colonial and racialized framework during the early to middle nineteenth century.[23]

From the sixteenth through the early nineteenth centuries, colonial religious administration helped to impose an Indian identity onto Ixtacalco and surrounding pueblos, since Ixtacalco formed part of a *doctrina de indios*. During the colonial period, *doctrina* or *doctrina de indios* referred to a protoparish meant for the exclusive pastoral care of Indians. As part of the Spanish crown's attempt to evangelize its possessions in the New World, the regular clergy had received papal dispensations that allowed them to serve as parish priests for Indians (such clergy were known as *curas doctrineros* or simply *doctrineros*), while they were expressly prohibited from serving as parish priests for non-Indians.[24] By separating the religious administration of Indians and non-Indians, the church and crown felt that *curas doctrineros* might better attend to the spiritual needs of Indians, whom Spanish theologians and jurists considered spiritual neophytes. Recalling the work of the Jesuit José de Acosta, Montenegro wrote, "The teacher of these Indians must be careful to uproot the vices and sins that tradition has made fast and to plant new flowers of Christian virtues. And for such an arduous and important undertaking, the evangelist must realize that his goal is nothing less than to transform ferocious beasts into beautiful angels."[25] The system of *doctrinas*, therefore, formed an integral part of the larger system of "two republics," a diffuse set of ideas, legislation, and institutions that attempted to maintain a distinction between Indian and Spanish society in the Americas, facilitating spiritual education as well as economic exploitation.[26]

For most of the colonial period, Franciscan friars administered San Matías Ixtacalco as part of the large Franciscan *doctrina de indios* of San José de los Naturales located in Mexico City.[27] Two Franciscan brothers served as resident ministers in Ixtacalco, located just over a league to the south of the capital, under the general authority of the *doctrina* in Mexico City. In 1771, however, as part of a scheme initiated by the archbishop of Mexico to reorganize Mexico City's parishes, the archdiocese transferred control of Ixtacalco parish from the Franciscan order to the secular clergy.[28] As part of the reorganization, Ixtacalco lost its formal status as an Indian-only parish, though the archdiocese still considered the parish heavily Indian and usually staffed it with priests bilingual in Spanish and Nahuatl.[29] An ecclesiastical census conducted in 1779, for example, determined the parish to be almost entirely Indian.[30]

Though Indians predominated in the parish, Ixtacalco was just a short walk or canoe trip from the center of Mexico City, the city with the largest non-Indian population in New Spain. Ixtacalco's proximity to the ethnically diverse capital, coupled with the town's colonial identity as an Indian pueblo, created problems for pastoral administration. But rather than being an anomaly, Ixtacalco's history highlights a number of issues in local religious practice that became prominent throughout Mexico in the nineteenth century. Foremost among these, both priests and parishioners questioned what constituted an Indian and how "Indianness" changed over time.

Notwithstanding its location near Mexico City, which priests in many rural parishes would have envied, during the early nineteenth century Ixtacalco's presbyters considered their assignment a sentence to be endured. The priests became involved in a variety of disputes with their parishioners, ranging from disagreements over fee payments for the sacraments to squabbles surrounding municipal politics.[31] Alcohol was often at the center of parochial discord. The short trip from the capital made the town a favorite destination for weekend visitors escaping the city, and their excursions often included a visit to one of the town's taverns. Sitting on a transportation route that extended south toward Xochimilco, the area also served as an entrepôt for shipments of pulque and *aguardiente*. Consequently, Ixtacalco had a reputation as a town particularly beset by the evils of drink. A number of the priests described their parishioners as depraved sots, and the clerics campaigned against drunkenness, revelry, and public disorder in the parish.[32] Travelers to the area also commented on the consumption of alcohol. On a canal trip through Santa Anita, a village under the authority of Ixtacalco parish, Fanny Calderón praised the beauty of the surroundings, but lamented the excesses of the locals. "Unfortunately," Calderón wrote, "these people generally end by too frequent applications to the jarro of pulque, or what is worse to the pure spirit known by the name *chinguirite* . . . which frequently terminates in their fighting, stabbing each other, or throwing each other into the canal."[33] Just after his ordination in 1800, Espinosa de los Monteros, the cleric who would become Ixtacalco's parish priest in the early 1830s, served as an assistant priest in one of the outlying communities of the parish, San Juan Nexticpac. At the time, the priest made an observation similar to Calderón's, noting that "the majority of parishioners were drunks, corrupted by their exposure to residents of Mexico City who came to Ixtacalco to amuse themselves. Moreover, during Lent, when others are taking their yearly confession and communion, the residents of Ixtacalco are all the more debauched."[34]

Ixtacalco's location near Mexico City influenced not just social commentaries on the parish, but also the relationship between the priest and his flock. According to the reports of priests and visitors to the area, many of the Indian parishioners in Ixtacalco and surrounding villages were becoming *indios ladinos*, speaking Spanish, wearing nontraditional clothing, and otherwise comporting themselves as mestizos.[35] Espinosa de los Monteros argued that "at least two-thirds of the town are mestizos."[36] In one sense, therefore, the "worldliness" of the capital impinged on the Indians of the parish and exposed their "natural" proclivities to drink, licentiousness, and violence. As Calderón noted, "it is neither in or near the capital that we can see the Indians to perfection in their original state. It is only by traveling through the provinces that we can accomplish this."[37] From the perspective of the parish's priests, Ixtacalco's Indian parishioners shed part of their Indian identity as they picked up bad habits from Mexico City. Their attitudes echoed the sentiments of some colonial jurists and theologians, who argued that Indians were *tabulae rasae* that might be inscribed with whatever virtues or vices they encountered. Though priests described an ongoing process of cultural *mestizaje*, which carried none of the optimism that would characterize later writing on the subject, the category "Indian" shaped parish activities throughout the nineteenth century.

How could this be? At a time when the juridical category "Indian" no longer existed in civil law, and when parish priests were forbidden to use such terminology in their records, why was pastoral care still influenced by an individual or a community's identity as Indian or non-Indian? The governing laws of the Mexican church remained the decrees issued by the Third Provincial Council held in 1585, and not until 1896 did Mexican prelates pass a new set of church laws that would be ratified by Rome.[38] In the meantime, parish priests relied upon colonial-era canon law to guide their work. Espinosa de los Monteros and other priests in "Indian parishes" also consulted seventeenth- and eighteenth-century pastoral manuals written for *párrocos de indios* (parish priests of Indians). In his *libros de miscelánea*, which were informal "how-to" books for his successors in the parish, Espinosa de los Monteros refers repeatedly to the writings of Montenegro and Manuel Pérez, two colonial pastoral authorities who wrote manuals for priests in Indian parishes.[39] That such a distinction between Indians and non-Indians conflicted with the new civil law did not concern parish priests such as Espinosa de los Monteros or the Mexican church hierarchy. In late 1822, for example, just months after Iturbide forbade the use of caste labels in parish registers, the Archdiocese of Mexico sent a protest to the civil government, noting that without knowledge of parishioners' caste, parish priests would have no way of determining whether or not they might apply marriage dispensations reserved for Indians.[40] The civil government soon relented and approved the use of caste labels when determining consanguinity levels for marriage.[41] The quick reversal by the authorities demonstrated that it would be difficult to eliminate caste labels from parish records by fiat, so long as canon law and local religious administration recognized caste.

In Ixtacalco, a variety of factors—from canon law to the manipulation of the pastoral relationship by parishioners—contributed to the persistence of Indian identity into the 1830s. Foremost among these was the attitude of Espinosa de los Monteros, who served in Ixtacalco from 1831 to 1832. He carefully documented his work as *cura* of Ixtacalco and reordered the parish archive in an attempt to pass on the institutional memory of the parish to his successors. Peppered amongst these notices in his *libros de miscelánea*, he left an eclectic assortment of personal observations on the parish and its parishioners. While the almost diarylike documents that he wrote were unusual for the time, the relationship of Espinosa de los Monteros to his flock was common. Like many priests in Indian parishes, Espinosa de los Monteros displayed a marked paternalism toward his flock, and he frequently used tropes of Indian difference that were prominent in the colonial period. He warned his potential successors about a wide range of his parishioners' behaviors, from the pervasive drinking of pulque and its consequences to the supposed naïveté of Indians, which—like Fanny Calderón—Espinosa de los Monteros argued was a mask that his Indian parishioners used to hide their true intentions or to escape culpability for some sin.

Despite the particularity of Espinosa de los Monteros's observations, which often displayed the priest's ironic humor, his writings should be read in the larger political context of the postindependence era. Like many of his fellow clerics during the first half of the nineteenth century, Espinosa de los Monteros understood the Mexican church to be under siege. As a priest whose career embraced both the colonial and national eras, he was attuned to the radical changes experienced by the church since the colony broke free from Spanish control.[42] In his biblical exegesis, the four winds of the Apocalypse were buffeting the church. Like the Apostles tossed around the Sea of Galilee in their small craft, Mexican Catholicism was also endangered by current events:

> With the introduction of foreigners and all kinds of books, we already have various doctrinal *Winds* and a variety of political opinions about the form of government. We are disturbed like the Sea of Genessaret and we will become even more so. We have proselytizers of various kinds that go about seeking converts. In the realm of politics there are those who want a federation, others centralism, and I think there are even some advocates of a monarchy, and between them all there are strong political and religious disagreements.[43]

Though he held hope for the future, in the short term Espinosa de los Monteros viewed the political environment grimly, and the increasingly difficult position faced by the Catholic Church, which was being ideologically attacked by liberals and financially attacked by both conservative and liberal governments, made him more inclined to look to the past to understand the present.

The guides that Espinosa de los Monteros referred to in his parish work both reflected and shaped his "traditional" ministry. He frequently cited colonial legal authorities and pastoral manuals as he reasoned his way through parish duties. More than any other issue, fee payments for religious services sent Espinosa de los Monteros searching for guidance in the texts of Montenegro and others. During the colonial period, many parish priests derived a substantial portion of their yearly income from payments for the performance of the sacraments (*derechos*).[44] In most cases, tradition and canon law obligated parishioners to pay fees for marriages, special masses, burials, and other Catholic rituals tightly woven into the social fabric. The price for a sacrament might be determined by an agreement between the priest and a particular community (in what were called *compromisos* or *convenios*) or by using a fee schedule (*arancel*) that the archdiocese approved and updated periodically, and priests and *doctrineros* zealously guarded their right to collect fees from their parishioners. The practice of demanding racially differentiated subventions for spiritual services dated back to the sixteenth century and was recognized in the Third Mexican Provincial Council (1585) and the earliest surviving *aranceles*. A new *arancel* issued by the archbishop of Mexico in 1767, for example, stipulated different fee schedules corresponding to categories within the caste system, and comprised four fee categories: Spaniards, *castas*, Indians working on haciendas (*"Indios de quadrillas y haziendas"*), and Indians attached to a landholding community (*"Indios de pueblo"*).[45] By issuing a new *arancel*, the archbishop hoped to minimize fee disputes between priests and parishioners. In an isolated, rural *pueblo de indios* an unambiguous fee schedule might place a shaky pastoral relationship back on solid ground. But in a parish such as Ixtacalco, with its ethnically diverse population and its proximity to Mexico City, an *arancel* could not eliminate the problem of contested caste identities. The new fee schedule clarified the cost of a *mulato*'s baptism (one peso as an offering), the price of an Indian's marriage (six pesos), or the cost of a Spaniard's burial (five pesos), but it could not determine whether or not an individual was in fact a *mulato*, Indian, or Spaniard; such questions were adjudicated at the baptismal font, on the street corner, and sometimes through detailed petitions sent to the archdiocesan secretary.

In this regard, very little changed in Ixtacalco's religious practice with the arrival of independence or the abolition of caste categories under civil law, for the town was still governed by a colonial *arancel* and Indian parishioners paid lower fees than non-Indians. Espinosa de los Monteros continued the practice while *cura* of Ixtacalco, even though he felt that most of his parishioners, including many of those who claimed to be Indians, were no longer "true Indians" and had become mestizos (half-Indian, half-Spanish) or *castizos* (three-fourths Indian, one-fourth Spanish). In 1831 he warned any unwitting future priest that in Santa Anita—the very hamlet that the cartographer García Cubas used in 1858 to present an idealized portrait of "Mexicanos" or Nahuatl-speaking Indians—almost all of the locals appeared to be mestizos or *castizos*.[46] In the main village of Ixtacalco, he wrote, "very rare would be the pure Indian."[47] Some of these parishioners, it seemed, claimed to be Indians in order to pay lower fees for the sacraments. Others claimed to be Indians in order to be allowed to marry at a higher level of consanguinity, a dispensation offered to Indians under colonial canon law. When conducting a parish census, he wrote, it is important to question thoroughly each father and mother to determine if he or she is a "pure Indian" or mestizo. Only rigorous questioning would ensure that all mestizos and Indians paid their proper church fees and completed the obligatory masses, fasts, and days of rest that were appropriate for their castes.[48]

On September 2, 1831, for example, José Ignacio and María de la Merced appeared before Espinosa de los Monteros in preparation for marriage. In the course of their discussions the priest "almost casually discovered that they were related in the fourth degree of consanguinity," and therefore could only be married without dispensation if they were Indians.[49] Both the woman's father and uncle told the priest, however, that the two were in fact *castizos*. Such a marriage, whether it was the result of miscommunication or outright subterfuge, troubled Espinosa de los Monteros. Not only would "false Indians" shortchange the parish and its priest of much-needed fees, but if José and María were *castizos* their marriage would violate canon law, and would therefore be a "bad marriage." In other words, as a sacrament it would lack efficacy, for it would confer no grace and the two would not truly be married in the eyes of the church. He concluded this entry on a rather cynical note, warning future priests, "don't believe it if the locals say they are Indians, not even if it says so in the parish registers and censuses," because the records "record what they [the Indians] say."[50] What is more, the priest noted, parishioners claimed Indian identity not only to escape higher fee payments or the need for a marriage dispensation, but also to receive land in the community.

But exploiting privileges for Indians carried a cost, since they rested on a foundation of colonial knowledge about Indians with an intellectual genealogy that could be traced back to the debate over the "nature of the Indian" in the sixteenth century. Such inherited knowledge about the mental faculties of Indian parishioners and their ability to be "good Christians" weighed heavily on Espinosa de los Monteros. Though he questioned the identity of many of his parishioners, he often wrote about how best to minister to these imaginary Indians that no longer existed in civil law and, apparently, hardly existed in his own parish. Espinosa de los Monteros observed, for example, that Indians could not be expected to complete a very difficult act of penance after confession. To order an Indian to fast, pray the Rosary, attend a number of masses, or return for additional confessions would be fruitless, he reasoned, since Indian penitents would not complete the penance out of forgetfulness or laziness. Referencing the pastoral manual of Montenegro once again, he suggested that the most appropriate penance for an Indian could be completed the same day as the confession, even upon leaving the confessional. Indians, he wrote, might even be given a penance that was in fact an obligation for all of the faithful, such as hearing mass on a holy day of obligation.[51]

By implication any discussion about the mental fortitude of Indians had political implications. Such possibilities were not lost on Espinosa de los Monteros, and he questioned the ability of Indians to provide accurate testimony in court cases, noting that in colonial Peru, the viceroy had ordered that the testimony of six Indians count only as much as one Spaniard's. In the new political environment, he wrote, if only two Indians could bring a charge against their *cura*, parish priests would be faced with innumerable troubles, "especially in places (such as this one), where there are so few Spaniards that can forthrightly and frankly tell the truth."[52] Virtuous Indians could be found everywhere, he wrote, "but they lack the fortitude and valor to tell the truth when a magistrate or town wants to hide or disfigure it."[53]

CONCLUSION

In theory, landmark political and legal documents such as the Plan de Iguala, the Constitution of 1824, and the Constitution of 1857 placed Mexicans on an equal legal footing, regardless of their ethnic identity. Indian difference, however, continued to be an axis upon which Mexican society revolved. The survival of colonial caste categories depended not only on individual interpretations of social difference, but also on the sedimentation of caste into key institutions and practices, such as parish administration and pastoral care. The legal pluralism that characterized the colonial era did not disappear with independence; local customs, canon law, and civil law shared jurisdiction over Mexico's inhabitants in the nineteenth century.[54] Moreover, contemporary social thought, contained in diverse sources ranging from pastoral manuals to liberal political treatises, helps explain how the label of "Indian" could appear, disappear, and then reappear in the historical record. Espinosa de los Monteros himself declared that by the 1830s most of Ixtacalco's parishioners were mestizos, but nearly thirty years later in his national atlas García Cubas claimed that the towns in and around the parish were composed "totally of Indians."[55]

During Espinosa de los Monteros's short tenure as parish priest of Ixtacalco, changes in civil law and politics appeared over a backdrop of deeply ingrained practices embedded in institutions such as the Catholic parish. The Catholic parish, in turn, was rooted in social structures, such as the Indian landholding community. As these elements of Mexican society were transformed at different rates and in different directions, contradictions developed within the term "Indian." The result was ambivalent for Ixtacalco's parishioners. Some were able to leverage the category of Indian to their own ends, securing lower fee payments or more lenient restrictions on marriage partners. But all religious dispensations for *indios* developed out of a colonial paternalism that distinguished Indians from other colonial subjects and questioned their ability to govern themselves autonomously. This legacy reached far beyond its religious origins, for the question of Indian difference translated clearly into the language of nineteenth-century Mexican politics: Could Indians form part of the modern polity?

NOTES

Chapter opening image source: AHAO, Parroquias, 1910–12.

1. Alonso de la Peña Montenegro, *Itinerario para párrocos de indios: Libros I–II* (Madrid: Consejo Superior de Investigaciones Científicas, 1995 [1668]), libro 2, trat. 1, prólogo, no. 1.

2. *Itinerario para párrocos de indios*, libro 2, trat. 1, prólogo, no. 3. Of course such legal categories, which might suggest a kind of benign paternalism on the part of the Spanish crown, also facilitated the control and exploitation of indigenous peoples.

3. Archivo Parroquial de la Santa Veracruz, "Plan del Sr. Coronel D. Agustín de Iturbide publicado en Iguala el 24 de febrero de 1821."

4. For a consultation on the decree, see Archivo General de la Nación (AGN), *Ministerio de Justicia y Negocios Eclesiásticos*, vol. 12, fols. 188–209, 1822; and Archivo Histórico del Arzobispado de México (AHAM), caja del año 1823, "Decreto de Agustín de Iturbide sobre la clasificación de personas en libros parroquiales," 1823.

5. Religious confraternities that had previously restricted their membership to a particular caste were also forced to comply with the decree. In 1822, for example, a government representative informed the brothers of a confraternity in Mexico City's San Sebastián parish that they should change one of their membership criteria from "must be Spanish" to "must be a Mexican citizen." AGN, *Ministerio de Justicia y Negocios Eclesiásticos*, vol. 7, fols. 77–166, 1817–1822, "Sobre la aprobación de las constituciones de Caballeros Cocheros del Señor Sacramentado, fundada en la parroquia de San Sebastián"; and AGN, *Ministerio de Justicia y Negocios Eclesiásticos*, vol. 5, fol. 253, 1822.

6. Fanny Calderón de la Barca, *Life in Mexico* (Berkeley: University of California Press, 1982), 382–83.

7. Jean Louis Berlandier, *Journey to Mexico during the Years 1826–1834*, trans. Josette M. Bigelow, Sheila M. Ohlendorf, and Mary M. Standifer, 2 vols. (Austin: The Texas State Historical Association, 1980), 1:140.

8. Calderón de la Barca, *Life in Mexico*, 378.

9. A debate over the place of indigenous peoples in Mexican society continues into the present and is at the heart of the neo-Zapatista struggle in Chiapas. Among the extensive literature on the topic, see Neil Harvey, *The Chiapas Rebellion: The Struggle for Land and Democracy* (Durham, NC: Duke University Press, 1998); and Jan Rus, Rosalva Aída Hernández Castillo, and Shannon L. Mattiace, eds., *Mayan Lives, Mayan Utopias: The Indigenous Peoples of Chiapas and the Zapatista Rebellion* (Lanham, MD: Rowman & Littlefield, 2003).

10. On the development of liberal thought and its relationship to the "Indian question," see Charles A. Hale, *Mexican Liberalism in the Age of Mora, 1821–1853* (New Haven, CT: Yale University Press, 1968), chap. 7.

11. Cited in Hale, *Mexican Liberalism*, 223.

12. For the debate surrounding communal landholding, see Hale, *Mexican Liberalism*, 224–45.

13. Francisco Pimentel, *La Economía aplicada a la propiedad territorial en México* (Mexico City: Imp. de Ignacio Cumplido, 1866), 186, cited in Raymond B. Craib, "A Nationalist Metaphysics: State Fixations, National Maps, and the Geo-Historical Imagination in Nineteenth-Century Mexico," *Hispanic American Historical Review* 82, no. 1 (2002), 52.

14. *El Universal*, December 15, 1848, cited in Hale, *Mexican Liberalism*, 243. As Hale notes, the article was likely penned by the archconservative Lucas Alamán.

15. This elite-centered discussion overlooks the ways that popular groups, including traditional Indian communities, sometimes embraced and appropriated liberal thought. See, among others, Peter F. Guardino, *Peasants, Politics, and the Formation of Mexico's National State: Guerrero, 1800–1857* (Stanford, CA: Stanford University Press, 1996); Florencia E. Mallon, *Peasant and Nation: The Making of Postcolonial Mexico and Peru* (Los Angeles: University of California Press, 1995); Guy Thomson, "Popular Aspects of Liberalism in Mexico, 1844–1888," *Bulletin of Latin American Research* 10, no.

3 (1991); and "Agrarian Conflict in the Municipality of Cuetzalán (Sierra de Puebla): The Rise and Fall of 'Pala' Agustín Dieguillo, 1861–1894," *Hispanic American Historical Review* 71, no. 2 (1991).

16. Mauricio Tenorio-Trillo, *Mexico at the World's Fairs: Crafting a Modern Nation* (Berkeley: University of California Press, 1996). See also his "1910 Mexico City: Space and Nation in the City of the Centenario," *Journal of Latin American Studies* 28, no. 1 (1996).

17. Antonio García Cubas, *Atlas geográfico, estadístico e histórico de la República Mexicana* (Mexico City: Imprenta de José Mariano Fernández de Lara, 1858). On the career of García Cubas and nineteenth-century Mexican cartography, see Craib, "A Nationalist Metaphysics."

18. On this point, see Craib, "A Nationalist Metaphysics."

19. For an introduction to the Third Mexican Provincial Council, see José A. Llaguno, *La personalidad jurídica del indio y el III Concilio Provincial Mexicano* (Mexico City: Porrúa, 1963); and Stafford Poole, *Pedro Moya de Contreras: Catholic Reform and Royal Power in New Spain, 1571–1591* (Berkeley: University of California Press, 1987).

20. The overlapping jurisdictions that characterized colonial Spanish America had been a hallmark of European legal culture since the Middle Ages. See Harold J. Berman, *Law and Revolution: The Formation of the Western Legal Tradition* (Cambridge, MA: Harvard University Press, 1983); and James A. Brundage, *Medieval Canon Law* (New York: Longman, 1995).

21. For a critical discussion of historical scholarship on the topic, see Robert H. Jackson, *Race, Caste, and Status: Indians in Colonial Spanish America* (Albuquerque: University of New Mexico Press, 1999), 3–22.

22. The documentation of Ixtacalco's religious history is spread across a number of Mexican archives, including the Archivo General de la Nación (AGN), the Archivo Histórico del Cabildo Metropolitano (AHCM), the Archivo Histórico del Arzobispado de México (AHAM), and the Archivo Parroquial de San Matías Ixtacalco (APSMI). I thank the parish staff of San Matías Ixtacalco for allowing me access to their small, but rich, repository. I also extend my deepest appreciation to the historians at the AHAM for their hospitality and assistance.

23. On the relationship between custom and other sources of law, see Víctor Tau Anzoátegui, *El poder de la costumbre: Estudios sobre el derecho consuetudinario en América hispana hasta la emancipación* (Buenos Aires: Instituto de Investigaciones de Historia del Derecho, 2001); John P. McIntyre, *Customary Law in the Corpus Iuris Canonici* (San Francisco: Mellen Research University Press, 1990); José Ángel Fernández Arruti, "La costumbre en la nueva codificación canónica," in Michel Thériault and Jean Thorn, eds., *Le Nouveau Code de Droit Canonique/The New Code of Canon Law. Proceedings of the 5th International Congress of Canon Law, organized by Saint Paul University and held at the University of Ottawa, August 19–25, 1984* (Ottawa: Faculty of Canon Law, University of Saint Paul, 1986); and Jorge Alberto González Galván, *El estado y las etnias nacionales en México: La relación entre el derecho estatal y el derecho consuetudinario* (Mexico City: Universidad Nacional Autónoma de México, 1995).

24. John Frederick Schwaller, *Church and Clergy in Sixteenth-Century Mexico* (Albuquerque: University of New Mexico Press, 1987), 4–5.

25. Montenegro, *Itinerario*, 336.

26. On the legal theory behind the system of two republics, see Woodrow W. Bo-rah, *Justice by Insurance: The General Indian Court of Colonial Mexico and the Legal Aides of the Half-Real* (Berkeley: University of California Press, 1983), chap. 3; and Colin M. MacLachlan, *Spain's Empire in the New World: The Role of Ideas in Institutional and Social Change* (Berkeley: University of California Press, 1988). On the early division of Mex-ico City into Indian and non-Indian parishes, see Roberto Moreno de los Arcos, "Los territorios parroquiales de la ciudad arzobispal, 1525–1981," *Gaceta oficial del Arzobis-pado de México* 22 (1982); and Edmundo O'Gorman, "Reflexiones sobre la distribu-ción urbana colonial de la ciudad de México," *Boletín del Archivo General de la Nación* 9, no. 4 (1938).

27. In the civil sphere, the pueblo of Ixtacalco formed part of the *parcialidad* of San Juan Tenochtitlan, one of two semi-autonomous Indian wards that was based in Mex-ico City but that also embraced surrounding villages. See Andrés Lira, *Comunidades in-dígenas frente a la ciudad de México: Tenochtitlan y Tlatelolco, sus pueblos y barrios, 1812–1919* (Mexico City: El Colegio de México, 1995).

28. Authorities referred to such a transfer of parochial administration from the reg-ular to the secular clergy as the secularization of a parish. The secularization of Mex-ico City's *doctrinas de indios* was part of a larger effort by the Spanish crown to curtail the power of the regular orders throughout its dominions during the second half of the eighteenth century. See David Brading, *Church and State in Bourbon Mexico: The Diocese of Michoacán, 1748–1810* (Cambridge: Cambridge University Press, 1994), chap. 4; Oscar Mazín Gómez, *Entre dos majestades: El obispo y la iglesia del gran Michoacán ante las reformas Borbónicas (1758–1772)* (Zamora: El Colegio de Michoacán, 1987); Virve Piho, *La secularización de las parroquias en la Nueva España y su repercusión en San Andrés Calpan* (Mexico City: Instituto Nacional de Antropología e Historia, 1981); and William B. Taylor, *Magistrates of the Sacred: Priests and Parishioners in Eighteenth-Century Mexico* (Stanford, CA: Stanford University Press, 1996).

29. See, for example, AHAM, caja 107, *Libro de curatos-vicarías del Arzobispado de México*, 1772–1784, "San Matías Yxtacalco." For a later census, see AGN, *Ayuntamien-tos*, vol. 187, "Padrón de Santa Ana Zacatalamanco" and "Padrón de los tres pueblos: San Juan Nexticpac, Santa María Magdalena Atlaxolpan, Asumpción de Aculco."

30. AHAM, caja 15, "Padrón del curato de Yztacalco, y pueblos de su jurisdicción hecho en el año de 1779."

31. One rumor suggested that in 1814 some of Ixtacalco's residents attempted to kill their priest by poisoning the wine he used to celebrate mass. AHAM, caja 51, *Li-bro de miscelánea tom. I de varias doctrinas morales, costumbres, observaciones, y otras notas pertenecientes al curato de Iztacalco, lo comenzó el actual cura Manuel Espinosa de los Monteros en mayo de 1831*, tom. 1, no. 56, f. 44, "Veneno." On the tenure of Manuel Morales (*cura* of Ixtacalco, 1811–16), see AHAM, *Libro de miscelánea*, tom. 1, f. 1. On the priest José María Bucheli (*cura* of Ixtacalco, 1813–29), see AHAM, *Libro de miscelánea*, tom. 1, f. 1, "Breve noticia de los curas clérigos de Ystacalco"; tom. 1, f. 35, "Caritativa pre-vención a un cura nuevo"; and tom. 1, no. 56, f. 44, "Veneno." The disdain that many of Ixtacalco's priests held for their appointment stemmed, in part, from the paltry in-

come the parish produced. After secularization, parish income for the years 1771–78 averaged only 400 pesos per annum, which placed it among the least lucrative curacies in the Archdiocese of Mexico. See Taylor, *Magistrates of the Sacred*, 480.

32. See, for example, Archivo Parroquial de San Matías Ixtacalco (APSMI), "Conatos de los curas contra la embriaguez y exesos de los paseos," 1782–1792 (1831–1832); and AHAM, *Libro de miscelánea*, tom. 1, no. 55, fs. 40–43, "Daños de embriaguez en Ystacalco," and tom. 2, no. 2, fs. 12–13, "Consumo de pulque." On the illegal importation of *aguardiente*, see AGN, *Aguardiente*, vol. 1, exp. 12, fs. 382–402, 1799.

33. Calderón de la Barca, *Life in Mexico*, 130.

34. AHAM, *Libro de miscelánea*, tom. 1, no. 1, fs. 1r–2v, "Breve noticia de los curas clérigos de Ystacalco."

35. On the declining use of Nahuatl in the town, see the report by the parish priest, José María Huerta, who reported to the archdiocesan secretary in 1845 that the native language of the parish was "Mexicano," but "today without exception all speak Spanish." See AGN, *Bienes Nacionales*, leg. 369, exp. 40.

36. AHAM, *Libro de miscelánea*, tom. 1, no. 10, f. 9, "Conviene que el cura haga un padrón de todos los vecinos de Ystacalco."

37. Calderón de la Barca, *Life in Mexico*, 379.

38. In 1771 Mexican prelates led by Francisco Antonio de Lorenzana (archbishop of Mexico, 1766–72) and Francisco Fabián y Fuero (bishop of Puebla, 1765–73) convened for the Fourth Mexican Provincial Council, which drafted new laws for the Mexican church, though their work was never ratified. In any case, the general outlines of parish administration and pastoral care from the Fourth Provincial differed little from those from the Third Provincial Council of 1585. On the Fourth Provincial Council, see Luisa Zahino Peñafort, ed., *El Cardenal Lorenzana y el IV Concilio Provincial Mexicano* (Mexico City: Universidad Nacional Autónoma de México, 1999).

39. Montenegro, *Itinerario*; Manuel Pérez, *Farol indiano y guía de curas de indios: Summa de los cinco sacramentos que administra los ministros evangélicos en esta América, con los casos morales que suceden entre los indios*, 1713. For a discussion of their work, see Taylor, *Magistrates of the Sacred*, 153–62.

40. AGN, *Ministerio de Justicia y Negocios Eclesiásticos*, vol. 12, fs. 188–209, 1822; AHAM, caja del año 1823, "Decreto de Agustín de Iturbide sobre la clasificación de personas en libros parroquiales," 1823.

41. Consanguinity refers to the proximity of kinship between marriage partners.

42. For a masterful study of clerical thought during this period, see Brian Connaughton, *Ideología y sociedad en Guadalajara (1788–1853)* (Mexico City: UNAM-CONACULTA, 1992).

43. AHAM, *Libro de miscelánea*, tom. 2, no. 8, fs. 7r–8r, "Tempestad contra la Yglesia."

44. In the early nineteenth century, one cleric estimated that an Indian parish of two thousand residents could be expected to generate approximately 500 pesos per year from such fees. See Taylor, *Magistrates of the Sacred*, 136–37.

45. Taylor, *Magistrates of the Sacred*, 135, 424–35.

46. On the supposedly ambiguous identity of Ixtacalco's parishioners as interpreted through language use, see AHAM, *Libro de miscelánea*, tom. 1, no. 73, fs. 59v–60r, "Castellano no aprendiendo y Mexicano olvidando."

47. AHAM, *Libro de miscelánea*, tom. 1, no. 45, f. 35v, "Caritativa prevención a un Cura nuevo."

48. AHAM, *Libro de miscelánea*, tom. 1, no. 10, f. 9r, "Conviene que el cura haga un padrón de todos los vecinos de Ystacalco."

49. AHAM, *Libro de miscelánea*, tom. 1, no. 54, fs. 40r–v, "Novios parientes." At the time, canon law allowed Indians to marry in the "third degree of consanguinity" (e.g., second cousins) or higher without seeking a dispensation from the hierarchy. All marriages involving non-Indians were restricted to the fifth degree or higher.

50. AHAM, *Libro de miscelánea*, tom. 1, no. 54, fs. 40r–v, "Novios parientes."

51. Holy days of obligation are those dates on which Catholics are required to attend mass in addition to Sundays. Mexican church law specified different requirements for Indians and non-Indians. AHAM, *Libro de miscelánea*, tom. 1, no. 18, f. 14v, "Penitencias que pueden imponerse a los yndios."

52. AHAM, *Libro de miscelánea*, tom. 1, no. 44, fs. 35r–v, "¿Que fee merezcan las deposiciones de los yndios contra sus curas?"

53. AHAM, *Libro de miscelánea*, tom. 1, no. 44, fs. 35r–v, "¿Que fee merezcan las deposiciones de los yndios contra sus curas?"

54. For a wide-ranging exploration of legal pluralism, see Lauren A. Benton, *Law and Colonial Cultures* (New York: Cambridge University Press, 2002).

55. García Cubas, *Atlas geográfico, estadístico e histórico*, Carta XVII, "Valle de México."

3

"Para formar el corazón religioso de los jóvenes": Processes of Change in Collective Religiosity in Nineteenth-Century Oaxaca

Daniela Traffano

The Feast of Peter the Apostle in Nochixtlan, Oaxaca, 1957. Note the image of the saint in the center carrying the papal cross symbolizing his role as the first pope. This feast was sponsored each year by the San Pedro neighborhood in Nochixtlán. Photographed by Ignacio Zanabria.

In the essay that follows I analyze a process of change in the structure of collective religiosity in a traditional society. That change implies the active presence of popular memory and historical actors' capacity to adapt in order to survive and to take advantage of new historical situations. This explanation is based on the social and cultural dynamics of the "reality" that is analyzed here and it is located in the "deep" history of nineteenth-century Mexico.[1] Specifically, I refer to the diffusion of the Laws of Reform in the state of Oaxaca during the nineteenth century and the consequences that these laws provoked in the social structure and in the organization of collective religiosity in indigenous communities.

In centering attention on the second half of that century, it is necessary to note that this period was characterized by the diffusion of the liberal doctrine and the promulgation of a new legislation. The separation of the church from the state was one of the basic principles of liberal politics and determined a profound and wide process of the secularization of society. The Lerdo Laws of 1856 and the nationalization of 1859 as well as the 1857 Constitution gave a decisive impulse to that process because these laws not only affected the patrimony of the church, but they also prohibited owners from the corporate administration of those goods on a civil level (via bans on governmental participation) or ecclesiastical levels (via confraternities).

We now know that since pre-Hispanic times a fundamental part of the existence of indigenous pueblos was organized around a religious cult, with the temple as the focus, as an expression of collective religiosity. Throughout the colonial period the confraternities took care of the material and spiritual aspects of community religious life. Historical and ethnographic sources show that during the twentieth century, confraternities, *mayordomías*, and Catholic associations were the institutions that gave voice, power, and influence to the community by offering resources to defray the costs of the temple, religious festivals, and pious sentiments.[2] Over the course of the nineteenth century, indigenous communities modified the structure of their collective religiosity by adding the *mayordomía* and Catholic association to the confraternity. Much work remains to be done on the historical processes behind these religious structural changes.

This essay analyzes each one of the religious institutions that were set up in Oaxaca during the nineteenth century in order to better understand the historical dynamics behind changes in indigenous religious practices and organization during Mexico's national period.

CONFRATERNITIES

The confraternity is one of the best-known and perhaps most important components of society in New Spain. Confraternities were introduced by missionaries in the sixteenth century and quickly became a means of aggregation, religious expression, and economic relations, and they continue to have a strong presence in both urban and rural settings. Confraternities were created for the veneration of a saint and were committed to disseminating and protecting its cult and worship. Additionally, a particular confraternity was charged with the goals of mutual aid, particularly concerning the death and passing of its members. Political and economic relations developed among confraternity members. The degree of wealth and prestige of a confraternity ultimately depended on its members, who were subordinate to their time and circumstances but nevertheless determined if a confraternity prospered or declined.

One can distinguish between indigenous confraternities and Spanish confraternities by focusing on some key characteristics. Spanish confraternities were usually organized in urban centers and were a medium through which economic resources were administrated and social networks strengthened. Indigenous confraternities were normally rural organizations whose functions were much more complex. As various authors maintain, the indigenous confraternity had two distinct levels of contact with pueblos: economic and spiritual.[3] Economically, a pueblo confraternity facilitated the organization of the goods and wealth of the community into what one might consider the community treasury. Spiritually, confraternities offered security and a sense of collective identity.

The confraternities responded, then, to a general necessity of the population and were characterized by their capacity for internal aggregation, which ran parallel to the larger community. The members were united around a saint, by pueblo and barrio, and represented organizations strictly tied to the economic and social dimensions of their respective territories. They were not characterized by a large, elaborate organizational structure, and the majority of the expenses were paid with community properties rather than from contributions from individuals who sought personal prestige. In Oaxaca, the income of confraternities came from sources similar to those of the community treasury: the work of the pueblo, crops, and livestock from communal lands.[4]

A tight bond existed between the goods of the confraternity and those of the community to the point of occasional confusion. Sometimes the pueblos assigned lands for cultivation and grazing to the confraternities[5] and these, in turn, financed the public works of municipalities or the lawsuits of the communities.[6]

In the state of Oaxaca between 1856 and 1862 liberal legislation established the means by which ecclesiastical goods could be confiscated by the state; community confraternity lands and livestock were disentailed and repartitioned. The application of this liberal reform determined the transformation of the confraternities and provoked a variety of situations in which the communities submitted to, applied, utilized, disobeyed, or violated those laws.

The testimonies of priests confirm that some confraternities were extinguished. In 1868 the priest of San Pedro Teozaocalco explained:

> There was a time when the branch of the confraternity, being regularly funded, helped the parishioners or titled mayordomos to satisfy their duties, masses, anniversaries and other costs of the cult as well as maintain the solemnity of the Church. None of these functions continue to exist. Consequently, everything that depended on the confraternity has ended and will not return again barring a special miracle from heaven.[7]

The Minas parish suffered the same fate. Offerings and shares of goods were reduced "because the livestock . . . was destroyed . . . due to the ill-fated laws of the reform."[8] Finally, in the pueblo of Tlacoatzintepec the parish priest explained the decrease of the emoluments as the result of the intervention of the *jefe político* of Cuicatlan who "has prohibited everything to the mayordomos and confraternities by giving authority to the presidents of each pueblo, all of whom are predisposed to make the confraternities and mayordomos disappear."[9]

Other testimonies take on an opposing political stance. For instance, the parish priest of the pueblo subject to Huahutla observed that his congregation was transformed for the better as a result of disentailment of church property, despite the fact that such measures led to church poverty. He stated that "the confraternities of livestock and money that were under the care and vigilance of the lord priest [*señor cura*] are now in the power of the authorities for their common use."[10] The priest of Villa Alta also argued along these lines and commented in 1868 that "the jefe político ordered the coup de grace to the festivals, dissolving the congregations that still survived, relieving the members of all obligations and responsibility and applying what used to be goods of the Church or confraternity to benefit common funds."[11]

These examples show that despite the laws that defined the suppression of the congregations, the citizens, as collective bodies, found ways to maintain communal properties that had belonged to the confraternities and to conserve their character of "shared utility."

There also existed pueblos where the confraternities simply survived with their property, which was perhaps reduced, but still officially in their power. This is the case of Cañadaltepec where between 1884 and 1898 the confraternity conserved various heads of livestock, retained some communal lands that belonged to the church, and sowed the "common" land for the benefit of the church.[12] Nevertheless, it appears that in general, the confraternities lost their properties and were able to survive the liberal winds by conserving a fund of cash and wax that they dedicated principally to the care of the cult and, sometimes, to supporting the shrine with materials and spiritual items. In Tuxtla, for example, the masses paid for by various confraternities represented a fourth of the monthly income of the parish,[13] while San Pedro Amuzgos, which at the end of the nineteenth century counted 1,309 inhabitants, counted a total of sixteen confraternities with a combined capital of 1,405 pesos. We find that in Huahutla a treasurer nominated by the priest collected money among the confraternities to buy musical instruments, showing how these organizations still found ways of meeting the material and spiritual needs of the community.[14] In Miahuatlan it was the fund of the Señor de Cuixla that financed the "composure of the standard and the five tin candleholders of that church,"[15] while in Juquila the money of the Virgin paid for the porters and the material of the works of the church and the *cabecera* (principal Indian pueblo in a region).[16]

The general impoverishment that occurred during this period changed the economic and social functions of the confraternity. It could no longer serve as the treasury for the community, nor could it facilitate mutual help for confraternity members. Rather, the material and spiritual energy of the group was concentrated from then on around the cult. The saint, the altar, his/her festival, the temple that housed him/her—all occupied the time and economic efforts of the devotees.

Concerning the internal organization of the confraternities, we find that mayordomos still directed the corporations. They collected alms and received the daily offerings with which they could ask and pay for the masses.[17] They collaborated with the priests in cases where the church and the laity shared the management of funds,[18] and in a special function, they received annually their positions and new responsibility.[19] There also existed an important relationship with the political authorities of the pueblos. In Juchitengo the civil authorities presided over the changing of the mayordomos of the confraternity of the Miracle, supervising the delivery of the wax and the cash of its collections.[20] In Santiago Atitlan the mayordomos of the saints offered the alms to the "justicia" of the pueblo in order to buy instruments.[21] Evidently the ties that united the authorities, and the feelings and manifestations of the community, tied the civil authority as the political representative of the people to the religious representative, the church, through its connection to the collectivity, the confraternity. What tightened the knot was the confirmation of the tight relationship among these entities that began with the colonial experience that had generated these three basic dimensions of indigenous reality.

Toward the beginning of the twentieth century, the Miter of Oaxaca decided to compile information about the situation of the archdiocese. To this end, it sent to the parishes a questionnaire about territories, the economy, and their parishioners. An important section of this document dealt with the diffusion and quality of devotion of the faithful and also with the canonically erected associations, brotherhoods, and *mayordomías*, their memberships, and the funds that they managed. Unfortunately, it is not easy to understand what distinction existed between these three types of organizations, and the responses of the priests do not clarify the situation. On the contrary, a notable confusion emerges from the priests concerning these three categories. Always taking into consideration the possible interchange or confusion of terms—religious association, brotherhood, *mayordomía*—I suspect that, in some cases, the fathers used the word "mayordomía" when referring to what I have called here a confraternity. Indeed, each one of these "mayordomías" corresponded to a saint and consequently to a festival. They were administered by a layperson who kept the name of mayordomo and, in the majority of cases, was the only person who collected or provided for the festival of its saint. The most important point, however, is that there is no explicit mention of an individual financing them, a characteristic element, as we will see further on, of the *mayordomías*.

In summary, during the second half of the nineteenth century the confraternity was in part transformed, yet persisted by adapting to changing conditions. By promoting and spreading a cult of a saint and attending to its festivals, the confraternity maintained its function as a means of expressing and manifesting collective religiosity. The structure of its leadership, which still fell on the figure of the mayordomo, suggests that a continuity with the colonial period was maintained. Nevertheless, since the confraternities were forced to relinquish a significant part and source of economic goods, the ways in which they made manifest their intentions were forced to change as well. Confraternities lost their capacity for mutual aid among members and in the majority of cases also their capacity to finance or help with the economic necessities of the community. Finally, the terminological confusion that emerges from the testimonies of priests at the beginning of the nineteenth century indicates that other institutions existed and that they shared with confraternities the landscape of the social and religious life of the pueblos.

MAYORDOMÍAS

For our purposes here I will define the *mayordomía* as a job or position that someone assumes in order to assure the completion of the festivals and other rituals relative to the saints of one's pueblo. This position is basically an individual responsibility that arose, according to some authors, as a consequence of the intervention of the colonial authorities against the collective payment of the necessary costs of the festivals and the impoverishment of the confraternities throughout the nineteenth century.[22]

Ethnographic studies of Oaxaca elaborated in the last decades of the twentieth century show that despite local particularities and the characteristics of the municipalities of each ethnic group, the *mayordomías* share common roots. In the twentieth century they were an instrument for the expression of collective popular religiosity, and as such, the *mayordomías* concerned themselves with the celebration of a saint and they characterized themselves as institutions based on individual patronage.[23]

The quality of ecclesiastical sources I used to analyze this institution made me reflect on its meaning and function in indigenous communities in order to contribute to the reconstruction of their history. These documents began to appear in the 1870s and they deal with ceremonies solicited and financed only by the mayordomos. It seems no reference was made about the existence of confraternities, brotherhoods, or associations. Certainly that omission could be the result of chance. The one clue we have for understanding this situation differently is that mayordomos alone opened the possibilities for assuming responsibility over and patronage of religious practices around local patron saints. In San Miguel Tlalixtac, for example, the mayordomos assumed the costs of the masses,[24] while in Ixcatlan and Jalapa the celebrations for the titular saints of the pueblos were paid for by the mayordomos with cash.[25] Finally, in Santa María Ozolotepec the mayordomos and the local magistrate (*justicia*) covered the costs of the fiestas and the magistrate covered the costs of the offerings (*ofrendas*).[26]

We can better understand *mayordomías* as individual patronage of collective fiestas, a fact that is confirmed when we observe the dimensions of their civil characteristics. The *jefe político* of Nochixtlan, for example, declared deliberately to the inhabitants of his district:

> Their customs are less exaggerated than before but nevertheless, some of them have reduced many individuals to misery through the costs of these [festivals]. For example, when the festival of some particular image occurs, the individual charged with voluntarily making it available goes into debt because he contributes such increased costs that his means are not enough to satisfy them. . . . The performance takes place with as much pomp as possible and the result of all this is a debt whose repayment forces one to sell one's farm tools, if he has them, his arable lands, his seeds or whatever he possesses. . . . The maintenance of all this comes out of the owner of the house of the one charged with this responsibility. Consequently it is indispensable to prepare all the flour necessary for bread, enough tortillas of maíz, chocolate, meat, a good deal of mescal, pulque, cigarettes and whatever else necessary, always in abundance. . . . It is customary that the day of the religious function all the most important personages, all the members of the municipality and the elders of the pueblo, called ancianos, attend the breakfast in the house of the mayordomo. All these costs indubitably ruin the said mayordomo; it is rather a precept among them that they consider it dishonorable when they cannot provide all the said costs.[27]

Returning to the questionnaire that was developed at the beginning of the twentieth century, we find testimonies on this situation. For example, the parishes of San Martín Tilcajete and of Jamiltepec note that the "existing mayordomías do not have funds and the mayordomos spend their own money to pay for the festivals they are responsible for."[28] The same situation we find in San Matías Jalatlaco where the parish showed that the *mayordomías* "do not have funds because if they did at one point they lost them with the law of disentailment."[29]

Taken together, the information suggests that the *mayordomías* constituted a phenomenon that emerged over the course of the nineteenth century. They coexisted and were confused with the institution of the confraternity from the 1860s on and can be considered a direct consequence of the impoverishment that the *mayordomías* experienced as a result of the Reform Laws.[30] This individualization of collective responsibilities was presented then as a response to the structural changes suffered by the "ancient" religious corporations and as an alternative form that allowed the pueblos to perpetuate the glorification of their particular patron saint and concurrently respond to the community demands of religious expressions that had been until then satisfied by confraternities.

CATHOLIC SOCIETIES AND RELIGIOUS ASSOCIATIONS

Jorge Adame Goddard and Manuel Ceballos Ramírez have reconstructed and analyzed the phenomenon of the Catholic Societies and situated their origins in urban areas around the 1860s.[31] Goddard shows that in Mexico City those conservatives who were no longer directly active in politics organized a group whose goal centered on promoting religious interests. For his part, Ceballos Ramírez argues that the foundation of Catholic Societies should be seen as an incursion of Mexican Catholics in the arena of social activities and action.

As in cities of Mexico, Zacatecas, Guanajuato, San Luis Potosí, and Veracruz, the Catholics of Oaxaca also were part of a national Catholic movement. In 1884 they founded in the capital of Oaxaca the Sociedad de Obreros Católicos (Society of Catholic Workers), discussed at length by Mark Overmyer-Velázquez in this volume. This society established various "círculos" (circles) of activity under the slogan of "religion, union and independence."[32] To this end the society had its members working in four distinct commissions that taught Christian doctrine, administered schools, regulated the economic administration of the society, and provided mutual aid. Doctrine was taught weekly in six temples throughout the city and in these sessions, a great number of catechisms written by Father Ripalda were distributed. Meanwhile two schools of primary instruction had been opened thanks to the cooperation and volition of members who had been solicited.

An effective administration of the contributions of the members of the society developed by those in charge of the treasury had given rise to an increase in funds within a matter of a few years, allowing them to establish a savings fund. The work of the commission of mutual aid had ensured that all the members who were in good standing by paying their dues and who happened to become ill would be cared for by guarantee of the statute. Through the work of the society and its principles of virtue and morality, of hard work and of respect for authority, many workers—and their apprentices—attended mass regularly on Sundays and festival days. Some members who lived out of wedlock married and others who had been given over to gambling and drinking "reformed" themselves.[33]

The Catholic Society of Ladies (Sociedad Católica de Señoras) was founded in the capital of Oaxaca in 1870. In the six years following, twenty-one "Foreign Societies" (Sociedades Foráneas), or societies outside the capital, were born in various other districts.[34] Through a statistic published in 1877 we know that the society of the capital counted at that time 113 active members, forty-five "cooperators," and eight benefactors. Their principal good works included teaching the doctrine to girls and adults in various churches. They formally arranged the sacramental union of more than twenty people who had been living out of wedlock, had given three workshops with the majority of the society's members in attendance, practiced days of religious retreat, established an endowed mass for the Immaculate Conception, cooperated actively in various solemnities, and sponsored various masses on distinct occasions. Likewise, the Catholic Society of Ladies had financially supported a school where girls learned reading, writing, handiwork, manners, home economics, and religious history. Finally, the society had taken care of the upkeep of the majority of the city's churches, bringing flowers, bouquets, altar clothing, and ornaments.[35]

For the most part, outside of the capital such activities varied little. The Catholic Societies were most active in teaching the doctrine, church upkeep, celebrating various festival days, ensuring that adults and children attended the sacraments, and attending to the sick. A brief flyer that was approved by the "Catholic Society" of Oaxaca City served as the code by which the women of the provincial societies established their spheres of activity. The first two articles explained that the Catholic Society had as its goal the moralization of the pueblos through means of religious instruction, observing the sacraments, help in necessities of life, propagation of good books, and the protection of the divine cult. To this end the members were expected to contribute alms each month. These contributions came to form part of the fund for catechisms for children and wax candles. After these costs were covered, the remaining funds were used for works of the commissions of the cult (i.e., physical worship and maintenance of churches) and to aid the sick and the poor.[36]

By establishing themselves in rural areas these Catholic Societies adapted to new religious demands that went beyond recuperating a Catholic social space that had been "usurped" by liberal politicians. These Catholic Societies expressed the demand for collective religiosity strongly tied to Christian doctrine in its most orthodox manifestations. To this end people gathered around the church and, in the name of their patron Virgin, pursued strictly doctrinaire goals. These associations were distinct not only because of their religious outlook and their individual, particular characteristics, but also because they facilitated a collective religiosity that was distinct from confraternities and *mayordomías* through their figure of a promoter, the organizational hierarchy of the members, their expanded funds, and their social goals.

In the first place, these "pious and charitable associations" were born from the initiative of a parish priest who likewise was charged with officially heading the associations. From Tlacolula, the parish, "desiring to foment the piety of its flock and to promote the cult of the Holy Virgin" in the name of "some pious persons," asked permission from the diocese to found the Brotherhood of the Most Pure Conception (Hermandad de la Purísima Concepción).[37] The regulations of the Association of Our Lady of the Cloister (Asociación de

Nuestra Señora del Claustro) stated: "The parish priest is automatically the rector of said association"[38] and the members "will give detailed accounts of the collection that they have made"[39] to the priest and he, in turn, had the responsibility to inform the diocese of these accounts each year.[40] On the other hand, the practical administration of the society remained in the hands of a hierarchy established by statutes and elected, under the supervision of the parish, by the community of members. In general this hierarchy included a president, a treasurer, and a secretary.[41]

With respect to property these associations were characterized by their lack of funds. Their income consisted primarily of voluntary donations. Accordingly these associations were incapable of reproducing or increasing their properties as the confraternities had done previously. They also did not delegate their necessary expenses to a single member as was the case with *mayordomías*. Neither do we see here the presence of grand festivals that involved the entire community: the funds collected served to pay for the annual or monthly mass of a venerated saint, to buy wax and necessary adornments for the saint's altar,[42] to help sick members,[43] or to buy doctrinal books.[44]

In the eleven cases that I have considered, the foundation of these societies was justified by the desire to promote the cult and devotion to an image of a particular saint: in Tlacolula, the Virgin of the Most Pure Conception (Virgen de la Purísima Concepción); in Teotitlan del Camino, that of Guadalupe; and so on. To this principal goal were added other justifications that specified further the intents of each association. In Santa Catarina Juquila, the promoter of the Apostolate of Prayer (Apostolato de la Oración) aspired to "moralize the customs of the faithful," while in Miahuatlan the Guadalupan Association had as its goal to stimulate its members at least to confess and commune at the festivals. The parish priest of Ocotlan was the rector of a pious and charitable association that, in the name of Our Lady of the Cloister, was organized for the assistance of its sick members so that there would be someone to accompany them during their suffering and to organize their funerals in case of death.[45] Likewise, the association dedicated to Saint Peter the Apostle in Etla was concerned with helping their brothers when they ailed and died. Nevertheless, its most urgent goal was "to form the religious heart of the youth through the teaching of the Christian doctrine."[46]

Therefore, during the second half of the nineteenth century, when the Catholic Church was losing power and legitimacy, the initiatives of the parishes were important because they were symbolic and made materially significant strides toward financing the expression of popular religiosity. The church actively promoted Catholic Societies as a reaction to the impoverishment of the parish economies and the ever-growing resistance of the citizens to provide offerings and dues to this institution.[47] Faced with the enormous costs incurred in iconic celebrations termed "profane diversions," the church preferred to invest in the parish priest who would be held responsible for the economy of the local associations. The structures and goals of these associations worked to foment strict religious devotion, maintain the material well-being of churches, and ensure that the dues corresponded strictly to liturgical functions.

These considerations were complemented by the logic that inspired the faithful to become "members." In the rhetoric of the manuscripts, the pious associations were a fundamental response to the secularization of society and presented themselves as the solution to "the anguished situation by whose terrible ordeal Our Mother the Holy Church is passing, by the relentless persecution on the part of the civil power, a power that strives to meet its depraved goals."[48] Finally, the same nature of these associations suggests that they were born to satisfy a spiritual demand of the populace. They filled a void left by the confraternities in the field of mutual aid and, in some cases, functioned as a precursor or complement to the schools of Catholic doctrine.

CONCLUSION

The Reform Laws and the 1857 Constitution were the protagonists of the official history of the second half of the nineteenth century. They played active roles in the development of a profound process of secularization that had a considerable impact on all the dimensions of life in Mexico. Focusing on the rural indigenous reality of the state of Oaxaca, I have tried to move my analysis to the level of "deep history" in order to be able to study the consequences of this process in the sphere of collective religiosity. I paid particular attention to the social and cultural aspects of the confraternities, *mayordomías*, and Catholic Societies that emerged during this period. These organizations aided in the expression of collective spirituality and constituted the means of aggregation and transmission of the religious and cultural values of the community.

Thus through the confraternities we saw that, although these organizations were able to adapt to the new laws and circumstances, they were so significantly impoverished that they inevitably had to suffer substantial changes in their collective and social goals. The confraternities survived, but in their struggle for survival, they lost their ability to respond to the material demands of the community, to guarantee assistance to their sick members, or to provide a funeral for the deceased. They could no longer celebrate the patron saint "as customary," a situation that gave momentum to the individualization of collective responsibilities and so to the development of the *mayordomías*. The festival of the saint continues to be a communal celebration. It currently is made possible thanks to individual patronage. This new custom's sustainability depends on the individual's capacity to pay for it. The *mayordomías* presented themselves, then, as a new form of administration of collective religiosity and could be seen as the result of a process of adaptation of the community to the phenomenon of the secularization of society.

Finally, the Catholic associations appeared as a response to other material and spiritual vacuums left by weakened confraternities. On one side, they guaranteed the satisfaction of the demands of mutual character of their members while, on the other, they ensured a renewed, sustained economy for the parish and the local church. Finally, their structures and goals were a reaction of Catholics to the secularization of society, of education, and, in general, of everyday life. In this sense the Catholic Societies were organized around an image with the object of propelling their devotion and teaching the Christian doctrine to children and adults alike. That image did not represent the entire community and promoting it became instead the task of a restricted group of people who, due to a profound change in the traditional structure of the expression of collective religion, would celebrate their festival so that the community did not fall into the disgrace and "pagan degeneration" that the church so feared.

Ultimately, the three institutions—confraternities, *mayordomías*, and Catholic associations—were born in a historical moment that created the distinct structural characteristics that allowed each organization to respond to the different needs of communities in particular ways. Though their origins lie in the changes provoked by a "legislative event" of the official history, their development, characteristics, and coexistence are a fundamental part of the "deep history" of the society here analyzed. Taken together, these organizations were social and cultural responses of the population to the processes of social secularization. This provoked substantial changes in the structure of the confraternity. This institution in turn diversified and essentially became the *mayordomía* and Catholic Societies. Together, the three shared a similar mission: they responded to both new and old demands and obligations—material, spiritual, symbolic—of the collective religiosity of the indigenous communities of Oaxaca.

NOTES

Chapter opening image source: Centro Fotográfico Álvarez Bravo, Fondo Ignacio Zanabria.

This chapter was translated by Martin Austin Nesvig with Lina del Castillo.

1. This is a reference here to the French school of the *Annales* and to the well-known concept of "deep history." See Fernand Braudel, *Las ambiciones de la historia* (Barcelona: Crítica, 2002). Evidently the first—the history of events—corresponds to the official history while popular memory remains one of the many dimensions that compose "profound" or "deep" history.

2. Translator's note: I have chosen to use the English term "confraternity" here for the Spanish "cofradía." Some corporate terms, like "mayordomía," seem better left in Spanish, given the cumbersome nature of English-language terms for it like "superintendency." Other terms that will be familiar to students and professional historians alike I have left in Spanish, notably "pueblo" and "barrio," since these are legal-social-cultural terms that have few if any direct English-language equivalents.

3. Charles Gibson, *Los Aztecas bajo el dominio español* (Mexico City: Siglo XX, 1967); and Rodolfo Pastor, *Campesinos y reformas: La Mixteca 1700–1856* (Mexico City: El Colegio de México, 1987).

4. María de los Angeles Romero Frizzi, *El sol y la cruz. Los pueblos indios de Oaxaca colonial* (Mexico City: CIESAS-INI, 1996), 227.

5. Marcello Carmagnani, *El Regreso de los dioses* (Mexico City: Fondo de Cultura Económica, 1988).

6. William B. Taylor, *Magistrates of the Sacred: Priests and Parishioners in Eighteenth Century Mexico* (Stanford, CA: Stanford University Press, 1996); Jesús Edgard Mendoza García, "Bienes de comunidad: Cohesión y autonomía de Santo Domingo Tepenene Oaxaca, durante la segunda mitad del siglo XIX. 1856–1910" (Tesis de licenciatura en etnohistoria, n.p., 1996).

7. AHAO, Diocesano, Gobierno, Parroquias, 1868. Distrito de Teposcolula. "Hubo un tiempo en que el ramo de cofradía siendo de muy regulares fondos ayudaba a los feligreses o titulados mayordomos a satisfacer sus funciones, misas, aniversarios y otros gastos del culto y solemnidad de la Yglesia que ya no existen, por consiguiente todo lo que de aquello dependía concluyó para no volver jamás sino para un milagro especial del cielo."

8. AHAO, Diocesano, Gobierno, Parroquias, 1888. Distrito de Ejutla. "Porque los ganados . . . se destruyeron . . . en virtud de las malhadadas leyes de reforma."

9. AHAO, Diocesano, Gobierno, Parroquias, 1869. Distrito de Teotitlan. "Ha prohibido del todo mayordomos y cofradías autorizando a los Presidentes de los respectivos pueblos, estén al tanto de lo dicho a fin de desaparecer las cofradías y mayordomos."

10. AHAO, Diocesano, Gobierno, Parroquias, 1862. Distrito de Teposcolula. "Las cofradías de ganado y dinero que estaban al cuidado y vigilancia del Sor. Cura ahora se hayan [*sic*] en poder de las autoridades para su uso común."

11. AHAO, Diocesano, Gobierno, Parroquias, 1868. Distrito de Villa Alta. "El Jefe Político dio el golpe de gracia a las fiestas, disolviendo las congregaciones que aun subsistían absolviendo a los cofrades de todas obligaciones y responsabilidad y aplicando a fondos comunes los que eran de la Yglesia o de las cofradías."

12. AHAO, Diocesano, Gobierno, Parroquias, Teposcolula, 1898.

13. AHAO, Diocesano, Gobierno, Parroquias, 1861. Distrito de Jamiltepec.

14. AHAO, Diocesano, Gobierno, Parroquias, 1862. Distrito de Teotitlan.

15. AHAO, Diocesano, Gobierno, Parroquias, 1862. Distrito de Ejutla.

16. AHAO, Diocesano, Gobierno, Parroquias, 1877. Distrito de Jamiltepec.

17. AHAO, Diocesano, Gobierno, Parroquias, cuentas presentada por los mayordomos del Señor de Cuixtla a lo largo de todo el periodo considerado (1862–1895), Distrito de Jamiltepec.

18. As is the case of the confraternity of the Virgin of Juquila.

19. In Tilantongo, distrito de Teposcolula, for example, where on February 2 "regularmente se cambia la cofradía del Dulce Nombre y entre los dos mayordomos pagan doce misas del mes y la misa de aniversario que se canta con vigilia al día siguiente." AHAO, Diocesano, Gobierno, Parroquias, 1898.

20. AHAO, Diocesano, Gobierno, Parroquias, 1873. Distrito de Jamiltepec.

21. AHAO, Diocesano, Gobierno, Parroquias, 1877. Distrito de Villa Alta.

22. John Chance and William B. Taylor, "Cofradías y cargos: Una perspectiva histórica de la jerarquía cívico religiosa mesoamericana," in *Suplemento del Boletín Oficial del Instituto Nacional de Antropología e Historia*, nueva época 14 (1987); John Chance, *La conquista de la Sierra. Españoles e indígenas de Oaxaca en la época de la Colonia* (Oaxaca: IOC-FOESCA-CIESAS, 1998), 274.

23. See, e.g., Jorge Hernández Díaz and Jesús Lizama Quijana, *Cultura e identidad étnica en la región huave* (Oaxaca: UABJO, 1996); Ingrid Geist, *Comunión y disensión: Prácticas rituales en una aldea cuicateca* (Oaxaca: IOC-INAH-FOESCA, 1997); Etzuko Kuroda, *Bajo al Zempoaltepetl* (Mexico City: CIESAS-Instituto Oaxaqueño de las Culturas, 1993); James Greenberg, *Religión y economía de los chatinos* (Mexico City: Instituto Nacional Indigenista, 1981); and John Monaghan, "'We Are People Who Eat Tortillas': Household and Community in the Mixteca" (Ph.D. diss., Univ. of Pennsylvania, 1987).

24. AHAO, Diocesano, Gobierno, Parroquias, 1875. Distrito del Centro.

25. AHAO, Diocesano, Gobierno, Parroquias, 1892. Distrito de Teotitlan.

26. AHAO, Diocesano, Gobierno, Parroquias, 1893. Distrito de Ejutla.

27. AHAO, Diocesano, Gobierno, Parroquias. Distrito de Nochixtlan. Teposcolula, Memoria del gobernador, 1872–1873: "Sus costumbres son menos exageradas que antes, y, sin embargo, algunas de ellas han dado lugar á que muchos individuos queden reducidos á la miseria con motivo de los gastos que hacen; por ejemplo, ocurre la festividad de alguna imagen, y el individuo encargado voluntariamente para disponerla se empeña en erogar gastos tan crecidos que sus recursos no bastan á satisfacerlos; se contrae compromisos para llenar sus deseos; se verifica la función con la pompa posible, y el resultado de todo es una deuda cuyo pago hace vendiendo sus útiles de labranza, si los tiene, sus tierras de sembradura, sus semillas ó lo que posee. Quizás se arrepiente de su hecho; pero ese arrepentimiento tiene lugar después de consumado. Y no se diga que los gastos que se hacen son puramente en los asuntos de Iglesia: calculados los que por tal motivo se verifican, los demás se ejecutan por la concurrencia que hay en la casa del encargado de la festividad, en la cual es costumbre que asisten a sus parientes, compadres, amigos, conocidos y cuantos deseen prestar servicios; la manutención de todos estos corre de cuenta del dueño de la casa durante los días de la función, y por tal razón es indispensable preparar toda la harina necesaria para hacer pan, suficiente cantidad de tortillas de maíz, chocolate, carne, mucho vino mezcal, pulque, cigarros y todo cuanto es indispensable, siempre con abundancia, y sin que se tenga en cuenta la posibilidad de cada cual: es costumbre que el día de la función religiosa concurran a tomar el de-

sayuno en la casa del mayordomo (nombre que se da al encargado de festividad) las personas más notables, todos los miembros que componen el municipio del lugar y los ancianos del pueblo, a quienes llaman los *principales*. Estos gastos arruinan indudablemente al llamado mayordomo; mas es un precepto entre ellos, y se consideran hasta deshonrados cuando no pueden hacer todos los gastos expresados."

28. AHAO, Diocesano, Gobierno, Parroquias, 1908. "La primera en el distrito de Ejutla y la segunda en el de Jamiltepec."

29. AHAO, Diocesano, Gobierno, Parroquias, 1908. Distrito de Oaxaca.

30. Chance and Taylor, "Cofradías y cargos."

31. Jorge Adame Goddard, *El pensamiento político y social de los católicos mexicanos; 1867–1914* (Mexico City: UNAM, 1981); and Manuel Ceballos Ramírez, *El catolicismo social: Un tercero en discordia. Rerum Novarum, la "cuestión social" y la movilización de los católicos mexicanos (1891–1911)* (Mexico City: El Colegio de México, 1991).

32. Margarita Dalton, comp., *Oaxaca, textos de su historia*, 4 vols. (Mexico City: Instituto Mora; Gobierno del Estado de Oaxaca, 1990), 4:45.

33. "Memoria sobre la Sociedad de Obreros Católicos de Oaxaca," in Dalton, *Oaxaca*, 1:42–55.

34. *Breve instrucción aprobada por la Sociedad Católica de esta ciudad, que servirá de reglamento a las señoras de las sociedades foráneas* (Oaxaca: Imprenta de San-Germán, 1899); AHAO, Folletería, Impresos religiosos, Diócesis de Oaxaca, Impresos varios.

35. *Estadística de la Sociedad Católica de Señoras de esta capital y de los distritos, correspondiente a los años de 1875 y 1876* (Oaxaca: Tip. de L. San Germán, 1877).

36. *Breve instrucción aprobada por la Sociedad Católica de esta ciudad, que servirá de reglamento a las señoras de las sociedades foráneas* (Oaxaca: Imprenta de San Germán, 1899).

37. AHAO, Diocesano, Gobierno, Parroquias, 1891. Distrito de Tlacolula.

38. AHAO, Diocesano, Gobierno, Parroquias, 1870. Distrito de Ejutla. "Es rector nato de la expresada asociación el Cura párroco que por tiempo le fuere."

39. AHAO, Diocesano, Gobierno, Parroquias, Teozapotlan Zaachila, 1884. Distrito del Centro.

40. AHAO, Diocesano, Gobierno, Parroquias, Tecomatlan, 1874. Distrito de Teposcolula.

41. AHAO, Diocesano, Gobierno, Parroquias, Miahuatlan, 1903. Distrito de Ejutla.

42. AHAO, Diocesano, Gobierno, Parroquias, Teotitlan del Camino, 1895. Distrito de Teotitlan.

43. AHAO, Diocesano, Gobierno, Parroquias, Santo Domingo Ocotlan, 1870. Distrito de Ejutla.

44. AHAO, Diocesano, Gobierno, Parroquias, San Pedro Etla, 1886. Distrito del Centro.

45. AHAO, Diocesano, Gobierno, Parroquias, Ocotlan, 1870. Distrito de Ejutla.

46. AHAO, Diocesano, Gobierno, Parroquias, Etla, 1886. Distrito del Centro.

47. See Traffano, *Indios, curas y nación*, chap. 4.

48. AHAO, Diocesano, Gobierno, Parroquias, 1886. "La situación angustiada por cuya prueba terrible pasa Nuestra Madre la Santa Yglesia, por la persecución sin tregua de sus enemigos capitales, el poder civil, para conseguir sus depravados fines."

4
Mexican Laywomen Spearhead a Catholic Revival: The Ladies of Charity, 1863–1910

Silvia Marina Arrom

Elaborately Framed Print of the Lord of Cuixtla, Oaxaca. The center of a colonial-vintage pilgrimage devotion in Oaxaca's southern sierra, this image is celebrated each May 3. In a tin shadow box, gold-colored foil, and glass frame surrounded by paper flowers, this image probably dates from the mid-twentieth century. His festival was previously an important trade fair featuring the sale of matched pairs of plow oxen.

It is difficult to believe that an organization that counted thousands of members and has lasted continuously from the mid-nineteenth century until the present could have left so little trace in Mexican history books. Although the religious order of the Sisters of Charity of St. Vincent de Paul is well known, the voluntary association of charitable laywomen, the Ladies of Charity of St. Vincent de Paul, is not. Established in Mexico City in 1863 and quickly becoming a vibrant national organization, the Asociación de Señoras de la Caridad de San Vicente de Paul is invisible in standard histories of nineteenth-century Mexico. The Ladies of Charity are also invisible in most histories of the church, perhaps because as lay volunteers they were only loosely tied to it. They are largely invisible in histories of charity and social welfare, despite their central purpose of assisting the poor. And they are invisible in histories of women, even though they may have been the largest female organization of nineteenth-century Mexico.[1]

50

The Manichean tradition in Mexican history helps explain this silence, because Catholic organizations were tainted by their association with the "evil" conservatives who lost the bitter war of the *Reforma* (1857–67). Broader intellectual fashions also contribute to this neglect. Historians of modern Latin America during the past half century preferred studying the lower classes to the elites, and were put off by the saccharine piety that characterized these groups. Historians of women focused on the left-wing feminist and labor movements. Fortunately, this situation is beginning to change. In the wake of liberation theology, historians are reevaluating the church by emphasizing the progressive Catholic movements that emerged after the promulgation of the *Rerum Novarum* encyclical in 1891. Recent works on Mexico explore the nineteenth-century antecedents to Social Catholicism, particularly the short-lived Sociedad Católica de México founded in 1868.[2] The disillusionment with the accomplishments of central states is leading scholars to reexamine the philanthropic initiatives of the private sector.[3] Inspired by the renewed interest in democracy, research on citizenship and civil society is recovering numerous forgotten nineteenth-century associations.[4] Revisionism has even reached the study of Mexican conservatism.[5] And historians of women are beginning to turn their attention to the right-wing organizations that often had as much support as their left-wing counterparts.[6] Yet the Ladies of Charity rarely appear in these works.

They should. The scant surviving documentation reveals that the Ladies of Charity were important historical actors.[7] They outlasted the Sociedad Católica de México, which was moribund by 1878. They outstripped their brother organization, the male Society of St. Vincent de Paul, which had far fewer chapters, members, benefactors, and clients. The strength of the ladies' association sheds new light on the feminization of religion and philanthropy, as well as on the deep Catholicism of urban middle-class culture. In particular, the Ladies' impressive growth in the second half of the nineteenth century challenges the dominant narrative of Mexican history that portrays that period as one when liberalism and secularization, usually conflated with modernity, prevailed over the dark forces of the past, supposedly represented by the Catholic church and its allies.

In the standard plot, the battered church was forced to retreat from the public sphere after its defeat in the War of the Reform. The victorious liberal state confiscated its properties, suppressed its religious orders, abolished its lay confraternities, took over its control of birth, marriage, and death, and substituted for it as the provider of education and poor relief. By silencing church bells and prohibiting priests from wearing clerical garb on the streets, the Reform Laws even banished the once ever-present religious sounds and sights from everyday life. In the intellectual sphere, the rise of the rational and scientific positivist philosophy further undermined religion and ushered in modernity.

This narrative of progressive secularization accompanied by the marginalization of the church and the weakening of religious belief is too simplistic. Despite the triumph of the Liberal Reform, the second half of the nineteenth century witnessed a Catholic revival embodied in new lay organizations that recuperated many public spaces for the church and deepened the commitment of the faithful. Yet even the historians who recognize the existence of a "Catholic Restoration" in Porfirian Mexico have missed its gendered dimension.[8] The Ladies of Charity were at the forefront of Catholic activism. These lay volunteers created a national network of local chapters, called "conferences," that mobilized thousands of philanthropic women in dozens of Mexican cities and towns to help the poor while simultaneously reinforcing their faith. In addition to their devotional activities, the Ladies offered extensive educational and welfare services that by the late nineteenth century reached a clientele numbering in the hundreds of thousands. By involving themselves in the daily lives of the masses and helping the church regain its influence, they also prepared the ground for the violent church-state confrontations of the revolutionary period.

FOUNDATION AND GROWTH

The Mexican Ladies of Charity were a branch of the international Dames de la Charité headquartered in Paris. The Dames were the second incarnation of the Confrérie des Dames de la Charité, the first organization founded by St. Vincent de Paul in the seventeenth century. Unlike his two religious orders—the male Congrégation de la Mission (also known as Vincentians, Lazarists, and, in Mexico, as Misioneros de San Vicente de Paul) and the female Filles de la Charité (known in Mexico as the Hermanas de la Caridad)—the original Ladies of Charity consisted of parish-based groups of pious laywomen who cared for sick and ailing paupers. This voluntary association lasted until the French Revolution, and it was refounded in 1840 as part of the nineteenth-century revival of the three Vincentian organizations.[9]

The rebirth of the Dames de la Charité was inspired by the creation of the male Society of St. Vincent de Paul. The first conference of laymen was founded in Paris in 1833 by a group of university students who dedicated themselves to visiting needy families in their homes to bring them material and spiritual aid. The young men believed that by practicing Christian charity they could help the poor while simultaneously combating the major problems of the nineteenth century: namely, the immorality, materialism, individualism, alienation, and class conflict that they blamed on the separation of the church from public life and the subsequent loss of faith. Their solution was to propagate the Catholic religion and Catholic values by establishing personal relationships with the destitute. In the face of the secularism and anticlericalism unleashed by the French Revolution, this new model of militant Catholicism found many adherents among upper- and middle-class youth. The conferences of laymen proliferated throughout Europe and eventually spread throughout the world. In an age when the "work of benevolence" was becoming increasingly female,[10] it held strong appeal for women as well.

The Ladies of Charity adopted the organizational structure of the men's conferences, performed similar charitable works, and copied much of their bylaws. The Ladies even applied for affiliation with the male society, but were rebuffed by its general council on the grounds that the statutes only allowed men to join. In practice, however, the nineteenth-century Ladies of Charity were the female counterpart of the male society. Indeed, although the Ladies had closer institutional ties with the church than the men, both organizations were affiliated with the order of Vincentian priests and initially worked in partnership with the Sisters of Charity, who referred needy families to the lay volunteers.[11]

It was in its second incarnation that the Ladies of Charity reached Mexico. The male Society of St. Vincent de Paul preceded them. The first conference of pious laymen was founded in 1844 by the medical doctor Manuel Andrade, who had become acquainted with the organization while studying medicine in Paris. Dr. Andrade also arranged to bring St. Vincent's two religious orders to Mexico, with the Hermanas de la Caridad arriving in 1844 and the Congregación de la Misión in 1845. The Ladies' conferences came later, owing to the initiative of the Vincentian priests.

The Ladies of Charity were apparently established more than once in Mexico because the early conferences did not survive the first chaotic stage of *La Reforma*. Although the first Ladies chapter was founded in Puebla in 1848 and scattered chapters followed in León, Huichapan, Nopala, Guanajuato, and Toluca,[12] these provincial conferences disappeared in the midst of the Three Years' War (1858–60), the abolition of Catholic confraternities in 1859, the suppression of male religious communities in 1861, and the exclaustration of nuns in 1863 (although the Sisters of Charity were granted a decade's reprieve because of their valuable nursing services in Mexican hospitals). The male conferences weathered the intense persecution of those years, not only by suspending their reunions or meeting clandestinely, but also by insisting that they were an apolitical welfare organization independent from the church that supported the Conservative cause.[13] The Ladies of Charity could not similarly claim to be autonomous. Unlike the men's Society, the Ladies association was not only founded and directed by the Congregación de la Misión, but its individual conferences were organized around local parishes and headed by the parish priest.[14]

Thus it was only after the conservatives ousted liberal President Benito Juárez in July 1863 that the Ladies of Charity reappeared in Mexico. They were reestablished the following month, on August 2, 1863, by Vincentian Father Francisco Muñoz de la Cruz, this time in Mexico City. The Ladies were now under the direct jurisdiction of the archbishop—a prudent move given that the Vincentian order had theoretically been suppressed in 1861, though in practice it persisted.[15] The association later recognized 1863 as its birthdate.[16]

The mission of the Ladies' conferences, as defined in the *Reglamento* they adopted in 1863, was to "visit the sick poor, provide them with spiritual and corporal relief, console them, and exhort them to take advantage of their illness to resign themselves to God's will." The corporal aid included bringing the patients medicines, food, clothes, and bed linens; paying their rent; washing them; "sweeping the room, making the bed and such"; and arranging for doctors and phlebotomists to provide medical care. The spiritual relief was achieved by praying with them, making sure they confessed, and preparing them to receive the last rites when the end was near. At the same time the Ladies were to see that the patients' families understood their Christian obligations, that they attended mass on Sundays and feast days, that the parents were married, and that the children were baptized, knew how to pray, and took first Communion.

The Ladies' mission was therefore twofold. First, they were to help remedy the widespread poverty and suffering that had been intensified by years of warfare. As the secretary general of the association explained at its first national assembly in 1864, "In a country such as ours which has been torn by over fifty years of civil war, . . . private individuals should be more solicitous of the poor."[17] Secondly, they were to help the church counteract the decay of Mexican Catholicism. Although the population was nominally Catholic, many Mexicans, especially in the lower classes, practiced an unorthodox version of folk Catholicism and had little contact with the institutional church. This problem was aggravated by a half century of ecclesiastical neglect caused by a shortage of priests working under an incomplete episcopal structure, followed by the virulent attacks on the church by anticlerical liberals. Having become separated from the state and its official support, the church was further threatened with competition when freedom of religion was declared in 1860. Consequently, it adopted a "missionary strategy" to regain its influence by establishing direct connections with the faithful and transforming Mexicans into devout practicing Catholics.[18]

The Ladies of Charity were agents of the church in achieving this "devotional revolution."[19] The 1863 bylaws envisioned them as intrusive visitors who became intimately involved in their clients' spiritual lives. In addition to their evangelizing efforts, the Ladies were supposed to foster Catholic values by dispensing moral advice and even insisting, for example, that boys and girls sleep in separate beds to avoid impropriety. Neither was the volunteers' guidance of the client families to end when the patient was cured. During Lent the Ladies were to visit all the people they had helped that year to exhort them to confess and receive Holy Communion. The Ladies were to prepare themselves for these good works by meeting in their small conferences regularly, usually once a week, to pray and discuss their activities. They also participated in spiritual retreats to strengthen their devotion and love for the poor, and celebrated the feast day of their patron Saint Vincent on July 19.

The volunteers received protection from the highest level of the Mexican church, as well as from the Congregación de la Misión. The association's annual assemblies were presided over by archbishops and attended by ecclesiastical dignitaries. The archbishop of Michoacán, Clemente de Jesús Munguía, presided the first year, and the archbishops of Mexico did so in subsequent years. Representatives of the Vincentian order made speeches to the gathered members and benefactors. In addition to discussing the organization's business, the assemblies included inspirational sermons and prayers.

The Ladies of Charity also received protection from the imperial regime, which apparently promoted the association as part of a plan to remake the Mexican welfare system in the French image. In 1865 Empress Charlotte's new General Council of Beneficence commissioned the translation and publication of two pamphlets describing the Parisian welfare system they wanted to emulate in Mexico. The Ladies of Charity were at its core, collaborating with the Junta de Beneficencia in each municipal ward to distribute home relief to the needy.[20] Although the Second Empire was cut short before it could implement this model, the Mexican Ladies benefited from the financial support of the imperial government while it lasted. For example, in 1865 Emperor Maximilian gave them 2,000 pesos to spend on their activities, and in 1866 they received 1,700 pesos from the government-run lottery.[21]

The Ladies of Charity flourished in this auspicious climate (see table 4.1). As required by their statutes, they held a national assembly each July during the week of Saint Vincent's feast day where they presented a report of the year's activities. The *Memoria* prepared for the first assembly of 1864 listed 566 active members. In addition, the association had obtained the backing of 839 "honorary members," or subscribers, who regularly contributed money but did not participate in the charitable works of the conferences. Already during their first year the Ladies of Charity had spread beyond their original base in

56   *Silvia Marina Arrom*

Table 4.1. Membership of the Ladies of Charity, 1864–1910

	Active	Honorary	Total		Active	Honorary	Total
1864	566	839	1,405	1888	7,344	10,601	17,944
1865	997	1,863	2,860	1892	13,371	25,120	38,491
1866	2,251	5,226	7,477	1895	9,875	12,777	22,652
1868	—	—	12,274	1896	11,264	18,550	29,814
1872	—	—	20,212	1901	14,933	21,047	35,980
1878	3,003	5,709	8,712	1907	17,921	28,991	46,912
1885	1,485	3,344	4,829	1909	18,034	24,338	42,372
1886	3,511	5,113	8,624	1910	20,188	23,018	43,206

Note: Statistics cover the fiscal year, which ran from July 1 of the previous year to June 30.
Sources: Vicente de Dios, *Historia de la Familia Vicentina en México*, 2 vols. (Salamanca: Editorial CEME, 1993), 1:544, 546, 550 for 1864, 1865, and 1868 and 2:641–46 for 1872, 1885, 1886, 1888, 1901, 1907, and 1909; *Memoria* (1865, 1867, 1879) for 1865, 1866, and 1878; *Rapport* (1893, 1896, 1897) for 1892, 1895, and 1896; and Moisés González Navarro, *La pobreza en México* (Mexico City: El Colegio de México, 1985), 62 for 1910.

the capital, which had twelve conferences, to establish another nine in central Mexico, with four in Toluca and one each in Puebla, Guanajuato, Zimacantepec, Tenancingo, and Santiago Tianquistengo. They had created a superior council in Mexico City to govern the emerging national network of local chapters. In the next two years the association continued growing dramatically, adding members as well as a second tier of regional councils (called Central Councils) in Guadalajara, Tenancingo, Toluca, Orizaba, Puebla, and Morelia. Although primarily an urban organization, it had moved beyond major cities to found conferences in small towns and even on an hacienda, the Hacienda de Treinta. By 1866 there were 2,251 active Ladies in eighty-seven conferences, including six composed of *niñas* training to become full-fledged members when they turned eighteen.[22]

Unfortunately, we know very little about the social background or life stories of these volunteers, and even less about their clients or how they were selected. The *Memorias* list the officers of each conference (or, in some reports, only the names of the Superior Council members), but rarely elaborate further. The Ladies included both married *señoras* and single *señoritas*. They appear to have been drawn from the middle and lower-middle classes as well as from a small elite. The 1863 *Reglamento* noted that "the principal ladies of each town" were ideal members of the association because, having "no need to work for their subsistence like the women of an inferior class," they could devote their time to charitable activities.[23] The officers included a few women with well-known surnames representing leading Mexican families, such as Señora Ana Furlong de Guerra, president of the Superior Council, and Doña Vicenta Montesdeoca, purveyor of Mexico City's Sagrario Metropolitano conference. Some women could evidently afford to contribute generously "from their personal wealth," as did Doña Antonia Frago de Tagle, who shouldered all the costs of caring for her "adopted families" (including paying one family's rent), and the Señoras Pilar and Soledad Tijera, who hosted a special dinner for one hundred paupers in their spacious home.[24] Yet most of the members' surnames are unknown to historians of the period,[25] and most of the individual donations praised by the annual reports are very small sums. Indeed, the 1864 *Memoria* noted that in Mexico City's twelve conferences "seamstresses are the majority of the *socias*." The 1865 *Memoria* noted that all seventeen members of the conference of San Antonio de las Huertas were seamstresses.[26]

It is therefore likely that the Ladies came from a similar range of backgrounds as the men who joined the Vincentian lay conferences. Since the male records consistently list the occupations of the members, we know that the male volunteers included artisans, shopkeepers, and even manual laborers along with members of well-to-do families.[27] Although it is likely that few of the Ladies held jobs and that most had servants to care for their homes and children while they engaged in charity work, this situation was the hallmark of the middle classes as well as the elites in nineteenth-century Mexico.[28] The butchers, bakers, pharmacists, and other shopkeepers who regularly contributed goods to the Ladies' works were also solidly middle class. Indeed, the large number of female volunteers and honorary members attests to the breadth of the organization's appeal, as well as to the depth of Catholic devotion among the upper and middle classes.

These Ladies achieved impressive results under the relative safety of the Second Empire. In the first year the 321 volunteers in the twelve Mexico City conferences alone served 2,240 sick and dying paupers by caring for them personally and "going to visit them at all hours." They arranged proper Catholic burials for the 156 who died. They gave out 45,678 ordinary food rations, consisting of rice, beans, peas, corn, chocolate, bread, and charcoal, as well as 3,000 extraordinary rations, consisting of milk, chicken, soup, desserts, and wine for special feast days. They distributed 6,820 medical prescriptions and 816 pieces of clothing, "the majority sewn by the ladies themselves." They raised 6,504 pesos for their good works by collecting alms in special boxes in local churches, soliciting their friends and neighbors, raffling off their handiwork, and giving money from their own pockets. They obtained donations in kind from local businesses. Their philanthropic efforts were aided by 517 subscribers, forty-six priests, and four Sisters of Charity, as well as by seventy-four doctors, eight phlebotomists, and six laundresses who provided their services free of charge. The association did not neglect its religious mission, either. In addition to the spiritual exercises performed for the members' own "moral improvement," the "exhortations of the lady visitors" had encouraged 911 confessions, ninety-seven confirmations, ten marriages, and two baptisms.[29] The provincial conferences reported similar activities, whose numbers grew exponentially in 1865 and 1866 as the membership expanded (see table 4.2).

The early *Memorias* also reported philanthropic initiatives besides those prescribed by the statutes. Echoing their centuries-old rule, the 1863 *Reglamento* only defined the Ladies' mission as the home visitation of the sick and infirm. Yet, with their singular "knack for invention"[30]—and following the precedent of the male conferences—the Ladies quickly expanded their clientele to include healthy paupers. For example, on Good Friday in 1864 the Ladies of the San Miguel parish in Mexico City served breakfast to three hundred children from the *escuelas gratuitas* (free schools). On Maundy Thursday the Ladies of the Sagrario parish organized a sumptuous dinner for one hundred paupers, twelve of whom sat at the head table with the parish priest. In Zinacantepec the "lady president," Doña Agustina Bracamontes, personally instructed fifty children in Christian doctrine and reading. In Tenancingo the Ladies provided assistance to "all the poor families that presented themselves." In San Agustín Tlalpan the Ladies provided meals for female prisoners, "served by the *socias* themselves," and obtained the release of several of the incarcerated. The Morelia conference visited with female prisoners to instruct them in Christian doctrine. The Jalapa visitors found a safe house for a woman whose husband beat her "cruelly," and then supervised the education of her five children "so the daughters would be good *madres de familia* and the sons would be good citizens." Several conferences paid the tuition for especially deserving girls to attend primary school.[31]

From the start the Ladies' conferences also began constructing their own welfare institutions. For example, the largest Mexico City conference in the Sagrario Metropolitano parish established an asylum for orphaned and abandoned girls, the Asilo de la Caridad de Nuestra Señora de la Luz. By June 1864 it was sheltering ten young women under the care of an impoverished but honest woman. "This small family was supervised by eight *Señoras socias* . . . who, rotating themselves in twos, provided lucrative and honest employment for the poor girls whom they educated and moralized . . . in order to remove them from the seductions of the world, even perhaps from prostitution, so that with time they will become excellent wives and tender mothers." By June 1866 the asylum was housing thirty-five girls.[32]

Although this shelter was the best known of the Ladies' early foundations, it was only one of many. Thus the Ladies of the Santa Veracruz parish conference opened a school for the local children. The Ladies of the San Miguel parish set up a soup kitchen. The Ladies of the Señora de Guadalupe parish founded a small clinic. In San Luis Potosí the Ladies established two *casas de misericordia* to house over eighty orphans. As other conferences followed suit,

Table 4.2.   Activities of the Ladies of Charity, 1866–1910

	1866	1878	1892	1895	1901	1910
Families Visited*	—	1,151	28,273	70,537	—	135,344
Sick	10,235	8,778	—	21,428	—	32,000
Dying Assisted	663	1,710	—	2,347	—	1,314
Burials*	—	—	—	—	—	3,141
Confessions*	2,622	15,273	—	—	—	—
Communions*	2,602	14,705	—	—	—	—
First Communions*	127	—	3,241	2,917	5,420	—
Confirmations*	312	—	198	279	1,005	—
Conversions*	—	11	110	173	865	264
Viaticums*	705	2,913	—	2,933	—	—
Marriages	29	150	—	298	378	1,253
Baptisms*	22	70	719	672	394	—
Devotional Sacraments*	—	—	—	31,390	—	—
Spiritual Retreats*	30	—	—	—	—	—
Children Instructed*	718	—	—	—	—	—
Ordinary Rations	135,900	385,110	893,852	1,036,588	2,903,000	1,779,849
Extraordinary Rations*	23,235	60,273	—	—	—	—
Additional Relief*	—	—	—	141,233	—	—
Prescriptions*	43,157	50,622	—	—	—	132,481
Items of Clothing*	3,457	8,664	—	—	—	27,000
Income (in pesos)	39,900	2,194	—	105,986	—	247,567
Expenditures	29,669	49,243	—	96,206	—	225,623

Notes: Starred categories do not appear in some years. Peso figures are rounded.
Sources: *Memoria* (1867), foldout chart; *Memoria* (1879), 52; *Rapport* (1896); Vicente de Dios, *Historia de la Familia Vicentina en México*, 2 vols. (Salamanca: Editor-ial CEME, 1993), 2:643–45 for 1892 and 1901; and González Navarro, *La pobreza en México*, 62 for 1910.

the association's asylums, orphanages, clinics, dispensaries, soup kitchens, and schools proliferated throughout Mexico.[33]

By providing a broad range of services for a broad range of paupers, the Ladies of Charity were building a mass base for their evangelizing efforts. Indeed, the association's revised bylaws published in 1911 applauded the expansion of the original narrow mission precisely because it enhanced the Ladies' ability to contribute to "the glory of God and the health of souls." Although noting that "St. Vincent established the Association of the Ladies of Charity only to aid the sick poor and to succor the corporal and spiritual needs of impoverished families," the *Reglamento* commended the Mexican Ladies for taking additional opportunities "to moralize the poor." In particular, it praised their work in "establishing Catholic schools . . . to give a Christian education to indigent boys and girls who wander the streets and plazas exposed to their perdition."[34]

Given that the Ladies' welfare services were inseparable from their religious mission, one might have expected them to suffer when the liberals returned to power. The defeat of the Empire and the execution of its hapless emperor in June 1867 did not, however, hurt the association appreciably. To be sure, the Ladies cancelled the annual assembly that would have been held in the midst of the change of governments.[35] And they never again enjoyed a close partnership with the state. Yet the association's membership statistics (table 4.1) show that it continued growing throughout Juárez's last presidency. In July 1868 the Ladies of Charity counted 12,274 active and honorary members, over five times more than two years earlier. They were supported by 101 priests and 171 medical doctors. And they had twelve central councils, including new ones in the far north and deep south of Mexico.[36] Their numbers approximately doubled by the time of Juárez's death in July 1872: the *Memoria* presented that month listed 20,212 active and honorary members, plus an unspecified number in conferences that failed to send their reports.[37] Evidently, the organization benefited from Juárez's strategy of trying to restore harmony in the war-torn country by ignoring the most radical anticlerical Reform Laws.[38]

The Ladies of Charity did not fare as well under the presidency of Sebastián Lerdo de Tejada (1872–76), who reversed his predecessor's conciliatory policy by vigorously enforcing and extending the anticlerical measures. Although little documentation exists for these years, it is clear that the membership dropped precipitously. The 1878 *Memoria* listed only 8,712 active and honorary members, a figure that apparently represents a partial recovery from an even lower point when several of the conferences had temporarily stopped meeting.[39] The difficult political climate explains some of the association's decline. In particular, the expulsion of the Sisters of Charity, decreed in December 1874 and carried out in the winter of 1875, affected the lay volunteers because they had cooperated so closely with the Vincentian sisters. Indeed, the 1863 bylaws stated that the Ladies "are assistants of the Sisters of Charity and shall always work under their direction."[40] Some of the decline may also reflect the flagging energy of the association's founder, Father Muñoz, who succumbed to death in 1877 after directing the Ladies for fourteen years and traveling throughout Mexico to help expand the network of conferences.[41]

The Ladies were nonetheless a force to be reckoned with, even with less than half the membership of 1872. Table 4.2 shows that in 1878 they cared for 10,488 sick and dying paupers, raised impressive sums of money, distributed large quantities of aid, and led numerous clients to take the sacraments. Moreover, the statistical summary in the 1878 *Memoria* tells only part of the story because it emphasizes the care of the sick poor. The reports of individual conferences show that the Ladies reached thousands more paupers, including indigent families that were "habitually succored," endangered youths who were protected, and children who were instructed in Christian doctrine, along with the people who attended their many primary schools, clinics, and shelters. One conference in San Luis Potosí had even established an employment agency to help its clients find jobs. The reports also mention the regular visiting of prisoners and patients in public hospitals. Thus, despite the militant separation of church and state that became the law of the land during the restored republic, the Ladies maintained a visible presence in public institutions as well as in serving the public.

Despite their dwindling numbers, the Ladies also kept the broad geographical network they had developed during happier years. In 1878 they had at least one hundred conferences affiliated with the twelve regional councils. They were now notably stronger in the Guadalajara region, with twenty-three conferences, than in the Mexico City area, which had nineteen. They also retained a foothold in northern cities such as Zacatecas, Monterrey, Durango, and Saltillo, as well as in southern ones such as Veracruz, Jalapa, and Orizaba.[42] Thus, although the number of volunteers had declined since 1872, the organization remained vigorous.

Indeed, the association had developed an efficient system to permit a reduced number of Ladies to maximize their impact. With only 752 more active members in 1878 than in 1866, they nonetheless spent some 20,000 more pesos on good works. Much of this money went to pay the employees of their welfare institutions, often single or widowed women struggling to make ends meet. The Ladies also used the Vincentian system of vouchers that, much like modern food stamps, their clients used to obtain food, clothes, and shoes directly from local shops.[43] With the assistance of these shopkeepers and employees, the Ladies did not have to provide all the institutional services or deliver all the goods themselves. The volunteers consequently achieved notable results with a limited membership.

Yet the Ladies did not sustain this momentum for long after losing their first director in 1877. Despite the friendly relations between the church and the state after Porfirio Díaz came to power in 1876, the association's membership continued to slide. Table 4.1 shows that it bottomed out in 1885, with only 1,485 active volunteers. Although it grew in the next few years, it did not fully recover until a new, energetic director turned his attention to reviving the conferences. The historian of the Vincentian family in Mexico credits Father Ildefonso Moral González, who came to that country in December 1891 as *visitador* (inspector) of the Congregación de la Misión and oversaw the Ladies association until his death in 1907, with initiating a new era of growth for the organization.[44]

The Ladies of Charity took off like wildfire under the stewardship of Father Moral. By 1892 the association counted 13,371 active members. Although these numbers dipped somewhat in the next three years, they quickly recovered and then surpassed their previous peak. In 1895 there were 9,875 active members in four hundred conferences throughout Mexico. With branches in nineteen states, the Ladies were broadly distributed across the nation, although they were strongest in Jalisco, home to nearly half their members. (See table 4.3.) They were backed by 12,777 subscribers and spent 96,206 pesos on good works, not including the value of in-kind donations. The Ladies reported aiding 21,428 sick people and visiting 70,537 needy families. They distributed more than a million meals. Finally, although the categories in table 4.2 are not entirely comparable for different years, the statistics demonstrate that the volunteers continued their religious ministry with enthusiasm. By this date their evangelizing efforts not only consisted of strengthening the faith of those who were nominally Catholic, but increasingly included converting Protestants as well. If their first conversion was in 1865, it was a rare achievement in the early years.[45] By 1895 the Ladies were responsible for persuading 173 Protestants to join the Catholic faith.

The organization's growth continued without interruption until the outbreak of the Mexican Revolution. A report of the international association listed 19,000 *niñas* in 1895, an indication that the Ladies were training a sizeable new generation of members.[46] By 1901 there were 14,933 volunteers and 21,047 regular contributors. In 1910, on the eve of the tumult, active membership had risen to a historic high of 20,188, with 23,018 subscribers. The volunteers visited 135,344 families and 32,000 hospital patients. They distributed 1,779,849 meals, 132,481 prescriptions, and 27,000 articles of clothing. In addition, they managed an extensive national network of elementary schools, asylums, cafeterias, clinics, and dispensaries. In 1909 these included

Table 4.3. Regional Distribution of the Ladies of Charity by State, 1895

Jalisco	4,341
Michoacán	979
Yucatán	920
San Luis Potosí	895
Mexico	788
Guanajuato	574
Sinaloa	380
Veracruz	281
Nuevo León	174
Zacatecas	104
Coahuila	91
Querétaro	73
Puebla	70
Chihuahua	60
Guerrero	59
Tabasco	35
Aguascalientes	23
Durango	14
Oaxaca	14
Total active members:	*9,875*

Source: *Rapport* (1896), tableau no. 7.

thirty-two hospitals, twenty schools, and seventeen orphanages throughout Mexico, with a large number concentrated in the Guadalajara region. The schools alone reached some 25,000 children that year.[47] The large scale of their operation was impressive, especially when compared with the limited services provided by the government.

Despite the visibility of their activities, the Ladies of Charity apparently did not encounter opposition from the Porfirian state. Historians have long known that, although President Porfirio Díaz left the anticlerical Reform Laws on the books, he quietly mended fences with the church. During his long reign (1876–1910) the number of priests increased, some religious orders returned, and prohibited parochial schools came out in the open.[48] Historians have also recognized that private philanthropy blossomed during the Porfiriato, as benevolent associations founded hospitals, asylums, and schools to supplement the meager resources of the government.[49] Less well known is how the militant Catholicism of the laity flourished, the extent to which these Catholics developed a parallel welfare system that indoctrinated the recipients of charity at the same time as it aided them, and the prominent role women played in spearheading this Catholic revival.

THE FEMINIZATION OF PIETY?

The leading role of women in the Catholic Restoration is highlighted by contrasting the Ladies of Charity with their brother organization, the Society of St. Vincent de Paul. Table 4.4 shows that the male conferences, although founded two decades earlier, never caught on as successfully. In 1865, their second year, the Ladies had already raised nearly as much money as the men and attracted more active members and subscribers: 2,860 women compared with 1,138 men. In subsequent years the Ladies' conferences dwarfed the men's. After reaching a peak of 2,824 active members in 1875, the men's conferences stagnated. By 1894 there were only 1,536 men active in 121 conferences, compared with 9,875 women active in some 400 conferences.[50] The Ladies not only had more than six times the number of active volunteers but some thirty times more subscribers. The Ladies had also developed a much larger network of shopkeepers donating goods, doctors donating services, and individuals donating money to help their charitable projects. Although the totals are difficult to determine, it is clear that the Ladies served many more paupers. For example, the 1,100 home visitations carried out by the male volunteers paled beside the 70,537 families visited by the Ladies. Then, as the female organization experienced explosive growth on the eve of the revolution, the male society languished. Their dwindling membership became the source of repeated concern in the society's reports, which lamented the "scarcity of *socios*" and especially the dearth of young male volunteers.[51] The Ladies of Charity were thus far more effective than their male counterparts in mobilizing Catholic activists, providing education and poor relief, building relationships with the poor, and winning hearts and minds for the church.

Why were women in the vanguard of this Catholic reform movement? Although it is tempting to argue that the success of the female organization re-

Table 4.4. Comparison between the Men's and Women's Conferences, 1865–95

	Active Members		Honorary Members		Families Visited		Expenses (pesos)	
	Men	Women	Men	Women	Men	Women	Men	Women
1865	791	997	347	1,863	374	—	17,743	16,767
1875/78*	2,824	3,003	640	5,709	714	1,151	23,793	49,243
1894/95*	1,536	9,875	432	12,777	1,110	70,537	54,170	96,206

*The first number refers to the men's conferences, the second to the women's.
Sources: The information on the men's Society is in *Reseña* (1895), 47; on the women's association in *Memoria* (1865, 1879) and *Rapport* (1896).

flects the feminization of piety in nineteenth-century Mexico,[52] there is a more complicated explanation for the disparity between the male and female conferences. Male piety flourished in other organizations. Devout laymen in the late nineteenth century published Catholic periodicals and founded devotional and mutual aid associations. In the early twentieth century they joined Catholic trade unions and attended Catholic conferences to find solutions to pressing social problems. In 1911 they proclaimed their fervor publicly by founding a Catholic political party, the Partido Nacional Católico.[53] Yet few men joined the Vincentian conferences.

The phenomenal growth of the Ladies of Charity is partially due to the conscious church strategy of mobilizing women to help it regain lost influence. The ecclesiastical hierarchy began promoting the formation of lay organizations after the *cofradías* (confraternities) were outlawed in 1859.[54] The Vincentian priests took up the call by founding the women's conferences, and the 1865 *Memoria* attributed the success of the Ladies of Charity during the first two years to the "zeal" of these missionaries.[55] The church increased its attempts to recruit laywomen after the expulsion of the Sisters of Charity left a glaring gap in Mexican welfare services. A pastoral instruction of 1875 called on "Catholic ladies" to join the conferences of St. Vincent de Paul to continue the work of the Sisters of Charity in providing for "the instruction of destitute children, the needs of ailing paupers in hospitals, and the relief of all sorts of misery."[56] According to the 1894 *Rapport* of the international Dames de la Charité, the Mexican chapter was the largest in "the world" (although perhaps this only meant outside of France) because the Mexican poor were "deprived . . . of the succor provided by the hospitaler communities."[57] Finally, the in-house history of the Vincentian organizations correlates the heyday of the Ladies of Charity after 1892 with the arrival of their new director, Father Moral.

Yet the church also issued appeals to Mexican laymen, with far less success. The pope offered the male volunteers the same indulgences granted to the Ladies.[58] In 1875 the archbishops of Mexico, Michoacán, and Guadalajara issued pastorals encouraging male parishioners to join the Society of St. Vincent de Paul.[59] Father Moral tried to revive the men's conferences, as did other ecclesiastical officials during the final years of the Porfiriato.[60] These efforts failed to produce the desired results.

We should therefore beware of narratives that erase the agency of the Ladies themselves. For if priests promoted the Ladies of Charity, it was laywomen who enthusiastically joined. Indeed, the women's initiative can be teased out of the self-effacing reports meant to portray them as mere followers of their priests. Already in 1865 the *Memoria* attributed the success of several conferences, such as the one in Mexico City's San Sebastián parish, "to the arduous work of its *señoras socias*, and principally the efforts of the ladies president, vicepresident, and treasurer."[61] The 1870 *Memoria* provides several concrete examples of the volunteers' energy, commitment, and resourcefulness. Praising their good works, the text states that "it is admirable . . . to see these good Ladies of Charity out on the streets even at inconvenient hours bringing medicine, food, blankets, and other necessities to their beloved patients." They risked their lives to nurse their charges through contagious illnesses, as did "one *socia* from Ocoyoacac," who, having caught a disease from a sick pauper, "in her delirium insisted that she faced death with contentment because she had been able to perform a work of charity." Furthermore, the report contains hints that some of the conferences were not founded by priests at all but by some of the strong woman presidents themselves. Thus the "president of the Association of Malacatepec" is praised for "founding it herself, reviving the Toluca organization to the point of duplicating its members and its income, . . . and today establishing a conference in Capuluhac." Evidently, the Ladies were not only willing handmaidens of the church, but also a driving force in the Vincentian lay movement.[62]

Since Mexican women joined the Ladies of Charity with such gusto, we should consider what this organization meant in their lives. Part of its appeal was that it provided middle- and upper-class women, who rarely worked outside the home, with a socially acceptable way to serve the larger society beyond their families. As women's education improved in the nineteenth century and the ideal of feminine seclusion declined, many ladies sought outlets where they could apply their talents. The growth of the conferences reflects the larger trend of the feminization of charity in nineteenth-century Mexico, likewise visible in women's membership on the boards of public welfare institutions as well as in their increased role in managing them.[63] Devout Catholic women welcomed this new organization that permitted them to work for their own salvation as well as the salvation of society. It is no coincidence that the exponential growth of the Ladies of Charity occurred, not only after the arrival of a new Vincentian director, but also immediately after the promulgation of *Rerum Novarum*, which energized members of the laity who wanted to participate in the project for Catholic renewal.

Moreover, after the suppression of religious orders, Mexican women had few comparable organizations they could join. Public welfare institutions had limited places for women as directors and board members. In 1869 laywomen flocked to the new Sociedad Católica de Señoras y Señoritas whose members engaged in social service activities similar to those of the Ladies of Charity. Indeed, by 1873 some twenty thousand women had joined.[64] The decline of the Sociedad by 1878 reduced that opportunity for women to perform "meaningful labor."[65] Although a few religious orders returned to Mexico during the late nineteenth century, they failed to flourish, for Mexican women were no longer drawn to the convent to the same degree as in the colonial period.[66] Filling a void, the Ladies of Charity gave thousands of Mexican women a structure for contributing to the common good without having to give up marriage and motherhood.

The Ladies' volunteer work helped expand the kind of activities that were acceptable for women of their social class, although without appearing to transgress traditional boundaries. Their activities were justified with a highly gendered discourse that—far from appealing to the equality of the sexes—instead emphasized women's special (that is, different) female condition and qualities.[67] The pastoral instruction of 1875 that called on women to join the conferences noted the special feminine disposition for serving the poor and sick.[68] So did the 1863 *Reglamento*, which explained that, in addition to having "greater compassion for the sufferings of others," women were already "accustomed to carrying out certain types of chores in their houses, and could thus more easily exercise them to benefit strangers." The bylaws added a further female advantage: "they are always at home and less distracted than the men, who are ordinarily occupied with their business and frequently out of the house and even the city."[69] The work of charity was thus constructed as a natural extension of women's domestic roles.

The volunteers were nonetheless engaging in a new type of female activism that placed them squarely in the public sphere. The conferences may have held their weekly sessions in the protected precinct of the parish church, but from there the volunteers went out into public spaces. They may not have been alone while visiting the dingy rooms of their "adopted" families or the filthy wards of public hospitals and prisons, since they usually worked in pairs, but they were not sheltered, either. In carrying out their good works they might be subjected to shocking sights and rude insults. For example, the triumphal story of one lady, who endured a dying patient's vulgar screams and after several tries succeeded in getting him to accept the last rites, was narrated in the 1865 *Memoria* as an inspiration to others.[70] Moreover, the Ladies were not restricted to a segregated female sphere. Their clients were male as well as female. The volunteers maintained close contact, not only with the priests who helped each conference, but also with the doctors, pharmacists, and lawyers who assisted them. (Indeed, the reports recorded the number of men associated with each conference—usually about one dozen—immediately after listing the number of members and subscribers.) The Ladies' fundraising efforts entailed not only organizing charity balls and raffling off donated items such as jewels, but also collecting alms in public plazas and approaching the leading men in the community, including a circus owner, Señor Chiarini, who donated the 910-peso earnings of one performance to the association.[71] Recognizing that the volunteers would be venturing into public spaces and interacting with men as well as women, the 1863 *Reglamento* defended the Ladies from potential critics by insisting that they would be protected by their modesty and unimpeachable virtue.[72]

The Vincentian conferences also provided an arena where women could become leaders, acquire new skills, and wield power. Whereas Mexican women were barred from voting and holding public office until the mid-twentieth century, they could do both as Ladies of Charity. Voting as equals in secret balloting,[73] the members of each conference elected a president, vice president, secretary, treasurer, purveyor, and librarian, as did the central and superior councils. The members voted to approve the entrance of new volunteers. After a six-month trial the *aspirantes* who proved their capacity to perform the demanding work of serving the poor were inducted, in the annual assembly whose ceremonies included the granting of a diploma to each new *socia*. In the process of running their associations and providing welfare services the volunteers also developed their organizational and financial expertise. Although aided by male priests, relatives, and supporters, the Ladies were gradually increasing their "social capital": the skills, self-confidence, and moral authority that come from participating in an international organization, attending meetings, exercising suffrage, holding elected office, making speeches, preparing reports, managing large sums of money, designing and implementing welfare services, and helping the church carry out a "devotional revolution."[74]

Finally, the Vincentian conferences were attractive to Mexican women because of the social opportunities they provided. Meeting in their local conferences regularly, year after year, the Ladies formed friendships and social networks that must have been deeply satisfying. The available lists of conference members show that women often joined in family groups, with mothers and daughters or sisters and sisters-in-law participating together. Yet the conferences also allowed the volunteers to interact with people they might not otherwise have met, both among their social peers and among their employees and clients. Although the personal bonds they forged with less fortunate members of society may have been paternalistic, the volunteers nonetheless created a Catholic community that united members of different social classes.

Men had less need for these outlets, for they had alternate sources of prestige and sociability, as well as alternate avenues for serving others, defending their faith, and reforming the modern world. They could do so through work, government service, or—for the most devout—the priesthood, options closed to women of the upper and middle classes. Men could also join the mutual aid societies, clubs, Masonic lodges, and political parties that were closed to their wives, mothers, sisters, and daughters. Moreover, many gentlemen were deterred from joining the conferences because of the kind of commitment they required. In the highly gendered world of nineteenth-century Mexico, the

Vincentian demands for regular face-to-face contact with the poor and for hands-on caregiving were considered more suited to women than to men. The time-consuming nature of volunteer work was perhaps the largest obstacle. The huge number of benefactors who helped the Ladies by contributing money, goods, and services indicates, however, that their work was widely supported by Mexican men as well as women. The men were simply more likely to support the female volunteers from behind the scenes.

Finally, after anticlerical liberals won the War of the Reform, Mexican men may have realized that their career advancement would be hindered by membership in a Catholic organization with close ties to the defeated conservatives. Indeed, at one point in 1861 the president and vice president of the male Society of St. Vincent de Paul, Teófilo Marín and Manuel Diez de Bonilla, had been imprisoned for their role in the Conservative opposition.[75] The female association was not similarly tainted. The Ladies' very anonymity and supposed subordination to their parish priests insulated individual officers from persecution. The importance of the political variable is confirmed by two recent studies of the St. Vincent de Paul Society in Chile and Colombia, which had far less conflictive relations between church and state. There, the male conferences continued growing at the end of the nineteenth century and there was less disparity between male and female Catholic lay organizations.[76] In Mexico, devout men joined the newer Catholic organizations, especially after the turn of the twentieth century, but shied away from the Vincentian conferences. In the second half of the nineteenth century it therefore fell to the Ladies to build a mass movement in support of their beloved church.

These structural factors, and not necessarily women's stronger devotion, help explain why the "rechristianization" of Mexico during the Porfiriato (as Ralph Gibson calls the similar recovery of the Catholic Church in late nineteenth-century France) had a distinctly feminine stamp.[77] Given the peculiarities of the Mexican case, women's lay organizations were the perfect vehicle for the church to recover lost influence. At the same time, changes in women's roles made the Vincentian conferences the perfect vehicle for proper ladies to contribute to the public good.

CONCLUSION

Austen Ivereigh's recent edited volume on *The Politics of Religion in an Age of Revival* helps rescue Latin America from the distortions of liberal historiography by showing that much of the area shared in the Catholic revival sweeping through Europe in the nineteenth century.[78] Yet the chapters on Mexico give the impression that it did not participate in the Catholic movements that mobilized society elsewhere.[79] On the contrary, the history of the Vincentian conferences suggests that the Mexican Catholic Church was far from a decadent, retrograde institution rescued for modernity only by *Rerum Novarum* in 1891. Decades earlier, Mexicans were the Latin American pioneers of a new kind of lay activism with a social conscience.[80]

Indeed, Mexican women created the largest association of Ladies of Charity outside of France. In the process of organizing to improve the lives of the impoverished masses, the volunteers also expanded notions of women's proper roles.[81] Actively participating in the public sphere, running voluntary associations, administering welfare services, and disseminating Catholic doctrine to strangers were new experiences for most Mexican women. Without overtly challenging social norms or claiming equality with men, the Ladies made themselves indispensable agents of Catholic social reform. Their effectiveness contributed to the late nineteenth-century ideology of *marianismo* that defined women as morally superior to men and served as a stepping-stone for the eventual improvement in women's status.[82]

The success of the Ladies of Charity demonstrates that, despite the triumph of the anticlerical Reform, Catholicism remained an important part of Mexican cultural life. Indeed, with the help of committed volunteers, the church by the end of the nineteenth century was on its way to recovering its prestige and influence. The twin attacks of the revolution and the defeat of the Cristero Rebellion halted the process and led to a decline of the conferences of St. Vincent de Paul,[83] yet they should not obliterate the memory of what these Catholic activists accomplished. By building an extensive network of local organizations to assist the poor, volunteers from the upper and middle classes created a large audience for their critique of secular liberalism and their vision of Catholic renewal. Their clientele included not only the paupers who received assistance but also the employees who provided it, not only the children in the charity schools but also their parents, not only the new members recruited into the conferences but also the benefactors who supported them. In this way, Mexicans of all social classes came together under a Catholic banner. By the late nineteenth century this constituency numbered in the hundreds of thousands, a potentially enormous base that could later be mobilized for political purposes.

Thus, if the Vincentian conferences were "feminized," they were not marginalized. They formed part of the growing Catholic network that paved the way for militant Catholic movements of the early twentieth century that would once again bring the church into a bloody confrontation with the state. Indeed, the regional concentration of the conferences, with their disproportionate strength in Jalisco and neighboring Michoacán (table 4.3), mirrors the eventual geography of the National Catholic Party and the Cristero Revolt.[84] The emergence of those movements is difficult to explain without understanding the vibrant Catholic community that lay activists—male and, above all, female—constructed after the *Reforma*.

NOTES

Chapter opening image source: Personal collection of Edward Wright-Rios.

1. Earlier versions of this paper were presented at a panel on "Catholic Sociability and Civil Society: Catholic Lay Organizations in the 19th Century" at the Latin American Studies Association meetings, Washington, DC, September 2001; at the Seminario de Historia Social of the Colegio de México in June 2002; and at the Harvard Boston Area Workshop on Latin American History in October 2002. I thank the participants of those sessions for their valuable comments.

2. See, for example, Jorge Adame Goddard, *El pensamiento político y social de los católicos mexicanos, 1867–1914* (Mexico City: UNAM, 1981); Manuel Ceballos Ramírez, *El catolicismo social: Un tercero en discordia: Rerum Novarum, la "cuestión social" y la movilización de los católicos mexicanos (1891–1911)* (Mexico City: El Colegio de México, 1991); and Randall S. Hanson, "The Day of Ideals: Catholic Social Action in the Age of the Mexican Revolution, 1867–1929" (Ph.D. diss., Indiana University, 1994). Laura O'Dogherty Madrazo mentions the conferences of St. Vincent de Paul as part of the flowering of lay organizations that characterized the "Catholic Restoration" of the Porfiriato, but gives the impression that they were exclusively male: *De urnas y sotanas: El Partido Católico Nacional en Jalisco* (Mexico City: CONACULTA, 2001).

3. See, for example, Ann S. Blum, "Conspicuous Benevolence: Liberalism, Public Welfare, and Private Charity in Porfirian Mexico City, 1877–1910," *The Americas* 58 (July 2001) and Cynthia Sanborn and Felipe Portocarrero, eds., *Philanthropy and Social Change in Latin America* (Cambridge, MA: David Rockefeller Center Series on Latin American Studies, Harvard University, 2005). In his mammoth history of Mexican social welfare, Moisés González Navarro refers to the Vincentian conferences, but presents them only as a late nineteenth-century phenomenon and does not distinguish between the male and female associations: *La pobreza en México* (Mexico City: El Colegio de México, 1985), 58, 61; and "Ejercicio Caritativo," 496, 502, 505–9 in vol. 4 of *Historia moderna de México, El Porfiriato: Vida social*, ed. Daniel Cosío Villegas, 3rd ed. (Mexico City: Editorial Hermes, 1973).

4. See review of the recent literature in Hilda Sábato, "On Political Citizenship in Nineteenth-Century Latin America," *American Historical Review* 106, no. 4 (Oct. 2001). Carlos A. Forment briefly mentions the Vincentian lay societies in his monumental survey of private associations, *Democracy in Latin America, 1760–1900: Civic Selfhood and Public Life in Mexico and Peru* (Chicago: University of Chicago Press, 2003), 260.

5. See, for example, William Fowler and Humberto Morales Moreno, eds., *El conservadurismo mexicano en el siglo XIX* (Puebla: Benemérita Universidad Autónoma de Puebla, 1999); and Erika Pani, "Democracia y representación política: La visión de dos periódicos católicos de fin de siglo, 1880–1910," in *Modernidad, tradición y alteridad: La ciudad de México en el cambio de siglo (XIX–XX)*, ed. Claudia Agostoni and Elisa Speckman (Mexico City: UNAM, 2001).

6. Recent studies have focused on Catholic women during the Mexican Revolution: Barbara Ann Miller, "The Role of Women in the Mexican Cristero Rebellion: Las Señoras y las Religiosas," *The Americas* 40 (January 1984): 303–24; Patience A. Schell, "An Honorable Avocation for Ladies: The Work of the Mexico City Unión de Damas Católicas Mexicanas, 1912–1926," *Journal of Women's History* 10, no. 4 (Winter 1999); María Teresa Fernández-Aceves, "The Political Mobilization of Women in Revolutionary Guadalajara, 1910–1940" (Ph.D. diss., University of Illinois at Chicago, 2000); and Kristina Boylan, "Mexican Catholic Women's Activism, 1929–1940" (Ph.D. diss., University of Oxford, 2000). See also Hanson, "The Day of Ideals," esp. 175–208, 579–600.

7. A recent history of the "Vincentian Family" in Mexico, which mostly focuses on the male and female religious orders, contains two excellent short chapters on the Ladies: Vicente de Dios, *Historia de la Familia Vicentina en México, 1844–1994*, 2 vols. (Salamanca: Editorial CEME, 1993). I am deeply indebted to Father Juan José Muñoz for giving me a copy of this work, which is unavailable in Mexico City outside the walls of the Convent of the Concepción. I have located only one study of the Ladies of Charity in Latin America: Karen Mead, "Gender, Welfare and the Catholic Church in Argentina: Conferencias de Señoras de San Vicente de Paul, 1890–1916," *The Americas* 58 (July 2001).

In addition, I have located some of the Mexican association's *Reglamentos* (1863 and 1911) and *Memorias* (for 1865, 1866, 1878, and 1921) in rare book libraries in the United States and Mexico, and have found information for the period after 1892 in the annual *Rapports* of the international organization, housed in the archive of the Lazariste Convent in Paris: *Reglamento de la Asociación de las Señoras de la Caridad instituida por San Vicente de Paul en beneficio de los pobres enfermos, y establecida en varios lugares por los Padres de la Congregación de la Misión con licencia de los ordinarios* (Mexico City: Imp. de Andrade y Escalante, 1863); *Reglamento para la Asociación de la Señoras de la Caridad . . . formado según su original de París y mandado observar por el Director General de la República* (Mexico City: Iglesia de la Inmaculada Concepción, 1911); *Memoria que el Consejo Superior de las Asociaciones de Señoras de la Caridad del Imperio Mexicano dirige al General de París, de las obras que ha practicado y cantidades colectadas e invertidas en el socorro de los pobres enfermos, desde el 10 de julio de 1864 a 30 de junio de 1865* (Mexico City: Tip. del Comercio a cargo de J. Moreno, 1865); *Memoria que el Consejo Superior de las Asociaciones de Señoras de la Caridad de México, dirige al general de París, de las obras . . . desde el 10 de julio de 1865 a 30 de junio de 1866* (Mexico City: Mariano Villanueva, 1867); *Memoria que el Consejo Superior de las Señoras de la Caridad de Méjico leyó en la Asamblea general verificada en la Iglesia de la Encarnación de esta capital el día 23 de julio de 1878* (Mexico City: Tip. Religiosa de Miguel Torner y Cía, 1879); *Memoria sobre la obra de la Señoras de la Caridad de San Vicente de Paul en México, año de 1921* (Mexico City: Imp. "La

Moderna," 1922); and *Rapport sur les oeuvres des Dames de la Charité pendant l'Année [1892/1893/1895/1896] Lu a l'Assemblée Générale* . . . (Paris: 95, Rue de Sèvres, 1893/1894/1896/1897).

8. The term is used by O'Dogherty Madrazo, *De urnas y sotanas*, esp. 21–50. See also Jean A. Meyer, *The Cristero Rebellion: The Mexican People between Church and State, 1926–1929*, trans. Richard Southern (Cambridge: Cambridge University Press, 1976), 6–10, 194–95; Ceballos Ramírez, *El catolicismo social*; and Hanson, "The Day of Ideals," 50–80.

9. On the original foundation, see Barbara B. Diefendorf, *From Penitence to Charity: Pious Women and the Catholic Reformation in Paris* (New York: Oxford University Press, 2004), esp. 203–16, 226–38. On the nineteenth-century refounding, see Edward R. Udovic, "'What About the Poor?' Nineteenth-century Paris and the Revival of Vincentian Charity," *Vincentian Heritage* 14 (1993).

10. I am here paraphrasing Lori D. Ginzberg, *Women and the Work of Benevolence: Morality, Politics, and Class in the Nineteenth-Century United States* (New Haven, CT: Yale University Press, 1990). On this point see also F. K. Prochaska, *Women and Philanthropy in Nineteenth-Century England* (Oxford: Oxford University Press, 1980); and Bonnie G. Smith, *Ladies of the Leisure Class: The Bourgeoises of Northern France in the Nineteenth Century* (Princeton, NJ: Princeton University Press, 1981), esp. chap. 6.

11. Albert Foucault, *La Société de Saint-Vincent de Paul: Histoire de Cents Ans* (Paris: Editions SPES, 1933), esp. 218; Société de St. Vincent de Paul, *Livre du Centenaire: L'oeuvre d'Ozanam a Travers le Monde, 1833–1933* (Paris: Gabriel Beauchesne et ses Fils, 1933); *Reglamento de la Sociedad de San Vicente de Paul, 1835* (Mexico City: n.p., 1851), 6, fn. 2; and *Reglamento* (1863), 16, 21–22.

12. De Dios, *Historia de la Familia Vicentina*, 1:146, 541–42.

13. On the history of the male Society, see Silvia Arrom, "Catholic Philanthropy and Civil Society: The Lay Volunteers of St. Vincent de Paul in Nineteenth-Century Mexico," in Sanborn and Portocarrero, *Philanthropy and Social Change*.

14. *Reglamento* (1863), esp. 13–14, 26–27.

15. De Dios, *Historia de la Familia Vicentina*, 1:145.

16. The canonical approval came on April 8, 1864; the date of the civil approval is unclear. De Dios, *Historia de la Familia Vicentina*, 1:541–43; *Memoria* (1865), 6; and *Memoria* (1922), 5.

17. De Dios, *Historia de la Familia Vicentina*, 1:542–53.

18. For an excellent discussion of the "missionary strategy" adopted by the Mexican church in the 1860s, see Hanson, "The Day of Ideals," esp. 13–15, 67–81.

19. The term was coined by Emmet Larkin for Ireland, where a similar process took place in the second half of the nineteenth century: see his "The Devotional Revolution in Ireland, 1850–1875," *American Historical Review* 77 (1972).

20. The Sisters of Charity were part of the Parisian municipal system as well, staffing Casas de Socorro that provided medical care and medicines. See *Estracto de los reglamentos generales de la asistencia pública y de los acuerdos de la Junta para el uso de las Hermanas, Comisarios y Señoras de la Caridad* and *Obras de Caridad que se practican en varios establecimientos de beneficencia* (both published in Mexico City: Imp. de J. M. Andrade y Escalante, 1865). On the imperial reorganization of the welfare system, see Silvia Arrom,

Containing the Poor:The Mexico City Poor House, 1774–1871 (Durham, NC: Duke University Press, 2000), 240–46. Note that Empress Charlotte's role in promoting the Ladies of Charity is not as clear as I thought when I wrote that book.

21. *Memoria* (1865), 6; and *Memoria* (1867), fold-out chart.

22. *Memoria* (1865), 4–6 and fold-out chart (which includes a summary of the 1864 report as well); *Memoria* (1867), 7; and De Dios, *Historia de la Familia Vicentina,* 1:544–49, 561. The 1896 *Rapport* explains that the girls' groups, the Enfants de Marie, were "puissantes auxiliaires des Dames, et . . . les premieres dignitaires de l'Oeuvre."

23. *Reglamento* (1863), 4.

24. *Memoria* (1865), 6–9, 15.

25. I thank Erika Pani for reviewing the membership lists with me and corroborating my own impressions.

26. *Memoria* (1865), 4, 10.

27. See discussion in Arrom, "Catholic Philanthropy and Civil Society."

28. See Silvia Arrom, *The Women of Mexico City, 1790–1857* (Stanford, CA: Stanford University Press, 1985), 7–8.

29. *Memoria* (1865), esp. 4.

30. De Dios, *Historia de la Familia Vicentina,* 1:546.

31. *Memoria* (1865) and (1867), 60; and De Dios, *Historia de la Familia Vicentina,* 1:545–46.

32. *Memoria* (1865), 7; and *Memoria* (1867), 10.

33. *Memoria* (1865) and (1867); De Dios, *Historia de la Familia Vicentina,* 1:547. Note that the dispensary, apparently a pharmacy, was called a *botica.* The clinics were called *hospitales* and *hospitalitos.*

34. *Reglamento* (1911), 47.

35. De Dios, *Historia de la Familia Vicentina,* 1:549.

36. In addition to the Superior Council that oversaw the conferences in the Mexico City area as well as governing the national association, there were Central Councils in Guadalajara, Toluca, Tenancingo, Puebla, Morelia, Orizaba, Jojutla, San Luis Potosí, Huamantla, Chilapa, Zacatecas, and Jalapa. De Dios, *Historia de la Familia Vicentina,* 1:550.

37. De Dios, *Historia de la Familia Vicentina,* 1:550–51.

38. For a history of church-state relations during these years see Mariano Cuevas, *Historia de la iglesia en México,* 5 vols. (El Paso: Ed. "Revista Católica," 1928), esp. 5:426–50; and Hanson, "The Day of Ideals," 44–62.

39. *Memoria* (1879).

40. *Reglamento* (1863), 21.

41. Juan José Muñoz, author of the chapters on the Vincentian volunteers, proposed the correlation between the decline of the Ladies of Charity and the death of the association's director. De Dios, *Historia de la Familia Vicentina,* 1:11, 556, 639.

42. Of the twelve Central Councils established by 1868, only Puebla failed to report to the Superior Council. Assuming that some of the conferences in that district still functioned, the number of active conferences would have been higher than the one hundred reported that year. *Memoria* (1879), 53.

43. *Reglamento* (1863), 22.

44. De Dios, *Historia de la Familia Vicentina*, 2:642, 645, 670.

45. *Memoria* (1865), 7.

46. *Rapport* (1896).

47. De Dios, *Historia de la Familia Vicentina*, 2:644–46. For an analysis of the nature of Vincentian welfare services, see Arrom, "Catholic Philanthropy and Civil Society."

48. See Cuevas, *Historia de la iglesia en México*, 5: chap. 6; and Hanson, "The Day of Ideals," 52–81.

49. See Blum, "Conspicuous Benevolence"; González Navarro, *La pobreza en México*, 35–146.

50. The number of female conferences, which looks suspiciously rounded, comes from the 1894 *Rapport*, 45, and thus represents the number reported to the international organization in 1893. The figures for the men are from 1894, *Reseña del Quincuagenario de la Sociedad* (Mexico City: Imp. y Lit. de Francisco Díaz de León, 1895), 21, 47, 50–57.

51. De Dios, *Historia de la Familia Vicentina*, 2:629–30.

52. On this trend see Margaret Chowning, "From Colonial Cofradías to Porfirian Pious Associations: A Case Study in the Feminization of Public Piety in Mexico" (unpublished paper presented at the Latin American Studies Association meetings, Washington, DC, 2001).

53. See Adame, *El pensamiento político y social de los católicos mexicanos*; Ceballos Ramírez, *El catolicismo social*; Hanson, "The Day of Ideals," 83–130; Pani, "Democracia y representación política"; O'Dogherty Madrazo, *De urnas y sotanas*; and De Dios, *Historia de la Familia Vicentina*, 2:627–28.

54. See De Dios, *Historia de la Familia Vicentina*, 1:516.

55. *Memoria* (1865), 8.

56. Quoted by Manuel Olimón Nolasco, "Proyecto de reforma de la Iglesia en México (1867 y 1875)," in *Estado, iglesia y sociedad en México: Siglo XIX*, ed. Alvaro Matute et al. (Mexico City: UNAM; Porrúa, 1995), 289. See the discussion of the 1875 Pastoral in Adame, *El pensamiento político y social de los católicos mexicanos*, 90–91. On the 1872 exhortations of the Mexican bishops, see De Dios, *Historia de la Familia Vicentina*, 1:551.

57. *Rapport* (1894), 45.

58. *Reglamento* (1863), 11–13; *Reseña* (1895), 26; and De Dios, *Historia de la Familia Vicentina*, 1:521.

59. *Reseña* (1895), 26.

60. De Dios, *Historia de la Familia Vicentina*, 2:629–30; and Ceballos Ramírez, *El catolicismo social*, 121.

61. *Memoria* (1865), 11. The Tacubaya conference was, however, described as practically directed by the president's husband, Joaquín M. de Ansorena: see *Memoria* (1865), 13.

62. Quoted in De Dios, *Historia de la Familia Vicentina*, 1:551. Diefendorf, *From Penitence to Charity*, makes a similar argument about the agency of women in founding the seventeenth-century Dames de la Charité, esp. 245–51.

63. For a discussion of these trends, see Arrom, *Women of Mexico City*, esp. chap. 1; and Arrom, *Containing the Poor*, 180, 228, 244–47, 260–61, and 267–68.

64. Cuevas, *Historia de la iglesia en México*, 5:383–84; and Adame, *El pensamiento político y social de los católicos mexicanos*, 19–27.

65. This term is from Mary P. Magray, *The Transforming Power of the Nuns: Women, Religion, and Cultural Change in Ireland, 1750–1900* (Oxford: Oxford University Press, 1998), viii. It is unclear from the secondary literature whether the women's branch of the Sociedad Católica disappeared along with the male Society, or whether it persisted, as hinted at by Ceballos Ramírez, *El catolicismo social*, 100, 106.

66. Adame, *El pensamiento político y social de los católicos mexicanos*, 105. It is worth noting that the appeal of convents was already declining by the late eighteenth and early nineteenth centuries. See Arrom, *Women of Mexico City*, 47–49.

67. For an analysis of a similar strategy in England, see Simon Morgan, "'A Sort of Land Debatable': Female Influence, Civic Virtue and Middle-Class Identity, c. 1830–c. 1860," *Women's History Review* 13 (2004).

68. Olimón Nolasco, "Proyecto de reforma de la Iglesia en México," 289.

69. *Reglamento* (1863), 4.

70. *Memoria* (1865), 7.

71. *Memoria* (1865), 6, 20.

72. *Reglamento* (1863), 4–5.

73. *Reglamento* (1863), 7.

74. Peggy Levitt describes a similar development of women's "social capital" in charismatic Catholic groups in the twentieth-century Dominican Republic: *The Transnational Villagers* (Berkeley: University of California Press, 2001), 161–62.

75. See Arrom, "Catholic Philanthropy and Civil Society."

76. Beatriz Castro, "Charity and Poor Relief in the Context of Poverty: Colombia, 1870–1930" (Ph.D. diss., Oxford University, 2001); and Macarena Ponce de León Atria, "La Sociedad de San Vicente de Paul en Chile: Nuevos vínculos con la jerarquía eclesiástica y los pobres urbanos, 1854–1870" and Sol Serrano, "Asociaciones católicas en el siglo XIX chileno: Política, caridad y rito" (unpublished papers presented at the LASA meetings, Washington, DC, 2001). In contrast, male conferences did not apparently catch on in Argentina: see Mead, "Gender, Welfare and the Catholic Church in Argentina," 100, fn. 23.

77. See Ralph Gibson, *A Social History of French Catholicism, 1789–1914* (London: Routledge, 1989), esp. 121, 227.

78. Austen Ivereigh, ed., *The Politics of Religion in an Age of Revival: Studies in Nineteenth Century Europe and Latin America* (London: Institute of Latin American Studies, 2000).

79. See review of Ivereigh by Hubert J. Miller, *Hispanic American Historical Review* 82 (May 2002), 428.

80. The Mexican men's conferences of St. Vincent de Paul were the first in Latin America. The Mexican Ladies' conferences were among the earliest in Latin America. They may have been preceded by those in Peru, which were referred to in the 1865 *Memoria*, 39, along with an association in Bahia (apparently in Brazil), which did not send a report to the central office in Paris. The 1893 *Rapport* listed branches of the Ladies of Charity in Costa Rica, Ecuador, Guatemala, Martinique, Peru, and Brazil. Karen Mead analyzes an Argentine association founded in 1889 that did not become

affiliated with the international body, apparently to avoid paying dues; "Gender, Welfare and the Catholic Church in Argentina," 100.

81. Mead found a similar trend in her study of the Argentine Ladies of Charity, "Gender, Welfare and the Catholic Church in Argentina."

82. For a discussion of this ideological shift, see Arrom, *Women of Mexico City*, 259–67.

83. In the 1920s the Ladies of Charity were overshadowed by a new Catholic Action organization, the Damas Católicas, founded in 1912. See Hanson, "The Day of Ideals," 24, 175–208, 579–600; Schell, "An Honorable Avocation for Ladies"; Fernández-Aceves, "The Political Mobilization of Women in Revolutionary Guadalajara," esp. chap. 3; and Boylan, "Mexican Catholic Women's Activism." The Vincentian lay groups never disappeared, however. In 1990 the women's organization, renamed Voluntarias Vicentinas, had some four thousand members; the men's conferences had approximately one thousand. De Dios, *Historia de la Familia Vicentina*, 2:638, 666.

84. Ceballos Ramírez, *El catolicismo social*, mapped a similar "eje geopolítico católico" in the first decade of the twentieth century and noted—without elaborating—its debt to the earlier proliferation of Catholic associations in that area. See also O'Dogherty Madrazo, *De urnas y sotanas*, 19, 98, 112–13; and Meyer, *Cristero Rebellion*, 70, 75, 85.

5
Liberal Religion:
The Schism of 1861

Pamela Voekel

Commemorative Sonnet from the Patron Saint Festival of Santa Catarina Loxicha, Oaxaca, 1899. Although images were more common mementos of religious festivals, village priests often ordered thousands of devotional poems printed on thin colored paper from urban printing workshops to sell at the celebrations. Note the militant tone typical of this period in the portrayal of Saint Catherine as the "vanquisher of error" (2nd and 4th stanzas).

Historians of Mexico's mid-nineteenth-century liberals have concluded that the movement's program of church-state separation amounted to an unambiguous secularization drive. Certainly the means suggest this end: between their initial success in the 1850s and their ultimate displacement by conservative forces allied with the French invaders, the liberals placed birth, death, and marriage rites under state auspices, ended the church's special privileges and prerogatives, and removed religious expression from the streets and corralled it into the home or the church building. But a closer look at the actors' own paper trail suggests a radically different interpretation of their motives. Far from seeking to remove religion from Mexican national life, they were instead consumed with refashioning the Catholic Church from within, with paring down its hierarchy and simplifying its liturgy without eliminating its central mysteries. In place of Romish excess they envisioned not a secular society but a Godly alternative.

78

Nowhere is this better illustrated than in the 1859 establishment of a schismatic Catholic Church under state protection. Prominent liberals cast the newly created constitutional clergy as critical messengers of a simple, ethical piety that blossomed in the Christian fraternity and God-given sentiment that would bind the fractured nation together. This schismatic national church would prove a resounding failure.[1] For with its stress on individual and unmediated conscience and its cult of masculine sensibility, this creed sanctified the male laity's leadership. In effect, with their very fervor for lay individualism, the reformed church's leaders put themselves out of a job. Their rapid disappearance combined with liberalism's subsequent and undeniably secular career has misled observers into ignoring the liberals' own interpretations of their fight. Mexican liberalism certainly spawned idol-smashing secularists, but it was born Christian.

THE SKULL BENEATH THE SKIN: CHRISTIAN JUSTIFICATION FOR REPUBLICANISM

David Brading poses the riddle of fervent liberalism succinctly when he asks, "For what cause did the proponents of possessive individualism and a market economy invite men to sacrifice their lives in a civil war?" Classical republicanism as an animating ideal was fraught with contradictions even at the time, for while the liberals billed themselves as the heirs of the French Revolution, their French opponents could make identical claims.[2] But long before the French took the field, the liberals had a decidedly more transcendent sense of mission: they were fighting an epic battle in the larger religious war that had wracked the Christian world for centuries.

Passions ran high because at the crux of this dispute between liberal and ultramontane Catholicism stood two fundamentally irreconcilable notions of how men connected to God; nothing less than salvation was at stake. While the ultramontane championed the indispensable mediation of the church and saints with the divine, liberals, as Melchor Ocampo explained, relied on "moral instincts by which each man sees inside himself (intuition this is called) his duty, on each occasion given by and in accordance with the infallible light, that, as a general rule, God has deigned to give him."[3] God had bestowed upon every individual "reason and conscience, without any motivation except to guide him." Now men were awakening to this spiritual gift and a "new humanity guided only by reason and love" was emerging, with new apostles who found themselves as persecuted as those of Christ.[4] Strict adherence to the dictates of this God-given conscience provided the fountainhead of moral sensibility, bestowing upon men the virtuous predisposition that manifested itself in compassion and charity toward all men as well as resistance to sensual, worldly temptations. According to reformed clerics, the battle then roiling the republic arrayed ignorant, slavish priests against "those sufficiently enlightened to understand the truth, those sufficiently virtuous to rise above the slander of the devout, those who listened to their conscience and followed it without vacillating."[5]

The church hierarchy, of course, represented the biggest threat to freedom of conscience. By the radical liberals' reckoning, the pope represented a feudal relic in a world aflame with democratic passion, a despot leagued with those twin enemies of progress: aristocracy and divine-right monarchy. After noting that the church preached fidelity to the cross but not to Christ, liberal Pedro T. Echeverría satirized the classic catechism. Taking on the voice of a mock conservative, his pamphlet begged the pope to liberate Mexico from the liberal heretics in the name of that unholy trinity, "the aristocracy, tyranny, and Mammon."[6] Other public champions of liberalism noted that absolute power was simply anachronistic in the nineteenth century: the world needed a pope willing to declare that democracy and the Bible shared the same spirit.[7] To the conservative assertion that despotism reigned supreme in non-Catholic countries, they pointed to the sad state of affairs in Rome, where the nobility had united with the papacy and a swarm of parasites lived from their abuses.[8]

Just as they devalued priestly access to the divine, these rational Christians likewise denied reports of communication with heaven through saints and miracles. In a typical instance, liberal journalists took on the supposed miracle of lush vegetation surrounding a cross in dry little town. Their investigation revealed the hidden tubing that brought water from a nearby convent, and they proudly publicized the subsequent dehydration when they disconnected it.[9] Likewise, the liberal army's official paper ridiculed the conservative troops' "superstition," noting that they attributed their successful defense of a particular plaza to the intervention of San Francisco.[10] Orations to render prisoners invisible to guards, miraculous powers attributed to Santiago's horse, chants to invoke lost objects or rid oneself of unwelcome guests—all this scattered the devotion rightly belonging to God alone and distracted from the valuable lessons to be learned from the saint's virtue and compassion.[11]

Moreover, a God who oscillated wildly between avenging wrath and miraculous mercy contravened the ethical truths found in scripture, which all men imbued with reason and conscience could read for themselves. "Millions of souls will divorce themselves from the bad clergy," the liberal press predicted, but not to become secular rationalists: to the contrary, they would "conserve the most powerful connection, the belief in just one Book."[12] All of the ambitious church councils, fatuous monarchs, the Vatican farm, canons, and even the church fathers' eloquence were not worth the science, truth, love, and, indeed, liberalism found on just one page of the Bible.[13]

It would be impossible to overstate the importance of the notion of Christian charity to liberal political thought in this era. In reform Catholicism, God granted men inborn feelings of compassion, sympathy, and benevolence as a way to guide them to virtue and to temper the worst excesses of natural reason. Moreover, while personal conscience splintered society into free individuals, this God-given *caridad* provided new social cement. Christian benevolence—not abstract republicanism or a common French enemy—could truly unite a fractured society into a nation.

The church's renewed emphasis on the exterior cult of worship constituted the biggest threat to this purified piety that would bind rich and poor together. Why give alms to an institution when they could go directly to suffering humanity and simultaneously make visible one's inner experience of God? And why give to a church that would most likely squander the money on useless distractions like the cult of the saints or elaborate decorations? Why indeed, thundered Ponciano Arriaga from the wellspring of his soul and the pages of the liberal Mexico City paper *El Monitor Republicano*:

> It would be bitter indeed to see inside a church on the day of its patron saint celebration curtains of rich silk, chasubles, gilded objects, ornaments of pure gold, branches of bright silver, incense holders, and chalices of emerald and other precious stones while there exists in the porticos of the same temple dedicated to the God of Love (*Díos de la Caridad*) a multitude of blind men, lepers, and the sick pallid with hunger, exhausted by misery, pulling themselves along the ground and extending their squalid hands for a handout, for the charity that one asks for in Christ's name and in the name of the same saint in whose honor they pay the noisy orchestra, Italian singers, and fire works . . . cover your face Holy Charity (*caridad santa*)! . . . nothing is true, nothing is just, nothing correct, nothing legitimate, especially not for the Christian clergy, without love (*caridad*) and good works.[14]

Far from tearing down the church to erect a secular utopia in its place, liberal intellectuals proposed a new religious *esprit social* that would replace the *esprit de corps* that had formerly reigned. Christian love and charity catapulted believers above petty corporate or party interests into a universal Christian humanism. "Christian charity" would save religion from an old society "grown so hopeless from the yoke of fanaticism that it wanted to break all religious bonds."[15]

That heartfelt religion animated the liberal project is hardly surprising: ENLIGHTENED Catholicism had flowered in late eighteenth-century Mexico, enjoying strong support from the preindependence church hierarchy and from postindependence intellectuals, as well as from a significant slice of the laity. As it did throughout the Catholic world, the ultramontane Catholicism of the mid-nineteenth century represented a sharp about-face from the sober, state-controlled churches that dominated the late eighteenth-century Catholic world.[16] Thus it was the institutional church, sidling toward papal infallibility and energetically promoting pilgrimage, the saints, and the cult of Mary, which had fundamentally changed in Mexico in the mid-nineteenth century.[17]

And indeed, although often demonizing the liberals as atheists and even communists, the conservative clergy also read the liberals' attacks not as philosophical secularism but rather as a specific religious misinterpretation, specifically the heresy of seventeenth- and eighteenth-century Jansenism.[18] Appointed by the crown in the late eighteenth century, Mexico City arch-bishops influenced by the Enlightenment had energetically preached their own version of Jansenist piety, adumbrating if not actually promoting the importance of conscience, the scriptures, and the early church councils' au-thority over the Holy Father. After independence, prominent liberal intel-lectuals like José María Luis Mora and José Joaquín Fernández de Lizardi took up the banner of this crusade; the *Reforma*'s liberal Catholics cited Mora in particular.[19] Certainly the freedom of conscience so central to Lizardi's and Mora's concerns was not part of the colonial-era bishops' and archbish-ops' agenda—worship should focus on Christ, yes, but he was certainly no martyr for democracy. Nevertheless, they had promoted many of the funda-mental tenets of the simple Catholicism that animated the liberal ranks dur-ing the *Reforma*.[20]

And their campaigns had affected the laity's pious sensibilities. Liberal Catholic intellectuals' contrast of true charity and benevolence with the frivo-lous and spiritually void exterior cult was echoed by mid-nineteenth-century testators. The pious bequests contained in 350 wills from each of the three pe-riods of 1710–20, 1810–20, and 1850–60 tell a story of increased concern for the poor and declining support for the pomp and splendor of the cult of wor-ship. Whereas during the period of 1710–20, only 33 of the 138 testators who made pious bequests gave specifically to the poor, one hundred years later 49 of the 65 testators who left gifts did so. In midcentury, 67 percent of Mexico City residents leaving bequests designated the poor as recipients, with over half of these giving exclusively to the destitute. The candles, bells, and rich cloth to adorn the saints faded from the wills, to be replaced by gifts given directly to the indigent.[21] Whether midcentury testators concerned with the poor defini-tively shared the liberals' theology and politics remains uncertain and perhaps ultimately unknowable, for to tacitly acknowledge *caridad* as an important social value was not necessarily to recognize radical liberals as its definitive exemplars.

But if Mexico's liberal Catholics had deep intellectual and social roots in their own country, they also knew themselves to be in conversation with all of Western Christendom. Religion and liberty were inextricably linked but cler-ical ignorance thwarted this simple truth, noted *El Constitucional*, citing such champions of liberal Catholicism as Chateaubriand, Abbé Felicité de Lamennais, and Pére Lacordaire.[22] In his highly influential *The Genius of Christianity*, the viscount of Chateaubriand flatly stated that "Christianity is opposed in spirit and determination to arbitrary power."[23] In 1830, Lamennais and Lacordaire founded the journal *L'Avenir*, whose motto "God and Liberty" summed up the tenor of the entire venture. The pope forced the men to make a statement of doctrinal submission in 1833 and Lamennais lived out his remaining years a bitter man, refusing to cede to papal authority, while Lacordaire went on to found *L'Ere Nouvelle*, which the staunch ultramontane Louis Veuillot sarcastically tagged "erreur nouvelle."[24] When asked his opinion on the separation of church and state, Lacordaire quipped that "It was not with a cheque drawn on Caesar's bank that Jesus sent His Apostles out into the world."[25] *El Heraldo* offered for sale to its readers Italian Giuseppe Mazzini's *The Pope in the Nineteenth Century*.[26] Their enthusiasm for this illustrious father of Italian nationalism is not difficult to fathom: in an 1834 letter to Lamennais, Mazzini rehearsed fundamental liberal Catholic beliefs: "The thought of the time rejects every intermediary between humanity and the source of life. In our epoch, humanity will forsake the pope and have recourse to a general council of the church—that is to say, of all believers. The papacy has destroyed religious faith through materialism far more degrading and fatal than that of the eighteenth century."[27]

If *El Heraldo* found Europe's liberal Catholic intellectuals inspiring, *El Siglo Diez y Nueve* found fellow believers closer to home. Giant of Peruvian liberalism Francisco de Paula González Vigil opined on the evils of papal pretensions and the virtues of Christianity's early centuries in the Mexican paper in 1857, displaying the movement's familiar juxtaposition of simple biblical ethics to the church's overweening power and unbridled hoarding of riches.[28] On receiving Vigil's eight-volume magnum opus *Defensa de la autoridad de los gobiernos y de los obispos contra las pretensions de la Curia Romana*, Pius IX is said to have exclaimed, "How is it that even in the land of St. Rose they persecute me? Well, to the Index with the diabolical work."[29] An 1851 papal brief prohibited the book and excommunicated Vigil. But Rome, a frustrated Vigil lamented, had mistaken his intentions: he merely wanted to separate Catholicism from "curalist pretensions so that it would remain Christian and humanitarian," not "decatholize Peru."[30] In a work published in Guadalajara in 1856, cleric José Ignacio Víctor Eyzaguirre denounced Roman Catholicism's detractors the world over, and joined Peru's ultramontane Catholic press in accusing Vigil of heresy; he laid the blame for the small country's "twenty years of anarchy" squarely at the feet of Peruvian liberals' fondness for rationalism and Jansenism.[31]

As historian Frederick B. Pike points out, in questioning papal authority and in vaunting apostolic Christianity as the only real religion, Vigil and his fellow liberals were less secular reformers than religious heretics who sought to mold the church's interior workings to their own democratic ideals; Peruvian liberals' decidedly religious heresy, Pike convincingly argues, added a measure of vindictiveness and bitterness to the country's political struggles, which became, in essence, religious ones—precisely, we might add, what happened in Mexico.[32]

With a clear understanding of the religious backstory, we turn to the liberals' most transparent attempt to impose a new religious order on the nation— the experiment of the constitutional clergy.

THE CONSTITUTIONAL CLERGY

The explicit link between a long-standing internal church battle and the larger War of the Reform was vividly demonstrated in 1859 by a renegade clutch of Mexico City clergymen. These priests could trace their own theological allegiance back to the reformed piety's late eighteenth-century heyday, but the revitalized ultramontane current had the upper hand in the capital archbishopric. Alarmed by the archbishop's "incendiary pastorals," the priests sent a representative to the liberal camp in Veracruz to request aid in their battle with the church hierarchy. The liberals, they hoped, would support their struggle to wean the faithful away from the "seditious ramblings of false ministers" and toward a true understanding of the sacrifice of the original martyr for democracy, Jesus Christ.[33]

In 1857, the state had appointed priest Rafael Díaz Martínez to head a statistical survey of the church, and he now found a warm reception among Veracruz's liberal defenders of "true religion." The republicans promptly extended the mantle of their protection to clergymen who dedicated themselves to "administering to souls and cultivating the Lord's vineyard."[34] Melchor Ocampo in particular waxed enthusiastic, lauding the virtuous lower clergy who "consoled the poor, visited the sick and tried, in keeping with their ministry, tried to end hunger, nudity, and misery." These reformed crusaders would improve that favorite liberal cause, public education, because instead of learning "rancid silliness and ultramontanism, the young would imbibe morality."[35]

As the government's agent in this endeavor, the Veracruz liberals further decreed, Díaz Martínez should encourage his fellow enlightened prelates to win their flocks to the liberal Constitution of 1857. The priests could reassure the public that the document adhered to Christian principles and that the new laws issued from Veracruz represented the triumphant return of the church's primitive democratic doctrines—an argument frequently heard during the 1857 Constitutional Convention, as historian Jacqueline Covo vividly illustrates. The founding document made vague references to state salaries for these liberal priests, but it also underlined the liberals' commitment to the separation of church and state. Thus it firmly promised little more than government protection from the decidedly hostile ecclesiastical superiors.[36]

Returning to Mexico City with the triumphant liberal forces on 1 January 1861, Díaz Martínez and nine other priests petitioned for three centrally located churches, citing as justification their valiant efforts to procure peace in the Republic and a record of blessing without charge over four hundred civil marriages as well as numerous baptisms and burials. La Merced, San Hipólito, and La Santísima were quickly turned over to them in early January.[37]

The opposition proved fast and fierce. In January of 1861, the lay voice of the ultramontane forces, *El Pájaro Verde*, informed the public that La Merced offered the sacraments without the ecclesiastical authorities' approval and that at least one priest had no license; La Santísima was now under civil, not ecclesiastical jurisdiction, the paper added.[38] The Cathedral Chapter, which had prudently followed the archbishop's advice to stop sermons during such trying times, now counseled a return to preaching to combat "the dissidents in La Merced who were leading even stalwart women away from true belief."[39]

Defenders of the conservative church even hovered outside church doors before mass, waylaying the faithful and informing them that the constitutional clergy had been officially excommunicated.[40] The conservative laity also stood firm, petitioning the government to keep the dissidents out of the parishes of San Miguel and Santa Veracruz.[41] Pasquinades tagging these liberal clerics as schismatics, Protestants, and excommunicated Catholics appeared on church doors one Sunday in February; in response, the following Sabbath churchgoers were greeted with a retraction. The Cathedral Chapter forcefully disavowed authorship of the preceding week's creed and noted that the laity committed no error in patronizing the dissidents, who were indeed true Catholics who strictly adhered to church dogma. While the liberal press gloatingly chalked up a victory for the "truly religious" in their battle with the "fanaticism" of the "vulgar superstitious," *El Pájaro Verde* stiffly noted that the Cathedral Chapter would not have voiced its opinions with a clandestine press; the retraction was entirely apocryphal.[42]

Not surprisingly, the forces arrayed against the dissidents in Mexico City took their cue from the church hierarchy, many of whom had been exiled by the victorious liberals.[43] From the very moment of the constitutional clergy's 1859 inception, the hierarchy had decried the reformed clerics' threat. Here was Satan's synagogue, a gathering place for the followers of Luther and Calvin, an invention of Jansenism and Regalism, the hierarchy warned, and

"the true Catholic would not be prisoner to this schismatic and impious propaganda . . . [but would instead] close his ears to the pompous prating of the
demagogic reformers and obey only the authorized voice of his pastors."[44]

With these clear instructions, the conservative newspapers *La Unidad
Católica* and *El Pájaro Verde* defended the faith in the bishops' absence, publishing lists of priests and deacons who had strayed from Mother Church as well
as the subsequent retractions, retorts, and wavering of many of those same
priests and deacons. When the liberal press called for a public discussion of the
accused *curas'* errors, the conservative newspapermen fired back that there was
nothing to discuss: the dissidents disagreed with their bishops, and no less an
authority than San Cipriano made it clear that when a schism occurred those
who broke with the hierarchy were the schismatics. The constitutional clergy
were no longer Roman Catholics.[45]

After four tense months, in early May the liberal priests beat a temporary
retreat from their three parishes, not returning again until September. The
now-chastened clerics confessed that they were few and that, alas, as the conservative Catholic press suggested, they might indeed fail on this second go-
around. But they attributed this possibility not to the tepid lay enthusiasm
charged by *La Unidad Católica*, but to clerical intrigue, the official church's
overwhelming wealth, and the continued disrespect for freedom of religion.
Intrigue was hardly the worst of it: the conservative clergy were in fact plot-
ting a Saint Bartholomew Day–type massacre, the liberals announced, an orgy
of violence in which they would "bathe themselves in the liberal heretics'
blood, as the fanatical French Catholics did in the blood of the Huguenots."[46]

Here the clerics expressed rumors that had earlier ricocheted around the
nervous city: red and green crosses mysteriously painted on doors and win-
dows on the eve of the anniversary of the conservative massacre of liberal soldiers and civilians at Tacubaya on 11 April 1858 had inspired the liberal press
to wonder if the Liberal Reform Club planned to butcher "the reactionaries"
or whether the conservatives planned to slaughter liberals in Mexico City, or
whether, indeed, the crosses were just an adolescent prank.[47] In a provocative
move, the *Pájaro Verde* had earlier denounced the Huguenot violence that had
provoked what it insinuated was a legitimate French Catholic outburst—the
convents sacked, the priests strung up, the faithful murdered during solemn
processions through the streets.[48] Clearly both sides of this civil war likewise
felt that they were skirmishing in a larger religious war.

The repression of external religious frivolities, the constitutional clergy's favorite battle in this war, must be seen in light of this long struggle for the soul
of the church itself. In December of 1860, the victorious liberals prohibited
the public procession of the Host to the homes of the sick and dying.[49] Liberal writers applauded the move: constitutional clergyman and *Monitor Repub-*

licano editorialist Juan N. Enríquez Orestes burlesqued the communicants at the cathedral who on their knees worshipped "the mules and the driver, who, with his hat on, drove the carriage that conveyed the Host." These fervent Mexicans reminded him of the "Israelites who worshipped the golden calf"—those oft-invoked idolaters.[50] He himself took the Host to the sick under his robes.[51]

In a world where religion was politics and politics had such deep religious hues, the law against the Eucharist's public procession and the constitutional clergy's naked satire quickly became flashpoints of conservative resistance. To the accusation that the lights, mules, sacristans, priests, and bells that accompanied the Host dignified "the most indifferent things and suffocated good sentiment," *El Pájaro Verde* took up cudgels in what it cast as a classic Catholic battle against heretics: the defense of Christ's real presence in the Eucharist. "Although God might be everywhere," it responded to the liberals' insinuations of exactly that, "He that is in the Host is not only God, but the man called Christ."[52]

But rather than addressing the Eucharistic issue with the rationalist arguments against transubstantiation, the liberal press took great pains to underscore that it challenged only the exterior trappings of religion and never the essential sacraments and doctrines themselves. The criticism stung nonetheless, as it was widely perceived to be attacking the central mystery of the faith, in the tradition of the Protestant heretic John Calvin. *La Unidad Católica* made sure readers understood this connection, noting that even the French king Louis XIV softened a law of religious tolerance by decreeing that Calvinists cease and desist from their provocative singing when the Eucharist passed; more recently, Napoleon had made Jews and Protestants adorn their houses for Eucharistic processions, the paper added.[53] The Wars of Religion raged on, far from Wittenberg and Geneva.

While the liberal and conservative newspapers wrangled, the female faithful took to the streets to defend the ultramontane church. Upward of 150 women from the parish of San Miguel petitioned the president to accompany the Host in January of 1861, an event widely reported in the papers. Even after the government flatly denied their request and reiterated its prohibition of public religious acts, the nocturnal processions continued.[54] In early February of 1861, the parish priest of La Santa Veracruz, Ateógenes Lombardini, was imprisoned and released the next day after an animated group of his female parishioners accompanied the Host out of the parish church into the streets.[55] Shortly thereafter, a neighborhood inspector arrested and imprisoned twenty-one women, one layman, and a priest as they amassed near the door of San Juan de Dios parish awaiting the Host's exit so they could "continue their scandals."[56]

Radical liberals no doubt remembered the petitions signed by thousands of Mexico City women who, along with groups of women from the provinces, had rallied to defend the bishops and church wealth and defeat the cause of religious freedom in 1856.[57] Over eight hundred Morelia women asked the government to release Clemente de Jesús Munguía and return him to his bishopric, noting that although laws and government were not the domain of their sex, they could indeed attest to his unassailable character.[58] The "beatas fanáticas" and "ancianas supersticiosas" who haunted liberal publications and their febrile imaginations, playing the role of the shadow army that foiled the advance of "true religion," were all too real.

The Mexico City women who processed with the Eucharist were simply one brigade in the larger battle between the sexes. "Who had not heard a seditious sermon, who did not have a wife, daughter, or mother who from the confessional brought discord into the domestic home?" asked the *Boletín del Ejército Federal* in response to its own question of who sustained the reactionaries.[59] Cultivated ladies crowned the brows of the assassins of Tacubaya the day of their triumphal entry into Mexico City, Ignacio Ramírez and Guillermo Prieto commented, "while scapulars and crosses reflected the animated gazes and furtive kisses." Women were mixed up in all of the reactionaries' endeavors, Ramírez and Prieto reported, so that if "we cease to combat them, we shall face the complete triumph of the reaction."[60]

As historian Margaret Chowning points out, one of the midcentury liberals' favorite tactics for discrediting the church was to associate it with women and effeminacy, as had their pre- and postindependence intellectual precursors.[61] To the accusation that Taumalipas's government representatives had processed through Mexico City's streets with the nuns of Santa Brígida with a cross and candles, Darío Balandrano reiterated his staunch support for *La Reforma* by distancing himself from its real and imagined enemies: "neither friars, sacristans nor skirts have influenced me," he insisted, "I am not Samson . . . and no Delilah's skirts have twisted my reason to prevent me from supporting the destruction of convents; I have fought for *La Reforma*."[62] The public celebration of religious holidays and customs like Day of the Dead not only threatened freedom of conscience, but it also provided an opportunity for women and effeminate men (*petimetres*) to strut and display themselves, Prieto reported.[63] Balandro's and Prieto's portrayal of the *Reforma* as a rational masculine force pitted against a superstitious and feminized enemy was a frequent trope in liberal publications: the *Boletín del Ejército Federal* saw in the current agitation of the patria "a sign of virility, a powerful force to break the bonds of religious superstition that have impeded its forward march."[64]

Ramírez and Prieto joined the liberal newspapers in gendering the press factions that squared off in Mexico City and in noting women's treacherous support for their opponents. *El Monitor* played Romeo; *La Unidad Católica*, in "pompous crinoline," primped as Juliet. The conservatives were depicted as awash in feminine silliness. *La Unidad Católica*, the coy Juliet, puffed superstition to the unsuspecting: water from San Ignacio for one sickness, earth from the Christ of Chalma for another, water from the well of Guadalupe instead of Holloway pills for yet another.[65] "Fanatical *beatas* and vulgar old women" served as *La Unidad Católica*'s oracles, *El Monitor Republicano* reported.[66] This war of religion was also a battle of the sexes.

But should we conclude from the constitutional clergy's sputtering beginnings that they were losing this war? The conservative press certainly thought so. *La Unidad Católica* noted that when the liberals passed their much-vaunted law declaring freedom of worship, no Protestants, Jews, or Muslims rushed to create their own temples. So, their opponents contested, the liberals had rifled through eighteenth-century French history to hit on a solution: the constitutional clergy, an influential group who had championed the French Constitution of 1791, with its mandate for a nonhierarchical church and simpler worship. This "exotic plant," this French import, was failing to thrive in Mexican soil, the conservative paper reported, and its ministers thus resorted to tactics such as the forced conscription of the faithful for mass; despite these radical measures, the pews remained sparsely populated.[67]

The conservatives may have been right. In Mexico City and in many of the provinces, the reformers appeared to be too few and far between to combat the church's vocal criticism and the laity's considerable hostility. A crowd pelted Guanajuato's martyrs for the "martyr for democracy" with rocks when they sallied into the streets, and the animosity continued when liberal officials summarily exiled the prelate they held responsible for the melee.[68] When a liberal law of 1861 declared that clerical supporters of the 1857 Constitution and the Reform Laws should occupy churches confiscated from the regular orders, Chiapas officials finessed the selection of a priest by noting that "the ancient and clearly democratic Don Climente Astillejo fit the bill, but given his weak eyesight, aches and pains, and advanced age, he simply could not fill the post."[69] And indeed within the year he was dead, leaving instructions that he was to be buried with "a cross in his right hand, the 1857 Constitution in the left, and letters from Benito Júarez under his robes."[70]

But while they were certainly a clerical minority and often the object of popular indifference and even hostility, these fishers of men were neither numerically insignificant nor entirely lacking in influence. Ever keen to downplay their numbers, *La Unidad Católica* estimated that in all of Mexico roughly one hundred clerics supported the Reform Laws and merely a dozen of these used the press or the pulpit to promote the reformed church; they also noted that these clerics hailed from only a few states, although we might note that the capital's press, even the conservative press, reported the goings-on of the reformers in many other, unspecified parts of the republic.[71] But this minimum of 100, an underestimation even by the conservative press's own reckonings, was no small number in a country manned by roughly 1,717 secular and 1,472 regular male clergy.[72]

And although perhaps not filling the pews, the constitutional clergy dominated an equally important pulpit during the liberals' brief stint in Mexico City: the press. And the press's importance in the battle for hearts and minds was certainly not lost on contemporaries. When the conservatives captured and summarily executed liberal personality Melchor Ocampo in early June of 1861, a mob chanting a popular couplet penned by liberal leader Guillermo Prieto sacked *El Pájaro Verde*, throwing the press into the street and burning it as an indifferent police force watched.[73] And when in December 1861 *La Unidad Católica* urged readers to defend the pope's temporal power, suggestively noting that he was surrounded by exiled clerics, it ran smack into Mexico City's press censorship tribunal, the Jurado de Imprenta, who accused it of inciting the public against the Reform Laws. The eleven-man committee, which included liberal *Siglo Diez y Nueve* editor Francisco Zarco, who had been arrested by the conservatives in 1858 and in 1860, and Federal District governor Juan José Baz, imprisoned author Florentino Saucedo and seized dozens of the offending articles.[74] The liberal and satirical *La Orquesta* opined that the press tribunal's agent had knocked on these conservative Catholics' door and awakened them from a dream that they were in Rome, not Mexico.[75] It was in front of this passionately contested tribunal of the reading public that liberals spelled out the tenets of this simple, ethic-based Christianity.

Under Juan N. Enríquez Orestes' leadership, the constitutional clergy's rhetorical flash lit up the headlines of *El Monitor Republicano*. No stranger to controversy, as a parish priest and later as a St. Vincent de Paul mission preacher in Zimapan, Enríquez Orestes had incurred the wrath of both the brothers and his own superiors, Archbishop Lázaro de la Garza y Ballesteros and Francisco de Paula y Veréa, bishop of Linares. These run-ins, he felt, sprang from the hierarchy's aversion to his simple sermons on the scriptural truths of equality and fraternity—sermons that won him a loyal following of liberals in Tulancingo, Zimapan, Jacala, Alfajayucan, and Mineral del Monte.[76] And indeed in Jacala, the city council had gone over the bishop's head to petition the government in 1856 to name Enríquez Orestes as the city's priest. Less than a year before, this liberal stronghold in Hidalgo had issued its *Acta de Jacala*, which adumbrated the Reform Laws and which historian Jesús Reyes Heroles later tagged as "the most complete document of its type for Mexican liberalism."[77]

As vital as the warring factions found the press, liberal intellectuals did not rely on newspapers alone to promote their religious vision. The hero priest of liberal novelist and pamphleteer Nicolás Pizarro Suárez's 1861 *El monedero* is a case in point. Together with a virtuous Indian artisan initially scorned by a beautiful aristocrat, Father Don Luis establishes La Nueva Filadelfia, a "Fraternal Colony" of hearty yeomen liberated from grasping foreign merchants and huge landowners. These humble republicans labor to their physical capacity and receive an education centered on the exact sciences and strict morality; a solid piety free of "superstitions" and the constant practice of mutual Christian love suffuses their brotherly interactions in this pastoral community.

No one abandoned this Christian utopia, the author explains, "because outside of it they could never find so much brotherly protection and such simple and true sociability purified by the truly divine influence of Christian love."[78] The simple injunction to love thy neighbor was emblazoned in gold on the community rotunda. Other than an avaricious Yankee named William Walker and the country's political chaos, the only menace to this idyll is the celibate priest's natural sexual urges; the approving author marries him to a devoted wife at the story's end. And indeed, although women farmed alongside the men, Nueva Filadelfia lacked the sexual edginess of some of its European utopian counterparts. This was no Fourierian phalanx: the patriarchal household reigned supreme and women could not miss a community gathering unless a husband, brother, or father accompanied them.[79] And indeed while singing the praises of a fictional rural parish priest strikingly similar to the literary examples above, eminent liberal Guillermo Prieto exclaimed, "What an energetic means to civilize, what a solid bond of national unity!"[80]

Nor was this connection confined to the capital's rarefied intellectual circles. Particularly in the north, the reformed church scored some major successes, garnering both lay and governmental support. Tamaulapis's liberal legislature granted Santa Bárbara parish priest and hacienda owner Ramón Lozano's petition to legitimize his three children in March of 1861, an event widely applauded in the state's liberal press and loudly decried as a scandal by Mexico City's *El Pájaro Verde*.[81] Stationed in Brownsville, Texas, bishop of Linares Francisco de Paula wasted little time, prohibiting the town's parishioners from any communication with the "disgraced priest Lozano" and declaring the sacraments he administered invalid.[82] Lozano, however, was not backing down, despite a small clutch of his own parishioners who circulated the bishop's edict to discourage church attendance. He noted that his clerical predecessors in the thriving town of perhaps ten thousand had been as fragile as he on the celibacy issue. And, perhaps more importantly, his children's legitimacy sprang from the Reform Laws, which he held in high regard.[83]

With the hierarchy poised to oust him from his post, on 12 May 1861, Lozano issued a manifesto of the new *Iglesia Apostólica Mexicana de Santa Bárbara de Tamaulipas*, noting in his parish baptismal record that his church had forever changed that day, "ceasing to be Romish." Fifty-three parishioners promptly signed this rousing statement.[84] The hierarchy behaved like wolves among sheep, the proclamation declared, and it was no longer possible to live in open struggle against conscience. This liberty of conscience and true Catholicism formed the cornerstones of the new church. Church canons that clashed with the Reform Laws were all banned. The Santa Bárbara rebels would indeed recognize Bishop Francisco de Paula's authority, but only after he had sworn to uphold the Constitution and the Reform Laws—an unlikely event indeed, as the bishop had worked assiduously and quite publicly to combat those same laws. In the meantime, Lozano would serve as head and "true pope" of his flock.[85]

The break sent shock waves through the hierarchy. From the archbishopric of Monterrey came a June pastoral letter warning parishioners that Lozano could no longer administer the sacraments; they would have to go to nearby Tula or Jicotencal. The edict begged those parishioners "who were still real Catholics" to help remove all obstacles to the reception of a new priest.[86] Monclova parish priest Narciso Villareal urged the parishioners to request a new priest and leave "the new Holiness to his fanatical delirium."[87] Although the hierarchy did eventually finagle a new priest into the parish in late July, Lozano refused to disappear, whipping off a spirited reply to Villareal.[88] Bishop Veréa had no jurisdiction over him and thus no right to suspend him for sexual incontinence: the Mexican Constitution had eliminated special tribunals and privileges. The scriptures and the example of the early church placed priests on the level of the bishops. And his parishioners—Catholics, not fanatics, he insisted—understood dogma and their own consciences well enough to know that the hierarchy erred.[89]

Reform enthusiasts like Lozano were joined by numerous clerics who most decidedly aided the liberals, but whose exact relationship to the official schism remains cloudy.[90] Enríquez Orestes' counterpart in the provinces, Francisco de P. Campa of Zacatecas, eagerly swore the oath to the 1857 Constitution and, until his dramatic public retraction, regularly contributed proliberal, anti–church hierarchy editorials to four newspapers, two of which were under his leadership.[91] Suspended by the hierarchy, Linares's liberal army chaplain Vicente Guevara was a cause célèbre with the constitutional clergy. During short–term president Ignacio Comonfort's brief reign, he had confessed several influential liberals shunned by the church and had then paid for his heroism, suffering prison and mistreatment after the conservative victory in 1858; he later contributed proreform articles to Mexico City's liberal press in 1861.[92]

In short, struggles over observance and authority within the church occupied a central role in the liberal-conservative competition for Mexico's hearts and minds.

And indeed the constitutional clergy would cleave to this conviction that they represented a valiant effort to restore the church rather than abandon it. As did many of the constitutional clergy after 1862, Enríquez Orestes sought financing from a nineteenth-century version of the NGO (nongovernmental organization): Protestant missionaries from the colossus of the north, in this case the Episcopalian Church.[93] Although his would-be patrons had high hopes for a Protestant church on Mexican soil, what shines out in the priest's rather shadowy funding quest is a man whose desire to reform the Catholic Church never wavered; he was no closet Protestant, although it is certainly not far-fetched to say that liberal Catholicism—with its distrust of clerical and saintly mediation with the divine—helped create the theological and cultural preconditions for others' conversion.

Enríquez Orestes and several colleagues had arrived in New York in 1864 highly touted by their sponsors as "men of intelligence and probity, and deserving of high regard."[94] Eerie tensions soon developed. The Mexican priests refused to say mass with their hosts, who found their actions and intentions "inscrutable"; would these erstwhile allies really "hold up a piece of dough and say it was Christ?" the Anglos wondered, concluding that they might indeed: Enríquez Orestes had defended the Catholic sacraments as indispensable to salvation and seemed more versed in "papal dogmatics" than his colleagues.[95] Body and blood of Christ, Orestes so believed; the Host was not a symbol of Christ's sacrifice, but the sacrifice itself. Some of the more astute Episcopalian missionaries grasped that their Mexican allies had no intention of ushering in a Protestant reformation: in Ciudad Victoria, where Enríquez Orestes had been so warmly received in 1864, Reverend A. E. Longson was introduced to a liberal army official in 1865 as an "anti-papist priest."[96]

The constitutional clergy counted staunch and influential liberal intellectuals like Ocampo, Prieto, Pizarro, and Ramírez in their camp; liberal pamphlets and even the Federal Army's own official bulletin rehearsed the fundamental tenets of the faith; under the fiery leadership of the prolific Enríquez Orestes they dominated the 1861 and 1862 liberal press. Yet for all this, even by their own reckoning they failed, for with few exceptions Mexico City congregants stayed away in droves. The hierarchy's vocal and explicit hostility, the satire heaped on it by *El Pájaro Verde* and *La Unidad Católica*, and, perhaps most importantly, the implacable distrust of this heresy displayed by many women—all of this proved too much to overcome.

Their own aversion to accumulation played a part as well; apostolic poverty was all very well in theory, but certainly no way to run a movement. "For supporting the Reform laws, where God's splendor shines," they explained, they had lost their welfare and resources to the point where they lacked even the money for mass; they feared they would end up as "ashes in the Laguna of Texcoco," although like good Christian martyrs they vowed not to falter.[97] Although the liberals offered explicit blueprints for proper priestly comportment and for the church's internal reorganization, starting with the pope's demotion, the Reform Laws nevertheless aimed at the separation of church and state, and at least a few liberals were unwilling to violate this tenet. As Francisco Zarco carefully explained, "Although the schismatics might rant and rave, and although we support their ideas, the government's job is not to endorse a particular sect."[98] Without government salaries or private donations, they had no way to support themselves.

This is hardly surprising given liberal Catholicism's stress on freedom of conscience and each enlightened individual's direct relationship with God. Priests—even virtuous fellow-traveler priests—were no godlier than liberal laymen, and except for the sacraments that these priests could provide, they were not really needed for real religion to flourish. As the liberal hero of Pizarro Suárez's *La Coqueta* tells a benighted elderly woman (almost synonymous in liberal discourse), "Priests are not religion . . . religion is the belief that each person has in the Divinity and in the mode in which to best honor Him . . . religion is good and necessary to society—priests are some good, some bad."[99]

France's constitutional clergy had to contend with noncompliant priests and their often female allies in places like the Vendée, but also with the official cult of reason, with its tendentiously secular rituals and de-Christianization campaigns. Perhaps ironically, the absolute centrality of Christian humanism to Mexican liberal discourse and the intellectual leadership's eloquent and oft-repeated defense of liberal Catholicism ensured that Mexico's constitutional clergy would be help-meets rather than leaders in this religious movement. It was Mexico's enlightened laity who led a godly campaign to save their simple ethical religion from the church. And if their own piety suggested to them that ordained priests were not absolutely central to this religion, an army to fight their dogged opponents most certainly was.

ONWARD CHRISTIAN SOLDIERS?: REFORMED RELIGION AND THE LIBERAL ARMY

Let us listen carefully to their liberal army's official bulletin, the *Boletín del Ejército Federal*, in 1858:

> We find ourselves in one of the phases of the great religious revolution that has agitated society since the sixteenth century . . . the Dominican Tetzel's scandalous

sale of indulgences encouraged another religious, a professor of theology in Wittenberg to take up the standard of reform and inspire Germany and all of Europe to combat Rome . . . their spirits were ready to fight this force that had corrupted even the purest Christians. The religious revolution then followed a slow path, conquering the sacred right of freedom of conscience . . . putting clerical riches into circulation . . . and reducing Rome to the point that it ceased to terrify Christian Nations. And when the revolution marches forward? What do Mexican clerics do? They ignite religious hatred, formulating anathemas against the innocent and denying them the sacraments. This clerical misconduct has irritated these families, and they have fled their altars; these people look for an asylum against this tyranny and disdain in God's great *misericordia*, in the reading of the holy writings where every unfortunate finds consolation and where doctrines abound to help them separate what truly comes from Jesus Christ and what comes from clerical passions and interests.[100]

This Christian army had a general befitting its stated religious mission. In his position as a commander of the liberal army, Santos Degollado, historian Enrique Krauze explains, "was a new incarnation of the armed man of religion" and "the finest example of the fusion between inner Catholicism and political liberalism"—an assessment shared by Justo Sierra, who claims that the general hoped the Reform Laws would mean the "resurrection of the church's prestige through returning it to the Gospel, poverty, charity, love, and the good."[101] In a letter to his son in September of 1860, Degollado, temporarily out of favor with Juárez, lamented the "ingratitude, reproaches, and calumniations" he had suffered at the hands of "our co-religious," but reiterated that "the sanctity of the cause" gave him courage; in an expression of his longing to imitate Christ's martyrdom he noted that "we should die like Hidalgo and Morelos died, because our blood falling on the eyes of the people (like that of the Divine Redeemer on the Blindman's eyes) will open them forever."[102] Just three days after accepting his position as general of the Federal Army in 1858, Degollado told the troops that "if the people ask me to lay down my arms, I will. But not to those adventurers who want to return to the status of Spanish colony; not to the privileged classes . . . not to those who would keep men's thoughts and actions in perpetual tutelage; not, in short to those hypocritical Pharisees who invoke the religion of Jesus Christ without really believing in it or observing its maxims of fraternity and peace."[103] The liberals, he roundly concluded in a March 1859 speech, were the true defenders of "the religion of the Crucified."[104]

Did the troops share Degollado's particular brand of religious passion? Florencia Mallon, whose thoughts on popular liberalism we would be wise to consider, would suggest a resounding "no." The liberals' intense hostility to religion, she argues, caused them to overlook the import of local religious rituals or read them as mere incitements to frivolous expenditures. A huge cultural rift thus yawned between these irreligious liberals and Indian and mestizo villagers whose community life centered on folk Catholicism. Where liberal populism centered on democratic representation and local autonomy, conservative populists happily connected religion to ritual, casting liberals as a threat to both and thereby winning peasant converts to their cause.[105]

But we may need to disaggregate the liberal army to evaluate its adherents' religious sensibility, perhaps along lines of geography; it would be odd indeed for a general like Degollado to send his troops to battle with rousing rhetoric that reflected little more than his own idiosyncrasies. In June of 1862, Enríquez Orestes joined the liberal army as a chaplain; in *El Monitor Republicano* he urged Mexicans to battle and likened liberal combatants to "Jesus Christ, who, infused with abnegation, went to Golgotha to offer himself in holocaust."[106] Several years later, the warrior priest, who referred to himself as a *fronterizo*, or border-dweller, wended his way to Ciudad Victoria and to yet another set-to with the church. Some of the town's laity in this bastion of liberal resistance to the French, however, breathed a sigh of relief: they finally had a spiritual leader who shared their piety and politics. Five hundred Ciudad Victoria residents declared that the bishop had denied them an official parish priest in revenge for their "democratic tendencies" and had even tagged them as non-Catholics. Enríquez Orestes had stepped into the void, much to the delight of this crowd, who harbored considerable hostility to the ultramontane church, having, after all, "borne witness to the injuries to the God of Charity (Misercordia) enacted by those who titled themselves his ministers." For these faithful, the clerical gadfly fresh from the battlefield and the big city was an "evangelical martyr," not the "false, impious imposter" of official church propaganda. They insisted he stay. The bishop should not even think of sending them another of the negligent, besotted priests of old.[107]

Constitutional clergyman Ramón Lozano also found the liberal cause to be a holy one and led his flock into battle. In early April of 1864, his followers rallied at his hacienda near Santa Bárbara, issuing a rousing manifesto against the fourth district's military and political chief's cavalier abuse of the military levy, and naming himself, citizen Ramón Lozano, in his place; many of the signers were among the fifty-three men who had signed on to his schismatic church. When the French seized the town in May of 1865, they targeted local liberal leaders, sacking Lozano's house and destroying the hacienda's store and his precious books and writing instruments. He likened them to "savage Comanches" outside of civilization's pale.[108] Later that month, he warned the citizens of the nearby town of Tula that they had but two choices in the battle with the French invaders: a sincere and fraternal embrace with other Tamaulipans who resisted these interlopers or a war to the death.[109] In 1869 he led a successful movement to change the town's name from Santa Bárbara to Ocampo, after his hero Melchor Ocampo. In the 1870s, he served as a senator in the state legislature.[110]

But if the liberal army's religious sensibility remains an interesting but open question, radical liberal intellectuals most assuredly shared Degollado's sense that their crusade was a holy one, as we have already seen. Thundering on the Alameda (the tree-lined promenade and park west of the central square in Mexico City) during the independence celebration of 1855, Guillermo Prieto announced that when God's word first came into the world, force dominated reason and particular interests reigned over the common good. From the cross Christ proclaimed man's liberty and announced the great revolution of love, fraternity, and equality.[111] This theme was frequently rehearsed. If Hegel's "spirit" was slowly unfolding through history to liberate mankind from tyranny, for Nicolás Pizarro Suárez this spirit was evangelical Christianity—a promise that gradually unfurled to destroy the despotic power of kings who claimed divine favor.[112] God's will, however, required human agency. This same author's political catechism, an official school textbook, offered some telling advice on resistance to tyranny to its young audience: "if your country's tyrant threatens you with cruel torments for not obeying his laws, resist, let him see you smile; this is what the first, real Christians practiced as they marched to their martyrdom."[113]

Taking the dais on the Alameda during the Independence Day celebrations, Ignacio Ramírez informed the crowd that the Roman Catholic Church, "pagan in the time of Cesar, feudal in the middle ages, and monarchical today," had met its match in Mexico's great hope for salvation: "the innumerable and good believers, who, loyal to the standard of the crucified . . . proclaim Him the symbol of love (*caridad*) and justice, and not of ambition and rancor; for that reason, they promise us that one day the first clerical blessing will be for democracy and their first anathema for intolerance and despotism."[114]

The liberals fought to define God and to reform religious practice in accordance with their definitions. They were anything but secular.

NOTES

Chapter opening source: AHAO, impresos religiosos, 1880–89.

Unless otherwise noted, all translations are by Pamela Voekel.

1. Jean-Pierre Bastian, *Los disidentes. Sociedades protestantes y revolución en México, 1872–1911* (Mexico City: Colegio de México and Fondo de Cultura Económica, 1993), 34. For more on the constitutional clergy's relationship to Protestant efforts in Mexico, see John Steven Rice, "Evangelical Episcopalians and the Church of Jesus in Mexico, 1857–1906" (M.A. Thesis, University of Texas at Pan-American, 2000); Fay Sharon Greenland, "Religious Reform in Mexico: The Role of the Mexican Episcopal

Church" (M.A. Thesis, University of Florida, 1958); and Alpha Gillett Bechtel, "The Mexican Episcopal Church: A Century of Reform and Revolution" (M.A. Thesis, San Diego State College, 1966).

2. D. A. Brading, "Liberal Patriotism and the Mexican Revolution," *Journal of Latin American Studies* 20:1 (May 1988): 28, 29, 40.

3. Melchor Ocampo, "Representación sobre reforma de aranceles y obvenciones parroquiales, dirigido al H. Congreso del Estado de Michoacán por el ciudadano Melchor Ocampo y que hizo suya el señor diputado D. Ignacio Cuevas (1851)," in *La religión, la iglesia, y el clero* (Mexico City: Empresas Editoriales, 1958), 45.

4. Melchor Ocampo, 15 September 1858, "Discurso de Melchor Ocampo," in *Documentos básicos de la Reforma, 1854–1875, Tomo 2*, intro. Mario V. Guzmán Galarza (Mexico City: Partido Revolucionario Institucional, 1982), 221–29.

5. Mexico City, 11 March 1861, *El Monitor Republicano*, 1, cols. 1–3.

6. Pedro Echeverría, *Catecismo de la doctrina clero-maquiavélica o sea del Padre Ripalda según lo observa y predica el clero mexicano* (Mexico City: Imprenta de la Reforma, 1861).

7. Mexico City, 15 November 1861, *El Heraldo*, 1, cols. 1 and 3.

8. Mexico City, 19 March 1861, *El Constitucional*, 1, cols. 3, 4.

9. Mexico City, 9 March 1861, *El Monitor Republicano*, 4, col. 2. For other examples of the satirical treatment of miraculous saints and holy men, see Mexico City, 16 April 1861, *El Heraldo*, 3, col. 3; Mexico City, 17 April 1861, *La Orquesta*, #14, 3, col. 2; Mexico City, 13 June 1861, *El Heraldo*, 3, col. 2; and Mexico City, 13 June 1861, *El Siglo Diez y Nueve*, no. 150, 3, col. 4.

10. Cuartel General en el Hospital de Belén de Guadalajara, 9 October 1858, *Boletín del Ejército Federal*, 2, cols. 2–3.

11. Mexico City, 10 July 1861, *El Monitor Republicano*, no. 3986, 1, cols. 5–6, p. 2 cols. 1–3.

12. Mexico City, 18 July 1861, *El Monitor Republicano*, no. 3994, 1, col. 1.

13. *Monitor Republicano.*

14. Mexico City, 18 March 1861, Ponciano Arriaga in *El Monitor Republicano*, 1, col. 4. Also see Mexico City, 12 March 1861, Ponciano Arriaga in *El Monitor Republicano*, 1, cols. 1–4, especially col. 2. Arriaga served as Defensor de los Fondos de Beneficencia under Juárez in 1861–62: see Silvia Arrom, *Containing the Poor: The Mexico City Poor House, 1774–1871* (Durham, NC: Duke University Press, 2001), 216.

15. Mexico City, 6 February 1861, *El Monitor Republicano*, 1, col. 3.

16. See Eamon Duffy, *Saints and Sinners: A History of the Popes*, 2nd ed. (New Haven, CT: Yale University Press, 2002), esp. 195–225.

17. In 1854, Pope Pius IX declared the dogma of the Immaculate Conception of Mary, an event that became a rallying point for Mexico's ultramontane Catholics: see, for example, Felipe Villarejo, *Sermón pronunciado en la solemne función que el comercio de esta capital dedicó a la declaración dogmática de la inmaculada concepción de María Santísima, el 23 de Septiembre de 1855* (Mexico City: Imprenta de J. M. Andrade y F. Escalante, 1855). Lázaro de la Garza y Ballesteros, *Carta Pastoral del Illmo. y Exmo. Sr. Arzobispo de México* (Mexico City: Imprenta de Vicente Segura, 1855). The conservative army's official bulletin noted that just as the people began to enthusiastically celebrate the Immaculate Conception, the liberals erased December 8, the day of Guadalupe, as a na-

tional holiday, see Toluca, 16 December 1860, *Boletín Oficial del Ejercito, Religión, Unión, Independencia*, 1, col. 4. The Month of Mary was also energetically embraced in Mexico: see, for example, Mexico City, 4 June 1861, *La Unidad Católica*, 2, col. 5.

18. Mexico City, 29 May 1861, *La Unidad Católica*, 1, cols. 1–3. *Suplemento Manifestación que hacen al venerable clero y fieles de sus respectivos diócesis y a todo el mundo católico, los Ilmo. Sres. Arzobispo de México y obispos de Michoacán, Linares, Guadalajara, y el Potosí, y el Sr. Dr. D. Francisco Serrano como representante de la mitra de Puebla* . . . (Celaya: Imprenta de G. Galván, 1859), 18, 25–26.

19. Mexico City, Ponciano Arriaga, 12 March 1861, *Siglo Diez y Nueve*, 1, col. 1.

20. Pamela Voekel, *Alone before God: The Religious Origins of Modernity in Mexico* (Durham, NC: Duke University Press, 2002), chap. 2.

21. Voekel, *Alone before God*.

22. Mexico City, 18 March 1861, *El Constitucional*, 1, col. 3.

23. J. Derek Holmes, *The Triumph of the Holy See: A Short History of the Papacy in the Nineteenth Century* (London: Burns and Oates, 1978), 60.

24. Caroline Ford, *Creating the Nation in Provincial France: Religion and Political Identity in Brittany* (Princeton, NJ: Princeton University Press, 1993), 101–2; Holmes, *The Triumph*, 112. Lamennais edited *Le Monde* with George Sand in 1837: see Bernard M. G. Reardon, *Religion in the Age of Romanticism: Studies in the Early Nineteenth Century Thought* (Cambridge: Cambridge University Press, 1985), 202.

25. Holmes, *The Triumph*, 76.

26. Mexico City, 30 May 1861, *El Heraldo*, 4, col. 1.

27. Joseph Mazzine, "Letter to Abbé Lammennais of 1834," 12 October 1834, in *The Life and Writing of Joseph Mazzine*, 6 vols. (London: Smith, Elder and Company, 1891), 3:42–43.

28. Mexico City, 5 January 1857, *El Siglo Diez y Nueve*, no. 3.005, 2, cols. 4 and 19; January 1857, 1, col. 2; and 20 January 1857, 2, cols. 1–2.

29. Frederick B. Pike, "Heresy, Real and Alleged, in Peru: An Aspect of the Conservative-Liberal Struggle, 1830–1875," *Hispanic American Historical Review* 47:1 (February 1967): 60.

30. Francisco de Paula González Vigil, "Apuntes acerca de mi vida (1857)," reproduced in "Escritos inéditos de Vigil," *Documenta* 3:1 (1951–55): 454, cited in Pike, "Heresy, Real and Alleged," 60.

31. José Ignacio Víctor Eyzaguirre, *El catolicismo en presencia de sus disidentes* (Guadalajara: Tipografía de Rodríguez, 1856), 11.

32. Pike, "Heresy, Real and Alleged," 50–74. For more on Vigil and Liberal Catholicism, see Frederick B. Pike, "Church and State in Peru and Chile since 1840: A Study in Contrasts," *American Historical Review* 73:1 (October 1967).

33. Mexico City, 15 August 1859, Rafael Díaz Martínez, Juan Nepomuceno Enríquez Orestes, Juan Francisco Domínguez, Manuel Aguilar, Manuel Estrada, and Cristóbal González Ríos (1859), reproduced in Mexico City, 5 October 1861, *El Monitor Republicano*, 1, cols. 4–6, p. 2, cols. 1–2. Justo Sierra reports that the liberals contacted the reformed clerics first, not the other way around: see his *Juárez. Su obra y su tiempo*, ed. Arturo Arnáiz y Freg (Mexico City: Universidad Nacional Autonoma de México, 1972), 180–81.

34. Mexico City, 13 March 1857, President's Order, AGN, Justicia Eclesiástica, vol. 181, fols. 1–32. Veracruz, 25 October 1859, Melchor Ocampo, Archivo del Arzobispado, sección arzobispado, caja 99, exp. 28.

35. Veracruz, Melchor Ocampo, 12 August 1859, Biblioteca Nacional, Colección Lafragua, vol. 467, fol. 163.

36. Jacqueline Covo, *Las ideas de la reforma en Mexico (1855–1861)*, trans. María Francisca Mourier-Martínez (Mexico City: Universidad Nacional Autonoma de México, 1984). Veracruz, 25 October 1859, Melchor Ocampo, Archivo del Arzobispado, sección arzobispado, caja 99, exp. 28.

37. Mexico City, 24 January 1861, Justino Fernández to Ministro de Justicia and Mexico City, Ramírez to S. Gobernador del Distrito Federal, 29 January 1861, AGN, Gobernación, leg. 1153 (1), caja 1389, exp. 4, no. 43; Mexico City, 29 January 1861, Gobernación, leg. 1153 (2), caja 1390, exp. 13, fols. 1–4v; Mexico City, 20 January 1861, *La Reforma*, p. 2, col. 4; and Mexico City, 19 January 1861, *El Siglo Diez y Nueve*, 3, col. 1.

38. Mexico City, 24 January 1861, *El Pájaro Verde*, 2, col. 4; and Mexico City, 9 February 1861, *El Pájaro Verde*, 2, col. 5. Historian Erika Pani reports that *El Pájaro Verde* got its start-up money from the bishop of Michoacán, Monsignor Munguía. See her *Para mexicanizar el Segundo Imperio. El imaginario político de los imperialistas* (Mexico City: El Colegio de México; Instituto Mora, 2001), 177, fn. 308.

39. Mexico City, 7 February 1861, Archivo Histórico de la Mitra, Actas de Cabildo, libro 87, fol. 11.

40. Mexico City, 13 February 1861, *El Monitor Republicano*, 3, col. 4.

41. Mexico City, 2 May 1861, *El Pájaro Verde*, 3, col. 1.

42. Mexico City, 23 February 1861, *El Siglo Diez y Nueve*, 3, col. 5; Mexico City, 23 February 1861, *El Movimiento*, 3, cols. 1–2; Mexico City, 25 February 1861, *El Movimiento*, 3, col. 5; Mexico City, 24 February 1861, *El Monitor Republicano*, 3, cols. 2, 3; and Mexico City, 23 February 1861, *El Pájaro Verde*, no. 43, 3, col. 4.

43. Brian Hamnett, *Juárez* (New York and London: Longman, 1994), 112. Archbishop Garza y Ballesteros was expelled on 17 January 1861 along with four colleagues. They were given three days to leave the country.

44. *Suplemento manifestación*, 18, 25–26.

45. Mexico City, 13 May 1861, *El Pájaro Verde*, no. 57, 1, col. 1; Mexico City, 14 May 1861, *El Pájaro Verde*, no. 58, 2, col. 5; Mexico City, 15 May 1861, *El Pájaro Verde*, 2, col. 3; and Mexico City, 17 May 1861, *El Pájaro Verde*, num. 61, 2, cols. 4–6.

46. José Ramón Malo, 2 May 1861, *Diario de sucesos*, 612; Mexico City, 10 October 1861, *La Unidad Católica*, 1, cols. 1–2; Mexico City, 22 October 1861, *La Unidad Católica*, 2, col. 4; and Mexico City, Juan Nepomuceno Enríquez Orestes, Juan Francisco Domínguez, Manuel Aguilar, Manuel Estrada, Cristóbal González Ríos, 5 October 1861, *El Monitor Republicano*, 1, cols. 4–6, p. 2, cols. 1–2.

47. Mexico City, 10 April 1861, *El Siglo Diez y Nueve*, 3, col. 3; and Mexico City, 10 April 1861, *La Orquesta*, tomo 1, no. 12, 2, col. 3.

48. Mexico City, 22 February 1861, *El Pájaro Verde*, no. 15, 1, col. 4.

49. Mexico City, January 1861, "Decretos y circulares del Gobierno del Distrito de México," AGN, Gobernación s/s, caja 482, exps. 6, 18; and Mexico City, 11 January

1861, *El Pájaro Verde*, no. 6, 2, col. 4. Also see Mexico City, 6 September 1862, Gobernación, sec. primera, 1862, caja 25, exp. 59, decretos y circulares.

50. Mexico City, 26 October 1861, Juan N. Enríquez Orestes in *El Constitucional*, 1, col. 3.

51. Mexico City, 10 December 1861, Juan N. Enríquez Orestes in *El Monitor Republicano*, no. 4139, 2, cols. 2–3.

52. Mexico City, 6 February 1861, *El Pájaro Verde*, no. 28, 1.

53. Mexico City, 10 May 1861, *La Unidad Católica*, 3, col. 5.

54. Mexico City, Señoras de la parroquia de S. Miguel to Señor Presidente, January 1861, AGN, Gobernación, leg. 1153 (1), caja 1389, exp. 4, no. 2, fols. 1–1v; Mexico City, Orden del Gobierno del Distrito, 31 January 1861, AGN, Gobernación, leg. 1153 (2), caja 1390, exp. 13, fol. 2v; Mexico City, Miguel Blanco to Ministro de Gobernación, 4 February 1861, AGN, Gobernación, leg. 1153, caja 1389, exp. 1, fol. 3; Mexico City, 8 Febrero 1861, *El Pájaro Verde*, no. 30, 2, col. 6; Malo, *Diario de sucesos*, 595–96; and Mexico City, 11 March 1861, *Trait d'Union*, 1, col. 4.

55. Malo, *Diario de sucesos*, 593.

56. Mexico City, 11 February 1861, *El Siglo Diez y Nueve*, tomo 1, no. 28, 3, col. 3.

57. Mexico City, 24 October 1856, "Protestan las mujeres contra la venta de los bienes del clero," *El Monitor Republicano*, 1, col. 1; Silvia Arrom, *The Women*, 42–43. Mexico City, 21 July 1856, "Las Mexicanistas Vueltas Bloomeristas," *El Monitor Republicano*, 3, cols. 2–4; *Representación que las señoras de Guadalajara dirigen al soberano Congreso Constituyente sobre que en la carta fundamental que se discute, no quede consignada la tolerancia de cultos en la república* (Guadalajara: Tipografía de Rodríguez, 1856); and *Representación de las Señoras de esta capital al Supremo Gobierno del Estado. Con motivo de las providencia dictadas últimamanete contra el Illmo. Señor Obispo de la Diócesis* (Monterrey: Imprenta de A. Mier, 1857).

58. Morelia, "Representación de muchas señoras de Morelia pidiendo se deje en libertad al Obispo de aquella diócesis para volver a ella," to Ministro de Justicia y Negocios Eclesiásticos, 26 September 1856, AGN, Justicia Eclesiástica, vol. 179, fols. 478–90v. This on f. 481.

59. Sayula, 11 August 1858, *El Boletín del Ejército Federal*, num. 14, 1, cols. 2–3.

60. 16 August 1861, Signed by Ignacio Ramírez and Guillermo Prieto: Guillermo Prieto, *Obras Completas XXIII. Periodismo Político y social*, 3, ed. Boris Rosen Jelomer (Mexico City: Consejo Nacional para la Cultura y las Artes, 1997), 332. [Same reference, but 4 September 1861, "el constitucional, la unidad cat y el monitor," 382–83.]

61. Margaret Chowning, "Liberals, Women, and the Church in Mexico: Politics and the Feminization of Piety, 1700–1930," unpublished paper delivered to the Harvard Latin American Studies Seminar, 2002, 3–4. Also see Pamela Voekel, "La feminización de la piedad barroca en la Ciudad de México, 1650–1850," paper prepared for the conference "Vida Urbana, Familia y Vida Cotidiana en América Latina," Universidad Católica, Lima, Peru, December 1999.

62. Mexico City, Darío Balandro to editors of *El Monitor Republicano*, 3 September 1861, *El Monitor Republicano*, no. 4041, 3, cols. 3–4.

63. Prieto, *Obras completas XXIII. Periodismo político y social*, 3, and *Obras completas XXIV, periodismo político y social*, 4:321–23—"La fiesta de todos santos," 321–22.

64. Guadalajara, 19 November 1858, *Boletín del Ejército Federal*, no. 29. 1, col. 2.

65. 16 August 1861, Signed by Ignacio Ramírez and Guillermo Prieto: Prieto, *Obras Completas XXIII. Periodismo Político y social*, 3, 332. [Same reference, but 4 September 1861, "el constitucional, la unidad cat y el monitor," 382–83.]

66. Mexico City, 14 October 1861, *El Monitor Republicano*, 2, cols. 3–4.

67. Mexico City, 29 May 1861, *La Unidad Católica*, 1, cols. 1–3.

68. José Ramón Malo, 1 April 1861, *Diario de sucesos*, 609.

69. San Cristóbal de las Casas, Chiapas, 7 March 1861, [?] to Minister of Justice and Public Instruction, AGN, Gobernación, leg. 1153 (1), caja 1389, exp. 10, fol. 1.

70. Mexico City, 27 November 1861, *La Unidad Católica*, 3, col. 1 (this report was reprinted from *La Tijera de San Cristóbal de las Casas*).

71. Mexico City, 16 December 1861, *La Unidad Católica*, no. 180, 1, cols. 1–3. *La Unidad Católica* reported roughly ten constitutional clergy operating in the states of Oaxaca, Jalisco, and Zacatecas. For other reports of the activities of the reformed clergy in these states and others, see, for example, Mexico City, 13 May 1861, *El Pájaro Verde*, no. 57, 1, col. 1; Mexico City, 18 July 1863, *El Pájaro Verde*, 3, cols. 4–5; Mexico City, 2 May 1861, *El Pájaro Verde*, 1, col. 1; and Mexico City, "Iglesia Mexicana," 13 June 1861, *El Heraldo*, 3, col. 3. More priests resisted the Constitution of 1857 than supported it, of course. On clerical opposition to the Reform program see Robert J. Knowlton, "Clerical Response to the Mexican Reform, 1855–1875," *The Catholic Historical Review* 50:4 (January 1965).

72. These numbers are from José María Pérez Hernández, *Estadística de la República Mejicana* (Guadalajara: Tipografía del Gobierno, 1862), 248.

73. D. José M. Vigil, *México a Través de los siglos, Vol. 5, La Reforma*, ed. Vicente Riva Palacio (Barcelona: Espasa, n.d.), 477; José Ramón Malo, *Diario de sucesos*, 619; and Sierra, *Juárez*, 282. Melchor Ocampo was killed on 3 June 1861.

74. Mexico City, "Que haremos por el papa," 27 December 1861, *La Unidad Católica*, no. 190, 1. Mexico City, Lazo Estrada to President of City Council, 28 December 1861, Archivo Histórico de la Ciudad de México, Jurados de Imprenta, 1829 a 1868, vol. 2740, exp. 48, fols. 1, 2, 4, and 6. When Baz, as an official representative of the president, had tried to enter the cathedral during Holy Week in 1857 to demonstrate the nation's patronage over the church, he was met by a humble choirboy who refused him entry: see Richard N. Sinkin, *The Mexican Reformation: 1855–1876: A Study in Liberal Nation-Building* (Austin: Institute of Latin American Studies, University of Texas at Austin; distributed by University of Texas Press, c. 1979), 135.

75. Mexico City, 2 January 1862, *La Orquesta*, #34, 2.

76. Mexico City, 26 March 1862, *El Monitor Republicano*, no. 4245, 1, col. 4; Mexico City, 6 April 1862, *El Monitor Republicano*, no. 4255, 1, cols. 1–6 and 2, cols. 1–2.

77. Jacala, "El ayuntamiento de Jacala pide se nombre para aquel curato al Br. Juan N. Enríquez Orestes," 6 December 1856, AGN, Justicia Eclesiástica, vol. 179, fols. 427–28v. Jesús Reyes Heroles is cited in Ana Lau Jaiven and Ximena Sepúlveda Otaiza, *Hidalgo, una historia compartida* (Mexico City: Instituto de Investigaciones Dr. José María Luis Mora, 1994), 136.

78. Nicolás Pizarro, *El monedero* (Mexico City: Imprenta de Nicolás Pizarro, 1861), 226–27. Novelist and pamphleteer Nicolás Pizarro Suárez (1830–95) worked in pub-

lic administration in the early 1850s and for the Ministry of Justice under the liberals in Veracruz: see Carlos Illades and Adriana Sandoval, *Espacio social y representación literaria en el siglo XIX* (Mexico City: Universidad Autónoma Metropolitana, 2000), 16. Erika Pani also underscores the importance of *caridad* to Pizarro's social vision in *El modedero*: see her "Para halagar la imaginación: Las Repúblicas de Nicolás Pizarro," in José Antonio Aguilar and Rafael Rojas, coordinators, *El republicanismo en Hispanoamérica. Ensayos de historia intelectual y política* (Mexico City: Centro de Investigación y Docena Económicas and Fondo de Cultura Económica, 2002), 424–46, especially 436, 439–40, 444–45. For more on Pizarro Suárez, see Luis Reyes de la Maza, "Nicolás Pizarro, novelista y pensador liberal," *Historia Mexicana* 6:4 (April/June 1957): 572–88.

79. Pizarro, *El monedero*, 122–23, 377, 588.

80. Guillermo Prieto (Fidel), *Viajes de Orden Suprema. Años de 1853, 54, y 55*, 3rd ed. (Mexico City: Editorial Patria, 1970), 285. For an example of this glorification of the reformed lower clergy, see Mexico City, 4 September 1856, *El Monitor Republicano*, 3, cols. 4, 5, 6.

81. Tampico, Governor Juan José de la Garza Edict, 1 April 1861, Archivo Documental del Instituto de Investigaciones Históricos de la Universidad Autónoma de Tamaulipas (hereafter AD-IIH-UAT), Decretos 1851–1929, Decreto #10; Ciudad Victoria, 20 April 1861, *El Rifle de Tamaulipas. Periódico Político y Literario. Segunda Época*, 1, col. 2; and Mexico City, 28 Mayo, 1861, *La Unidad Católica*, 3, col. 1.

82. Santa Bárbara de Tamaulipas, 6 June 1861, Ramón Lozano to *El Rifle de Tamaulipas*, printed in Ciudad Victoria, *El Rifle de Tamaulipas. Periódico Político y Literario. Segunda Época*, 22 June 1861, 2, cols. 1–2. *La Unidad Católica* ran Bishop Veréa's suspension of Ramón Lozano, see 24 June 1861, 3, cols. 4–5 and 5, cols. 1–2. Also see, New York, 29 June 1861, Pedro Obispo de Guadalajara to Sr. Dr. Lázaro de la Garza, Archivo Histórico del Arzobispado, Serie Correspondencia, caja 103, exp. 18, fols. 1–6.

83. Santa Bárbara de Tamaulipas, 6 June 1861, Ramón Lozano to *El Rifle de Tamaulipas*, printed in Ciudad Victoria, *El Rifle de Tamaulipas. Periódico Político y Literario. Segunda Época*, 22 June 1861, 2, cols. 1–2.

84. Santa Bárbara de Tamaulipas, 12 May 1861, Archive of the Parroquia de Santa Bárbara Martir (APSBM), Ocampo, Tamaulipas, Libro de Bautismos de 1854–1862, fol. 245.

85. Mexico City, 23 June 1861, *El Siglo Diez y Nueve*, 3, cols. 3–4; Mexico City, 4 June 1861, *El Heraldo*, 3, cols. 2–4; and Mexico City, 15 June 1861, *La Unidad Católica*, 3, col. 4. and 18 June, 1, cols. 3–5.

86. Monterrey, 20 June 1861, Circular of the Gobierno Eclesiástico del Obispado de Monterrey, AD-IIH-UAT, sin clasificación.

87. Narciso Villareal, *Cuatro palabras al Presbítero D. Ramón Lozano, cura propio de Santa Bárbara, para que no descanse tranquilo en sus errores* (24 July 1861) (Monterrey: Imprenta de A. Mier, 1861), 4, 7, 10, 13. Also see, Monterrey, 24 September 1861, Archivo Municipal de Monterrey, Actas de Cabildo, vol. 999, fols. 140–140v.

88. Santa Bárbara de Tamaulipas, 12 May 1861, APSBM, Ocampo, Tamaulipas, Libro de bautismos, in the parish's record book.

89. Ramón Lozano, *Contestación á las cuatro palabras del Cura de Monclova, D. Narciso Villareal* (Ciudad Victoria: Imprenta de Sebastián Perrillos, 1861), 1.

90. See, for example, Taxco, Juan de Oehla to Ministro de Justicia, 7 September 1858, AGN, Justicia Eclesiástica, tomo 146, fols. 126–31. José María Encinos to Consejo del Gobierno, 13 June 1850, AGN, Justicia Eclesiástica, vol. 171, fol. 158. Tehuacan, General José Maria Cobos Report, 4 February 1860, AGN, Justicia Eclesiástica, tomo 146, fols. 447–49.

91. Francisco P. Campa, *Protesta y retracción del Presb. Francisco de P. Campa ante su dignísimo prelado el Illmo. Sr. Dr. D. Francisco de P. Veréa, Obispo de la Diócesis de Linares* (Guadalajara: Imprenta de Rodríguez, 1857), 2. Francisco P. Campa, 1857, Archivo Histórico del Arzobispado, Secretaria arzobispal/libros de gobierno, caja 167L, exp. 2., fol. 413. *Gran ascencio aerostática del Presbítero Ciudadano Francisco de P. Campa en busca del espíritu santo, para que concurra á los juzgados de la república* (Guadalajara: Imprenta de Dionisio Rodríguez, 1857). José Gutiérrez Casillas lists priests who supported the ecclesiastical desmortization as well as those who acted as chaplains in the liberal army, including one Ignacio Traspea, who ran with a band who profaned churches; see his *Historia de la iglesia en México* (Mexico City: Porrúa, 1974), 308–10.

92. Mexico City, "El pres. don Vicente Guevara pide se le satisfagan sus sueldos como capellán del 6 batallón de Linea," 16 November 1857, AGN, Justicia Eclesiatica, vol. 182, fol. 194; and Mexico City, Ministro de Hacienda to Ministro de Justicia, 19 November 1856, AGN, Justicia Eclesiatica, vol. 182, fol. 196.

93. New York City, October–November 1864, Declaration of Rev. Orestes to Rev. Doctor Cove and Reverend Smith, Archives of the Episcopal Church, Austin, Texas (hereafter AEC), R.G., Nacional Council RG 73: (Domestic and Foreign Missionary Society)—Mexico Records, 1864–1952, Miscellaneous, 1864–1879, RG 73–15, fol. 1.

94. New Orleans, 17 October 1864, Elijah Guion, Daniel Shaves and A. Vallas to the bishops, clergy and laity of the Protestant Episcopal Church in the United States, AEC, RG 73: Nacional Council (Domestic and Foreign Missionary Society)—Mexico Records, 1864–1952, Miscellaneous, 1864–1879, RG 73–15, fol. 1.

95. Cleveland, Ohio, E. C. Nicholson to S. Dennison, 1 May 1865, AEC, RG 73: National Council (Domestic and Foreign Missionary Society)—Mexico Records, 1864–1952, Miscellaneous, 1864–1879, RG 73–7, E. C. Nicholson Papers, 1864–5, fols. 13–13v, 15.

96. José Miguel Barragán Sánchez, "Pequeño diario portatil 1864. Memorias de un guerrillero durante la intervención francesa," *Archivos de Historia Potosina* 3:8 (January–March 1977): 237.

97. Mexico City, 7 October 1861, *El Monitor Republicano*, 1, col. 1. *La Unidad Católica*, of course, shredded these men's pretensions to poverty, claiming that in his capacity as an inspector of the inventory of La Merced, Enríquez Orestes had been granted the best ornaments and sacred vessels of the entire inventory project: see Mexico City, 9 August 1861, *La Unidad Católica*, 2, col. 4.

98. Mexico City, 22 June 1861, Francisco Zarco in *Siglo Diez y Nueve*, 1, col. 1.

99. Nicolás Pizarro, *La Coqueta* (Mexico City: Imprenta de Ana Echeverría de Pizarro e Hijas, 1861), 74.

100. Cuartel General en el Hospital de Belén de Guadalajara, 19 October 1858, *Boletín del Ejército Federal*, #25, 2, cols. 1–3.

101. Enrique Krauze, *Mexico. Biography of Power. A History of Modern Mexico, 1810–1996*, trans. Hank Heifetz (New York: Harper Collins Publisher, 1997), 157; and Sierra, *Juárez*, 288.

102. Mexico City, 13 August 1862, *El Monitor Republicano*, 3, cols. 4–5.

103. Colima, Santos Degollado, "Proclama que el general Degollado dirigió al Ejército Federal con fecha 30 de Marzo de 1858," printed in Ernesto de la Torre Villar, ed., *El Triunfo de la república liberal, 1857–60* (Mexico City: Fondo de Cultura Económica, 1960), 56–57.

104. Santos Degollado, "Proclama que el general Degollado expidió a los vecinos de la Ciudad de México, el 21 de Marzo de 1859," in Ernesto de la Torre Villar, ed., *El Triunfo*, 91.

105. Florencia Mallon, *Peasant and Nation: The Making of Postcolonial Mexico and Peru* (Berkeley: University of California Press, 1995), 93–94.

106. Mexico City, 9 June 1862, *El Monitor Republicano*, 1, col. 6.

107. Ciudad Victoria, 15 January 1864, "Respuesta que los Católicos de Ciudad Victoria dan a los avisos que desde Monterrey les dirige el Padre D. José María Hinojosa," AEC, RG 73: National Council (Domestic and Foreign Missionary Society)— Mexico Records, 1864–1952, Miscellaneous, 1864–1879, RG 73–15, fol. 1.

108. Santa Bárbara de Tamaulipas, 3 April 1864, Ramón Lozano and Benigno el Valdés (and signed by five hundred or so others) to Jefatura Política y Militar, original in Archivo Histórico, Municipalidad de Miquihuana, Tamaulipas, caja 3, fols. 1–4. I want to thank Juan Díaz Rodríguez, the head of the historical collection at the IIH-UAT in Ciudad Victoria, for providing me with a copy of this document.

109. Santa Bárbara, 23 May 1865, Ramón Lozano to Señor Teófilo Ramírez, in Ciudad Victoria, *Boletín de Campana*, 31 May 1865, 2v, col. 2.

110. Joaquín Meade, *La Huasteca Tamaulipeca*, tomo 2 (Ciudad Victoria: IIH-UAT, 1978), 69; Ciudad Victoria, 4 June 1870, *La Reconstrucción. Periódico oficial del Gobierno del Estado de Tamaulipas*, 2, cols. 2–4 and 3, col. 1; Ciudad Victoria, *La Reconstrucción. Periódico oficial del Gobierno del Estado de Tamaulipas*, 21 January 1871, 4, cols. 2–3; and Ciudad Victoria, 17 September 1871, *Seminario de los debates del Congreso de Tamaulipas*, 2–3.

111. "Oración Cívica pronunciado por el ciudadano Guillermo Prieto de la alameda de México, el día 16 de Septiembre de 1855," 5.

112. Nicolás Pizarro, *La libertad en el orden. Ensayo sobre derecho público en que se resuelven algunas de las más vitales cuestiones que se agitan en México desde su independencia* (Mexico City: Imprenta de Ana Echeverría de Pizarro e Hijas, 1855), 9.

113. Nicolás Pizarro Suárez, *Catecismo político constitucional* (Mexico City: Imprenta de N. Chávez, 1861), 94.

114. Ignacio Ramírez, "Discurso cívico pronunciado el 16 de septiembre de 1861 en la alameda de México, en memoria de la proclamación de la Independencia," in Ignacio M. Altamirano, ed., *Obras de Ignacio Ramírez*, tomo 1 (Mexico City: Editora Nacional, 1960), 131.

6
Priests and Caudillos
in the Novel of the
Mexican Nation
Alejandro Cortazar

Vigil for a Dead Young Girl, Probably in Nochixtlan, Oaxaca, Unknown Date. Note the numerous framed images displayed above the cadaver. Some of them, such as the Sacred Heart of Jesus and what appears to be Our Lady of Perpetual Succor, were particularly popular in the nineteenth and twentieth century. The small tin-framed prints on the right appear to be souvenirs from local shrines. Photographed by Ignacio Zanabria.

Mexican historians of the early nineteenth century began analyzing the epic political and military trajectories of the two principal caudillos that made independence possible: Priest Miguel Hidalgo, who initiated the movement in 1810, and Agustín de Iturbide, a royalist whose pact with insurgent Vicente Guerrero consummated independence for the Mexican nation in 1821. The historical judgments generated during that period ranged from a radically liberal posture as seen in Zavala and Bustamente, to a moderately liberal one as in the case of Mora, and then finally to a radically conservative vision enunciated by Lucas Alamán. Yet regardless of their ideological divergences, all of these historical accounts came to one common conclusion: despite the ruthlessness of his campaign, Iturbide was indubitably the "liberator of the nation."[1] This historical judgment did not heal the wounds of revolutionary discord. On the contrary, the political passions of both contemporary political actors and the general population were inflamed. From the moment Iturbide was deposed from his imperial throne in 1823, numerous functionaries and journalists debated the issue of who should rightfully assume historical paternity of the nation: the liberals proclaimed Hidalgo; the conservatives, Iturbide. This debate raged into the 1850s and became especially virulent in 1854, the year that a conservative backlash made up of powerful clerics and military elites was frustrated in its desire to establish a monarchy. These conservatives had placed their hopes in one Antonio López de Santa Anna, a caudillo who was ultimately deposed by militant Ayutla revolutionaries.

In 1855 a new group of political leaders emerged. The majority were mestizos who had little or no previous involvement with the recent failures of the early republic. These men embarked on a decisive political agenda focused on generating social reforms. This project particularly angered the upper clergy who had monopolized a significant portion of the nation's wealth up until that moment. This new initiative, distinct both in its political origins and in its anticlerical position, was transcendental. From this moment forward, a new dialectical discourse emerged concerning the essence of Mexican cultural identity that became the ideological sustenance that lent continuity to the politics of the state. Mexican historians searched for an official historical account about the ideas and facts of independence that would illuminate a possible path toward political and religious conciliation for the new independent community—a path that would ultimately lead to economic, social, and cultural change. Given cleric Hidalgo's role in the independence movement, what role did priests as characters play in the conciliatory nation-building novels written during Mexico's nineteenth century? This essay aims to demonstrate the importance and the trajectory of the priest as a mediating figure in the Mexican novel and in doing so prove the critical role that the priest figure and the novel played in the formation of a Mexican discourse of national cultural identity.

HIDALGO THE CLERIC, HISTORY, AND THE HISTORICAL NOVEL

The new group of liberal reformers that gained power in the 1850s proclaimed Hidalgo father of the nation for one fundamental reason. They sought to reify local, popular religious beliefs over the historical and religious traditions that the upper echelons of the established Catholic Church in Mexico sought to impose. This guiding premise resulted in a historical discourse that favored the cleric Hidalgo as the first republican to further the revolutionary cause under the banner of the Virgin of Guadalupe as the quintessential symbol of a religious tradition that had emerged in the Americas and whose spiritual power was believed to shelter and protect the Indians and the inhabitants of New Spain. Above all Hidalgo was portrayed as the parish priest who turned to religion in order to provide daily charity that benefited the community. The liberal reformers' ideological slant also had serious repercussions for the historical portrayal of Iturbide as the consummator of independence. Iturbide became an opportunist who had initially betrayed the cause of independence by declaring war on the insurgents. Only after he had the support of the upper clergy did Iturbide switch sides, become an insubordinate royalist, and proclaim himself emperor.

The political-ideological effervescence begun in the mid-1850s occurred at the same time that deep social fissures riddled the Mexican nation's ability to unite and progress, at least from the perspective of its novelists. The traditional social structure that had existed up to that time included a tiny aristocracy, an upper clergy associated with a military that enjoyed a military judiciary accountable only to itself, a weak middle class, and an overwhelmingly large segment of the population living in poverty. Economically, the country faced a crisis after years of internal fighting and external intervention.[2] Literature and the plastic arts appear to have remained stagnant with little incentive to continue. Only a few writers continued to produce poetry and short narratives—genres representative of an indelible literary tradition already established in Mexico.

Juan Díaz Covarrubias was one of these writers. He proposed to write a series of historical novels and suggested that this was a "much more useful genre and one through which one can test one's creative skills."[3] Díaz Covarrubias's literary content was inspired by a nationalist psyche—a fervent emotional state that ennobled his intense desire for national liberty and progress for Mexico. He observed his surroundings and reflected on history in order to understand how he could best disseminate his instructive message intended to idealize the nation. As a liberal Catholic conscious of Mexico's religious tradition, Díaz Covarrubias turned first to the origins of independence and the figure of the priest not only to vindicate Hidalgo but also to emphasize this cleric's leading role as the first republican caudillo and to espouse a doctrine of charity, progress, and social equality.[4] Díaz Covarrubias's sympathy for Hidalgo was already evident in his sharp critiques of the clergy and the conservative party in his "Civic Discourse" ("Discurso Cívico"), a speech he delivered on September 15, 1857. If the clergy and the conservative reaction had exalted the figure of Iturbide both from religious pulpits and from political offices, Díaz Covarrubias would use the historical novel to exalt Hidalgo as a legendary village priest, a missionary, liberator of the oppressed masses who lacked a voice in government, and, ultimately, the true father of the Mexican nation. From then on the figure of the priest, understood by Mexicans as a necessary element for peace, equality, and progress, would come to be more than this for a series of writers in the nineteenth century. This supposed "true" priest was to be simultaneously a master of peace and social progress, friend, and brother. In the realist novel, the priest also became the confessor of and adviser to the protagonists of the tradition of social-political events.

PRIEST AND CAUDILLO IN THE MEXICAN NATION

In *Gil Gómez el insurgente*, Díaz Covarrubias narrates a story of two brothers, Fernando and Gil Gómez, who live in a village near Xalapa. Gil Gómez was adopted in childhood by Fernando's father and does not know his true origin. He is thin and tall with long legs and big ears, astutely aware of the natural environment, although not very dedicated to his studies. He serves as sacristan in the parish church and appears to have no other future. Fernando, on the other hand, is blessed with intelligence, artistic dexterity, and an impressive physique. He falls in love with Clemencia, a young woman with artistic talents but also ill with a rare pulmonary disease that weakens her health while her beloved engages in a campaign with the royalist army. Fernando enrolls in the royalist army with the help of his uncle Rafael's intervention. Gil Gómez cannot conceive of living without Fernando's company and escapes from his home to search for his brother. After a several-hour journey, he stops at a roadside inn to eat and to feed his horse. To his surprise, however, nothing remains in the inn because a priest who "appeared to have a voracious appetite" had monopolized all the provisions.[5] In the afternoon Gil arrives at another inn and discovers that that same priest who had preceded him was staying there. Again, the priest took all the provisions for himself with the excuse that he had not eaten in a day and a half, inspiring Gil Gómez to attack the hypocritical and conniving priest. Gil nevertheless holds back, thinking that somehow something could be solved through a dialogue that makes allusion to Christian charity. He tells the priest, "the monastery has done well in choosing for its business a person so dignified as yourself," to which the priest responds that one should love one's neighbor as oneself, "stressing the pronunciation of the last two words, and continued gobbling down his food."[6]

In this first encounter the ingenuous young man does not find the help he needs to fulfill his material needs from the priesthood. Instead, he encounters only gluttony. If, according to the author, at the beginning of the century the population of New Spain had suffered from a "frightening difference between classes,"[7] little had changed by the time of the Reform when Díaz Covarrubias wrote his novel. Robert Knowlten argues that during this period, "the population was made up by a well organized, traditional and assertive clergy, an ignorant and ill-fed populace, and a weak middle-class, impotent in its attempts to fill the gap between the privileged few and the many needy."[8] And while the populace was "ill-fed," this was in part because for many years the "well organized clergy" saw to it to feed itself first. Consequently, Díaz Covarrubias made the priest into a synecdoche for a gluttonous priesthood that ate well while the populace went hungry.

Like so many individuals who would follow Hidalgo in the insurgency of 1810, Gil Gómez, the narrator tells us, was the "son of misfortune but not of crime."[9] He was orphaned by his father before his birth and later abandoned by an unhappy mother who had nothing with which to feed him.[10] Curiously, he would be raised with an instinctive nature that would serve him in adversity, both within and outside of his surroundings. For example, when he begins boarding school and discovers that his classmates are hatching a plot against him, Gil Gómez hides himself in the dormitory and smashes the room's lamp when they enter. He manages to escape and closes the door from the outside. As a result of his actions, Gil witnesses how the same aggressors, amidst darkness and confusion, attack each other. Unfortunately for them, these aggressors are punished by the father superior who had caught them in the middle of their disturbance. After this event, the boy Gil Gómez, who had "at first been designated as a victim was later considered a caudillo in all subsequent tricks and rebellions."[11]

During his search for his brother, Gil Gómez arrives at night in a small village where he stumbles upon an insurgent soldier, Juan Aldama. Aldama fights with Gil because he thinks he is a royalist spy. Gil Gómez neither flees nor begs for mercy because he does not understand what the supposed spying was about nor does he even know where he is. Aldama notes the bravery and honesty of Gil Gómez and takes him to Hidalgo where he finds shelter and time to heal the wounds he suffered during the fight.

Gil Gómez is a coming-of-age story. The title character is confronted with a world of intrigues and realizes that the men who should be united in leadership for the common cause of Mexican independence actually were bitter enemies who shared only the irreconcilable differences that came with competition for positions of power. Another factor that changed Gil Gómez's worldview was the unexpected and spontaneous speed with which the priest Hidalgo helped him, offering to feed and house him in addition to bandaging his wounds.

The contrast between the actions of Hidalgo and those of the gluttonous priest whom Gil Gómez met previously amazes Gil. This wonder should be understood as a textual surprise—that is, a literary effect that the author employs to vindicate the figure of Hidalgo. Hidalgo was a priest who, as seen in the novel, decided that instead of living a contemplative, speculative life celebrating masses and "works of the parroquial notary," he preferred to find ways of converting "theology into charity."[12] By 1857, Mexican novelists such as Díaz Covarrubias were continuing to reshape the figure of Hidalgo as father of the Mexican nation.

From Díaz Covarrubias's point of view, collective Mexican consciousness did not reflect the "true" religiosity of the priest Hidalgo. Perhaps ignorance, or the immediate negative effects of the Reform, or even the attacks of the clergy and their reaction to liberal policies were to blame. Consequently, in his "Civic Discourse" proclaimed in 1857 to commemorate independence, Díaz Covarrubias exhorted his fellow citizens to "understand the true spirit of religion . . . that the true humble religious figure taught in small villages, modest parishes or even deserts. The Christianity of processions and showy practices that the aristocratic clergy of the cities teach has more in common with wealthy medieval lords than the apostles of Jesus Christ."[13] This was not an attack directed against religion but rather a critique that reinforced the justification for the Ley Lerdo of 1856, which had accused the church and its intermediaries as a corporate agent and accumulator of lands that were not used for the productivity of the nation.[14]

What better source of support and show of political-literary moral rectitude could one find to counter corrupt church practices than a priest who had taken up the cause for independence under the patronage of the Virgin of Guadalupe? Even more than an icon of Catholicism, the Virgin of Guadalupe was viewed as the mother of all Mexicans. How could the clergy tap into this deeply held belief within the traditional and collective consciousness of Mexicans? History and concurrent reality reflected each other. Neither Díaz Covarrubias's speeches nor his fiction attempted to relive memories, but rather they reflected the actions of the "father" (Hidalgo) so that others could follow his examples.

The insults of the anti-Reform clergy had their origin in the attacks proclaimed by the viceregal government to control desires for independence. Díaz Covarrubias evokes these royalist anti-independence strategies by citing an 1810 letter of Viceroy Venegas that said that Hidalgo and his supporters had committed sacrilege to praise the "sacrosanct image of the Virgin of Guadalupe, patroness and protectress of this kingdom, in order to dazzle the unsuspecting with the appearance of religion, which is nothing other than impudent hypocrisy."[15]

According to Díaz Covarrubias, the viceroy miscalculated along with the anti-Reform clergy when he sought to denigrate the image of Hidalgo by calling him a "heretic" and otherwise insulting him and his cause. Yet his claims of treason and avarice did not have the immediate effect he sought. On the contrary, the forces of Hidalgo had grown so large that the royal forces commended themselves to the Virgin of Remedios as the protectress "against enemies of the Catholic faith and public tranquility."[16] The royalist forces thought that the Virgin blessed the high clergy "so they could carry out the campaign, 'armed with saber and pistol and with a crucifix in hand, like bishops in the times of crusades.' They circulated innumerable pamphlets, invectives and anathemas against the 'heretic' priest, the 'frenetic and delirious monster,' the 'impious, abominable enemy of God.'"[17] If the War of Independence took on the tones of a holy war, the truth is that more than holy it was a war that legitimated itself through appeals to a religious icon. The Virgin of Guadalupe was triumphant because her image inspired thousands of Indians and campesinos to believe in an instinct of liberty that since the conquest had been shackled by material deprivation. Only religion had provided temporary relief.

While the royalists parodied the independence movement as a holy war, both sides made it into a political war. Yet to understand the narrator of Díaz Covarrubias's novel, one must see independence as fundamentally a social war on the part of Hidalgo and the other insurgent caudillos. The vindication of the human condition of the colonized Indian was linked into the independence movements through Hidalgo's struggle to vindicate and recuperate a lost nation.

If the narrator turns to history in order to discern the voice of the reactionaries, he also turns to historical documents (in this case, pamphlets) by which Hidalgo defends himself from and responds to his aggressors not in a violent manner but in a clear and serene way, asserting the transcendental nature of his revolution—that "our constant insomnia is due to our efforts to maintain our religion, our law, our nation and the purity of our customs." To this the narrator reacts by telling his readers, "what a noble defense and what unjust accusations! What complete lies and what false calumnies!"[18] This is a reflexive assertion, a "felt" history (here narrated in a novel) that vindicates the person, the thinker, and the caudillo by citing the historical figure himself. It is, symbolically, the vindication that confers moral and political authority on the author and the mestizos of the Reform as the new Gil Gómezes, combatants who have "sworn to defend the most holy of causes."[19]

Gil Gómez, the boy, is designated captain for his honest and brave attitude. During the campaign, owing to his wise habits and instinctive nature, he manages to save Hidalgo from a spy's attempts to poison him. The priest and the caudillo of independence come together in one man as the man-hero who saves his father protector and who ultimately defends the "most holy of causes." Because he missed the affection of his brother this man-hero begins his journey, a choice that ultimately destines Gil to save Hidalgo's life. The two brothers—two young men destined to become involved in a war on different sides—are united by bonds of brotherhood. Gil Gómez assumes the responsibility delegated to him by converting himself into a man-hero who will have to bring to fruition the task of reconciling a national family separated by foreign customs and interests ostensibly contrary to those of Mexicans.[20]

In his novel *Sacerdote y caudillo* (1869), Juan A. Mateos also turns in large part to historical texts in order to recreate his fiction about Hidalgo and independence. Most notable in his work is the idea of turning to "felt" history in order to make reference to the Gil Gómezes as the symbolic "father figures" and to vindicate Hidalgo as a father of Mexican nationality. The nationalistic expression of the liberal consciousness that was embodied in this novel as an idea of "independence united to religious sentiment" served as an "attack of high politics."[21] This was an idea that only time could confirm one way or another. The triumph of the liberals over Maximilian in 1867, by combining two empires, thus revived anew the rancor against Iturbide. This triumph also referred the victors to the origins of Mexicanness historically, traditionally, and geographically, and revived belief in the religious icon, the Virgin of Guadalupe. Finally, it also reminded Mexicans of the liberating impulse of one man—Father Hidalgo. Ultimately, this triumph lent a new initiative to Mexican nationality. The idea and sentiment behind this history and tradition sought to shape a collective consciousness. These attempts faltered when faced with the reality of a community that was socially fragmented and unequal.

Díaz Covarrubias refers to Hidalgo in a nostalgic tone as a missionary priest whom all other priests should imitate; however, Mateos refers to this Hidalgo apparently in reaction to his political sentiment of the moment, highlighting the actions of a historical character who left his missionary function in order to succeed at independence.

A series of novels were produced, even before those of Mateos, that would reintroduce the theme of the missionary priest with the idea of discerning a modern and progressive community. Given the conflict-filled political, economic, and social circumstances, and recognizing the deeply rooted common sentiment of Mexicans, other writers would seek to conceptualize reconciliation. They (re)created a community modeled on a common understanding of history, customs, culture, and inclination to social "progress." They needed a guide to accomplish this common understanding and conciliation and turned to a representative of religious faith—a master priest, guide, and counselor to others.

THE VILLAGE PRIEST AND THE PROGRESS OF THE COMMUNITY

The only novels published during the actual period of the War of the Reform (1857–60) are those of Díaz Covarrubias. At twenty years of age he thought that perhaps they would call him a child or insane for "writing in Mexico in this tragic epoch of social collapse and pretending to be read by the fierce red light of destructive fires and thunder of cannons."[22] The truth is that the unpredictable and risky life one lived in society also influenced his personal life.[23] With the soul of a romantic who was conscious that he could die at any moment, he thought that to write about Mexico would be the best form of vindicating himself to himself and to others. But he did not live long enough to be able to accomplish this goal. His novels directly criticized a bad administration and brought attention to the corruptions of the higher clergy. Consequently, Díaz Covarrubias was assassinated by the conservative army while he lent his aid as a physician to the opposing side. It is no coincidence that only after 1861, once the civil war had ended, did writers like Manuel Payno, Nicolás Pizarro Suárez, and others begin to publish novels again.[24]

In his novel *El monedero* (1861), Pizarro Suárez centers the plot on the years 1846–48 when the United States Army invaded and occupied Mexico City. The fundamental purpose of this novel was to put into perspective the ideas and political actions of the Mexicans who participated in this drama in order to reflect on the idea of protecting the sovereignty of the nation. Faced with the overwhelming state of panic, destruction, and sense of impotence among many, the critical voice of the narrator attacks those he considers responsible for having permitted such circumstances: "Let the factions who devour the entrails of Mexico enjoy this result!"[25]

The origin of these circumstances, according to the novel, appears to have emerged from the actions of the ill-fated monarchists with a "spirit of imitation" of Spanish customs who were only interested in assuring their social status under the tutelage of a conservative government. According to the narrator these monarchists "proclaimed the defense of property, of religion and of family, although for all the world this was clear hypocrisy, and there was no shortage of persons who wore this mask in order to hide their intentions, because in all parts, but especially in Mexico, politics is a continuous carnival."[26]

Before the Reform both the revolutionary party and the conservative party—as could easily happen with any other political party in the world according to the narrator—proclaimed themselves the defender of family, religion, and liberty. Yet neither party could establish continuity based on these concepts. Both remained in a stagnant, decayed administrative system that merely adopted the modern ideological concept of "liberty" that in practice was not made reality. On the contrary, "liberty" as conceived by these political parties implicated class interests that neglected the profound social reality of Mexicans.

Given these circumstances, "the difficulty has existed and will continue to exist for considerable time," says the narrator of *El monedero*, "in applying the consequences of a just and ordered liberty to a regime of society."[27] Some intellectual reformers subsequently deliberated on how to make the reach and practical significance of those concepts more specific and in accord with the reality and the necessity of the Mexican people. A proper dissemination of the concept of "liberty" would require that social "equality" be added to it. And since social equality requires rights and responsibilities of citizens, what better way to discern this world than through the relationship to a common sentiment—in this case, a religious sentiment. Thus the novelists foresaw those with whom they could share this feeling—as a unifying means of community—by using the figure of the priest as a guide and director. These novelists made a biblical analogy between an apostle of brotherhood and charity and those who would be Mexico's conciliators.

Given this line of argument, the objective in *El monedero* is to create an ideal community for all: a community based on a Christian association separate from the great urban centers and one that integrates those degraded by the social vices and evils of poverty, politics, the system of levy, racism, and religious fanaticism. The directors of this idealized community in *El monedero* are Fernando Hénkel and Father Luis. Fernando is an Indian who is orphaned and lost in Mexico City as a child when his father is taken through the levy. Luis is a village priest in a very poor region of the country. He himself suffers from the lack of basic needs that he tries to supply to the people he seeks to aid. Cutting through the historical reality of the years 1846–48 (the U.S. invasion; the apathy of the conservatives; the insidious division of social classes; the devastated economy), the fiction of the work reflects a symbolic creation—a rather utopian one at that—of a communitarian association called New Philadelphia with a structural plan of living space and buildings for religion, education, a nursery school, a communal eating place, and a place for art and social recreation. The regulations dictate that the family should be the structural basis of this association and consequently all the directors must be married. Here social equality leaves behind class barriers and the gendered division of labor since all were to identify themselves as "members" equally compensated according to labor.

If the "pueblos have never really been free," this was due in great measure to the mire of ignorance and the vices that afflict them, says Father Luis. He suggests that "actions must show the most advantageous way a family can be united . . . with the help of Providence I intend to do this."[28]

In *El monedero* one finds a priest "with the faith of a patriot" and "the countenance of a saint, reading the happiness of Mexico for a near future." This is a priest for whom the idea of equality extends to love, justice, and progress through the practice of his faith. He conceived of his faith as the result of "THE TRUE RELIGION" and "HOLY LIBERTY."[29] Faith and happiness: concepts of religious character that have been sustained by history. These concepts, in order to be disseminated favorably, had to be first present in the collective memory of the community. In the books of inscriptions of this new

Christian association, Father Luis says to Fernando, "You will notice that to all the Indians who do not have a last name I have given names of our heroes [Hidalgo, Morelos], so that they never forget the sacrifices that they made for our liberty.[30]

This "never forget" creates a historical memory projected through the person of Father Luis. Like the first caudillos, Luis embarks on his priestly mission as a protector of Indians and servant of liberty with the religious character of his words made into charity.[31] With New Philadelphia thus established, Luis the priest and caudillo of social equality shows his "partners" that "God sent his gifts without distinction for all his children and the church cares nothing for material goods."[32] But while this comes to fruition in New Philadelphia, the reality of the nation was quite different. Toward the end of the novel, ten years later (in 1858), the annual report of New Philadelphia tells of the following: "In the ten years that have passed had we had efficient protection from government officials the number of colonies would have multiplied. Contrary to this, it seems that we are being persecuted with taxes, contributions, and levies that frequently take away from us a father or a youth who could have soon formed his own family, when they are caught outside the colony."[33]

A priest plants the seed for the solution to the political and social problem of the nation. This "village" reformer priest lives happily as director of the community and far surpasses the tradition of a high clergy who, with the support of the conservative party, had obstinately maintained itself unchanged and in power. As the narrator observes, "in the ecclesiastical hierarchy, as in all careers of society, those who work the most are the ones who enjoy the least."[34] This novel was written in the middle of a civil war and the conservative forces that fought in this war were financed in part by the clergy. At the same time that the clergy launched its verbal attacks and declared war on the "impious" and "heretical" liberals, writers who sympathized with the liberal cause reminded the clergy about what they saw as the true function of the religious character of the men of the Catholic Church in Mexico.

During the period of civil war from 1858 to 1860, and throughout the nineteenth century, the Laws of the Reform and the constitution did not articulate the necessary and convincing mechanisms for them to be peacefully exercised.[35] If the church felt betrayed by the decree of freedom of worship and the dissolution of its traditional ties with the state that were promulgated by the Constitution of 1857, no less did the campesinos and indigenous communities rebel at seeing their communal lands expropriated—through the Ley Lerdo—when they were exposed to a state of intensified poverty and were forced to seek shelter in a system of peonage that was the only means for sub-

sistence. As one historian has explained, "the Indians distrusted the anticlerical and, in their vision, antireligious politics of the liberal party, since the
church had provided them at the least with hope and festivals and they had received from it education and material benefits that they had not received from
any government."[36]

Ignacio Manuel Altamirano had been a witness to and participant in this
tension—as an Indian who later was educated and became a liberal combatant,
politician, and journalist—and delivered his reflections on the matter in his
novel *La navidad en las montañas* (1871), both as narrator and through the voice
of his protagonist, the brother priest.

This novel relates the events and circumstances of Christmas Eve of 1860.
The narrator is described as a "political exile, a victim of passions, who perhaps was going in pursuit of the death that the participants in the civil war so
easily decree for their enemies."[37] He finds himself on the road, sad and soli-
tary, and meditating on the past Christmases of his childhood, in the village
with his family, and in his later youth surrounded by friends in the hustle of
the city. The narrator consoles himself by remembering that "his journey
would end in a small village of hospitable and poor mountain people who
lived from the produce of agriculture and who enjoyed a relative well-being
thanks to being far from the large centers of population and as a result of the
kindness of its patriarchal customs."[38] Altamirano thus foreshadows the basic
tensions and plot of the novel that the captain–narrator later complements
with his intervention as the protagonist.

From the perspective of the author, and from the first moment, *La navidad
en las montañas* suggests a context and idea similar to that of *El monedero* by
Pizarro Suárez—a community in harmony based on work, order, and distance
from big cities. The main difference between the two novels is that in order to
create a new social structure in *La navidad*, the idea of the community is conceived from a collective, traditional sentiment—the nostalgic evocation of
memories tied to the religious tradition that Christmas Eve commemorates.
Altamirano distinctively refers to the "harmony" of the "patriarchal customs"
as the sustenance of the modern, new elements necessary for what he considers to be the true progress of villages.[39] His fictional form is motivated by lo-
cating and promoting original customs. This form has an added element of
surprise embodied in the captain-narrator who realizes that the priest of the
small village was Spanish.

It was well-known that among village priests some were criollos and the
majority mestizos. During the Reform, the clergy was formed principally of
criollos. Accordingly, the literary reference to the ethnic origin was used to refer to the origin of Christianity in New Spain. To the great surprise of the

captain-narrator, the priest reflects and laments, "with pain," he says, to realize that with respect to origins,

> Now have ended the beautiful times of the heroic missionaries who, risking their lives, went to remote regions to bring the light of civilization with the Christian word, and in which the friar was not the otiose priest that one saw passing his days in the comforts of a sedentary and easy life, but was instead a hard-working apostle that went to the far-away mission to wear the crown of evangelical victories, converting the savage villages to Christianity, or who went to martyrdom, to fulfill the precepts of Jesus.[40]

Three years previously the priest had arrived in the same small village in the mountains with inhabitants "in a state much like idolatry and barbarism." He explained to the captain that, with his mission as a "working apostle," he instantly assumed the function of "schoolteacher, doctor, and municipal advisor."[41] He taught people to read and write and imparted ideas about work and economic progress, including how to improve mental and physical health. He obtained this improvement of the community through executing his plan for social liberty, equality, and brotherhood.[42] Indeed, he suggested that everyone should treat him as an equal, as a "brother priest" because "that formula of 'sir priest' displeased him because it was too high-flown."[43] His faith is practical; he defends it and ensures that all the changes in the town are due to that faith and religion. When the captain expresses his surprise at the accomplishments realized in such areas of the country and the speed with which they occurred, the priest responds: "*It is true that I have not proposed all of those reforms in the name of God or pretended to be inspired by Him*; my dignity is opposed to that fraud. *But evidently my character as a priest gave authority to my words. The mountain people would not have found them in the mouth of a person of a different class.*"[44]

The narrator-captain led the Christian work he hoped to accomplish, but that he never had witnessed before, fighting in favor of the Reform. He was not a fanatic spawned by the promulgation of the Constitution of 1857. If the church imposed taxes and tithes, it also "sold" hopes and happiness, above all to the pueblos where there surged forth an entire series of religious festivals in honor of one saint or another. Daniela Traffano details in her essay in this volume how indigenous communities in Mexico continued to rely heavily on traditional forms of community religion even if the administration of saints' festivals was altered by necessity. Altamirano also refers to this in his novel.[45] Such customs were often based in the quagmire of material necessity in an uncertain, unaffordable world. If through these means there existed a fanaticism so strong that Catholic believers repudiated the Reform, how could the liberals correct such a situation if with the same Reform they only offered ideas that in reality intended to deprive indigenous communities of their customs of subsistence, their land, and their Catholic faith? Consequently, emotion moves Altamirano to the point of questioning the value of those Christmas memories of traditional festivity—transient and now diffuse—before this precious moment that exemplifies Christian virtue: "Blessed Christmas that reserved for me the greatest happiness of my life and which is having encountered a disciple of the sublime Missionary, whose coming to the world is celebrated today!"[46]

The brother-priest accomplished his reforms in that small town in the mountains over a period of three years during which, paradoxically, the nation had been torn by a civil war. This "greatest happiness of his life" the captain feels at that moment regenerates his faith in the Reform. He acquires a new attitude, wishing that he and the legislators and other politicians knew how to understand that "the simple sanction of the freedom of conscience is not enough to remove abuses, to illustrate to the masses and to make possible the philosophic idea of modern men, which is, if possible, to found the building of public prosperity on top of free religious principles."[47] In 1871, thirteen years after the beginning of the civil war, and despite the conclusive victory of the liberal party in 1867, sociopolitical discord still continued—between the various factions within the same party—adding to an insuperable economic crisis and discrediting the laws of the Reform.

Altamirano interpreted this problem and wanted to go beyond it, not from a political perspective, which might have aggravated the tension between the church and the liberal factions, but rather by reevaluating the function of Catholicism as a mediator of Mexican cultural identity and tradition. This was an attempt to understand the deep causes of the backwardness of the rural pueblos by turning ideas into actions. He was not interested in ideas intended to cause discord between liberal ideology and conservative ideology. The liberal ideology attempted to impose a new system of laws that, contrary to what was expected or desired, really promoted the economic progress of a few and left the majority of the population in poverty. To this Altamirano proposed a liberalism based in social Christianity aimed at alleviating rural poverty and misery.

From 1867 on liberal politics would establish the figure of Hidalgo as the indisputable father of the nation. Accordingly, from this point on the celebration of September 16 would displace the countless fiestas of saints as the principal national event. This responded not only to the decision to make September 16 into an official event but also to the reality that this event represented a solemn act of communion for all Mexicans in which religious, patriotic, and historical sentiments converged. In order to exalt this cluster of feelings the organizers of this event would take on the task of introducing the civic act with a representation of the *grito* (shout) and the pealing of the bells that the priest Hidalgo had rung to announce independence. This representation would likewise form a definitive part of the collective memory of the nation. So if from that moment the church had lost its political power it had not likewise lost its spiritual power and continued to gain the confidence of the populace (by incorporating the *grito* into civic political culture). With the arrival of Porfirio Díaz in power in 1867, the church would recuperate its political influence, although not in the direct form it once had but rather as an institution in service to the executive power. With this alliance the church regained certain privileges and Díaz maintained an indispensable alliance in order to propagate, through faith, the new order of government.

THE SOCIAL FUNCTION OF THE
SCOLDING GOODWILL CLERIC

In the 1887 novel *La bola*, Emilio Rabasa projects a vision of a priest who both demonstrates goodwill and reprimands. This character, instead of continuing on a philosophy of progress, takes on the role of a counselor whose angry attitude rejects an equality that, in his view, only caused moral degradation of the individual. Such equality intensified preexisting vices and social ailments like economic ruin, military, civil, and political corruption, and the use of violence and blackmail to obtain power. Accordingly, Rabasa referred to the context of the Reform and proposed that the Laws of the Reform and the Constitution of 1857 only caused social chaos. The nation could not count on citizens who neither understood nor followed those same laws. In his view they only caused corruption and were manipulated by bureaucrats along with the passions and ambition of crude and uneducated men. Consequently, the author conceived the civic action of the citizenry as a parody of tradition. In *La bola* he refers particularly to the celebration of September 16 with its traditional *grito* as evoking Mexican nationality due to its historical, political, and religious resonance. At the beginning of the novel the narrator says "[a]t dawn the children jumped out of bed thanks to the thundering of the fireworks that the government had wasted so much money on . . . more than public festivities it appeared like the frenetic beginning of a tremendous riot."[48]

If the narrator, Juan, foreshadows the negative prophetic character of his story, it is because he wants the reader to see the intransigent state of the nation, of "eleven million opinions that have agreed that there is nothing better than the tolling of bells, drum rolls, explosion of firecrackers and snorting of brass."[49] This is a participation of collective conscience, a tradition in which, by political decree, the religious and political spirit was reconciled under an act of all Mexicans. Indeed, the narrator Juan says that the village priest took it upon himself to loan to the organizing committee the curtains that would serve to drape the bandstand where the civic discourse would culminate. He explains that "in the center [of the curtain] one saw the portrait of father Hidalgo . . .; on the sides of the portrait and a yard away, two thick sashes were hanging with the national colors, and crowning the portrait of the liberator an eagle boldly spread out its wings of cut paper."[50] Particularly notable in this commemoration is that at the hour of carrying out the national duty, the head of the small town, Mateo Cabezudo, will be defeated and humiliated by Jacinto Coderas, who imposes his power as the new political chief of San Martín. The director of the newspaper *La Conciencia Cívica*, Pérez Gavilán, takes advantage of the circumstances by referring in a note to the affronts committed against the local hero and urging the hero to raise arms against the government. On the other hand, the trustee Abundo Cañas tries to blackmail Juan into serving as secretary to Coderas. Then, although he resists it, Juan will have to join "la bola" given that it represents his best option in order to be close to his beloved Remedios, the niece of Cabezudo.

In his first essay as a "bolista," on the side of Cabezudo's people, in which they attack Coderas and his allies, Juan falls gravely wounded and loses consciousness. Then a woman, "Bartolita la revendedora," finds him and takes him in her cart to the house of the priest Marojo. The narrator, Juan, relates how well this priest cared for him, who in his ministry "followed his duties strictly, gaining renown with his good works."[51] He remembers, among other things, that on this occasion "the good elderly man scolded me sweetly for having gotten myself in such dire straits." This priest "was not a great preacher but he had the necessary talent to teach by example, an objective system that is not easy to apply with frequency, especially in small towns."[52]

Father Marojo's "goodwill" was driven by an "objective system" based on application of the faith according to circumstances and not on the spontaneity of faith as his literary predecessors had done. Two good examples of such spontaneously inspired faithful priest characters in previous novels are the brother-priest of *La navidad* and Father Hidalgo. The liberal political party that had instituted Hidalgo as the father of the nation had arrived at its ideological transformation; the political party was now different and Rabasa similarly transforms the meaning of the figure of the priest. Could it be that now literature and religion went beyond the simple desire to represent (indirectly) the sociopolitical reality of the author?

Noting what Rabasa's narrator says about Father Marojo, it suggests that his character had anticipated his own time. With his intervention as an adviser and scolder, with a practical, methodical system, Father Marojo was projected as a mediating priest figure channeling a government order that conceived of the nation as an organ subject to evolutionary ideas by way of the simultaneous act of integration and differentiation. For Father Marojo, los Cabezudos, los Sorias, los Coderas cannot be redeemed, and they do not deserve to "integrate" because their condition does not allow it.

If at any moment Juan describes Father Marojo as a priest who "has the necessary talent to teach by example,"[53] the truth is that in his story he only presents a Father Marojo who criticizes and gives his opinion about the types of protagonists that represent tradition and the circumstances of his surroundings. Toward the end of the century, the Catholic priest was close to the dictatorship, and, as anticipated with the example of Father Marojo, he became a critic of society with an attitude similar to that of the Porfirian regime—and that of the narrator Juan himself—one of serving as a guardian judge over society.

The political period that sets the scene for the context of this story is one in which people pay more attention to the ideas and actions of transition (supposedly a transition toward social progress) than to tradition and experience. Father Marojo's observations remain at the level of official discourse. What does transcend is the action of the government that "recognizes and confirms the rank of colonel that *la bola* gave to Mateo."[54] For Father Marojo this is simply inconceivable and irrational. His final advice is more of a complaint in the form of a lamentation. It is likewise a breath of hope deposited in Juan, who, different from all San Martín, is the only young man who can save himself. Directing himself to him, Father Marojo says, "[t]his is a country of consummated acts . . . the country of aberrations. . . . This country has no remedy."[55]

Years later, Juan would refer to this attitude of wisdom and rejection of the inherited sociopolitical disorder as a moralizing Periquillo (the "itching parrot"—*periquillo sarniento*—the title of the ostensible "first" Mexican novel, by José Joaquín Fernández de Lizardi, in the late colonial era) in order to sustain his aversion to a reality in which he only wanted to redeem himself and begin his life anew, dedicating himself to work in his "little lands" and, although "sad, depressed and alone," confident in recuperating his integrity, self-esteem, and his own worth.[56]

CONCLUSION

From the moment of Hidalgo's "grito" in the actual history, the priests and caudillos of novels and fiction were characterized, above all, curiously, particularly, as an essential vehicle of their religious mission—that is, turning charity into direct contact with the "popular" classes. But the attitude and manner of directing themselves to their subjects had changed over time. If Rabasa referred to the context of the Reform in order to show the poison of the tradition of irrational acts taken to their extreme by corrupt men who lacked culture or manners, this was without doubt with the aim of delivering a message of and for his times—a positivist message through a creative technique that rejects both idealism and social ineptitude.

Freedom of thought (in the case of Díaz Covarrubias) begins and later evolves into what becomes a freedom of ideas and action in order to show a possible world of social reform (Pizarro Suárez). This social reform that comes to refer to the origin of a religious "mission" (Altamirano) is ultimately refuted by the religious action (Rabasa) that while simultaneously offering charity rejected freethinking, requesting as well strict observance of social order.

The figure of the priest in Mexican literature is one that is shielded by the principle of goodwill and that evolved with the changing political leanings of authors who sought to use the medium of the novel to influence change over their immediate surroundings. These authors were well aware of the religious tradition in Mexico, and all the novelists examined here knew to announce their instructive message in order to have better access to social consciousness. They utilized a discourse that alluded to the theological thesis of the redemption of the world through a man-god who intercedes on earth. They personify this redeemer in the figure of a priest who, with the help of providence, serves as the spiritual force that guides the man-hero to fulfill the destiny of the nation.

Finally, with his sarcastic rejection of those "eleven million opinions that have agreed that there is nothing better than the tolling of bells, drum rolls, explosion of firecrackers and snorting of brass" to celebrate Independence Day, Rabasa sends a fruitless message. He does not understand that it was not about ambitions or political juggling but rather a historical-religious sentiment that created a national identity. It was an act of communion that did not discriminate according to race, social position, sex, or even religious cult. This act of collective consciousness reminds us and continues to remind all of the "millions of opinions" that culturally Mexicans are Catholic because they live historically—and from September 16, 1810—as *Mexicans*.

NOTES

Chapter opening image source: Centro Fotográfico Álvarez Bravo, Fondo Ignacio Zanabria.

This chapter was translated by Martin Austin Nesvig with Lina del Castillo.

1. María del Carmen Vázquez Mantecón, "El discurso de un patriota a propósito de la consumación de la Independencia y de su héroe (1821–1852)," in *El nacimiento de*

México, ed. Patricia Galeana (Mexico City: Archivo General de la Nación; Fondo de Cultura Económica, 1999), 112.

2. Robert Knowlton, *Los bienes del clero y la reforma mexicana, 1856–1910* (Mexico City: Fondo de Cultura Económica, 1985), 31.

3. Juan Díaz Covarrubias, *Gil Gómez el insurgente o la hija del médico* (Mexico City: Porrúa, 1991), 3: "género mucho más útil y en el cual se pueden más ensayar las fuerzas."

4. Díaz Covarrubias considers the texts of Mexican history by Bustamante, Zavala, and Alamán to lack objectivity (*Gil Gómez*, 82–83). His proposal is to describe historical reality from inside out: the psyche, nature, customs, desires, and hopes of the populace. As a writer, Díaz Covarrubias proposes the following: express what has been heard in contact with "the simple people of the pueblo," in the sketches (heartbreaking for him) on the history of Mexico by "expressing what has been felt kissing while crying our miserable flag of Iguala" ("expresar lo que h[a] sentido al besar llorando nuestro desdichado pabellón de Iguala"), *Gil Gómez*, 4.

5. Díaz Covarrubias, *Gil Gómez*, 71: "parecía tener un apetito voraz."

6. Díaz Covarrubias, *Gil Gómez*, 75, "—El convento ha hecho muy bien en elegir para sus negocios a una persona tan digna como su paternidad, que lleva por nombre la caridad que se encierra en esas hermosas palabras de las obras de misericordia: 'Dar a comer al hambriento.'—En efecto, 'amarás al prójimo como a ti mismo'—dijo el padrecito recalcando la pronunciación sobre las dos últimas expresiones, y sin dejar un momento de engullir."

7. Díaz Covarrubias, *Gil Gómez*, 80: "una diferencia espantosa de clases."

8. Knowlten, *Los bienes*, 31.

9. Díaz Covarrubias, *Gil Gómez*, 35: "hijo de la desdicha y no del crimen."

10. Metaphor of the son of "the conquest": son of a father he never had and an abnegated mother: "un hijo de *la chingada*."

11. Díaz Covarrubias, *Gil Gómez*, 43: "primero había sido designado como víctima, fue considerado como caudillo en todas las travesuras y motines."

12. Enrique Krauze postulates that "there were many Hidalgos in Hidalgo, all equally eccentric. In his ministerial army (in the parishes of Colima, San Felipe and finally Dolores), he showed that he was not fond of work in the parish notary office nor of celebrating many masses. In contrast he enjoyed preaching, adapting his theological duties and taking very seriously confession of the sick and dying. He sought to convert theology into charity. This parental aspect of the priest was manifested above all in his dealing with Indians: he knew their language and taught them grammar and skills." ("Había muchos Hidalgos en Hidalgo, todos igualmente excéntricos. En su ejercicio ministerial (en la parroquias de Colima, San Felipe y, finalmente, Dolores) mostró que no era afecto a los trabajos de notaría parroquial ni a celebrar muchas misas; en cambio le gustaba predicar adaptando sus deberes teológicos y tomaba muy a pecho la confesión de enfermos y moribundos. Es decir, buscaba convertir la teología en caridad. Este aspecto paternal del Cura se manifestaba sobre todo en su trato con los indios: sabía su idioma y les enseñaba artes y oficios.") From *Siglo de caudillos: Biografía política de México (1810–1910)* (Mexico City: Fábula Tusquets Editores, 2002), 53–54.

13. Juan Díaz Covarrubias, "Discurso cívico," in *Obras completas*, estudio preliminar, edición y notas por Clementina Díaz y de Ovando, 2 vols. (Mexico City: UNAM, 1959), 1:22: "que se comprenda el verdadero espíritu de la religión, . . . que enseña en las aldeas el modesto párroco o en los desiertos el sufrido religioso, y no ese cristianismo de procesiones y prácticas exteriores que enseña el clero noble de las ciudades, el canónigo rico y perezoso que tiene más de gran señor de la edad media que de apóstol de Jesucristo." The judgment of historians of this era and recently as well agrees that his novels, but in particular this discourse, made the clergy and the conservative party hate Díaz Covarrubias, to the point that they did not respect his life in his capacity as an auxiliary medic and he was shot together with other liberal prisoners by conservative forces in 1859.

14. See, for example, Knowlton, *Los bienes*.

15. Díaz Covarrubias, *Obras*, 1:11. This is part of a letter from the archbishop of Mexico directed to "the priests and vicars of the churches of this diocese" dated October 31, 1810, and here I refer to the complete paragraph from the cited letter: "Digan ustedes, pues, y anuncien en público y en secreto que el cura Hidalgo y los que vienen con él intentan engañarnos y apoderarse de nosotros, para entregarnos a los franceses y que sus obras, palabras, promesas y ficciones, son iguales o idénticas con las de Napoleón, a quien finalmente nos entregarán si llegaran a vencernos; pero que la Virgen de los Remedios está con nosotros, y debemos pelear con su protección, contra estos enemigos de la fe católica y de la quietud pública."

16. Díaz Covarrubias, *Gil Gómez*, 134: "contra estos enemigos de la fe católica y de la quietud pública."

17. Krauze, *Siglo de caudillos*, 58: "para la campaña por los mismos sacerdotes del alto clero que, 'armados de sable y pistola, y con el crucifijo en la mano, como los obispos en los tiempos de las cruzadas', hacían circular innumerables folletos, invectivas y anatemas en contra del cura 'hereje', 'monstruo frenético y delirante', 'abominable', 'impío', 'enemigo de Dios', a quien su propio amigo Abad y Queipo había decidido excomulgar."

18. Díaz Covarrubias, *Gil Gómez*, 141–42: "el objeto de nuestros constantes desvelos es del de mantener nuestra religión, nuestra ley, la patria y pureza de costumbres" and "¡Qué defensa tan noble y acusaciones tan injustas! ¡Qué desmentida tan completa a calumnias tan falsas!"

19. Díaz Covarrubias, *Gil Gómez*, 147: "jurado defender la más santa de las causas."

20. One understands here also the metaphor of the "ideological-political conciliation" of the nation between insurgents and royalists and, consequently, between liberals and conservatives.

21. Mateos, *Sacerdote y caudillo*, 328: "la independencia unida al sentimiento religioso, era" and "un golpe de alta política."

22. Juan Díaz Covarrubias, *El diablo en México y otros textos*, edición de Clementina Díaz y de Ovando (Mexico City: UNAM, 1989), 145: "escribir en México en esta época aciaga de desmoronamiento social, y pretender ser leído a la luz rojiza del incendio y al estruendo de los cañones."

23. He was orphaned from his father at age nine. On moving with his two older brothers and mother from Xalapa to Mexico City in 1848, the family encountered

harsh economic travails. In 1854 he fell deeply in love with a young woman from the middle class, Lucía, who only snubbed him and showed him disdain. With the death of his mother in 1857, Díaz Covarrubias must have felt a deep sense of emptiness to the point of feeling socially disconnected.

24. Altamirano shows that on the conclusion of the administration of Comonfort "volvió a atrasarlo todo la guerra, esa guerra fatal que ha pesado sobre este país como una maldición, y que ha cegado las fuentes de su riqueza material, así como ha paralizado su movimiento intelectual" (*Obras completas* XII, 1:66). If one considers that up to then Pizarro Suárez had already written his novel *La coqueta* and most of *El monedero*, it is not surprising that this author had preferred to postpone the publication of his novels in order to avoid possible reprisals on the part of the clergy and conservative party.

25. Nicolás Pizarro Suárez, *El monedero* (Mexico City: Imprenta de Nicolás Pizarro, 1861), 273: "¡Gócense en este resultado las facciones que devoran las entrañas de Méjico!"

26. Pizarro Suárez, *El monedero*, 30: "proclamaron la defensa de la propiedad, de la religión y de la familia, y aunque para todo el mundo era clara la hipocresía, no faltaron personas que se pusiesen aquella máscara para encubrir sus intenciones, porque en todas partes, pero en México especialmente, la política es un continuo carnaval."

27. Pizarro Suárez, *El monedero*, 30: "la dificultad ha sido y será por mucho tiempo" and "aplicar las consecuencias de una libertad justa y ordenada al régimen de la sociedad."

28. Pizarro Suárez, *El monedero*, 81: "los pueblos nunca han sido realmente libres" and "[m]ostrarles con hechos cuál es el modo más ventajoso con que pueden unirse las familias, . . . lo que con el auxilio de la Providencia intentaré yo hacer."

29. Pizarro Suárez, *El monedero*, 82: "con la fe del patriota" and "el arrobamiento del santo, leyendo en un cercano porvenir la dicha de México" and "LA VERDADERA RELIGIÓN" and "LA SANTA LIBERTAD."

30. Pizarro Suárez, *El monedero*, 227: "Notarás que a todos los indígenas que no tienen apellido les he puesto al inscribirlos los de nuestros héroes [Hidalgo, Morelos], para que nunca se olviden los sacrificios que hicieron por nuestra libertad."

31. He notes that throughout the work, all the religious messages and references evoked by Luis were taken from the Bible.

32. Pizarro Suárez, *El monedero*, 346: "Dios envía sus dones indistintamente para todos sus hijos, y que la Iglesia para nada quiere los bienes materiales."

33. Pizarro Suárez, *El monedero*, 615: "Si en los diez años que han transcurrido hubiéramos contado con la protección eficaz del gobierno, se habrían multiplicado las colonias, pero lejos de esto, parece que se nos persigue con las alcabalas, contribuciones y levas, que frecuentemente nos roban un padre de familia, o un joven que pronto la habría formado, cuando los pillan fuera de la colonia."

34. Pizarro Suárez, *El monedero*, 384: "en la jerarquía eclesiástica, como en todas las carreras de las sociedad, los que más trabajan son los que menos gozan." [sic]

35. T. G. Powell finds that in the "month of March in 1857" the jefe político of Ixmiquilpan, Mucio Barquera, helped four haciendas of his district to regain some lands that campesinos had been occupying. Barquera had barely finished this when a

lawyer tried to unify the indigenous communities of the district in a league whose principles were considered by the jefe político to be "communist ideas." See his "Los liberales, el campesinado indígena y los problemas agrarios durante la Reforma," in *Actores políticos y desajustes sociales*, ed. Romana Falcón (Mexico City: El Colegio de México, 1992). The similarities here are reflected, and the rejection implied, in the ideas and person of Pizarro Suárez: liberal lawyer, defender of Indians and individuals marginalized by society through nationalist sentiment shielded in sociopolitical and Christian ideas. The problem of lands, as is well known, had to continue with continuous uprisings, and the only method that the government found to resolve the problem was through military action.

36. Powell, "Los liberales," 98–99.

37. Altamirano, *La navidad*, 95: "un proscrito, una víctima de las pasiones, [qu]e iba tal vez en pos de la muerte que los partidarios en la guerra civil tan fácilmente decretan contra sus enemigos."

38. Altamirano, *La navidad*, 95: "que terminaría [su] jornada en un pueblecillo de montañeses hospitalarios y pobres que vivían del producto de la agricultura, y que disfrutaban de un bienestar relativo merced a su alejamiento de los grandes centros populosos, y a la bondad de sus costumbres patriarcales."

39. In 1869 Altamirano had referred in his literary writings to the novels of Pizarro Suárez. Particularly he had praised *El monedero* and the social function of the priest Luis. It is curious that in *La navidad* the author alludes to personages similar to European writers but he scarcely mentions Pizarro Suárez. It could have been in part because he wanted to avoid polemics and misunderstandings, as apparently happened with the work of Pizarro Suárez when Gabino Barreda (godfather of Mexican positivism) identified it as having a "tint" of communism.

40. Altamirano, *La navidad*, 95: "Habían acabado ya los bellos tiempos . . . de heróicos misioneros que, a riesgo de su vida, se lanzaban a regiones remotas a llevar con la palabra cristiana la luz de la civilización, y en que el fraile era, no el sacerdote ocioso que veía transcurrir alegremente sus días en las comodidades de una vida sedentaria y regalada, sino el apóstol laborioso que iba a la misión lejana a ceñirse la corona de las victorias evangélicas, reduciendo al cristianismo a los pueblos salvajes, o la del martirio, en cumplimiento de los preceptos de Jesús."

41. Altamirano, *La navidad*, 98: "en un estado muy semejante a la idolatría y a la barbarie," "apóstol laborioso," and "maestro de escuela, y médico y consejero municipal."

42. Altamirano, *La navidad*, 98: "— ¿De manera, señor cura—pregunté—que usted no recibe dinero por bautizos, casamientos, misas y entierros?" Three years of war and, curiously, three years of civil reform in this small village where its leader lives not as a politician nor as a sedentary priest of the city but above all as "cultivator and artisan."

43. Altamirano, *La navidad*, 103: "hermano cura," "desagrada esa fórmula, demasiado altisonante," and "señor cura."

44. Altamirano, *La navidad*, 103: "Sin mi carácter religioso quizá no habría yo sido escuchado ni comprendido. Verdad es que yo no he propuesto todas esas reformas en nombre de Dios y fingiéndome inspirado por él; mi dignidad se opone a esta superchería; pero evidentemente mi carácter de sacerdote y de cura daba una autoridad

a mis palabras, que los montañeses no habrían encontrado en boca de una persona de otra clase" (my emphasis).

45. Altamirano, *La navidad*, 109: "nada es más común que ver esas larguísimas caravanas de peregrinos indígenas que, con todo y familia, se dirigen a pueblos lejanos, abandonando los trabajos agrícolas en busca del santo famoso a quien van a dejar el producto de sus miserables trabajos de un año."

46. Altamirano, *La navidad*, 99: "¡Bendita Navidad ésta que me reservaba la mayor dicha de mi vida, y es el haber encontrado un discípulo del sublime Misionero, cuya venida al mundo se celebra hoy!"

47. Altamirano, *La navidad*, 109: "La simple sanción de la libertad de conciencia no basta para desterrar los abusos, para ilustrar a las masas y para hacer realizable la idea filosófica de los hombres modernos, que es la de fundar, si es posible, sobre los principios religiosos libres, el edificio de la prosperidad pública."

48. Emilio Rabasa, *La bola/La gran ciencia* (Mexico City: Porrúa, 1991), 3: "Al alba los chicos saltaron del lecho, merced al estruendo de los cohetes voladores en que el Ayuntamiento había extendido la franqueza hasta el despilfarro . . . más que regocijo público, parecía el comienzo frenético de una asonada tremenda."

49. Rabasa, *La bola*, 6: "once millones de pareceres, que han convenido en que nada hay mejor que el repique de campanas, redoble de tambores, estruendo de cohetes y bufido de latones."

50. Rabasa, *La bola*, 6: "En el centro [de la cortina] se veía el retrato del padre Hidalgo . . .; a los lados del cuadro y a una vara de distancia, colgaban dos anchas fajas con los colores nacionales, y coronando el retrato del Libertador desplegaba atrevidamente las alas un águila de papel recortado."

51. Rabasa, *La bola*, 109: "cumplía con sus deberes estrictamente, extendiéndose más allá por sus buenas obras."

52. Rabasa, *La bola*, 109: "[n]o era gran predicador; pero tenía el talento necesario para enseñar con el ejemplo, sistema objetivo que no es fácil aplicar con frecuencia, especialmente en los pueblos cortos."

53. Rabasa, *La bola*, 109: "tenía el talento necesario para enseñar con el ejemplo."

54. Rabasa, *La bola*, 163: "reconoce y confirma el grado de coronel que *la bola* le dio a Mateo."

55. Rabasa, *La bola*, 163–64: "—Este es el país de los hechos consumados—me dijo al fin—, el país de las aberraciones. . . .—Este país no tiene remedio—siguió diciendo el cura con notable disgusto."

56. Rabasa, *La bola*, 170: "pequeñas tierras" and "triste, abatido y solo."

7

"A New Political Religious Order": Church, State, and Workers in Porfirian Mexico

Mark Overmyer-Velázquez

Up-and-Coming Clergymen in Oaxaca circa 1903. Trained amidst the late nineteenth-century surge in militant Catholic revivalism and the emergence of Social Catholicism, this group of priests served as key conduits of new ideas in provincial Mexico. For example, José Othón Núñez y Zárate (no. 4) studied in Rome, distinguished himself as a journalist-priest and organizer of Catholic workers, and served as bishop of Zamora, Michoacán (1909–22), and archbishop of Oaxaca (1922–42). Unknown photographer.

Capital cannot do without Labor, nor Labor without Capital. Mutual agreement results in the beauty of good order; while perpetual conflict necessarily produces confusion and savage barbarity. Now, in preventing such strife as this . . . the efficacy of Christian institutions is marvelous and manifold. First of all, there is no intermediary more powerful than Religion (whereof the church is the interpreter and guardian) in drawing the rich and the working class together, by reminding each of its duties to the other, and especially of the obligations of justice. Thus Religion teaches the laborer and the artisan to carry out honestly and fairly all equitable agreements freely entered into; never to injure the property, nor to outrage the person, of an employer; never to resort to violence in defending their own cause, nor to engage in riot or disorder; and to have nothing to do with men of evil principles.

—Pope Leo XIII, *Rerum Novarum:*
On the Condition of the Working Classes, 1891

Now that times have changed, a new era has begun, I hope, in the political religious order. From the conquest to the French intervention, the

> [Catholic] church was politically active in Mexico. Under the present cir-
> cumstances with the [Reform] laws in place, the church does not have the
> political power it once had. In my opinion, it is time to establish a regime
> that allows the church to follow the path of its counterpart in the United
> States. That is to say, completely unconcerned with politics and related
> matters.
>
> —Archbishop Gillow of Oaxaca to President Porfirio Díaz, 1892

A series of anticlerical laws set in motion by Mexico's 1857 Constitution left
Roman Catholic prelates and priests struggling to keep their religious faith
alive within the walls of the country's churches and seminaries. Despite the
state's attempts to weaken the church, Mexican society and government continued to be predominantly Catholic throughout the era of President Porfirio
Díaz (1876–1911, commonly referred to as the Porfiriato). In fact, the moral
teachings and social conventions of Catholicism continued to pervade and
shape the daily lives of Mexicans.

Oaxaca de Juárez exemplified the resurgence of Mexican Catholicism and
the critical role it played in the formation of the state capital's encounter with
modernity during the Porfiriato, even in the wake of the liberal reforms of the
1850s and 1860s. Including the fundamental contribution of the church and
religion in a study of Mexico's modernizing processes challenges and complicates their past treatment as secondary and epiphenomenal "stand-in[s] for
more pressing matters."[1] Furthermore, it undoes notions that the process of
modernity necessarily equates a teleological narrative of progress from religious to secular worldviews.[2] Oaxaca's Catholic Church contributed to the
Porfirian capitalist project by attempting to cultivate productive and acquies-
cent laborers. The church hierarchy hoped that by instilling the city's workers
with a combination of a capitalist work ethic and Catholic morality they could
achieve the double result of strengthening their membership base and allying
themselves with the economic agenda of the Porfirian state.

In Oaxaca City, the 1895 federal census recorded that, of the city's 32,437
inhabitants, 32,301 were practicing Catholics, 107 were Protestant, and the remaining handful identified themselves as "deists, free thinkers, and spiritual-
ists."[3] Given the predominance of Catholics in the capital city, leaders and followers of the church needed to reconcile their conservative attitudes and
practices with the newly developed projects of Díaz's government. The Porfirian history of Oaxaca City exemplifies these tensions between church and
state and underscores the unique and influential relationship the president had
with the political and religious life of his hometown.

Like other provincial cities in Latin America during this period, Oaxaca
City, the capital of the southern state of Oaxaca, located 350 miles southeast

of Mexico City, was the center of modernity for the majority of the region's population. Connecting the periphery to the center, provincial capitals like Oaxaca City showcased modernizing and state-building projects. Oaxaqueños witnessed myriad political, economic, social, and cultural changes engineered by the city's celebrated son, President Porfirio Díaz. More than sixty years of family ties to the state capital by Don Porfirio and his predecessor, President Benito Juárez, brought the state and especially Oaxaca City squarely into the modernizing activities of the era. During the Porfiriato the people of Oaxaca City witnessed the significant transformation of their state capital. For example, after years of renewed political stability and moderate financial recovery, the arrival of the Mexican Southern Railway in 1892 supported a mining boom in the region and a period of economic and demographic growth.[4]

Mexico's nascent involvement in an increasingly capitalist and industrialized world prompted Catholic leaders to address the labor and living conditions of the country's workers. Whereas anticlericalism characterized the liberal government's approach to modernization in the decades prior to the Porfiriato, Díaz directly involved the church in his designs of economic development. As such, the church played an integral role in Mexico's experience with modernity at the turn of the century. This essay examines the precarious intersection of religion, work, and state politics during the tenure of Oaxaca's archbishop, Eulogio Gillow, a friend and business partner of Díaz. After serving as the state's bishop from 1887 to 1891, Gillow was appointed the region's archbishop. Although absent for part of the Mexican Revolution (1910–20), he served as archbishop until 1922.

The notion of modernity in Oaxaca City included the seemingly incongruous roles of the church and the city's workers. Traditional historiography of the nineteenth century has long stressed the anticlericalism of Mexican modernity, assuming that the church and religion faded before the modernizing project. Yet in Oaxaca, the Mexican government and Catholic Church worked in tandem to construct a modern Mexico fueled by the labor of the country's workers. After years of anticlerical measures, the Porfirian process of reconciliation between church and state made the two institutions strange but complementary bedfellows. The liberalization of both institutions in a period of capitalist expansion depended upon the exploitation of Mexican workers, and the relationship between Díaz and Gillow and Oaxaca City's workers epitomized this dynamic. There is little in the literature that connects the state with religious institutions, let alone religious practices. Most often, the church tends to disappear after the Reform period (1855–75) and then reemerge during the Cristero War of 1926–29.[5]

Born in 1841 to a wealthy industrialist and a member of the Spanish nobility, Eulogio Gregorio Gillow y Zavalza, Oaxaca's religious leader for most of the Porfiriato, embodied the era's trend of reconciliation between church and state.[6] Equally well versed in his economic and ecclesiastical commitments, Gillow was poised to benefit from and influence Díaz's modernizing agenda. Gillow biographer Manuel Esparza notes: "Without a doubt, what complicates the historical judgment of Archbishop Gillow is the fact that he was simultaneously a religious hierarch and a Porfirian landowner."[7]

In the decades before becoming Oaxaca's bishop, Gillow received an extensive education in business and religion. At the early age of ten he accompanied his father to London's first world exposition, where the elder Gillow hoped to promote his business, which was tied to the mechanization of Mexican agriculture. In his teens and twenties, Gillow followed a distinguished path of university education. He attended academic institutions in Oxford, Paris, Bonn, and Salamanca, and finally earned his doctorate in law, political economics, and ecclesiastical diplomacy in Rome. Mexico's Catholic Church sent him as its representative to the Catholic Congress in Belgium in 1864. The Congress was one of three Congresses convened by Belgium's Catholic authorities in an attempt to rally the church's strength in the face of the country's anticlerical Liberal party. In 1866 Pope Pius IX named him his privy chamberlain supernumerary (an advisory position) and then his domestic prelate in 1869. Gillow met Díaz in 1877 at Mexico's first regional exhibition of industrial agriculture, which the Oaxacan prelate helped organize and which would later serve as a model for other such exhibitions in Mexico.[8] Eight years later, after Gillow arranged for Mexico's archbishop to marry Díaz and Carmen Romero Rubio, President Díaz sent Gillow as the representative of the Federal District to the New Orleans World Exposition of 1885, where he worked closely with the president at the headquarters of Mexico's delegation.[9]

By the time Gillow assumed the see of Oaxaca, he had managed to forge strong relationships with Rome and Mexico City and to establish himself as a leader in the business and Catholic communities of Mexico. Gillow drew on these qualities to modernize the ranks of Oaxaca's Catholic Church and workers and to improve relations with the city and state governments.

THE CHURCH IN THE REFORM ERA

After Benito Juárez and the leaders of the Revolution of Ayutla ousted Antonio López de Santa Anna in 1855 from his long-held position as Mexico's conservative leader, they turned their attention to revitalizing the nation. A series of brutal civil wars and an invasion by the United States (1846–48) had sabotaged attempts to consolidate the nation after its independence from Spain in 1821. Among other measures legislated in the 1857 Constitution, the leaders of Mexico's new government drafted several harsh anticlerical reforms meant to curtail the power of the church. Since the colonial period, the leaders of the Catholic Church had closely allied themselves with conservative, centralist forces in the government. Juárez and his coterie of liberal politicians deemed the church's extensive properties, tithe collection, and political influence detrimental to the formation of the Mexican nation.

In the years before the 1857 Constitution, the government passed two major anticlerical laws. The Ley Juárez (1855) abolished ecclesiastic and military *fueros*, which had exempted the clergy and military officers from trial in civil courts. The Ley Lerdo (1856) forbade groups (principally the church) from owning or administering property not used in everyday activities. The church was allowed to retain its churches, monasteries, and seminaries, but it was forced to divest itself of other types of urban and rural properties, while keeping the proceeds of the sales.

Following the War of the Reform—yet another bloody civil war dominated by ideological battles between liberals and conservatives (1858–61)—the Juárez government issued a series of decrees intensifying the separation of church and state and further subordinating the church to the Mexican government. These decrees became law in the 1874 Constitution. The Juárez government nationalized church properties and retained the proceeds from further sales. The confiscation of church properties at public auctions by the federal government and private individuals took place throughout the Reform era. In Oaxaca City alone, the federal government confiscated 1,102 church properties in this period, or nearly 80 percent of the region's total.

In 1857 President Ignacio Comonfort signed two other statutes into law imposing further prohibitions on the church and secularizing ecclesiastical activities. In a radical break from over three centuries of church control, the registration of births, marriages, and deaths as well as the administration of cemeteries would now fall under civil jurisdiction. The Ley Iglesias required the church to administer the sacraments at reduced rates to a largely poor population.

While an otherwise occupied neighbor to the north fought a bloody civil war, French troops, after years of fighting, installed Napoleon III's puppet emperor, Maximilian of Hapsburg, on a throne in Mexico City (1864). The defeat of Benito Juárez and his armies provided government and church conservatives with a brief opportunity to regain some of the political ground that they had lost during the previous years of liberal reforms. The overthrow of the French army and Maximilian's execution only three years later thus sounded the death knell for the church. The partial recuperation of church control over its lands and rituals enjoyed during the French occupation government ended when Juárez resumed power in 1867. Conservative Catholics considered the years of the restored republic (1867–76) and the presidency of Sebastián Lerdo de Tejada (author of the Ley Lerdo, 1872–76) a "religious tyranny."[10]

Although Lerdo's successor Díaz supported the laws of the Reform, church leaders looked hopefully to him for reconciliation with the government. Their wish would come true in part, but not without enormous efforts by both clergy and laypersons. On the eve of the Porfiriato, the Catholic Church was in disarray; it lacked economic and human resources and had lost many of its churches and institutional centers. Even in the primary archdiocese of Mexico, the government did not allow its archbishop to return to his see until 1871. Oaxaca fared little better—the state and its capital city devoted few resources to the ailing religious community. Until Gillow's arrival in 1887, closed seminaries and abandoned churches greatly hindered official church activities in the state capital. The city retained merely twenty-nine priests out of only ninety-eight in the entire diocese,[11] a radical decline from the late colonial period; in 1792 priests and other ecclesiatics had represented 11.7 percent of the working population of Oaxaca City, whereas by 1875 this figure had fallen to 1.2 percent.[12]

RECONCILIATION

During the Porfiriato the Mexican Catholic Church experienced a revival. Although it would never regain its pre-Reform status, the church emerged from the years of Díaz's rule a much stronger and more influential institution. In Oaxaca, as elsewhere in the republic, church leaders like Gillow shifted their focus from emulation of the gospel in daily practice to social reform. In the state capital, leaders concentrated much of their reform efforts on the relationship with the capital's artisans. They hoped to confront what they saw as the detrimental effects of modernity by inculcating morality and bringing an end to vice and poverty among the popular classes.[13]

The Porfirian reconciliation between church and state emerged from a series of radical changes in the international and national church and government hierarchies. Appointed in 1878, Pope Leo XIII worked quickly to assuage relations between Rome and anticlerical governments in Europe and around the world. There has been a tendency in the historical literature to equate the late nineteenth- and early twentieth-century period of industrialization and state formation with secularization. Yet, the era that Anthony Gill refers to as "Neo-Christendom" witnessed an increase in the power of the Catholic Church around the world as bishops adopted flexible political positions vis-à-vis their government counterparts. Church leaders developed workers circles as a way to strengthen their ties with a growing workforce in what they envisioned as a bulwark against the influence of socialism, thus preserving "Catholicism's ideological hegemony."[14] In addition to Mexico, the church government in places like Brazil, Argentina, and Colombia regained some social and political privileges lost during the era of liberal reforms. As Pamela Voekel has argued for the early independence period in Mexico, the revitalized Porfirian church needs to be reconsidered not as the government's handmaiden and a hindrance to modernization, but as integral to the processes of modernization on both ideological and material levels.[15] That is, especially in places such as Oaxaca City, church and government leaders worked to mutually advance each other's modernizing designs.

After conducting a successful appeal to improve relations with the Apostolic See to Chancellor Bismarck of Germany, the pope communicated to Díaz a similar request with Mexico. Eager to benefit from a stabilized ecclesiastical institution, Díaz had already been acting to ameliorate interactions between church and state. For example, in 1881 the president requested that Gillow marry him to Carmen Romero Rubio, a devout Catholic and daughter of Manuel Romero Rubio, a prominent cabinet member in the Díaz government as minister of Gobernación. Although Gillow declined the honor, he convinced Mexico's archbishop, Pelagio Antonio de Labastida, to do so, thus joining Díaz with a conservative Catholic supporter of Maximilian and strong critic of the 1857 Constitution. In fact, Díaz openly proclaimed himself a proud Catholic in private, but the Reform Laws forbade him from making religious proclamations as Mexico's head of state. Gillow also served as confessor to the first lady.

By the 1890s, the state-church reconciliation of the Porfiriato had begun to come to tangible and dramatic fruition. For example, in 1891, the pope named Gillow archbishop of Antequera (the diocesan and colonial name for Oaxaca City), and published the papal encyclical *Rerum Novarum* (literally, "Of New Things"), concerning the relationship of the world's working classes to emergent capitalist economies. As the Mexican Southern Railway made its way to Oaxaca in the following year, Mexico heralded its new liberal archbishop, Próspero María Alarcón, who replaced Antonio Labastida, a staunch monarchist. Then, on October 12, 1895, the church celebrated the coronation of the Virgin of Guadalupe, Mexico's patron saint and powerful symbol of the country's syncretic fusion of indigenous and European religious traditions.[16]

The construction of nearly five thousand new churches, schools, and seminaries, as well as the creation of several new bishoprics, accompanied this succession of fundamental changes in Mexico's Catholic community. The country's official Catholic paper, *La Voz de México*, which had previously spoken cautiously of the new economic and social policies of the Díaz government, now enthusiastically supported the president in his 1900 presidential reelection campaign. The paper lauded Díaz as a representative of "all that is serious, respectable, and honest in Mexican society." *La Voz de la Verdad*, Oaxaca's official Catholic paper and the voice of Gillow's diocese, similarly praised Díaz: "The presence of General Díaz at the head of our nation's government signifies peace, an indispensable and crucial factor without which the progress of Mexico, its indisputable advancement and prosperity, would quickly decline."[17]

The church was similarly reinvigorated in Oaxaca under the modernizing and reorganizing efforts of its archbishop, Gillow. Throughout the colonial and early independence periods, the Catholic Church had flourished in Oaxaca City. Ecclesiastical architecture dominated the capital, dotting most blocks with one of thirty-three churches. Gillow oversaw the rebuilding and revitalization of the physical and human infrastructure of his diocese. In an 1888 letter to Díaz, Gillow celebrated his early achievements as bishop. He wrote that "belligerent priests have been removed from their parishes. I have received no further complaints [from their parishioners]. I am reforming the rules of the Catholic workers society in order that the workers always remain subject to ecclesiastical authority and refrain from all interference in [state] politics."[18]

This letter and the many others like it between the two friends reveal the importance of their relationship, especially in the realm of reconciliation and development of the church, and the broad and influential reach of Gillow into secular society. In order to maximize administrative efficiency, Gillow divided the city into three parishes, each with ten thousand inhabitants, appointed priests to the capital's seventeen remaining churches, and reorganized the diocesan seminary. He also managed to return some secularized property to church control and received permission for priests to wear their robes in public.[19] The latter concession provided a powerful symbol increasing the visibility and presence of the church in daily life. By 1910 the number of churches in the state had risen to 1,340, representing a ratio of 774 inhabitants per church.[20]

Reconciliation between church and state on a municipal level reached its pinnacle in Oaxaca City with the celebration of the Virgin of Guadalupe and the coronation of Oaxaca's own patron saint, La Virgen de la Soledad. Starting in 1896, Gillow linked parishioners to the nation's saint by arranging annual Virgin of Guadalupe celebrations in all of the city's parishes.[21] On the eve of Mexico's fourth national Catholic Congress, hosted by Gillow in 1909, the Vatican decreed that a colonial-era statue of the Virgin be crowned as La Virgen de la Soledad.[22] According to local newspapers, thousands of people attended the event, including high-ranking ecclesiastical and civic officials. Similarly to the following year's celebrations of Mexico's centennial independence from Spain, the lavish events surrounding the Virgin's coronation on January 18 by Gillow and a representative of Pope Pius IX symbolically linked the main event to notions of modernity and economic progress. On coronation day floats with costumed people staged in tableaux vivants formed scenes from Oaxaca's past, present, and future. Floats symbolizing commerce, Christian enlightenment, mining, and progress and industry paraded past throngs of onlookers. Together, all the floats clearly portrayed the city's Catholic and business communities on a common course of progress and civilization. Anticipating the theme of the Catholic Congress, several displays highlighted the evangelization of Oaxaca's indigenous inhabitants. Members of Oaxaca's Catholic Workers Circle joined the show, where they rubbed elbows with a group of the city's prominent industrialists and their children from the Zorilla, Varela, Murgía, and Tejada families. The following year "all classes of society" in the city repeated the celebration with nine days of pomp and circumstance.[23]

In 1904 Oaxaqueños filled the streets of the capital to celebrate the visit of the pope's representative, Domingo Serafini. The author of an article in the official bulletin of the diocese proclaimed that he had "never seen in Oaxaca such spontaneous and universal enthusiasm as the population demonstrated on the afternoon [of the arrival of Serafini]." Other articles reinforced that image. One proclaimed that "religious sentiment lives, filling with vigor the hearts of the great majority of the [church's] members. It is revealed in extraordinary occasions like the grand demonstrations of faith, of piety, of fervor during which one's heart cannot help but be inundated by ineffable comforts."[24]

Despite the resurgence of physical manifestations of Catholicism, the Reform Laws continued to impinge on the formal church structure. Government officials wrote hundreds of impassioned letters to Gillow's predecessor, Bishop Vicente Fermín Márquez y Carrizosa, bemoaning their absence from the church and requesting absolution of sins committed (for example, private acquisition of church properties) in the name of the laws of the Reform. Indeed, an article in *La Voz de la Verdad* complained that the "ordinary family regimen of modern society" was to blame for the decline of Christian morality in the capital. The article went on to exclaim that families, losing their connection to Catholicism, needed to raise Christian children and not just "simply procreate like animals."[25]

Scores of letters to the diocese from city inhabitants reveal the degree to which people thought about Catholicism and, more importantly, the extent of their concern for personal salvation. The handwritten letters, largely from lawyers and government officials, requested that the church accept a retraction of their oath to the anticlerical laws of the Reform. Thus the official secular posture of the state had created a tension among government workers who wished to remain loyal to their Catholic roots. Luis G. Córdova and Manuel Mendoza, both civil servants, wrote to repent their "allegiance to the laws of the Reform" and to proclaim that "now as always my beliefs impassion me to live always in the bosom of the church of Jesus Christ."[26]

Other state employees, like Demetrio Sodi and Jesús A. Vásquez, wanted to have their cake and eat it too. Representatives of Oaxaca's state council and the city's mayor, respectively, each petitioned for a "license" from the church to work simultaneously for the state and pay their allegiance to the church, an arrangement explicitly banned by the 1857 Constitution. Sodi in particular hoped to avoid "the scandal that has resulted for other [government workers] with faith." In both cases the bishop granted their wish as long as they pledged they "would not attack the laws, finances, and rights of the church or its authorities."[27]

Other supplicants confessed that they had purchased church property auctioned according to the Ley Lerdo. Juan Bautista claimed that he had been "ignorant of the business of disentailing and selling church buildings" and that he "had been tricked" by the government into purchasing a formerly church-owned house in 1872. Ten years later Bautista asked to sell it back to the diocese for what he had paid. In that same year Colonel Vicente Lozano wrote: "Wishing to ease my conscience as a Catholic, I admit to owning four houses that were the church's property but were disentailed due to the Reform Laws. I took advantage of these laws, buying [the houses] at a [government] auction." After declaring the shame that he felt for his actions, Lozano asked that church leaders pay him only what they thought was fair for the four houses.[28]

The intensity and pervasiveness of the reaffirmation to Catholicism underscore the importance of the church in the everyday lives of Mexicans during the Porfiriato. The rush by civil servants to repent their oath of allegiance to liberal doctrines exposed challenges to the state's secular modernizing agenda. Oaxaca state and capital employees could not simply relinquish their ties to the church in favor of a liberal government. Instead, they found ways to bridge their religious convictions and their civic duties.

The Díaz regime needed to find a way to to include the Catholic Church in its visions of modernity. How could the state mobilize the powers of the Catholic Church to meet its own political and economic ends? For Oaxaca, the response came in the person of Archbishop Eulogio Gillow and his connection to the city's workers.

GILLOW: THE PORFIRIAN COMPROMISE

On November 18, 1887, Gillow entered Oaxaca City for the first time as its new bishop. In a symbolic gesture before his official reception, Gillow stood on the ruins of the chapel of San Juan de Dios (neglected during the decades of anticlerical governments) and proclaimed to an enthusiastic crowd of civic and ecclesiastical dignitaries his intention to restore the building. Listening among the other government officials in the audience, Miguel Castro, former governor of Oaxaca and a strong supporter of the Reform Laws, must have taken notice of this historic moment of rapprochement between the government and the Catholic Church.

Like his municipal government contemporaries, Gillow radically restructured the church's infrastructure and administration. In addition to rebuilding and newly adorning many of the city's churches, Gillow conducted extensive pastoral visits (*visitas pastorales*) in the towns and villages of the state, during which he claimed to have administered the sacrament of confirmation to over six hundred thousand Oaxacans.[29] In his first decade as archbishop, he expanded and rationalized the administration of the church. For example, in 1901 he institutionalized regular meetings with the clergy of the diocese. Clergy residing in the city were to meet with him on the first and third Monday of every month to discuss church matters; those outside the city would meet with Gillow's vicar (*vicario foraneo*). Additionally, Gillow required clergy to take an examination every five years in order to renew their registration in the capital.

Gillow reinforced this administrative modernization with the publication of two church periodicals. In January 1896, after the archbishop installed printing presses in his newly created Sociedad Protectora de la Buena Prensa, the editor, Lorenzo Mayoral, printed the first copy of the newspaper *La Voz de la Verdad*. As the state's official paper, it connected Oaxaca's Catholics with their international brethren with articles like "Bismarck and Catholicism" and "Baptisms in China" as well as provided information on church activities throughout the region and in the capital city. In addition to publishing daily news items, *La Voz de la Verdad* editorialized about the "immorality of the masses" and the "yankeeization" of Mexico by Protestants and entrepreneurs from the United States. *La Voz* also ran a weekly column entitled "For Ladies," which prescribed "proper social conduct" for the city's female population.[30] Most important was the newspaper's support for Díaz and his policies. As noted above, *La Voz de la Verdad*, along with other Mexican Catholic presses, praised the Porfirian government's efforts at promoting peace and prosperity in the country. With a correspondent in Mexico City by 1908, it claimed a weekly run of more than four thousand papers.

In March 1901 Gillow published the first edition of *El boletín oficial y revista ecclesiástica de la provincia de antequera*, which promoted the "uniformity of doctrine and the unity of religious and social action among the state's clergy."[31] Accordingly, the publication served as a kind of trade journal for local clergy, emphasizing doctrinal and social renewal and clarity. In tandem, *La Voz de la Verdad* and *El Boletín* highlighted Gillow's effort to modernize his diocese's infrastructure and to mediate church-state relations.

In addition to the rhetoric of the church's official publications, Gillow's relationship with the municipal and state governments was varied, but ultimately positive throughout the period. Despite the often belligerent official attitude of the government and the restrictive Reform Laws toward the Catholic Church, Díaz, Oaxaca's state governors, and city officials maintained amicable, if not openly cordial, relationships with Gillow and granted him concessions over property and church powers. Gillow's ties with General Martín González (1894–1902) and Emilio Pimentel (1902–11) represent the two, albeit moderate, extremes of relationship he had with the state's governors.

Despite vehement objection from some of his clergy, including his would-be successor, Othón Núñez, Gillow maintained a friendly relationship with Governor González, on one occasion inviting the governor to celebrate his birthday. As he did on many matters, Gillow corresponded with Díaz following González's inauguration. The archbishop assured the president that church-state relations in Oaxaca would continue to contribute to the state's progress: "I do not doubt that in this new period that is beginning I will have the fortune to preserve the best relations with the civic powers, and united both of us have the intention, each in his own sphere of influence, to work for the progress and benefit of the state."[32]

In contrast, Gillow and Emilio Pimentel did not profess to be friends. In fact, they had officially met only once, when Pimentel arrived to the city to assume the governorship. Pimentel's close friend, Ramón Ramírez de Aguilar, the *jefe de hacienda* of the neighboring state of Puebla, lamented this lack of contact. He noted that with previous governors Gillow always had maintained a friendship and that Pimentel's predecessors had "never had reason to complain, because [Gillow] had always kept within his own sphere of power, never wanting to meddle in that of the government's."[33] Pimentel blamed the distance between himself and the archbishop on a state tax levied on church properties. Apparently Gillow viewed the tax as an unfair fiscal imposition. Pimentel maintained that he had been just upholding the law. Nevertheless, despite this disagreement, Gillow and Pimentel continued to correspond on official matters and avoided confrontation.

Although the church expansion projects of the archbishop provoked criticism among members of the city's government, the two groups usually came to an amicable settlement of differences. In one example of his ability to circumvent conflict, Gillow managed to convince the city to remove a tax on work done on the border of the cathedral's property. In June 1903 city officials attempted to enforce legislation that required a license for a worker constructing a tombstone near the cathedral's atrium. Gillow intervened and argued that, despite the government's assertion otherwise, the atrium was not a public space but belonged instead to the church, as guaranteed by Article 14 of the federal constitution. Municipal authorities agreed with Gillow's argument and released the worker from any licensing obligations.[34]

Gillow's unique educational and business background, along with his close personal ties to Díaz and other members of the federal government, made him an excellent intermediary between the state capital's church and government leaders. He would deftly utilize this unique position to transform the relationship between the city's artisans and the church.

OBREROS CATÓLICOS AND THE NEW CAPITALIST ECONOMY

In 1910 Mexico's wage-labor class reached 15 percent of the population. This was not the case in Oaxaca, where most of the state's laborers continued to work as rural peasants. For example, of the 11,605 textile workers in the state, only 570 worked in factories; the rest labored as individual producers in small cottage industries selling their wares at regional markets. Independent artisans or proprietary producers dominated the capital city's worker population.[35] Despite the arrival of the Mexican Southern Railway and the development of the port at Salina Cruz, the predominance of indigenous artisans in the state impeded the development and expansion of regional markets. Unlike in states in northern Mexico, industrial modernization in Oaxaca never flourished. Consequently, Gillow's relationship with workers in Oaxaca City focused on people working in a variety of crafts as independent producers in jobs that, with little variation, had existed since the colonial era.

Only a small percentage of the region's workforce labored in factories in the city and the Valle Central. Textile factories in San José and San Agustín in the districts of Etla and Xía in the Sierra Juárez, as well as beer, cigarette, and shoe factories in Oaxaca City, employed all told a mere 1,360 workers at their highest point at the turn of the century.[36] Most laborers in the capital worked in

small, independently owned shops with a handful of people, mostly close relatives. A comparison of municipal census records from 1875, 1895, and 1901
bears this out. Through those Porfirian years, little change occurred in the
makeup of the city's artisan population. Positions included hat, tortilla, and
candle makers; copper, iron, and brick workers; and street cleaners, day laborers, servants, water carriers, and tailors. Some new occupations emerged during the period, such as photographer and telegraph and railroad worker.[37]

Although Charles Arthur, the United States consular agent in Oaxaca City,
was always quick to recommend the hardworking and inexpensive workers of
the state, he neglected to mention to his foreign colleagues that they also
worked under deplorable conditions.[38] Divina Providencia, a group of small
business owners petitioning the city for a change in taxation regulations, described the state of the capital's workforce: "The workshops are in a grave state,
almost to the point of complete deterioration . . . [worsening] the already em-
barrassing condition of the working class, who in place of deserving protection from the authorities to guide them through the rough path of their daily
needs, feels weakened and afraid, unable to provide the onerous contribution
of daily bread to their families."[39]

In addition to sharing this difficult position as members of the workforce,
women laborers suffered an unequal wage when compared to their male counterparts. Moreover, business owners permitted women to work in only a
handful of trades: in addition to jobs as clothes washers and bakers, women
worked in the capital's small hat, cigar, and match factories. Their wages most
closely approximated those of men at La Sorpresa cigar factory. There they
earned a daily wage of 40 centavos to the men's 50 (both barely enough to afford the city's growing rent and food costs). In most other industries women
received only half of what their male coworkers were paid for the same
amount of labor.[40] This gender inequality persisted throughout the state.[41]
Women in the city's workforce also exemplified other trends in capitalist expansion. The introduction of women workers into small factories and the
deskilling of labor were both examples of economic modernization beginning
to appear throughout Mexico.

Combined with government and church pressure, this historically entrenched, highly differentiated workforce undermined the organizing power of
labor unions in the city.[42] Instead, worker groups looked to the various mutual
societies (in existence since the colonial era as *cofradías*) in the capital for social
and financial support. In the last decades of the nineteenth century, mutual societies began to flourish throughout Mexico. The societies functioned largely
as patronage organizations headed by elite politicians and entrepreneurs. They
organized job training, basic education, recreational activities, and occasionally
emergency funds for their members.

THE *RERUM NOVARUM* AND THE
CÍRCULO CATÓLICO DE OBREROS DE OAXACA

In 1891 newspapers throughout Mexico published the encyclical of Leo XIII, *Rerum Novarum: On the Condition of the Working Classes*, issued that same year, which had emerged from the Vatican's concern over industrialization and new class relations.[43] Church leaders feared that the forces of capitalism, devoid of Christian influence, would cause "chaos, greed, revolution, and great suffering among the masses." Consequently, *Rerum Novarum* evaluated the socioeconomic climate at the end of the nineteenth century as much as it prescribed social action.[44] Yet the Catholic Church, still reeling from anticlerical reforms earlier in the century, realized that it could recover some of its lost power by aiding the state's developmentalist projects and establishing social programs for the working poor. In the case of Oaxaca, creating a "new political religious order," Gillow augmented aspirations to political power with social action; however, this did not mean that church leaders removed themselves from state and national politics. On the contrary, ecclesiastical elites worked within the Porfirian system to gain concessions. The formation of Catholic workers circles aided reconciliation with the state and increased the institutional status of the church.

Unlike in Europe, where socialist movements had already taken hold, in Mexico, according to historian Manuel Ceballos, *Rerum Novarum* "awoke the consciousness of Catholics to social problems."[45] During this period of rapid industrialization, Catholic workers circles sprouted up throughout Latin America. Circles formed in response to the *Rerum Novarum* in places like Buenos Aires and Bogotá, where the Jesuit-sponsored circle, in addition to providing a bank, school, and other social services, supplied a constituent base for the governing Conservative Party.[46]

Archbishop Gillow and Oaxaca's Catholics followed this larger regional trend. Gillow's most significant contribution to church-state reconciliation came with an intervention in the city's artisan community: his creation of the Círculo Católico de Obreros de Oaxaca (Catholic Workers' Circle, CCOO) in 1906. The CCOO served as an institution where workers encountered the imbricated modernizing designs of both the Catholic Church and the Mexican government. Limited in their options and familiar with the long-standing existence of guilds and mutual aid societies, workers in Oaxaca City turned to the CCOO for financial and social benefits. At the same time, however, the CCOO not only supported the city's artisan population, but also acted as a powerful organizational tool for the church (and city government) to educate and discipline that population. The Círculo emerged from a multinational effort by the Catholic Church and secular elites to become more involved in a growing industrialized world. In Mexico, as in other countries in Latin America, the church combined its commitment to the living and labor conditions of workers with its efforts to support the developmentalist projects of the government.

In Oaxaca City, Gillow's Círculo Católico de Obreros de Oaxaca not only became the dominant labor organization in the capital but also epitomized the archbishop's intermediary position between the social advocacy of the Catholic Church and the economic projects of the Mexican state. The CCOO was also part of a larger effort of Gillow's to discipline and order the church's laity through the creation of new brotherhood organizations throughout the state and cultivate fervent personal dedication to Catholicism and Rome's primacy.[47]

The impulse for a workers circle in Oaxaca City already existed prior to the founding of the CCOO. In 1885 church and secular elites in the state capital had founded a predecessor to the CCOO.[48] Like other workers circles from the era, La Sociedad de Obreros Católicos sought to "moralize workers" through Christian teachings and social and financial support. In its second year of operation the society united four other Catholic worker groups in the capital to form a consortium. Headed by prominent officials like former and future governors Francisco Meixueiro and Miguel Bolaños Cacho, the society's board strengthened the influence of the state over the church and workers.

La Sociedad de Obreros Católicos eventually gave way to Gillow's Círculo Católico de Obreros de Oaxaca. From its official beginning on New Year's Day of 1906, the CCOO epitomized the fusion of liberalism and Catholicism that marked the Porfiriato. The CCOO's cooptation of municipal workers contributed to the suppression of union activity and helped promote the state's modernizing agenda. On the opening night, hundreds of workers filled the theater in the Carmen Alto Convent, the headquarters of the Círculo. Jesús Acevedo, Juan Varela, Ramón Pardo, Federico Zorrilla, Wenceslao García, Nicanor Cruz, and other members of Oaxaca City's ruling elite also attended in support of the inauguration. These men and others received honorary membership in the Círculo and served on its board of directors.

The CCOO quickly became the dominant labor organization in the capital. Workers and *gremios* (trade unions) had little alternative but to join the Círculo if they wanted any support. In its first year, membership in the CCOO exceeded 1,000 workers, reaching a high of 1,781 in 1910, with workers joining it through their *gremios*. The Círculo represented twenty-eight of the capital's *gremios*, each with varying degrees of administrative organization. Some, like the carpenter, tailor, and shoemaker *gremios*, supported their own board of directors within the CCOO.[49] Others with smaller numbers of members joined as part of a larger conglomeration of *gremios*. The 1907 regulations of the CCOO sought to promote the ideals of "God, Morality, Work and Union," as its motto proclaimed. The regulations required that workers be at least fifteen years of age, be professed Catholics, and be of good standing in society. They also were obliged to attend meetings, carry out Círculo-related tasks, strictly adhere to religious teachings (i.e., the observation of Catholic sacraments), attend festivals, avoid vice (gambling, drinking, and inappropriate reading material), and pay monthly dues.[50] Above all, the circle and its workers would remain "uninvolved in any form of politics."[51] This last stipulation was congruent with the general stance of the Catholic Church during the Porfiriato, which advocated political detachment as a way to gain concessions from the state. In reality, of course, the reverse was true. Although removed from official party politics, Gillow took great pains to maintain his influential relationships with local and national politicians.[52]

Failure to comply with the CCOO's regulations would result in penalties for the members involved. Depending on the severity of the infraction, penalties could include fines and expulsion. In return for their commitment to the Círculo, however, members would enjoy access to religious instruction for themselves and their families, some financial support in case of sickness and death, assistance from a prisoner advocate if needed, and the right to deposit money in the Círculo's savings account.

On the one hand, Gillow and the directors of the CCOO purported that these benefits would shore up the "moralization" of the workers. On the other hand, working together, church and government leaders sought to foster disciplined and obedient workers in support of the expanding capitalist economy.[53] Therefore, the elite and middle class focus on reforming the hygienic, moral, and educational standards of the city workers was in fact an attempt to construct a modern work ethic.[54]

From the outset Archbishop Gillow spared no expense to make sure that his new organization supported a "moralizing" environment. Chapter 10 of the CCOO's regulations mandated the construction of a recreation center, named "Festive Chapel." Gillow spent 7,365 pesos on the center, a space free of "gambling and other vices," filled instead with chess tables, ball games, and a reading room with books on religion, industry, arts, and economy. The center provided workers access to dramatic productions, a choral society, and a gymnasium with showers, and it also served as the clubhouse for sports teams, including the baseball team, "los Gillow." Federico Zavala, CCOO director and city councilman, hoping to curb the "degenerative" appetites of popular groups, held regular "anti-alcoholism" classes for workers and prisoners at the center and city jail. According to one newspaper, an average of four hundred workers attended the center on Sundays, the only day it was open during the week (it was, of course, closed on workdays).

Gillow also encouraged celebration and revelry among the CCOO's members, but, as with the recreation center, only in Círculo-sanctioned events and spaces. He hosted an annual fiesta for CCOO members and directors at his mansion in the neighboring town of San Felipe del Agua, an event more spectacle than party. Like carnival, it allowed workers one monitored day in the year to engage in activities otherwise prohibited. Accompanied by live music, streetcars and carriages transported workers and city elites alike to Gillow's home. Nearly five hundred people feasted on barbecued meat and played sports. In an ironic disregard of official behavior, Gillow donated an entire cask of pulque "as a gift for his beloved workers."[55] As witnessed earlier, the Círculo often participated in municipal celebrations, joining parades down the capital's main streets. The CCOO's individual *gremios* would display brightly colored flags adorned with symbols of their trade as well as that of the Workers Circle. Other gala events included annual festivals in honor of the Círculo's patron saints, the Virgin of Guadalupe and Saint Joseph. Government elites intended the parades to serve as symbols of the city's advancement with all social classes united along the path of progress.

In another attempt to moralize workers, the CCOO established a savings bank to encourage the "modern quality" of thrift among its members. Chapter 3 of the Círculo's regulations stipulated that a mutual aid savings bank be established for the benefit of workers. The requirement adhered to the pope's entreaty in *Rerum Novarum*, encouraging workers to save some of their wages in the ultimate hope of purchasing and owning property. "Many excellent results will follow from this," the pope remarked. "Property will certainly become more equitably divided."[56] The directors of the CCOO had more modest aspirations. In order to combat the "slow but sure ruin" encouraged by the practice of usury in the capital, they actively promoted a volunteer savings program. Advocates for wage saving argued that workers poorly managed their money, often paying as much as 12 percent interest on loans. In times of a financial crisis, an editorial in *La Voz de la Verdad* claimed, working-class families were left with no other recourse but "begging and crime."[57] Gillow contributed 5,000 pesos of his own money to the workers' bank. CCOO members could voluntarily submit weekly quotas of 5, 10, or 20 centavos. Those depositing 20 centavos would receive 1 peso a day for two months in case of sickness. Members contributing 10 and 5 centavos a week would receive 50 and 25 centavos, respectively, in case of debilitation.[58] By 1910 CCOO members had saved 1,528 pesos in the mutual aid bank.

In 1907 a branch of the CCOO run out of the Iglesia de las Nieves started two specialized aid groups to promote savings. In the first group, the church started a mutual aid society for women workers called "The Needle." This branch society met every Sunday to "help women free themselves of usury." The Workers' Cooperative Society Union started that same year at the Iglesia de las Nieves, but focused on exposing artisans to the alleged social and cultural sophistication of the middle class. The group established a store next to the church—a "cooperative society of consumers"—where members could build credit by investing money to buy goods over time. In theory, the store, run by middle-class merchants, would beneficially influence the lives of workers as they "saw that their (middle-class) partners were better dressed, fed, and housed than they were." A review of the cooperative society in the *Oaxaca Herald* noted that "although some workers would continue to succumb to the [habits of] vice on Sundays, they could still [because of the cooperative society] maintain their family in an honest and decent manner."[59]

While state governor more than two decades earlier in 1882, Díaz had sought to aid the working poor by institutionalizing pawnshops in the city. Before the inauguration of the Monte de Piedad, the city's official pawnshop, dozens of unregulated pawnshops (*casas de empeño*) existed throughout the capital. Consistent with the modernizing trends of the era, Díaz attempted to control the *casas* by establishing regulations in 1881. Like all other new ordinances in commercial areas of the capital, these regulations required *casa* owners to pay regular taxes and obtain an annual license. Furthermore, an appointed municipal "expert" visited the pawnshops weekly in order to authenticate the prices of items for sale. The official pawnshops also helped channel funds to municipal coffers. By 1903 the four branches of Monte de Piedad together earned over 11,000 pesos for the city each year.

Oaxacan leaders hoped to develop a kind of fiscal morality among artisans and workers in order to foster a "culture of capitalism." Thus their attempts to improve the financial status of the city artisans—mutual aid savings banks and state-run pawnshops—also served a crucial interest of the state. In promoting the long-term benefits of saving and credit, these institutions prepared workers to be consumers—vital players in a growing capitalist economy. Although the low wages of Mexican workers prevented them from being a real economic force in the country, it is clear that the state and Catholic Church had more than thrift in mind when establishing these financial institutions. For example, in his work on nineteenth-century Bogotá, David Sowell demonstrates that in addition to providing much-needed funds for the city, savings banks also served to "instill 'progressive' thinking among the populace, which some leaders thought might help the region keep pace with other nations of the Atlantic community."[60]

THE PURIFICATION OF WORK

In addition to promoting a "culture of capitalism" and a respect for thrift, the CCOO encouraged a "proper" work ethic among its members. It presented prizes to *gremios* with the best record of attendance and good conduct. Editorials in the CCOO's official newspaper, *La Voz de la Verdad*, condemned the vices of truancy and tardiness. In reference to the spontaneously celebrated holiday San Lunes (Saint Monday), one editorial proclaimed to workers the virtue of fulfilling their duty: "Duty, regardless of its nature—be it spiritual or temporal—is sacred, and for that reason demands completion. . . . Saint Monday is one of the worst enemies of the worker because it reduces a day of work, of labor, into a day of idleness, dissipation, drunkenness, and crime!"[61]

The editorial continued by listing "great men" of Latin American and world history—Bolívar, Hidalgo, Washington, and Pasteur—as examples of those who, as a result of fulfilling their duties, have done "great things in the eyes of God and humanity." Other editorials similarly constructed a rigid dichotomy between the good of the workshop and the evil of the tavern. According to an officer of the CCOO, Trinidad Sánchez Santos, the notion of work as purification of the soul stemmed from the biblical story of Jesus as the worker who cleansed the world of its sins. In his speech before the CCOO's third-anniversary celebration, Sánchez was "breathless" at the "brutal ignorance" in which most working-class people lived. "What then," he asked, "is the duty of the Catholic worker in such dire circumstances? I do not hesitate to declare it: the struggle. But not the struggle against the legitimate interests of capital, which have sacred rights, but the struggle against error that is precipitating the working world into incalculably profound abysses."[62] Furthermore, argued *La Voz de la Verdad*, workers needed to be vigilant against the "tyrannical" influences of non-Christian unions like those in Germany and France. The paper warned CCOO members that bosses in these unions would start strikes without a care for the workers, and then pocket the benefits for themselves.[63]

Yet, despite the exhortations of Sánchez and others that workers harmoniously labor for the glory of capitalism, truancy and other work-related "vices" continued to plague modernizing elites. Workshop leaders complained to local newspapers that their workers were dishonest and arrived late. Popular groups often thwarted elite attempts to shape and regulate their lives.

Gillow's success at promulgating Social Catholicism and preempting worker unrest in the capital fell short in the surrounding districts. Despite his attempt to propose a branch of the CCOO in the textile factories mentioned above, workers, unhappy with the deplorable conditions and the imposition of a quota for religious festivals, went on strike. Gillow would later blame the workers' radicalism on the "evils of socialism, which influence the students and workers of diverse nations and disturb the social order and the tranquility of families."[64] The Vista Hermosa factory in San Agustín Etla witnessed the most unrest. In 1907 editors of *La Unión* chided the workers for proclaiming their allegiance to "our compatriots of Río Blanco," which the newspapers alleged to be their only reason for striking.[65] More, of course, had been at stake. The previous year had seen the bloodiest days of labor unrest in the Porfiriato. In one of many incidents, textile workers in Río Blanco, Veracruz, burned down the company's store as a symbol of their poor treatment and low wages. Federal troops sent by Díaz brutally resolved the strike by firing into a crowd of protestors. Workers in Oaxaca, forced into mutual societies by an absence of options and threatened by violence from the state, lacked the support to form unions. In 1912 President Madero received a series of reports indicating that only two unions existed in all of Oaxaca's twenty-six districts. All other listed labor organizations were legally sanctioned mutual aid societies. Significant union activity in the state would not appear until the 1920s with the start of organizations like the Confederation of Socialist Leagues of Oaxaca (CPSO).[66]

SEALING THE DEAL: THE FOURTH CATHOLIC CONGRESS

The conclusions reached by Archbishop Gillow and other local church leaders at Mexico's Fourth Catholic Congress, held in Oaxaca City in January 1909, signaled the apex of church support for the Porfirian goals of economic development. During the Mexican Revolution (1910–20) church-state relations would once again fall into disrepair. Yet this congress, the last one of the Porfiriato, highlighted the extent of the Catholic Church's resurgence during Díaz's reign. The previous three conferences, held in Puebla (1903), Morelia (1904), and Guadalajara (1906), had all focused their agendas on the development of Social Catholic action. The conferences marked the solidification of a new current of Social Catholicism in Mexico. Earlier in the Porfiriato, Catholic-supported labor organizations had developed in principal cities throughout Mexico.[67]

In addition to promoting the continuation of Social Catholic action in Mexico, the ostensible focus for the Oaxaca City congress was the "Indian problem." As in Mexico's other southern states (e.g., Chiapas and Yucatán), indigenous groups dominated Oaxaca's population. Church and state leaders searched for ways to transform this "backward, ignorant, vice-ridden, and unhygienic" population into productive workers and citizens.[68]

Yet this congress, unlike the previous three, focused on how to mobilize the resources of the church in support of the economic projects of the Díaz government. Whereas the preceding conference in Guadalajara had emphasized improving workers' wages and living conditions, its Oaxacan successor instead sought to reinforce the domination of landowners and industrialists. Conference participants, predominantly laypeople, including government representatives, published the conclusions of the conference, which amounted to 177 separate articles.[69] The conference report only nominally addressed issues of improving worker wages (articles 69 and 146). In a reversal of previous conference decisions, the report promoted company stores (*tiendas de raya*) as beneficial to both manager and worker and encouraged owners to make a profit from their sales (articles 81–83). Other issues that marked changes in direction from previous conferences included new forms of punishment for workers and increasing concessions to employers and landowners (articles 25, 26, 28, 91).[70] "These and other conclusions," writes Manuel Ceballos, "give the impression that the Oaxacan congress was attempting to establish and fortify the Porfirian order as the necessary norm."[71]

CONCLUSION

The revolution overthrew Díaz in 1911 and initiated the decline of the Catholic Church of Oaxaca's close relationship with the federal government. In 1914, three years after President Díaz had fled Mexico for Europe, Archbishop Gillow escaped to the United States, fearing persecution by the revolution's Constitutionalist "First Chief," Venustiano Carranza. Gillow had performed the marriage ceremony for the son of Carranza's enemy, General Victoriano Huerta.[72] In 1921 Gillow eventually returned to his diocese, where he attempted without success to rescue it from financial dilapidation. He died the following year. By that year the city's workers had switched their allegiance from the defunct CCOO to secular mutual aid societies and had, amidst a less restrictive institutional and governmental climate, started to join the city's first unions.

Limited in their alternatives, Oaxaca City's workers had turned to the Círculo Católico de Obreros de Oaxaca for much-needed social and financial support during the late Porfiriato. Unlike labor unions, however, the Círculo did not advocate to improve the low wages or harsh labor conditions of its members. Instead, the CCOO facilitated Archbishop Gillow's pact with Porfirio Díaz to discipline and inculcate "proper behavior" in the city's workers, behavior that included cultivating a culture of capitalism.

The efforts of Gillow to reform and rationalize Oaxaca's Catholic Church in conjuction with and support of Díaz's developmentalist plans reveal the extent to which the state's main religious institution played a fundamental role in the Porfirian project to modernize Mexico's workers. Furthermore, the case of Oaxaca's Porfirian Catholic Church provides a clear example of the religious dimension of the construction of modernity.

NOTES

Chapter opening image source: AHAO.

I dedicate this chapter to my father, Daniel L. Overmyer, a historian of Chinese religions. All translations are mine unless noted otherwise.

1. On the study of religion in the social scientific and historical literature see Patricia Pessar, *From Fanatics to Folk*: *Brazilian Millenarianism and Popular Culture* (Durham, NC: Duke University Press, 2004), 6–7.

2. In his work, Talal Asad criticizes scholarly conventions that assume a transition to secularism in modern societies. See his *Formations of the Secular: Christianity, Islam, Modernity* (Stanford, CA: Stanford University Press, 2003).

3. *Resúmen del primer censo general de habitants*, Secretaría de Fomento, Colonización e Industría. Dirección General de Estadística de la República Mexicana, 1896.

4. For a detailed discussion of the city and its encounter with Porfirian modernity see Mark Overmyer-Velázquez, *Visions of the Emerald City: Modernity, Tradition, and the Formation of Porfirian Oaxaca, Mexico* (Durham, NC: Duke University Press, 2006).

5. In a few studies, most notably Paul Vanderwood's recent narrative history of Porfirian-era Tomochic, the church, as both a cultural and political actor, plays a predominant role in the analysis. See *The Power of God against the Guns of Government: Religious Upheaval in Mexico at the Turn of the Nineteenth Century* (Stanford, CA: Stanford University Press, 1998). See also Edward Wright-Rios, "Piety and Progress: Vision, Shrine and Society, Oaxaca, 1887–1934" (Ph.D. diss., University of California, San Diego, 2004). My thanks go to Wright-Rios for comments on an earlier version of this chapter. Other works include: Pamela Voekel, *Alone before God: The Religious Origins of Modernity in Mexico* (Durham, NC: Duke University Press, 2002); Jorge Adame Goddard, *El pensamiento político y social de los católicos mexicanos, 1867–1914* (Mexico City: Universidad Nacional Autónoma de México, 1981); Jean-Pierre Bastian, *Los disidentes: Sociedades protestantes y revolución en México, 1872–1911* (Mexico City: El Colegio de México, 1989); Jean-Pierre Bastian, *Breve historia del protestantismo en América Latina* (Mexico City: Casa Unida de Publicaciones, 1986) and "Metodismo y clase obrera durante el porfiriato," *Historia Mexicana* 33: 39–71; Manuel Ceballos Ramírez, *Historia de Rerum Novarum en México, 1867–1931*, 2 vols. (Mexico City: Instituto Mexicano de Doctrina Social Cristiana, 1991) and *El catolicismo social: Un tercero en discordia* (Mexico City: El Colegio de México, 1991); and Laura O'Dogherty Madrazo, *De urnas y sotanas: El partido católico nacional en Jalisco* (Mexico City: Consejo Nacional para la Cultura y las Artes, 2001).

6. Gillow's father, Tomás Gillow, originally from Liverpool, England, was a wealthy jeweler, entrepreneur, and landowner. He introduced new agricultural equipment from England to Mexico and established Mexico's first agricultural society in 1860. Gillow's mother, Doña María J. Zavalza y Gutiérrez, was the ex-marquise of Mexico's Selva Nevada.

7. Manuel Esparza, *Gillow durante el Porfiriato y la revolución en Oaxaca, 1887–1922* (Tlaxcala: Talleres Gráficos de Tlaxcala, 1985), 169.

8. Gillow also worked closely with Thomas Braniff, the British manager of the Ferrocarril de México.

9. Díaz continued as the country's de facto leader during Manuel González's term as president.

10. Juárez did gradually permit some church leaders to return to their posts with lessened powers. Goddard, *El pensamiento*, 8–17, 95–96.

11. Esparza, *Gillow durante el Porfiriato*, 24.

12. Manuel Esparza, *Padrón de capitación de la ciudad de Oaxaca, 1875* (Oaxaca: Gobierno del Estado de Oaxaca; Documentos del Archivo 1, 1983).

13. In his detailed study of Oaxaca's Catholic Church during this period, Wright-Rios maintains that prelate Gillow and his closest adherents successfully implemented a local version of modern European Catholicism in Oaxaca City. He goes on, however, to explain that this was not the case outside the state capital. Mixed results ensued as indigenous villagers grafted long-standing local religious traditions onto the new structures and practices promoted by Gillow. See Wright-Rios, "Piety and Progress," esp. chap. 3.

14. Anthony Gill, *Rendering unto Caesar: The Catholic Church and the State in Latin America* (Chicago: University of Chicago Press, 1998), 32–36. Late nineteenth-century reforms among the Mexican Catholic Church closely paralleled reforms during the same period in Europe. See Frances Lannon, *Privilege, Persecution, and Prophecy: The Catholic Church in Spain, 1875–1975* (Oxford: Clarendon Press, 1987) and Ralph Gibson, *A Social History of French Catholicism, 1789–1914* (London: Routledge, 1989).

15. Voekel, *Alone before God*, esp. 1–16.

16. Although no government functionary officially attended the lavish celebrations, the mere fact that they took place in the nation's capital served to bridge the gap between church and state. For historical treatment of the Virgin of Guadalupe, see David Brading, *Mexican Phoenix: Our Lady of Guadalupe: Image and Tradition across Five Centuries* (Cambridge: Cambridge University Press, 2001) and Jacques Lafaye, *Quetzalcoatl and Guadalupe: The Formation of Mexican National Consciousness, 1531–1813* (Chicago: University of Chicago Press, 1976).

17. *La Voz de México*, 7 October 1899; and *La Voz de la Verdad*, 19 November 1899. Until the 1890s the Catholic press continued to challenge Díaz's attempts at reconciliation. The success of new policies as well as a burgeoning economy convinced editors of Catholic publications, however, to support the government, albeit with caution. See Ceballos Ramírez, *El catolicismo social*, 50.

18. Letter to Porfirio Díaz from Bishop Eulogio Gillow, 17 February 1888. Colección Porfirio Díaz, Mexico City (hereafter CPD), Legajo 0013, Caja 0004, Documento 001951.

19. Jorge Fernando Iturribarría, "La política de conciliación del General Díaz y el Arzobispo Gillow," *Historia Mexicana*, vol. 14, no. 1, 100.

20. The national ratio of people to churches was much higher at 1,211 to 1. Francie Chassen-López, *From Liberal to Revolutionary Oaxaca: The View from the South, Mexico, 1867–1911* (State College, PA: Pennsylvania State University Press, 2004), chap. 5, 31.

21. CPD, 1896; L 40, C 7, D 388.

22. On the day before the coronation, Canon Agustín Echeverría's "official" history of the Virgin of Solitude appeared in the *Oaxaca Herald*. The story tells of a

mule driver transporting goods from Veracruz to Guatemala "thirty years after the landing of Cortés on Mexican soil." As he approached Oaxaca City (then Antequera), he noticed a lone mule from another train alongside his own. After searching for the mule's owner at length and without success, the driver, "being a conscientious man," decided to turn it and its burden over to the authorities. Yet, before the driver could make it to the city, the mule collapsed. When the mayor arrived at the site he opened a package strapped to the mule, and inside was an image of the Virgin inscribed with the words "Our Lady of Solitude at the foot of the cross." According to Canon Echeverría, "The mule rose again, relieved of its burden, but then trembled and died." Oaxaca's bishop quickly came and delivered the miraculous Virgin to the capital. Over the centuries, people flocked to the Virgin to benefit from her reputed healing powers. In 1683 the city began construction of a church dedicated to the Virgin. In the next century, Augustinian nuns came from the state of Puebla to act as the statue's caretakers. *Oaxaca Herald*, 17 January 1909. The Virgin, on display at the Templo de la Soledad in Oaxaca City, continues to attract pilgrims and followers to this day. For a comprehensive discussion of the coronation see Wright-Rios, "Piety and Progress," chap. 4.

23. *Álbum de la coronación de la santísima Virgen de la Soledad que se verá en Oaxaca* (Oaxaca: Talleres de Imprenta, Encuadernación y Rayados de La Voz de la Verdad, 1911); *Boletín oficial y revista eclesiastica de la provincia de Antequera*, Oaxaca: La Voz de la Verdad, 4 April 1909 and 18 January 1910.

24. *Boletín oficial y revista ecclesiastica de la provincia de Antequera*. Oaxaca: La Voz de la Verdad, 15 March 1901 and 22 November 1908. These "official" reports also served to stake claim to the church's growing influence among the city's faithful.

25. *La Voz de la Verdad*, 1 June 1896.

26. Archivo de la Arquidiócesis de Oaxaca (hereafter AA), Diócesis, Gobierno, Correspondencia, 1876–1912, letters from 14 June 1876 and 13 July 1876.

27. AA, letters from 8 July 1876 and 22 December 1882.

28. AA, letters from 23 April 1882 and 22 March 1882.

29. Gillow spent thousands of pesos of his own money sprucing up the diocese. On the city's cathedral alone he spent 9,000 pesos for an ornate curtain from Rome, 5,000 pesos for candles from Paris, and an undisclosed sum for twelve bronze busts representing saints and church fathers. *Boletín oficial y revista ecclesiástica de la provincia de antequera*, vol. 5, no. 28, 1 October 1908. For a description of his journeys in the Oaxacan countryside, see Eulogio Gillow, *Reminicencias* (Mexico City: Imprenta del Sagrado Corazón de Jesús, 1919). It is important to cast a critical eye on Gillow's proclamations. Although he was responsible for much change in Oaxaca's church, he often portrays his success in a careerist manner, one that calls into question the veracity of his claims.

30. See Overmyer-Velázquez, *Visions of the Emerald City*, chaps. 4 and 5 for a discussion of the Catholic Church's attitudes on "proper" gender roles.

31. *Boletín oficial y revista ecclesiástica de la provincia de antequera*, 15 March 1901.

32. Eulogio Gillow to Porfirio Díaz, December 1894. Cited in Manuel Esparza, *Eulogio Gillow y el poder: La correspondencia privada como fuente de la historia* (Oaxaca: Carteles Editores, 2004), 15.

33. Ramón Ramírez to Eulogio Gillow, November 21, 1907. Cited in Esparza, *Eulogio Gillow y el poder*, 11.

34. AHMO (Archivo Histórico del Municipio de Oaxaca), Orden 03, Grupo documental Secretaría Municipal, Leg. 1903.3, Exp. 3, 1903.

35. I avoid the term "working class," because there did not exist a cohesive workers' consciousness or movement in the state capital. John Womack's term "proprietary producer" or "artisan" better describes the type of workers in Porfirian Oaxaca City. I am grateful to John Womack for his comments on an earlier version of this chapter.

36. Archivo General del Poder Ejecutivo del Estado de Oaxaca, Oaxaca City (hereafter AGPEO), Special data for the 1903 Universal Exposition at Saint Louis, MO, 1903, Fomento, Leg. 7, Exp. 13, 1902; Anselmo Arellanes Meixueiro, *Los trabajos y los guías: Mutualismo y sindicalismo en Oaxaca, 1870–1930* (Oaxaca: Instituto Tecnológico de Oaxaca, 1990), 46–53.

37. Esparza, *Padrón de capitación de la ciudad de Oaxaca, 1875; Resumen del primer censo general de habitantes*. Secretaría de Fomento, Colonización e Industría. Dirección General de Estadística de la República Mexicana, 1896; AHMO, *Padrón para elecciones*, Orden 03, Grupo documental Secretaría Municipal, Leg. 1901.11, December 1901; and AGPEO, Office of General Statistics, Industrial Statistics, Fomento, Leg. 37, Exp. 3, 1902.

38. National Archives II, College Park, Maryland (NAII), Oaxaca, Oax., Consular Posts, RG 84/Stack 35/Row 07/Compartment 02—Miscellaneous Record Book—Vol. 3: see letters from 12 and 29 December 1904.

39. AHMO, Orden 03, Grupo documental Secretaría Municipal, Leg. 1882.1, Exp. 1.

40. AGPEO, Office of General Statistics, Industrial Statistics, Fomento, Leg. 37, Exp. 3, 1902; AGPEO, Name, quantity, and value of products or articles of industry in the city of Oaxaca de Juárez, Fomento, Leg. 37, Exp. 3.

41. Francie Chassen-López, "'Cheaper Than Machines': Women and Agriculture in Porfirian Oaxaca, 1880–1911," in Mary Kay Vaughn, ed., *Women of the Mexican Countryside, 1850–1990: Creating Spaces, Shaping Transitions* (Tucson: University of Arizona Press, 1994), 27–50.

42. A weak and disorganized labor movement (hence vulnerable to employer domination) persisted throughout most of Mexico during the Porfiriato, especially in nonindustrial centers like Oaxaca. See Alan Knight, *The Mexican Revolution*, 2 vols. (Cambridge: Cambridge University Press, 1986), 1:431–32.

43. As we can see from the above quotation, the pope relies on tropes of nature and the body to argue for the "natural" harmony among social classes. Throughout the text, he describes a "natural" social order of class and gender, one that, according to him, requires divine intervention from the Christian God if it is to survive. This powerful motif adroitly fuses the Christian doctrine of stewardship with the immediate needs of social action and service. *Rerum Novarum* (On the Condition of the Working Classes, 1891): Encyclical of His Holiness Pope Leo XIII (New York: The America Press, 1936).

44. John Molony, *The Worker Question: A New Historical Perspective on Rerum Novarum* (Hong Kong: Gill and Macmillan, 1991), 2–3.

45. Ceballos Ramírez, *Historia de* Rerum Novarum *en México*, 123.

46. David Sowell, "Political Impulses: Popular Participation in Formal and Informal Politics, Bogotá, Colombia," 15–29; and James A. Baer, "Buenos Aires: Housing Reform and the Decline of the Liberal State in Argentina," 129–52, both in James A. Baer and Ronn Pineo, eds., *Cities of Hope: People, Protests, and Progress in Urbanizing Latin America, 1870–1930* (Boulder, CO: Westview Press, 1998).

47. Wright-Rios argues that "Gillow should be understood first and foremost as an important conduit and facilitator of militant modern Catholicism in Mexico." Wright-Rios, "Piety and Progress," 238.

48. For guidance, society founders also turned to the predecessor of *Rerum Novarum*, Pope Leo XIII's 1884 encyclical, *Humanum Genus*. In the earlier encyclical the pope argued that the best way to defend the Catholic Church against its secularizing enemies was to foster the growth of Christianity among the working class.

49. The *gremios* represented builders, potters, quarriers, carpenters, tanners, shopkeepers, copper workers, cart drivers, deliverymen, sculptors, blacksmiths, tinsmiths, printers, plasterers, gardeners, soapmakers, general laborers, musicians, painters, bakers, silversmiths, watchmakers, tailors, hatmakers, saddlers, weavers, shoemakers, and a group of assorted workers.

50. Undoubtedly inappropriate reading material meant the newspaper and propaganda issued by the city's Protestant community.

51. *Reglamento del Círculo Católico de Obreros de Oaxaca* (Oaxaca: La Voz de la Verdad, 1907).

52. In 1909, as part of a resurgence of national political involvement, which included the construction of new schools and churches, the holding of national conferences, and the publishing of periodicals, the Mexican Catholic Church formed the National Catholic Circle (CCN). The CCN imitated contemporary European political parties and involved itself in the growing Mexican electoral crisis. In 1911 the CCN became the National Catholic Party, the predecessor of the National Action Party, or PAN—the party of president Vicente Fox Quesada.

53. For Gillow and Oaxaca's church leaders the CCOO also, and perhaps most importantly, functioned as one of the many new religious associations and sodalities established during the Porfiriato and meant to rally the state's Catholics around the revitalized church. See Wright-Rios, "Piety and Progress," chap. 5.

54. William French, *A Peaceful and Working People: Manners, Morals, and Class Formation in Northern Mexico* (Albuquerque: University of New Mexico Press, 1996), 36 and 67–68.

55. Pulque is a frothy-white alcoholic drink made from the fermented juice of the agave cactus. *La Voz de la Verdad*, 24 June 1907.

56. *Rerum Novarum*, 26–27.

57. *La Voz de la Verdad*, 18 August 1907.

58. These deposits and benefits were significant considering that workers earned an average of 3 pesos per week.

59. *Oaxaca Herald*, 10 March 1907.

60. David Sowell, "La Caja de Ahorros de Bogotá, 1846–1865: Artisans, Credit, Development, and Savings in Early National Colombia," *Hispanic American Historical Review* 73:4 (1993): 617, 623, 635.

61. AHMO, Orden 22, Grupo documental Biblioteca, Annual message read by Governor Emilio Pimentel, 1904.

62. Trinidad Sánchez Santos, *El obrero católico ante el socialismo revolucionario. Discurso ante el Gran Círculo Católico de Obreros, celebrado el día 20 de enero de 1909 en la Ciudad de Oajaca* (Oaxaca: La Voz de la Verdad, 1909).

63. *La Voz de la Verdad*, 30 August 1908.

64. Esparza, *Gillow durante el porfiriato*, 86.

65. *La Unión*, 14 July 1907.

66. Ruiz Cervantes and Arellanes Meixueiro, "Por los orígenes del movimiento obrero en Oaxaca," 385–86.

67. The central cities included Guadalajara, Mexico City, Morelia, Leon, Aguascalientes, and Zamora.

68. *Oaxaca Herald*, 31 January 1909.

69. In the first three congresses only a few laypeople attended. By contrast, the Oaxaca conference included seventy-eight laypeople out of ninety total participants.

70. The conclusions of the conference are published in the *Boletín oficial y revista ecclesiástica de la provincia de antequera*, May, June, and July 1909.

71. Ceballos Ramírez, *El catolicismo social*, 227.

72. Francisco José Ruiz Cervantes, "Carlos Gracida, los primeros años difíciles: 1914–1919," *Esbalones* No. 1, January–July 1991, 34.

8

Rights, Rule, and Religion: Old Colony Mennonites and Mexico's Transition to the Free Market, 1920–2000

Jason Dormady

Poster Advertising Patron Saint Festivities in Ixtlán, Oaxaca, 1902. Produced on thin colored paper, posters such as this were plastered on walls to announce the schedule of religious and celebratory activities. The poster reveals recent innovations in local religious institutional culture designed to ensure greater orthodoxy in Oaxaca. Instead of mentioning the town's traditional brotherhoods, it stresses the role of two new Catholic associations closely controlled by the clergy, the Apostolates of Prayer and of the Cross.

In 1989 the Partido Revolucionario Institucional (PRI), Mexico's entrenched ruling party, made much of the connection between human rights and the rule of law when amending the 1917 Constitution to remove restrictions on religion and clerics. Mexico could not advance, said the party technocrats, as long as a gap existed between the laws on record and the state's enforcement of those laws. President Carlos Salinas de Gortari (1988–94) later commented on this situation, writing, "domestic changes allowed us to promote initiatives in favor of changes . . . related to one of the fundamental human rights, the freedom of religious belief. A country could not be truly democratic without out full recognition of that liberty."[1] There was no longer room in modern Mexico for *obedezco pero no cumplo* (I obey but do not comply)—the practice of writing laws but unofficially (and at times officially) disregarding them. The rule of law became the order of the day regarding freedom of worship, and all Mexicans, regardless of religion or clerical status, could now freely (and at times be required to) participate in the state regardless of previous exclusions.

But what of Mexicans whose religious liberty relied on the disregard of the law and strict separation from the state? Through either explicit agreements or tacit acceptance postrevolutionary Mexico had allowed a broad range of religious practices to flourish in the hidden niches of its loosely crafted empire. In the case of the Old Colony Mennonites a signed agreement between the colonists and the state guaranteed exemptions from Mexican law and protection from state supervision. However, with the modernizing reforms of Salinas de Gortari, groups such as Mexico's Mennonites lost the protection previously afforded them. The group that had sought shelter in the shadow of the Mexican Revolution found the rules suddenly changed, and rather than protect religious rights, the enforcement of the law led to their violation.

MODERNIZATION OF CHURCH/STATE RELATIONS

In 1991, President Salinas de Gortari's press secretary issued a full-color English-language booklet called *Carlos Salinas de Gortari—A Portrait*. The publication appeared during the debate over the North American Free Trade Agreement (NAFTA) and Mexican attempts to persuade the U.S. Congress to support the treaty. NAFTA was to be Salinas's crowning triumph, modernizing Mexico via free market economics. The task for Salinas de Gortari, then, was to convince the U.S. Congress, with all of its preconceptions of Mexico's backwardness, that his nation was indeed a modern state and a viable economic partner for the Colossus of the North. One token of that worthiness that Salinas de Gortari and the technocrats of the PRI chose to focus on was the rule of law and the observation of religious human rights. "Salinas de Gortari has stressed that national modernization will only be achieved according to law because 'it is the law that warrants change in our political and economic life. . . .' Thus, the President has assumed the commitment to reaffirm the rule of law by means of strict constitutional principles."[2] Enforcing laws would inspire investor confidence and progress, and where laws failed to meet "the new reality of Mexico,"[3] the rule of law demanded they change. The regulations governing the relationship between religions and the state fell in that category. Nevertheless, Mexico had not always been so relaxed regarding this relationship.

Mexico's revolutionary constitution of 1917 drew heavily on nineteenth-century liberal traditions to impose tight restrictions on religion. These controls included limiting the number, nationality, and political participation of clergy, minimal church property ownership, and bans on religious education. While such restrictions had been largely ignored during the tenure of President Álvaro Obregón (1920–24), they were strictly enforced under the presidency (1924–28) and later political influence (1928–34) of Plutarco Elías Calles. Calles firmly rejected the participation of religious organizations, particularly the Roman Catholic Church, in politics. In spite of the revolutionary credentials of many devout Catholics, Calles implacably opposed religious education and public ceremony to the point of passing laws in 1926 to enforce the provisions of the 1917 Constitution.[4] Devout Catholics rose in rebellion, and the ensuing violence led to a bloody insurgency known as the Cristero War (1926–29) as well as the stimulation of militant Catholic political opposition.[5]

After a 1929 deal between the Mexican state and the Catholic Church as well as the softening of the state's stand on religion by conservative president Manuel Ávila Camacho (1940–46), backroom deals flouted constitutional provisions and the rule of law. Preserving constitutional restraints on paper allowed the Catholic Church to function in Mexico while the state's legal sword of Damocles hung ready in case the church ever posed a threat.[6] While these unconstitutional side deals largely involved the powerful Catholic Church, the presence of yeshiva schools as well as Mennonite, Mormon, and mainline Protestant schools shows the state's flexibility regarding non-Catholic religious entities. By 1988, the reality of religious organizations in the national life moved Salinas de Gortari to modify the anticlerical clauses of the 1917 Constitution.

In 1989 the assistant to President Salinas, José Córdoba Montoya, began drafting modifications to the 1917 Constitution. Using the French, Polish, and U.S. Constitutions as models, Córdoba Montoya sought a balance between religious separation and participation in politics by clerics.[7] The only way that Salinas saw to ensure such human and civic rights was to eliminate the informal ties that linked both the religious and antireligious under the banner of the ruling party.[8] "Things in Mexico are going to change," Salinas told newsmagazine *Tiempo* in June of 1990. "We will confront new threats to human rights regardless of where they come from. Society and the state both demand the rule of law."[9] Yet not everyone in Mexico was crying out for the intervention of the state and the rule of law to protect their religious liberties. In fact, for some groups the expansion of the modern state meant yet another blow to religious freedom.

MENNONITES AND THE REVOLUTIONARY STATE

Mennonites in Mexico are a cultural curiosity that has piqued the interest of writers and scholars intrigued by the perceived oddity of Northern Europeans speaking German in a land of Indians and mestizos. Cast out of Catholic Holland as heretics and driven to Poland, Prussia, Russia, and finally to Canada, many Mennonites finally settled in the postrevolutionary, nationalist, anticlerical, traditionally Catholic nation of Mexico. The Mennonite tale—from Holland to Chihuahua—is a grand epic, but it also illuminates key aspects of modern Mexican history.

Mexico's northern state of Chihuahua lay devastated by 1920. Not only had thousands perished or fled due to the revolution between 1910 and 1920, but thousands more died in 1917 as the Spanish Flu swept across the desert state. In addition, torrential rains and flooding had combined with depopulation and rampant banditry to reduce Chihuahuan agricultural productivity by three-fourths.[10] Mexico's desire to rebuild Chihuahua, however, was not the only reason for seeking colonists.

Mexico also fretted that its largest state's border with, and ties to, the United States made postrevolutionary Mexico vulnerable. The United States already had a history of seizing Mexican possessions and military adventurism on Mexico's borders. Mexican president Sebastián Lerdo de Tejada (1872–76) commented on the position of Chihuahua under these circumstances by saying, "Between weakness and power—the desert."[11] Though the desert had initially served as a valuable buffer zone for Mexico, under Mexican president Porfirio Díaz (1875–1911), U.S. and British investment in that arid, sparsely populated region grew to formidable railroad and land holdings as well as agricultural and commercial ties. Linked to the United States and the rest of Mexico, the north was no longer an isolated buffer zone. Between 1877 and 1910, Chihuahua's population rose by 227 percent (including fifteen thousand U.S. citizens). Historian Friedrich Katz even calls the northern Mexico of that era "one of the most 'modern' regions of Mexico."[12] With proper supervision, argued the Porfirians, the north could once more serve as an engine for the Mexican economy.

After the revolution the new government so feared invasion from the United States that it included provisions in its 1917 Constitution to prevent U.S. aggression. Article 27 prohibited ownership of property by foreigners within 100 kilometers of the international border. The last thing a weakened Mexico wanted was another Texas where U.S. citizens settled in Mexico and then called for annexation to the United States.[13]

Drawing on the Porfirian-era *1883 Law Pertaining to the Colonization and Demarcation of Uncultivated Lands*, the postrevolutionary administration of Álvaro Obregón began its own program to attract revitalizing non-U.S. immigrants and investment to northern Mexico.[14] Said Obregón in his 1920 election manifesto:

> For the development of the natural riches of my country, I propose to extend an
> invitation to all men of capital and enterprise, nationals and foreigners, who are

disposed to invest their capital in the development of the said riches, based on a spirit of equity, with the result that there will be obtained for our national treasury and for the workers who cooperate with the said capital, participation in the benefits which logically must accrue to each.[15]

One area of "natural riches" that he clearly intended to develop was agriculture. In 1919, while maneuvering for the presidency in Guadalajara, Obregón laid out his agricultural vision for Mexico. "In nations with so many products like ours, agriculture must be considered as the major source of riches for sustaining the government," declared the then–military leader. "We must conclude that it is imperative that only the amount of land needed to cover the pre-supposed basic consumption of this nation be dedicated to this class of products (beans, maize and wheat) and that the rest should dedicate itself to the exclusive cultivation of marketable products," said Obregón.[16] A pragmatic representative of Sonoran revolutionaries, President Obregón envisioned a streamlined market-based export farm economy, fueled by "men of capital and enterprise, nationals and foreigners." Highly productive "pequeños agricultores," or yeoman farmers, using modern machinery would propel Mexico into the better future of Obregón's dream. These farmers were to use agricultural techniques just like in modern Sonora and Sinoloa, where "no farmer uses a wooden plow" and their "modern systems of production and agriculture are true examples for the rest of the States of the Republic."[17]

Reflecting on Obregón's position, historian Jean Meyer said, "His main aims were national unity and national reconstruction, and he was to run the country like a big business."[18] "Big business" may be an overstatement, but Obregón's efforts eventually bore fruit, drawing more foreigners to Chihuahua than Porfirio Díaz had managed to attract in his thirty-four years of dictatorial rule.[19] Many of those immigrants imported by Obregón were the Old Colony Mennonites.

Seeking desperately for a new land in which to settle, the Old Colony Mennonites of Canada fit hand in glove with Obregón's vision for Mexico. Calling themselves the Altkolonier, the Old Colony Mennonites were a particularly conservative division of Anabaptist Protestants, shunning modern conveniences, military service, and state intervention in community affairs and education. However, in early twentieth-century Canada, increased state intervention in their religious affairs and discrimination toward their German language pushed many Altkolonier to seek a new land of religious liberty—one they found in Mexico.

In 1921, President Obregón announced his law on immigration in the Presidential Decree of January 27, 1921 (one day before a delegation of Mennonites arrived for a land hunting expedition in Mexico) and the Provisional Law for Concession of Exemptions to Colonists. In them, the Mexican government agreed to cover the cost of transportation of all equipment, furniture, and farm implements from the Mexican border to their destination and removed tariffs and taxes at the border. In exchange, the colonists needed to "certify" that they would "dedicate themselves to agriculture."[20] The traditionally agricultural Mennonites eagerly signed.

After touring several Mexican states, the Mennonites proceeded to Mexico City where they met with A. I. Villareal, the minister of agriculture and development, and entered into negotiations with President Obregón. Though Obregón was anxious to persuade the Mennonites to settle in his nation, he was also "at first reticent [sic] to endorse the clause referring to sectarian schools and the exclusive use of German."[21] When the Mennonites explained that they could not settle in Mexico without those exemptions, the chief executive relented and issued a letter known as the Privilegium. In part, it reads:

1. You are not obligated to military service.
2. In no case are you required to make oath. [sic]
3. You have the most far-reaching right to exercise your religious principles and the rules of your church, without being in any manner molested or restricted.
4. You are entirely authorized to found your own schools, with your own teachers, without the government in any manner obstructing you.
5. Concerning this point, our laws are most liberal. You may administer your properties in any way or manner you think just, and this government will raise no objection if the members of your sect establish among themselves economic regulations which they adopt of their own free will.

It is the particular wish of this government to favor colonization by elements of order, morality, and toil, such as the Mennonites, and it will be pleased if the foregoing answers are satisfactory to you, in view of the fact that the aforementioned franchises are guaranteed by our laws and that you enjoy them positively and permanently.[22]

With this short official document, the Mennonites settled the Hacienda Santa Clara near the whistle-stop of San Antonio de los Arenales in the Bustillos Valley of Chihuahua. From the initial five thousand five hundred settlers in 1922 at the Santa Clara Colony, the population grew and congregations split until they were occupying colonies in Chihuahua, Durango, Zacatecas, Campeche, Coahuila, and Tamaulipas by 2000.

The benefits of the Mennonite presence were apparent after only one decade. Part of the Mennonite contribution to this agricultural-led export program was introducing high-quality draft horses and farm equipment, such as iron plows, to central Chihuahua. Eventually, the immigrants phased out draft horses in favor of animals suited to the desert climate. Nevertheless, the initial introduction of high-grade equipment paved the way for improvements: By 1930 the state of Chihuahua, traditionally wedded to cattle production, now had the most farm machinery operational in Mexico outside of the breadbaskets of the Bajío and the Central Valley.[23]

In addition to introducing high-grade farm implements, the Mennonites also brought cash. Over the first years of colonization the Canadians brought in $4 million (U.S.) that they invested in land, equipment, and savings. This sort of investment stimulated bank growth, brought in non-Mennonite German colonists, and attracted others from northern Chihuahua and South Texas who invested in branch operations of gasoline, machinery, hardware, and lumber to meet the needs of the Mennonites and the growing non-Mennonite community.[24] Inevitably, that level of investment fed on itself, driving a population explosion. From around three hundred people in 1921, the small town of San Antonio de los Arenales (the locus of settlement) boomed until it became its own municipio (corporate municipality) in 1927 when the name was changed to Cuauhtémoc in the spirit of nationalism. By 1930 the town had a population of around nine thousand Mennonites and fourteen thousand Mexicans.

The Mennonites also started supplying hogs to slaughterhouses in Monterrey for direct export to the United States.[25] This contribution made Cuauhtémoc the leading swine producer in Chihuahua by 1935.[26] The colonists bolstered Mexican farming and ranching in other ways as well. By 1948, 96 percent of all oat production in the Mexican states originated with the Mennonites who had been oat growers in Canada. Not only did it serve as superior fodder for cattle and horses, but the rise of oat production also coincided with the 1940s effort by the central government in conjunction with the Rockefeller Foundation to fight hunger in general and encourage oat consumption as part of a "balanced" diet.[27] Indeed, nutrition was identified by the government in educational texts as the "most grave and urgent concern facing the government of the Republic."[28]

The Mennonites also aided the state in its push to increase dairy consumption. In 1929 a Mennonite of the Manitoba colony in Cuauhtémoc returned from working for cheese makers in the Mormon colonies of northern Chihuahua. After some initial failures, the Mennonites hit on a successful system and soon marketed their cheese through wholesalers in Chihuahua City and the Mormon colonies. By 1936, Mennonites had removed the middlemen and were directly marketing cheese all over Mexico. Because cheese was considered a luxury item in highland Mexico, the influx of affordable Mennonite cheese propelled the market forward with little effort on the part of the Mennonites.[29] Also, the Mexican demand for milk steadily increased by 0.9 percent per year until 1960, a favorable trend for Mennonite herders.[30]

The Mennonites benefited the local government as well. The boom in the Bustillos Valley area—from three hundred residents to twenty-three thousand in ten years—required a Herculean expansion of the local infrastructure. The Mennonites, however, took charge of building their own (as well as many public) roads, wells, streets, homes, and irrigation projects, relieving the government of those costs in a hope of ensuring that they not "owe" the state. It also added to their luster as the ideal immigrants and a model for the new Mexican.

The influx of immigrants also brought in hundreds of children. However, since the Mennonites took charge of the construction and conduct of their own schools, this was yet another obligation not put on the Mexican state. They also participated in community-wide work projects, such as water and roadwork, to benefit non-Mennonites in the surrounding area. They did all of this while still paying taxes to the state and national governments.

Such large-scale investment and growth meant one crucial thing for the local economy of Cuauhtémoc—jobs. For hundreds of Mexicans returning from the United States (either forced or voluntarily) during the Depression, the opportunity to find work in Cuauhtémoc was a great boon.[31] Educated Mexicans found work with the colonies as translators, sales representatives, or writers since many Mennonites refused to learn Spanish beyond basic phrases. The Mennonites relied upon the expertise and labor of less-educated Mexicans for the harvest of corn and beans and then leased the harvested ground out to the locals as pasture. This situation, however, created something of a patron/client relationship, reminiscent of the colonial and neocolonial hacienda economy.[32]

In this new patron/client relationship the Mexicans often got the upper hand. Geographer Harry Leonard Sawatzky describes the situation where the Mexican laborer worked for a Mennonite long enough to gain his trust and then asked for a loan. The laborers repaid the loan, but then later asked for a second loan, this one of more value. Thereafter the laborer defaulted on his patron and sought a new boss. While this may be reminiscent of pre-Revolution practices, the Mennonites, whose religious culture made them eager to forgive and reluctant to seek revenge, seldom acted against the defaulting person. Yet because of their early need for labor and the scarcity of that resource, the Mennonites repeatedly fell victim to such practices.[33]

This picture of Mennonite settlement appears, at a glance, to be a near utopia for the central government: colonists with no political position and no disposition toward crime and violence revitalized a marginally productive agricultural area, inviting further investment and settlement that led to a general state of prosperity. The government benefited from exports, foodstuffs, and taxes while the locals thrived on employment opportunities, an increase in market variety, and a growth in available goods and services. This cozy situation, however, hinged upon one very important point: the arrangement between the government and the colonists was illegal and unconstitutional. The Mennonites and their children's entire future hinged on good faith that Mexico would not enforce the provisions of its constitution and on Mexico's pattern of *obedezco pero no cumplo* that served as a shield for the Mennonite religious tradition.

Specific constitutional breaches that caused later tension between the state, Mexicans, and the Mennonites existed in the area of education, religion, civic duties, and land. In education, the Mennonite religious schools clearly violated Article 24 of the 1917 Constitution, which was an injunction against any sort of doctrinal discussion at school. They also ignored the mandatory promotion of participatory democracy and nationalism. The Obregón Privilegium also exempted the schools from the state inspection mandated by the same article.

Regarding religion, since Mennonite bishops were Canadian they violated Article 130's prohibition of foreign-born clergy. Mennonites also carried out religious marriages, which were not always registered as civil marriages. Furthermore the group refused to petition the secretary of the interior every time it needed to build a new chapel and provide the necessary blueprints and inventory of contents. Regarding citizenship, the children of the Mennonites born in Mexico became Mexican citizens (Article 30), but the "Privilegium" excluded them from the obligations of Article 36 such as National Guard service and voting in district elections. Their failure to participate in such should have invoked Article 38 and removed their rights of citizenship—an action that was never taken.

Finally, land ownership was an issue. The 1917 Constitution (Article 27) expressly regulates religious institution ownership of land and buildings and denies the acquisition of land for future use to parties administered by religious groups. The Mennonites operated a system whereby they held land and money for buildings, supporting widows and helping new married couples as a communal religious organization. Article 27 also forbids the foreign ownership of land unless authorized by the secretary of foreign relations, and gives wide-ranging powers to the states to pass and enforce land laws. Obregón violated all those constitutional principles by allowing Mennonite ownership. Most importantly, Article 33 states "no foreigner shall mix in the political business of the nation, in any manner." Simply by taking land that could have gone to Mexicans, the Mennonites stirred the pot of a long-standing political and social dispute that figured prominently in the revolution.

The government attempted to alleviate this tension about Mennonite land ownership by avoiding references to the Mennonites in widely circulated publications. For example, though the Mennonites participated in the development of the Durango/Canatlán agricultural region (the most advanced and prosperous after the Laguna area of Gómez Palacio—and the most ejidal), no mention of them is made in the extensive *Geografía del Estado de Durango* of 1929, while other ethnic agrarians are mentioned, including "españoles."[34] Historian Martina Will points out that while the colonization of the Mennonites was touted as a sign of the progressive Mexican state, the "Privilegium" those colonists received was not publicly published. According to one official, this was for "reasons of public order . . . so as not to awake jealousy in the Mexican campesinos."[35] Locally, the presence of the Mennonites provoked tensions with Mexican squatters and *ejiditarios* (communal landholders of state-sanctioned ownership), and the central government came down squarely on the side of the Mennonites.

Using the 1926 Law on Colonization, the Mexican state settled an agricultural colony in the Bustillos Valley near the Mennonites, only to see it collapse under severe debt and convert to an *ejido* to write off that debt.[36] Local activists then tried to expropriate land already cultivated by Mennonites, only to be met with state-sponsored brutality. In 1930, unknown gunmen assassinated agrarian leader Andrés Mendoza, a local farmer advocating the expropriation of Mennonite land. By 1932, twelve other agrarian leaders in the area followed him to the grave, bringing agrarian agitation in the Bustillos Valley to a near halt.[37] However, in an attempt to lessen the "danger" of the Mennonite presence and try to encourage more "mixing," the state opened thirty *ejidos* bordering the colonies.[38]

The arbitrary and controlled manner in which the state directed land reform is highlighted by another complaint registered by another foreign landowner. In January 1921, the same month and year that Obregón met with the Mennonites and granted them exemptions and land, he met with E. C. Houghton, a U.S. manager of the Corralitos ranch in Chihuahua. The purpose of Houghton's mission was to discuss why new squatters with no history of settlement on the land were expropriating that ranch. To Houghton, the president replied that he was "obliged to respect the sovereignty of States and the legal actions of all governors and would not . . . go against him unless he found that the Governor(s) of the Agrarian Commission of the State had exceeded their authority." Houghton later protested to the government that his land was unfairly targeted while "Mennonites from Canada were preparing to buy 'the very lands that were occupied by Mexicans.'"[39] Responding to such criticism, Governor Enríquez said that it was impossible for him to evict the squatters on the lands of the U.S. citizen since they had already built homes and begun cultivation. Nonetheless, the removal of squatters from Mennonite land was not an obstacle for the state or central governments then or later. The American ranch simply did not fit into the state vision of Obregón, while the Mennonite enterprises did.

Chihuahua was not the only center of Mennonite-ejidal disputes in Mexico. By 1924 the expansionist Mennonites had spread to Durango in the municipio of Canatlán and founded the Hague Colony. There, Mexican squatters occupied and planted 6,500 acres of colony land in 1935, then petitioned the state to have the land redistributed to them. In 1936, however, President Lázaro Cárdenas ordered the Mexican squatters off the Mennonites' land. The squatters tried once again in 1937, but the governor of Durango ordered the president of the municipio to halt the expropriation of the land after the central government contacted him and ordered a halt to taking land from Mennonites. Clashes in Durango occurred again in 1941 and 1947, with the Mexican squatters being "more or less gently dislodged" each time.[40]

Such disputes over land redistribution continued into the 1960s. In 1962, colonists in the La Batea Mennonite colony in Zacatecas found that Mexican squatters had planted corn on uncultivated land held in reserve and designated for expansion for future Mennonite families. The squatters had also done the same on the land of a neighboring hacienda and used that location as a base to farm Mennonite land. After complaints from the Mennonites, the neighboring hacienda owner destroyed the squatters' water pipes and had federal soldiers tear down their houses. The Mennonites then petitioned the state of Zacatecas to have the squatters removed, and after a short investigation, the governor sided with the Mennonites. It turned out that the squatters were ejidal landholders who were not farming their own ejidal grants because they had already leased them to the Mennonites in clear violation of Mexican law.[41] After leasing their land, the *ejiditarios* then squatted on the Mennonite property in the hopes of having the state expropriate the land, attempting to put themselves in the roll of landlords and designate the Mennonites as tenant farmers.

Even Lázaro Cárdenas (1934–40), known for his generous distribution of land to peasants, passed up opportunities to remove the Mennonites. The Land Law of August 1935 decreed that all land and buildings belonging to "churches" and "cults" should revert to the state. This law was supposed to supersede all other Mexican laws on land and property in the hands of religious groups. However, the Mennonites appealed to the German representative in Mexico City, Hugo Natus, and the Nazi consul arranged a visit for them with the president. That December the Mennonites were declared exempt from the new land law in presidential decree 6-330. In addition, he ordered the states to cease their inspection and closure of Mennonite schools and to respect the Privilegium set down by President Obregón.[42]

Not all cases of tension between Mexicans and Mennonites occurred in the nonviolent halls of municipal offices and the courts. As noted above, banditry was rampant in Mexico after the revolution as landless, armed gangs roamed the countryside. The situation was no different in the areas of Chihuahua and Durango where the Mennonites settled. Sawatzky and Will describe the banditry in Chihuahua and Durango as particularly tense during the 1920s when the central government still had not established a rule of law on the "frontier," as well as during the 1930s when the United States forcibly returned laborers to Mexico. In both Chihuahua and Durango, the Mexican government deployed troops to the area on behalf of the Mennonites. While this lowered the incidence of petty crime, armed bands started to group together with heavier weaponry to raid Mennonite settlements. After the particularly appalling murder of the entire Schellenburg family in 1933, troops received authority to act as judge, jury, and executioner in the field.[43]

When bandits again menaced Durango Mennonites in 1936, a delegation visited Lázaro Cárdenas in Mexico City. His reply came in a letter to the governor of Durango, Severino Ceniceros, in June of 1936. It reads in part: these "colonists constitute an important factor for the economic development of that State and to respect that fact with strict justice, it behooves you, with all rigor, to reprimand the aforementioned crimes and to mete out to the people and patrimony of the colonists the protection to which they have a right."[44]

The religious culture of the Mennonites, which required isolation and autonomy from the government, relied implicitly on the flexibility of the state and the flouting of Mexican law. The period following the Mexican Revolution was particularly fertile ground for such an arrangement when the economic interests of the state trumped the liberal and revolutionary desires of the rural citizenry—at least in this particular case. Such was the nature of the Mexican empire after the revolution when the struggle to solidify Mexico and Mexican culture was still being debated. The struggle to define Mexico in economic terms through the perpetuation of Porfirian notions of progress and productivity allowed the growth of religious cultural diversity beyond the traditional Catholic or folk Catholic definition of community. Because of the flexibility allowed the Mennonites due to their economic power, they survived in a niche sheltered from the prevailing ideological winds, be they anticlerical or antiforeign. However, when the protector of their religious culture shifted—namely, Mexico's economic policy—they were in for another trial of their faith.

FREE TRADE, MENNONITES, AND MEXICO

By 1988, Mennonites had settled across six Mexican states and counted a population of approximately sixty thousand people with a birthrate that doubled their population every eighteen years.[45] For many of those Mennonites, their space in Mexican society still depended on an informal and illegal agreement with the government reached over sixty years earlier. The constitutional changes and societal shift that Salinas proposed affected them profoundly, for if informal relationships with the state were prohibited, what would become of their exemptions from Mexican law and the separatism that the Old Colony Mennonites held so dear?

With the Salinas-era formalization of Mexican relations with religious groups, Mennonite exemptions from military service were revoked in 1990 for those born in Mexico. This shattered at least two extraconstitutional agreements made with the Mexican state. In addition to the Privilegium from the Obregón years, the Ávila Camacho administration, as part of its 1942 National Defense Decree, exempted the Mennonites from Article 31 of the Mexican Constitution calling for mandatory military service and registration for the National Guard.[46] In the 2000 Mexican Federal Code, the Law on Religious Association and Public Worship states that religious conviction "does not exempt in any case any citizen from fulfilling the laws of the country. No one can assert religious motives to avoid the responsibilities and obligations prescribed by the law."[47] This includes participation in the National Guard.

This military program, resembling U.S. Selective Service, opens up various state benefits to male Mexican citizens when they produce proof of enrollment in the system. One such service is the issuance of passports, a problem that concerns Mennonites in recent years due to their increased numbers working as migrant laborers in the United States and Canada.[48] Even "modern" Mennonites who had separated from the Old Colony groups that wished to cooperate fully with the state but who still desired conscientious objector status were affected, since Mexican law recognized no such status.[49] Apparently the push for religious human rights only went so far as to include the religious in the state, not exclude them from it.

Another significant change in Mennonite-state relations was the government's decision to bring Mennonite education under the control of states. Under the Salinas administration, the state set goals to modernize the education system because "it is the only way to increase competitiveness," meaning that children needed to be trained in educational competition and sports so they could develop the free market mentality of the new Mexico.[50] In 1992, Mennonite education fell under state supervision, and states like Durango and Chihuahua began to express concern about the quality of Mennonite education, if not Mennonite society as a whole. For example, in 1995, the state of Chihuahua issued a report, carried out by the Educational Services of the State of Chihuahua (SEECH), on the quality of Mennonite education. "Without the intention of being critical and negative," states the report, "looking at their daily life [the Mennonites] causes great wonder and even repugnance among civilized people." It goes on to state that such practices as public flatulence and clearing the nose onto the ground in public, as they do in the fields, is the result of "the lack of adequate education or anyone to teach them the good customs and norms that will help them live well with others and amongst themselves."[51] The duty of the state of Chihuahua, then, is to bring the Mennonites into a system that can assimilate them to societal norms. From paragons of progress to health and public safety threats, the Old Colony Mennonites have traveled a hard road in Mexico as their contribution to progress has expired.

By 2000 the transition to state supervision, however, was not complete and not all Mexicans were convinced that there was value in forcing Mennonites into the public school system. As one observer put it, the traditional schools covered all their own costs, and though the level of education was below state demands, "they are instructed by persons in the things that interest them."[52] By the mid-1990s the Mennonite schools had split into two divisions—traditional schools, run by the strictest remnants of the Altkolonier, and the modern schools, incorporated into the various state education systems but still based in Mennonite communities with only Mennonite students. This division, however, reflects a corollary fractionating within the very communities themselves and a shattering of the Old Colony structures.

Another blow to the Mennonites was the privatization and dismantling of Mexico's National Company of Popular Foodstuffs (CONASUPO) between 1988 and 2000. CONASUPO was the state entity that purchased agricultural products at subsidized prices and redistributed them to the public. Such an agency was a guaranteed buyer for many farmers, including the Mennonites, who were no longer large producers, no matter what their level of efficiency was.[53] During its existence CONASUPO purchased corn, beans, and wheat from the Mennonites.[54] The state company even had a specialized division dedicated to the purchase and distribution of milk—a major Mennonite product.[55] While high-volume production is usually a feature of private agribusiness purchasers, CONASUPO was a guaranteed market, no matter the volume of the production. Thus, as CONASUPO privatized and shut down purchasing centers, small producers lost this avenue for acquiring cash because few other buyers appeared for "inefficient" small farmers—a problem not limited to the Mennonites. Unfortunately, privatization of CONASUPO was not the only move to strike the Mennonites hard.

As previously noted, Mennonite rental of Mexican ejidal land gave Mennonite colonies access to land beyond their own overworked and overpopulated holdings. However, in July of 1992, the process of ejidal ownership was brought to a halt, allowing individual Mexicans to sell land, including to foreigners. While this step legalized what Mennonites had been doing for sixty years, it also allowed large agribusinesses to compete with the Mennonites for the arable land that *ejidos* occupied. Already land hungry due to their sky-rocketing population and lack of capital to compete with agribusinesses, many Mennonites had no choice but to become itinerant laborers within Mexico or migrant laborers in the U.S. or Canada like millions of other Mexicans, or leave Mexico permanently to farm in Bolivia and Belize. For those Mennonites who chose to remain as farmers, some became employees of large corporations, such as Cargill Grain Company, that dictate what seed they can use and lease land and modern equipment to them at inflated prices.[56]

When the rule of law, state efficiency, and economics met religion, education, and land, the Mennonites found themselves adrift in a world of global issues while trying to maintain local cohesiveness. As the Mexican government formalized relations with religious groups, it ended the informal agreements that had previously reserved a special place in Mexican society for the Mennonites. As the stresses of this new relationship contributed to the division of the community, many Mennonites emigrated from Mexico, abandoned their beliefs, or fell into poverty. Moreover, state efforts to streamline agriculture also moved the Mennonites to the fringes of Mexican society, along with other small producers. No longer privileged dynamos of imperial economics, the Mennonites descended into a new life as economic vagabonds.

While the new economies of Mexico and the United States exchange dollars and pesos across a new free trade zone, Mennonites use a more organic form of economic exchange—milk. Short on land, resources, and cash, many Mennonites have returned to a barter economy where they exchange milk for goods and services and wander the streets of Mexican cities, selling cheese, sausage, eggs, and bread when they have it, or just begging for change.[57] The last decade of the twentieth century saw a new chapter for the conservative Altkolonier Mennonites. At times, the quest for a new livelihood even brought Mennonites into the alternative Mexican economy of narcotics.

"More than 100 Mennonites are in prison for drug dealing, and that is only the tip of the iceberg," reported Jacob Funk, a radio producer with the Mennonite Family Life Network in Winnipeg, Canada, in the *Mennonite Brethren Herald*.[58] What Funk recognized in 2000, however, customs officials in Canada and the United States had discovered as early as 1989: Mexican Mennonites moving back and forth as migrant laborers to Canada are one of that country's leading importers of narcotics. Supplied by "a Mennonite family in Chihuahua," immigrants with dual citizenship load trucks with drugs, easily crossing with looser NAFTA standards, and move "an estimated 1,000 to 2,000 pounds of marijuana" into Canada each month, especially to the major migrant provinces of Ontario and Alberta.[59] The expanded Salinas/Bush "war on drugs" discovered that one of Mexico's key tourist attractions and rural icons was deeply involved in a "Mennonite Connection" of smuggling.[60]

Mennonites do not have to be involved directly with hauling the drugs to profit from the narcoeconomy of northern Mexico. In June of 2002 the Mexican attorney general's office uncovered an entire service industry of Mennonite machine shops that offer their services to smugglers. Charging from $1,200 (U.S.) for filling tires with marijuana to $7,000 for special compartments in motor vehicles, the Mennonites have used their welding and mechanical skills to act as craftsmen for the drug trade. These shops, made up of Mennonites working in family units, are often indistinguishable from the farm equipment repair shops that lie scattered around Cuauhtémoc, Chihuahua.[61]

Drug smuggling is just one example of societal change occurring among Mennonites in Mexico, even among those integrating into Mexican society. As more and more conservative Altkolonier flee to South and Central America, those left in Mexico are torn between tradition, modernization, and mixing with their Mexican neighbors. An April 2002 visit to a colony in Zacatecas by President Vicente Fox displayed the degree to which the Mennonites remaining in Mexico are now integrating with mainstream Mexican society. Lines of bonneted children singing in Spanish greeted the president, presenting him with a basket of cheese, after which a Mennonite Norteño band provided entertainment. "I am very proud," Fox told the crowd "of this variety of diverse origins that we have in our country—of this getting along in plurality."[62] Variety and diversity, it seems, are more welcome in Mexico as it becomes less "foreign."

CONCLUSION

Mennonites' settlement and their consequent history in Mexico are a natural extension of the pattern of governing power in Mexico, not an aberration. That Mennonite settlement violated Mexican constitutional norms in deference to economic concerns is perfectly in line with the Sonoran revolution, headed by the northern revolutionaries seeking to make Mexico an agricultural economic power. Furthermore, the Old Colony Mennonite condition of economic collapse, drug trafficking, and flight from Mexico reflect the establishment of constitutional rule of law—once again as a consequence of state economic policy.

Mexico is often portrayed as a victim of empires—Europe, the United States, and world systems of capitalism in general. But what of the Mexican empire? Joining dozens of cultures, agricultural systems, classes, and interests is an act of empire, and the act of welding that brought that empire together is the political history of Mexico. Augustín Iturbide, the first ruler of an independent Mexico, was not the last emperor to rule that land. With Mexico's great revolution, an elite circle of Sonoran leaders and revolutionary generals along with the official party they put in place pragmatically merged groups or played them off one another, making extraconstitutional concessions for the benefit of the central government. By trying to be all things to all sectors, the central elite kept a balance of power within their empire, trading favors for a monopoly on economics, violence, and power.

After the collapse of the economy in 1982 and the consequent ascension of the Ivy League technocrats in Mexico, certain members of the economic elite promoted the rule of law to encourage foreign investment so that Mexico would become an international player and the ruling party would receive the funds it needed to stay on top. President Carlos Salinas took the gamble. This meant that in some cases, groups previously exempted from supervision, such as the Mennonites, were made to conform to the new constitutional amendments. In other cases, it meant that the constitution had to change so that those groups would not be outside the formal reach of the state. The changing of this extraconstitutional norm in Mexico is the ultimate victory for the Sonoran revolution of centralized unification, affecting even the religious culture of Mexico. The shift to constitutional rule of law supplanted relativism as the new centralization.

The Mennonites' tale as told here is also a story that links all of North America in a great epic of modernity, religion, and empire. Driven from the nation-building project of the Canadian Confederation in the early twentieth century, the Mennonites sought refuge in Mexico, rejecting the United States as too assimilationist for their needs. Arriving in Mexico, they carved a niche in an informal society still struggling to define the national identity and codify *mexicanidad*. Unfortunately, as global economics reached deeper into the heart of Mexico, protection for the closed religious community faded. This time an alliance between the three North American powers called NAFTA placed Mennonites in a precarious position, moving them once more to seek refuge, most recently in the wilderness of Central and South America. How far, and how long, can they run?

NOTES

Chapter opening image source: AHAO, Folletería, 1900–10.

Unless otherwise noted, translations are by the author.

1. Carlos Salinas de Gortari, *Mexico: The Policy and Politics of Modernization* (Barcelona: Plaza y Janés, 2002), 257.
2. *Carlos Salinas de Gortari—A Portrait*, Presidency of Mexico, Office of the Press Secretary to the President (Mexico City: Talleres Gráficos de la Nación, 1991), 22.

3. Fernando Serrano Migallón, *Toma de Posesión: El rito del poder* (Mexico City: Porrúa, 1988).

4. On Catholics in the revolution see Robert Quirk, *The Mexican Revolution and the Catholic Church* (Bloomington: Indiana University Press, 1973). Quirk's discussion of Catholic social doctrine and the creation of unions as well as the governing of Jalisco is particularly informative. See also Jennie Purnell, *Popular Movements and State Formation in Revolutionary Mexico* (Durham, NC: Duke University Press, 1999), 20–21. She argues that the Catholic Church was the heir to one style of nineteenth-century liberalism in its desire for a less intrusive state and small-scale land ownership.

5. For the Cristero War, see Jean Meyer, *The Cristero Rebellion: The Mexican People between Church and State, 1926–1929*, trans. Richard Southern (London: Cambridge University Press, 1976). For the bitter reaction that later grew up to the repression of the Cristeros, consult Salvador Abascal, *Mis Recuerdos: Sinarquismo y Colonia María Auxiliadora* (Mexico City: Editorial Tradición, 1980).

6. See Roderic Ai Camp, *Crossing Swords: Politics and Religion in Mexico* (Oxford: Oxford University Press, 1996).

7. Manuel Chac and Raquel Pastor Escobar, *Ha vuelto Dios a México: La transformación de las relaciones iglesia estado* (Mexico City: UNAM, 1997).

8. This is not to say that the Catholic Church itself, or any other religion, fell under the official umbrella of the PRI. Jorge Castañeda claims leaders in the Catholic Church had a certain amount of influence. See his *Perpetuating Power: How Mexican Presidents Were Chosen* (New York: The New Press, 2000). In addition, groups such as the Luz del Mundo in Guadalajara or the community of Nueva Jerusalén in Michoacán had significant local power in the party. Regarding the Luz del Mundo, see Renée de la Torre, *Los hijos de la luz: Discurso, identidad y poder en La Luz del Mundo* (Guadalajara: Universidad de Guadalajara, 1995). For more on Nueva Jerusalén, see Sam Quiñones, *True Tales from Another Mexico* (Albuquerque: University of New Mexico Press, 2001).

9. *Tiempo*, June 6, 1990.

10. Luis Aboites, *Breve historia de Chihuahua* (Mexico City: El Colegio de México; Fondo de Cultura Económica, 1994), 141–43.

11. Enrique Krauze, *Mexico: Biography of Power*, trans. Hank Heifetz (New York: Harper Collins, 1997), 6.

12. Friedrich Katz, "The Liberal Republic and the Porfiriato, 1867–1910," in *Mexico Since Independence*, ed. Leslie Bethell (Cambridge: Cambridge University Press, 1991), 74, 89.

13. Jean Meyer, "Revolution and Reconstruction in the 1920s," in *Mexico Since Independence*, 213. Meyer notes that American intervention and invasion were a perceived threat through at least 1926.

14. Velia Patricia Barragán Cisneros, *Mennonitas: Etnicidad y derecho* (Durango: Serie Cuadernos Jurídicos No. 17, 1996), 11.

15. Harry Leonard Sawatzky, *They Sought a Country: Mennonite Colonization in Mexico* (Berkeley: University of California Press, 1971), 53, fn. 52. From the Silvestre Terrazas Collection, Bancroft Library, UC–Berkley. Translated by Harry Leonard Sawatzky.

16. Narciso Brassols Batalla, *El pensamiento político de Álvaro Obregón* (Mexico City: Editorial Nuestro Tiempo, 1967), 135.

17. Batalla, *El pensamiento politico de Álvaro Obregón*, 135.

18. Meyer, "Revolution and Reconstruction," 204.

19. The *Quinto Censo General de la Población* for 1930 shows more U.S. Americans, Canadians, Europeans, Asians, and North Africans in Chihuahua than in 1910. The census asks all *extranjeros* their origin and then puts them in categories by nation (like Canadian and United States) and therefore I lumped the others according to broad geographic categories for expediency. The author recognizes the dubious quality of counting in the early Mexican censuses. It is more likely, however, that the 1930 census undercounted rather than overcounted.

20. Martha D. Chávez Quezada, "La colonización menonita en el estado de Chihuahua" (Tesis de licenciatura en economía, UNAM, Mexico City, D.F., 1948), 17.

21. Sawatzky, *They Sought*, 39. Sawatzky extracts this observation from the personal writings of the Mennonite delegation.

22. Sawatzky, *They Sought*, 39

23. Sawatzky, *They Sought*, 61.

24. Sawatzky, *They Sought*, 125–26. The $4 million figure is an estimate of several bankers that Sawatzky uses as his source. That sort of investment at 1925 rates in the United States would have measured $42,520,000 (U.S.) in 2000. Sawatzky characterizes the German population that arrived in Cuauhtémoc as "adventurers," "former officers" in the Mexican Army, and "German-Jewish Peddlers."

25. Sawatzky, *They Sought*, 207.

26. Secretaría de Agricultura y Fomento, *Regiones económicos de la República Mexicana* (Mexico City: Talleres de la Oficina de Publicaciones y Propoganda, Tacubaya, 1936), 62.

27. Chávez Quezada, "La colonización menonita," 70–71. That these were food grade–quality oats is confirmed by Sawatzky's notation (209) that the Quaker company, working out of Mexico City, was an early purchaser of Mennonite oats. The year 1947 saw the publication of a study carried out by the Rockefeller Foundation and the Instituto Nacional de Nutriología stating that Mexico was deficient in its consumption of riboflavin and niacin—two well-known benefits of oats.

28. Juan Ventosa Roig, *La alimentación popular* (Mexico City: Secretaría de Educación Pública, 1947), 84.

29. Sawatzky, *They Sought*, 140–41.

30. P. Lamartine Yates, *Mexico's Agricultural Dilemma* (Tucson: University of Arizona Press, 1981), 25. Yates notes that after 1960 milk consumption leveled off to a 0.3 percent yearly increase while new state price controls served to discourage dairy herders from increasing productivity.

31. Aboites, *Breve historia*, 150.

32. Sawatzky, *They Sought*, 327–28.

33. Sawatzky, *They Sought*, 327–28.

34. *Geografía del estado de Durango* (Mexico City: Talleres Gráficos de la Secretaría de Agricultura y Fomento, 1929). Also see *Atlas ejidal de Durango* (Aguascalientes: Instituto Nacional de Estadística, Geografía e Informática, 1991).

35. Martina Will, "The Mennonite Colonization of Chihuahua: Reflections of Competing Visions," *The Americas* 53 (1997), 357. While the Mennonites retained a copy, Will notes that the first official Mexican copy was not published until 1944 in a collection of laws issued by the secretary of agriculture.

36. Aboites, *Breve historia*, 155; Chávez Quezada, "La colonización menonita," 18.

37. Aboites, *Breve historia*, 152.

38. Chávez Quezada, "La colonización menonita," 92.

39. John Mason Hart, *Empire and Revolution: The Americans in Mexico Since the Civil War* (Berkeley: University of California Press, 2002), 359–60.

40. Sawatzky, *They Sought*, 195.

41. Sawatzky, *They Sought*, 195. The practice of renting Mennonites' *ejidos* began in Durango as early as 1935.

42. Sawatzky, *They Sought*, 151–52.

43. Sawatzky, *They Sought*, 147; Will, "The Mennonite Colonization of Chihuahua," 353. Sawatzky also draws attention to the fact that Mennonite pacifism prohibits execution as a means of judicial punishment. Thus they were placed in the precarious position of relying on the state to solve their problems with violence, which they could not do as Anabaptists.

44. Barragán Cisneros, *Mennonitas*, 25. From "Correspondencia Particular del Presidente de los Estados Unidos Mexicanos."

45. Larry Towell, *Shared Lives: The Communal Spirit Today* (New York: Aperture Foundation, 1996), preface.

46. Concodoc—Proyecto de Documentación sobre Conscripción y Objeción de Conciencia, 1998.

47. Cámara de Diputados, Ley de Asociaciónes Religiosas y Culto Publico, 2002.

48. Barragán Cisneros, *Mennonitas*, 44.

49. U.N. Commission on Human Rights, 1995, *Report of the Secretary-General Prepared Pursuant to Commission Resolution 1995/83* (and Addendum) (Geneva: United Nations, 1995). The report recognizes conscientious objection as a basic human right of freedom of choice, conscience, and religion.

50. Carlos Salinas de Gortari, Speech at Rice University, Baker Institute of Foreign Policy, March 15, 2002.

51. Reynaldo Lastra Hernández, *La educación menonita* (Chihuahua: Servicios Educativos del Estado de Chihuahua; Talleres Gráficos del Gobierno del Estado, 1995), 11–12.

52. Barragán Cisneros, *Mennonitas*, 44–45.

53. Sawatzky, *They Sought*, 211–12. Sawatzky notes early interaction with Almacenes Nacionales, a government entity that also ran small-volume purchase programs.

54. Jeffrey Lynn Eighmy, *Mennonite Architecture: Diachronic Evidence for Rapid Diffusion in Rural Communities* (New York: AMS Press, 1989), 59.

55. *CONASUPO Ahora*, Coordinación de Communicación Social de CONASUPO (Mexico City: CONASUPO, 1984), 11

56. Larry Towell, *The Mennonites* (New York: Phaidon Press, 2000), preface.

57. Towell, *Mennonites*, preface.

58. "Mexican Mennonites Hungering for Hope," *Mennonite Brethren Herald*, 11 August 2000.

59. Tim Rotheisler, "Drug Smugglers in Sheep's Clothing," *Alberta Report*, 26 May 1997.

60. Train tours of the Copper Canyon region of Mexico often boast a stop in Chihuahua to see the Mennonites and buy crafts and cheese from them.

61. *El Heraldo de Chihuahhua*, 21 June 2002. *La Jornada* reports that the other support business with which the Mennonites are involved is arms trafficking. See Marislava Breach and Ruben Villapando, "Mueren seis personas al enfrentarse dos familias en la sierra tarahumara," *La Jornada*, 27 March 2002.

62. Vicente Fox, speech delivered on 5 April 2002 to Mennonite colonists in the Municipio Miguel Auza, Zacatecas.

9
Visions of Women: Revelation, Gender, and Catholic Resurgence

Edward Wright-Rios

Image of Our Lady of Juquila, Oaxaca. The Virgin of Juquila is today perhaps the second most important Marian devotion in Mexico after the Virgin of Guadalupe, but she has been an important pilgrimage image in Oaxaca since the seventeenth century. Her feast was once a key economic event where inland residents purchased items from the Pacific Coast and traded horses. This small likeness was probably purchased by a visitor at her remote mountain shrine in the mid- to late 1800s, and graced a wall or home altar in its simple tin-and-glass frame.

In the late 1920s a woman named Matilde Narváez faced a momentous decision. Narváez lived in Juquila, Oaxaca, a town situated in the mountains above the state's Pacific Coast boasting a very popular, colonial-vintage devotion to the Virgin of Juquila. In the summer of 1928, however, the elderly spinster received news that Nicha, an Indian girl from the nearby village of Ixpantepec, was speaking to the Virgin Mary in a remote cave. Like many devout locals she must have wondered what Marian apparitions within her parish could mean. Was God trying to communicate with the faithful through a poor indigenous child? If so, what action should she take? Narváez probably plumbed the depths of her faith, and mulled her extensive knowledge of Catholic lore. Her choice ultimately destroyed a personal reputation burnished over many years, and it still elicits divergent opinions among individuals who remember her. For Narváez's part, once she embraced the seer's visions as legitimate divine miracles she did what came naturally—she led. Within a few weeks of her initial

178

visit to the mountain grotto where Nicha held consultations with the Virgin, Matilde Narváez emerged as the energetic spokeswoman of the visions, the docent at the apparition site, and the epistolary champion of an upstart devotion to the Virgin of Ixpantepec before antagonistic ecclesiastical authorities.

A member of a mestizo landowning family, Narváez had much to lose. Her biography reads like a casting call for the Hispanic archetype of the black-clad, fanatically proclerical, unmarried *beata* or *ratón de iglesia*.[1] For over three decades prior to Nicha's visions she had gained recognition for her fidelity to the church. Older residents of the town still recall her as Doña Matildita the Catholic schoolmarm, the benefactress of the pilgrims' hostel beside the Virgin of Juquila's shrine, and the organizer of local women in defense of the faith.[2] Archdiocesan correspondence from the period and present-day oral testimony suggest that she possessed a formidable personality, resolutely pursuing her goals and promoting her beliefs despite considerable social pressure. Among Juquila's Catholics she was an exemplar of unshakable piety, a tireless church activist, and a homegrown religious intellectual. As one of the most prominent women in the region, she was the chief local interpreter of church doctrine aside from the curate.

Matilde Narváez occupied a classic position of female authority in Mexican society—she was the confidant of curates. Ausencio Canseco, the parish priest from 1902 to 1933, noted that he and his predecessor had boundless confidence in her as a devout role model and ally. Evidence of their trust in her competence and loyalty resides in their appointment of Narváez as the principal of Juquila's Catholic school in the early years of the twentieth century. Canseco even safeguarded church funds with Narváez during the revolution. The pairing of young priests and older female parishioners appears repeatedly in Catholic culture and replicates the symbolic dyad of Christ and the Virgin as the mother-son/male-female duo of divine action. This construct bears expectations of social roles and behavior. Clergymen are to emulate the chastity, compassion, and divine vision of Christ; devout women are to act the part of the Virgin, purified and humbled through a life's travails, obedient, and purged of sexual identity.[3] Within parishes women who develop close relationships with priests gain prestige and a time-honored social identity as intimates of one of Mexican culture's salient paternal figures, "el padre." Especially in rural parishes, priests occupy a key node of influence that extends beyond their religious duties. As a result, prominent laywomen gain a palpable degree of power by virtue of their ties to priests.[4] People seeking the priest's support in spiritual matters, social arrangements, and issues of political and economic import often try to secure the backing of well-known Catholic women. In a community like Juquila (both during Narváez's lifetime and in the present day) where shrine-related activities reside at the hub of local economic life, the curate and individuals in his confidence are even more important.[5]

Women like Narváez throughout the Catholic world were crucial agents of the church's revitalization in the late nineteenth and early twentieth centuries.[6] After the sundering of church-state linkages, parish management grew increasingly dependent on the establishment and maintenance of bonds between activist women and priests. Particularly in rural areas where priests were few and anticlerical politics sometimes removed them from communities entirely, devout women provided religious continuity. The Oaxacan clergy viewed them as the local protectors of the faith and the natural champions of Catholic renaissance. The archdiocese's official organ, *El boletín oficial y revista ecclesiástica de la Provincia de Antequera*, encouraged parish priests to spark the spiritual renewal of irreligious communities through female parishioners. The *Boletín* spoke of priests harnessing female devotional and social energies: first in acts of devotion, then in religious education, and ultimately in the re-Christianization of modern society.[7]

In this context what can Matilde Narváez's decision to defy her curate after years as his loyal henchwoman reveal about female social mobilization in the nineteenth and twentieth centuries? And what can her life teach us about Mexican women as religious leaders and thinkers during the period? What follows is a discussion of women, prophecy, and local religion inspired by her actions. Scholars of Catholicism, particularly in European case studies, have documented the feminization of Catholic practice and the predominant role of women as agents of Catholicism's resurgence during this period. My research suggests that women played a similar part in Mexico's history, vastly outnumbering men in the new militant lay associations that became a driving force of the nation's oft-cited "Second Spiritual Conquest."[8] The standard explanation for this phenomenon is that liberal nation-states provided little outlet for female initiative and social energy, and failed to deliver promised socioeconomic equity. Instead they offered women "republican motherhood"—essentially a rephrasing of patriarchal norms circumscribing women to the hearth and child-rearing. According to liberal propagandists, the idealized object of female social action was the shaping of new generations of patriotic male citizens. Women at times challenged patriarchy by tapping into the social and moral power within this construct, but it greatly restricted their freedom to participate in public life. Recent historical scholarship in Mexico and Latin America during the nineteenth century suggests that women's social prerogatives often lost ground in fledgling nation-states.[9] The embattled Catholic Church, however, offered women opportunities for education, prominent positions in religious institutions, socially acceptable public roles of significant prestige, settings for female fellowship beyond the home, and an outlet for their spiritual and intellectual energies.

This contrast between what modern states and the church offered women represents a compelling argument for the prevalence of women in ranks of the Catholic faithful, but there remains something unsatisfactory about the suggestion that Catholic action was women's default option amidst the advance of modernity and more intrusive patriarchy. Narváez's case suggests that perhaps there was more to this issue. Her actions demonstrate that the nineteenth century opened Catholicism to female initiative and leadership in a more profound manner. Women like Doña Matildita experienced a new and deeper level of empowerment within local Catholicism and periodic militant discourse, and deployed this authority to transform the church rather than simply avail themselves of opportunities provided by the clergy. In addition, Catholic piety and the church's fierce rejection of modern error emerged as crucial tools for women contesting social norms within the church and civil society.

To examine these issues this essay focuses on three aspects of the apparition movement that coalesced around Nicha and devotion to the Virgin of Ixpantepec. First, it explores the prophecies of a late-colonial seer known as La Madre Matiana. According to a local critic and observer of the controversial events at Ixpantepec, popular beliefs concerning these legendary prognostications fueled credence in the girl's claims. The colonial visions allegedly experienced by a humble Mexican woman in the 1770s (Matiana del Espíritu Santo) predicted the upheavals of independence and subsequent unrest, as well as the nineteenth-century setbacks experienced by the Mexican church. But they also foretold the church's ultimate triumph after a bloody conflict and the emergence of a fervent expiatory movement led by devout women. These prophecies became a staple of popular devotional literature and Catholic propaganda after the mid-nineteenth century. Matiana's visions and their interpretation by church militants propagated a potent gendered combination of Catholic intransigence and apocalyptic anticipation. This current of ultramontane discourse held up women not only as vessels of unwavering piety, devout obedience, and orthodox belief, but also as the vanguard of the church's victory over Satan's latest inspirations—liberal constitutions, religious indifference, and anticlericalism.

Women like Matilde Narváez found the exalted Catholic feminism expressed in Matiana's visions empowering and employed its juxtaposition of female purity and male depravity in local struggles. Thus this essay proceeds from an examination of Matiana's prophecies to a discussion of Narváez's role in the promotion of Nicha's visionary experiences in the late 1920s and early

1930s. Finally, it proposes that the resonance between Matiana's prophecies, Nicha's visions, local natural disasters, and religious political violence in 1928 inspired Matilde Narváez to lead a local devotional movement that challenged Catholic patriarchy. In this case, local apparitions and popular prophecy convinced a trusted Catholic activist to break with the clergy and seize an independent role in what she believed were world-changing miraculous happenings. By way of this woman's fateful decision and initiative this essay suggests that militant Catholicism's attraction for energetic women resided in its ability to inspire women to see themselves as important agents of Christian social transformation and religious leaders in their own right. The ramifications of this level of motivation, however, did not always suit the clergy.

LA MADRE MATIANA

In the 1970s and early 1980s Hilario Cortés, an elderly jack-of-all-scribal-trades, began writing a history of his hometown, Juquila, and the surrounding villages of the region. As a young man in the early twentieth century he was the protégé of Juquila's pastor, Ausencio Canseco. In all likelihood he received his primary education and learned the catechism at the Catholic school run by Narváez in the early 1900s. As a youth Cortés assisted the curate when he visited sick parishioners. He made his first journey to Oaxaca City with Canseco in 1912, and briefly fled Juquila with the priest when insurgents (*carrancistas*) attacked Juquila 1919.[10] Cortés entered Oaxaca's seminary in the 1920s, but discontinued his education when church-state tensions temporarily closed the institution. Subsequently he worked as a teacher, peripatetic municipal secretary, letter writer, healer, and funeral prayer leader. Present-day residents of Juquila recall him as "the penguin" because he waddled about town dressed in a black suit and hat with a matching umbrella dangling from his arm. In 1928 this local historian joined locals rushing to the apparition site. He never finished his opus, but among the extant fragments of his manuscript is his analysis of Nicha's visions and the devotional movement she inspired dedicated to the Virgin of Ixpantepec.

According to Cortés, there were no miracles of divine or diabolical origin. At several decades' remove he depicted the entire episode with a distinct smug disdain, depicting a backward Indian village's moment of fame before a rapid, and deserved, return to obscurity. He claimed that a conniving Nicha availed herself of a moment of intense popular unease and deceived thousands of believers with her fraudulent visions and consultations with the Virgin. The sham began in the summer of 1928, he asserted, when Nicha returned to Ixpantepec from her daily collection of firewood and flowers in the mountains, claiming to have been surprised by the Virgin inside a cave near town. She alleged that Mary instructed her to tell the people of Ixpantepec to construct a temple and render homage to her at the site. Nonetheless, Cortés claimed, many people refused to give credence to the girl's testimony, prompting her to issue threats of imminent divine punishments. Cortés never mentioned Narváez specifically. But given Father Canseco's testimony about her crucial role as the chief interpreter/promoter of the visions, in all likelihood Cortés was thinking about her when he wrote that the eerie congruence of Matiana's colonial prophecies, Nicha's dire warnings, and local earthquakes in 1928 inspired people to hail the indigenous girl as the "Second Juan Diego."[11]

Thus Cortés's testimony suggests that in order to understand the emergence of a twentieth-century devotion to the Virgin of Ixpantepec we need to explore the history of colonial-era visions. The details relevant to the life of the legendary seer known as La Madre Matiana and her visions are sketchy. A search for sources on the prophecies nets a small but curious catch that can be divided in two categories: popular references making light of the Catholic superstition, and devout commentaries interpreting the prophecies and their relevance to historical events. In the first group Matiana was a subject of the legendary caricaturist José Guadalupe Posada, a Revolutionary-era satirical newspaper appropriated "La Madre Matiana" as its title, her moniker became a euphemism for death (as in La Flaca, La Pelona, etc.), and she emerged in mordant rhymes (*calaveras*). In a 1930s broadside, titled "The Doctrine of Madre Matiana," she appears as a rotund, one-eyed fortune-teller with copious freckles and a sagging lower lip. The verses accompanying her likeness lampoon Catholic prayer and Mexican fatalism in an acid commentary on post-Revolutionary politics.[12] Thus Matiana is enshrined in Mexico's rich tradition of irreverent satire as the face of doom-and-gloom Catholic fanaticism rendered female.

Our interests lie more with the texts that engaged her prophecies seriously. At least three of these texts on the prophecies probably influenced the apparition movement centered on Nicha and the Virgin of Ixpantepec in 1928. They include an 1861 pamphlet published in Mexico City claiming to be the original text of the prophecies; an 1889 book by Luis Duarte published by the capital city's Círculo Católico, including an allegedly faithful copy of an 1857 text of the prophecies and in-depth commentary; and a 1910 article in Oaxaca's official archdiocesan organ.[13] The 1861 pamphlet noted that numerous versions of Matiana's prophecies were in circulation throughout Mexico. Many people in Oaxaca probably read about them in cheap popular printings or heard retellings of Matiana's prophecies. Narváez must have been very familiar with Matiana's visons. Chapbooks and pamphlets on the famous prognostications were probably sold alongside lithographs of the Virgin of Juquila, prayer books, and scapulars at Juquila's annual pilgrimage fair. In addition, preachers leading yearly revival missions at the shrine most likely held forth on Matiana's visions. It is also probable that Narváez knew Duarte's analysis. This book may have also shared shelf space with shrine mementos, or found its way into the parish archive thanks to one of Juquila's priests. It is almost certain that Narváez read the article in the archdiocese's *Boletín oficial*.[14]

In spite of their distinct origins these three texts are remarkably consistent in their renderings of the prophecies. The 1910 Oaxacan article only glosses them, citing the Duarte text as the definitive interpretation of the visions. Duarte truncated Matiana's prophecies into discreet ideas/issues and composed nineteen separate chapters examining each of these points, but the prophecies as Duarte included them are nearly identical to those in the 1861 pamphlet. According to these sources, Matiana's prophecies emerged from Jeronymite convent oral history. Matiana apparently died in the late eighteenth century due to ardent acts of penance, but she entrusted the details of her visions to two disciples. They in turn passed on Matiana's experiences to María Josefa de la Pasión de Jesús, also known as Madre Guerra, whose testimony on January 18, 1837, is the alleged source text of Matiana's prophecies.

Matiana lived most of her life as a servant (*criada*) in various convents. Of humble origins in Tepoztlan, the young Matiana caught the eye of a nun at San Juan de la Penitencia. While in this woman's service the girl began to gain a reputation for miracles. When her benefactress died, she lived briefly in another convent before receiving word from the Virgin that she should join the sisters of the Jeronymite order.[15] There a demented, gluttonous nun hired the budding visionary as a personal servant. Matiana reputedly embraced her station with great abnegation, forfeiting her meager wages and allotment of food to her voracious mistress, and subsisting on stale bread that fellow servants proffered. In addition, she took up the leadership of a floundering devotional sodality in the convent emphasizing care of the sick and personal humility. Apparently the visionary's stature grew such that the prioress obeyed the *criada*, and viceregal ladies sought her insights into the future.[16]

In moments of rapture, Matiana communicated with the Virgin. Within the Jeronymite convent the Virgin instructed Matiana that a new order would emerge dedicated to el Desagravio de Jesús Sacramentado (the Expiation of the Blessed Sacrament). As described by Madre Guerra, the new aggregation of religious women was to be something of a superorder, with three initial Jeronymite members and others selected from different convents. The new order, Matiana learned, would be the last establishment of a religious order before the final judgment. These nuns dedicated to acts of expiation would lead a movement of religious renewal emphasizing fervent devotion to the Body of Christ in order to placate the righteous anger of God fired by the sins of men and the inequities of society. The Virgin, Madre Guerra stressed, promised Matiana that the founding members of the order would attain the same stature as the original apostles. Through these nuns' fervent personal piety and the acts of expiation they inspired among others, Mexico would regain divine favor. Old religious orders would resurrect their primordial fervor, lax churchmen would rediscover their pastoral zeal, and sinners would plead for mercy.

Aside from instructing her on the establishment of the Hermanas del Desagravio, the Virgin showed her seer the source of God's looming wrath. Matiana witnessed a secret meeting in hell where demons frustrated by the Christian peace reigning during the seer's lifetime gathered: "They formed a congress, and together they made the constitution and the legal code; and Lucifer directed the demons to spread those constitutions throughout the world to pervert everyone."[17] Matiana glimpsed the outcome of this assault; she saw the violence and destruction of Mexico's Wars of Independence and the expulsion of the Spaniards. She envisioned Iturbide's blundering imperial venture, the Parián Riot in 1828, the assault of North American armies, and the attendant invasion of Protestant sects and Masonic orders. She also foretold Mexico's suffocating indebtedness to American creditors. And most galling, Matiana perceived the exclaustration of the nation's female religious orders.

Thus these pamphlets suggest that Matiana anticipated the dawn of a painful period in which Mexico and faithful Catholics would suffer martyrdoms, poverty, humiliation, and persecution. She presaged epic battles and fire in the streets of Mexico City, but at some vaguely defined point in the future, just prior to the emergence of the new order of nuns in October of a year ending in 8, Mexicans would reunite with their Spanish brethren and reestablish a trans-Atlantic Catholic empire ruled by a Spanish king living in Mexico. Facing a vigorous Hispanic devotional and military phalanx, the Anglo-Americans and their heretical sects would retreat without struggle or the money owed to them. The restored monarchy would rule from a new palace next to the Basilica of the Virgin of Guadalupe, and the Hermanas del Desagravio would take up residence in the shrine's cloister. Furthermore, all previously cloistered nuns throughout the nation would rejoin their congregations and find that their convents had miraculously returned to their exact condition prior to expropriation. Thenceforth all of Mexico's religious orders would prosper in peace and unity.

Pondering these prophecies today it is difficult to suppress the notion that they represent a fabrication of intransigent Catholics pining for the return of monarchy, church-state unity, and the definitive defeat of liberalism in Mexico. The publication of the earliest known Matiana texts in the late 1850s and early 1860s amidst intense liberal-conservative violence and the promulgation of the 1857 Constitution and the Reform Laws arouses suspicion. Matiana's prophecies could be a product of conservative propaganda. They invoked a colonial society of religious and social harmony and juxtaposed this idealized past with the turmoil that Mexicans experienced between 1810 and 1860. The prophecies portrayed civil strife, foreign invasion, and economic turmoil as divine punishments for the nation's separation from Spain and church teachings due to a satanic plot ensconced in ascendant liberalism. In this light the visions foretold that an Armageddon-like conflagration was in the offing. Matiana's visions, however, also provided the possibility of redress—*el desenojo de Dios* (the unangering of God)—through female-led expiatory fervor. If Mexicans returned to the bosom of the church and devoted themselves to acts of ritual indemnification, God's righteous anger could be calmed. The theme of society being at odds with divine will, and thus courting world-ending disaster, has been an apparition staple for millennia. But amidst the advent of secular modernity the "dragons of the apron [i.e. Masons], the basilisks of liberalism, and the great serpents of materialism" emerged as the great enemies of Catholic civilization.[18] The faithful, however, could "help" the Virgin's efforts to stave off divine punishment if they demonstrated remorse and repentance. In this chiliastic worldview the church emerged triumphant regardless; either society would turn away from the blasphemous resistance against God and his church, or God would extirpate the wicked and resurrect the church himself.

Liberals probably saw Matiana's prophecies as a transparent ploy by their opponents to scare the nation's superstitious public. Militant Catholic interpreters, however, portrayed criticisms as proof of their veracity—prophets and visionaries, they assured their readers, were often mocked in their own time. But Catholic texts sought to reassert the contemporary relevance of Matiana's prophecies, fuel fears of the United States and Protestantism, strengthen the laity's identification with Hispanic Catholicism, and generalize notions of Christian civilization's perilous existence. Furthermore, they gave even greater importance to devout females as the protectors of Catholic purity, devoting extensive attention to women and girls as the Virgin's stalwart visionaries and depicting faithful women as the catalysts of male repentance.

Luis G. Duarte's *Profecías de Matiana acerca del triunfo de la iglesia* represents a dramatic recasting and amplification of the visions.[19] In contrast to the popular publications of Matiana's visions, this book donned the trappings of official ecclesiastical scholarship. Aside from Duarte, a reputedly learned Catholic named Antonio Martínez del Cañizo provided explanatory footnotes and secured canonical license to publish the book and ecclesiastical opinions supporting the prophecies. *Profecías* linked Matiana's prophecies to late nineteenth-century European visionary lore, burgeoning intransigent devotionalism, and the church's critique of secular modernity. Duarte argued that Matiana had foreseen the Mexican experience of an international anti-

Catholic, Masonic/demonic conspiracy that emerged first in France and subsequently enveloped the world. Successive chapters of Duarte's book employed the various themes in Matiana's prophecies as starting points for the author's disquisitions on historical events and contemporary issues. Duarte wove Matiana's prophecies into the fabric of the period's European-inspired Catholic militance. Much of the text is taken up with the visions of other Catholic seers, primarily European girls and women, whose visions echoed Matiana's warnings of an impending great chastisement and subsequent Catholic renaissance. Modern societies, particularly educated men, Duarte averred, were in a state of rebellion against God, and thus invited annihilation. Nevertheless, during the great impending conflict some men would experience religious conversions when they realized that relics and Catholic images hidden in their clothing by their wives, sisters, or daughters had spared their lives.

From Matiana's emphasis on expiation, Duarte discussed the Virgin's historical role as the "General" of Catholic forces against the faith's enemies. He linked the seer's call for acts of ritual indemnification and veneration of the Eucharist to the chief devotion of late nineteenth-century militant Catholicism, the Sacred Heart of Jesus.[20] Intertwining the visions of different European seers and notions of Christ's sufferings occasioned by society's iniquity, he argued that through Mary's advocacy and the blood of her martyrs, God's vengeance had been repeatedly postponed. Yet the modern era had occasioned such extensive irreverence that the Savior's heart suffered as if impaled by numerous weapons. The Virgin, he claimed, feared that mankind would only respond to the lash of divine retribution, and yet she beseeched the world through her stalwarts, laywomen and nuns. Duarte cautioned that the dates of the impending chastisement given by seers had passed thanks to Mary's intercession and the prayerful pleas of her devotees. But, he suggested, the world had become so blinded by the quest for secular power and riches that only mass repentance and expiation as described by Matiana could avert impending punishment.

Discussing the Hermanas del Desagravio and their apostle-like status, Duarte underscored the special role of Mexican women in Catholicism's epic struggle. Women throughout the world opposed the faith's enemies with "manly vigor," and Mexican women's part in the larger struggle was particularly laudable. First, they clung to Catholic virtues and nurtured the faith in their children. Second, they contended with recalcitrant fathers and husbands in a heroic struggle to steer men aright, "despite the depravation that surrounds them without contaminating them."[21] Hence the establishment of the Hermanas del Desagravio, the emergence of new saints from their ranks, and their pivotal role in the church's triumph represented a grace bestowed upon

Mexicans of the "pious sex" by the Virgin Mary in recognition of their exemplary sacrifice.

In April 1910 the Oaxacan curia endorsed Duarte's interpretation in the archdiocese's official organ.[22] Prophecies, the archdiocese argued, were God's method of conveying to the faithful the outlines of his divine plan. This text did not offer a new analysis, but it glossed both Matiana's pronouncements and Duarte's book, underscoring the church's position that the Mexican visions had all the hallmarks of divine prophecy. It was only natural, the archdiocese maintained, that God should inform impious nations of what awaited them. Pondering the state of affairs in Juquila in the late 1920s, the respected Catholic educator and others who were inclined toward visionary thinking would have found ample evidence that a great crisis was upon them.

THE VIRGIN OF IXPANTEPEC

Nicha's visions could not have arrived at a more delicate time for the Oaxacan church. The Mexican Revolution had thrown the state into political disarray.[23] All over the state local factions allied themselves with the various national groups vying for power and availed themselves of the weakness of state governments to settle old scores. A coalition of regional strongmen and Porfirian elites attempted to isolate Oaxaca from the penetration of the emergent revolutionary government in 1915 and 1916 but could not hold back the Constitutionalist forces that occupied Oaxaca's major cities and towns.

In the 1920s various local leaders maintained control of their respective satrapies, and as a result instability endured as local groups tried to position themselves as best they could in light of tumultuous national politics. In the late 1920s the Oaxacan church conducted careful diplomacy to navigate the difficult period of the Cristero Revolt (1926–29) and intense federal government anticlericalism. Oaxaca did not experience a powerful, religion-infused peasant rebellion like Mexico's Center West, but it was far from calm. The church struggled to safeguard resources and maintain its presence throughout the region as some local politicians parroted the anticlericalism characteristic of the Calles administration. In the state capital the curia faced antichurch demonstrations and state-sponsored cultural activities designed to compete with religious services and festivals. But for the most part the city remained at peace although on a few occasions street violence between factions was narrowly avoided.[24]

Beyond Oaxaca City parishes lived their own histories of civil-religious conflict. Village priests felt besieged by economic, political, and religious challenges. As in other parts of the country, federal statutes required that priests turn over church buildings to village committees in 1926. Responding to other laws emerging from the anticlerical regime of President Plutarco Elías Calles, local officials published edicts regulating the number of priests and summoned clerics to the state capital to be registered. Many Catholics feared this represented a step toward the complete removal of priests from their communities. Municipal governments sometimes sought to "reconcentrate" priests to their own liking or remove them from their jurisdiction altogether, and individuals availed themselves of the church's predicament to pilfer parish wealth and prosecute legal claims against priests.[25] Clerics also complained of the waxing power and malevolent intentions of regional tax collectors. In some areas, particularly the region surrounding Miahuatlan and Juquila, small bands proclaiming allegiance to "Christ the King" attacked towns and villages. The skeletal reports in Oaxaca's newspapers indicate that the peak of Oaxacan *cristero* activity coincided with the emergence of the Virgin of Ixpantepec.[26] The press alleged that a priest and thirty-five armed men sacked Juquila's public offices and destroyed the municipal archives on September 9, 1928.[27] Throughout Oaxaca's southern sierra federal patrols searched for local *cristeros* and occasionally harassed clergymen. Some priests went into hiding, and some of them fretted that Indian communities would lapse into apostasy, Protestants would establish beachheads of heresy, and some of their clerical brethren would conspire with the state.

Father Ausencio Canseco spent much of the 1920s and early 1930s trying to safeguard the church's interests in the region. In Juquila proper he struggled with local municipal officials who sought to tax pilgrims, expropriate shrine funds, and plunder the Virgin of Juquila's accessories. Simultaneously, the local economy floundered as pilgrims and peddlers stayed away due to unsafe rural travel.[28] The archdiocese depended upon Canseco to quell other problems in the region as well. He traveled to the neighboring parish of Tututepec to mediate conflict between the town's curate and civil authorities. In 1927 he visited another nearby parish, Teotepec, to investigate a colleague's collusion with local civil officials and defiance of the church hierarchy's suspension of religious services. Supplying documentary evidence, villagers wrote to the archdiocese that their curate was a schismatic, and expressed fears that the sacraments and rituals officiated by this priest were invalid and thus imperiled their souls.[29]

As pro-church and anticlerical interests squared off in Juquila, and rumors of a schismatic movement filtered through the region, Matilde Narváez's role as the right-hand woman of the parish's curates also suffered. During the revolution Canseco entrusted 1,900 pesos of shrine capital to the faithful spinster to protect these funds from marauding soldiers and nosy officials. When he sought to recover them in 1926, however, Narváez informed him that she no longer had the money. Apparently, she had spent it over the years while living with her mother. Canseco claimed to be shocked and exasperated by her betrayal: "The news hit me like a lightning bolt in the noblest part." After a few years pressuring Narváez to repay the money, Canseco involved archdiocesan authorities in the early 1930s. The issue festered as Narváez and her family agreed to pay the debt in cattle, but kept postponing their transfer. The issue must have seasoned the subsequent conflict over the Virgin of Ixpantepec, but neither Narváez, Canseco, nor the archdiocese indicated that it influenced their divergent interpretations of Nicha's visions. Nonetheless, the priest and his longtime ally were simultaneously arguing over the disappearance of money and the appearance of Mary.[30]

The Chatino village of Ixpantepec is approximately 15 kilometers from Juquila. It was then, and remains today, a very small and poor community. Coffee production began in the region during the late nineteenth century and became quite prominent by the mid-twentieth century, but due to its poor soils and relatively high elevation Ixpantepec was not among the communities where this crop took hold.[31] Unlike in Juquila, civil authorities in Ixpantepec enjoyed a good relationship with the clergy. Hilario Cortés described the town as a monolingual Chatino backwater, whose residents "have not castilianized themselves and live without evolving."[32] Residents subsisted on corn farming, the production of maguey and its fermented products, and cold-climate fruit collection. Nicha lived with her mother; her father had died some years before the apparitions.

Narváez produced two key documents related to the case: a report in April 1932 narrating the emergence of the apparitions and describing Nicha's visions, and a desperate letter to the archbishop in 1934.[33] She also made the arduous trek to Oaxaca City in April 1930 to argue Nicha's case personally before the curia, but no record of this meeting survived. In the 1932 letter Narváez sought to sketch a basic history of the apparitions and convince archdiocesan authorities of an orthodox, fervent gathering of the faithful communicating with the Virgin through a blessed seer. She emphasized Nicha's simplicity, miraculous foresight, and precocious understanding of the faith. The exact date when the young girl first reported seeing the Virgin remains a mystery, but her visions probably began in the early summer of 1928. Narváez provided the earliest concrete date and a description of the early mood of anticipation and excitement in Ixpantepec. She wrote that after an earthquake on July 16, 1928, Nicha and the Virgin discussed the supernatural implications of the tremor, and the girl relayed to others that Mary wanted them to beseech Christ for forgiveness and worship the Blessed Sacrament at her temple—that is, the cave. Mary, the girl said, could no longer restrain God and her son, whose patience and goodwill had been exhausted by society's depravities. The earthquake was a warning, Nicha said, and the Virgin beseeched the faithful to devote themselves to acts of repentance or face divine chastisement. At some point after this date, Ixpantepec's civil authorities sent word to Father Canseco, asking him to come to the pueblo and witness the happenings before the cave. We do not know what prompted village officials to inform their pastor, but a large earthquake on August 4, 1928, leveled most of the region's public architecture and may have inspired this action. To make matters worse torrential rains followed the seismic disaster, destroying remnants of adobe structures and soaking residents who were forced to live in the open.[34]

According to Narváez, Father Canseco rushed to Ixpantepec upon hearing news of the apparitions. Many of the parish seat's devout followed closely on his heels, including Doña Matildita at the head of a group of women. Up to this point the apparitions had been primarily a Chatino event. Aspects of Narváez's testimony hint that indigenous religious beliefs infused the girl's visions and their local interpretation. A present-day informant in Ixpantepec claims that her grandfather, a Chatino religious specialist, treated Nicha when she returned in hysterics after one of her visions.[35] Once the clergy and Juquila laity became involved, however, the apparitions rapidly became a regional phenomenon. Upon his arrival Canseco said a mass of rogation in Ixpantepec and then proceeded to the apparition site with the village authorities, many of the town's residents, and visitors in tow. When he arrived at the cave Nicha informed him that the Virgin was indeed present, prompting him to lead the crowd in the Rosary, but no one aside from the girl saw the apparition. Nicha told the priest and those gathered before her that the Virgin requested that Canseco perform thirteen special masses for her during the month of August. Narváez implied that Canseco may have initially thought the girl's visions were legitimate miracles, noting that he took care to perform the masses stipulated by the Virgin, celebrating some at the grotto and others in private due to the suspension of services.

Not long after the regional emergence of Nicha's visions large numbers of pilgrims thronged the trails leading to the village from September 1928 until at least January 1929; significant numbers of pilgrims may have continued to arrive in the early 1930s. Both detractors and supporters commented on a basic pattern of activities at the foot of the cave. Visitors and devotees gathered in a flat area in front of the cavern and prayed, sang, performed penance, and made personal offerings to the Virgin. Many of them conferred with Nicha and she in turn relayed their questions and supplications to the Virgin through an angel. Some individuals left the apparition site with the Virgin's responses scrawled on treasured pieces of paper.[36] Narváez never mentioned other seers beyond Nicha, but Father Canseco and the Oaxacan press claimed that many visitors experienced visions. Soon reports surfaced of more apparitions in the nearby towns of Temascaltepec and Nopala, and a three-stop pilgrimage circuit emerged. According to Canseco, some visitors saw nothing, others saw silhouettes of saints and the Virgin in the shadows caused by hundreds of flickering candles, and still others reported vivid three-dimensional apparitions of sacred figures and the entire celestial court. According to Narváez, devotees massed before the grotto first focused their attentions on All Saints Day (November 1), an important feast in the local ritual calendar associated with the end of the Chatino calendric cycle. Nicha prophesied that the Virgin would reveal herself to the faithful by this date. When this failed to occur, believers hoped for a dramatic apparition on the feast of the Immaculate Conception (December 8) and lobbied Father Canseco to perform more rituals that Nicha claimed had been required by the Virgin in order for her to appear. The curate refused to participate, and this date also passed without the hoped for public apparition.

Our sources are silent on what caused the curate to turn against Nicha and Narváez, but his interpretation of the apparitions emerges from letters sent to his superiors in 1929.[37] Canseco argued that he had gone to Ixpantepec to investigate the happenings rather than participate. He omitted mention of the masses and Rosary with the devotees, slighted the believers, labeling them *los interesados* (the interested party), and emphasized the bizarre visions experienced by visiting pilgrims.[38] He documented doctrinal irregularities/parodies, visions of freakish animals and sharply dressed devils, and unflattering portrayals of the clergy. In general, Narváez depicted an orderly gathering of the devout and the priest described visionary chaos. Canseco was clearly troubled by the apparitions. He did not simply argue that Nicha had deceived a host of ignorants as Cortés did years later. After cataloging the strange and ominous experiences of his informants, Canseco had probably concluded that the apparitions were demonically inspired, but left the final judgment to archdiocesan authorities, stating, "The fact of the apparitions of the divine images is true, very true . . . it is necessary to determine if the cause of these apparitions is good or bad; either it is God through the ministry of his angels, or it is the devil planning some evil outcome."[39] Present-day oral history sources claim that he "conjured" the apparition site and determined that Satan was afoot.[40] Canseco's definitive interpretation is abundantly clear in subsequent correspondence.

Aside from remarkable detail concerning pilgrim visions, Canseco's testimony reveals a gendered dimension to the conflict over the Virgin of Ixpantepec. In his letters he slighted all of the females involved in the apparition movement, showing that his principal opponents were local women. In a let-

ter in May 1930 he described Narváez as "the fomenter and soul of that disturbance . . . suggesting that those diabolical visions were actual apparitions of
the Holy Virgin. Even worse this doña Matilde has been teaching that within
the stone of the cave resides the very person of the Holy Virgin."[41] Thus
Narváez appears as an insubordinate busybody inculcating pilgrims with doctrinal error, but Canseco also revealed her leadership role at the apparition site
and profound influence on beliefs emerging from Nicha's visions. He portrayed Nicha as an unreliable waif controlled by an overbearing mother.
Canseco underscored suspicious statements made by the girl. For example, he
alleged that Nicha announced that the Virgin wanted her to safeguard all alms
collected at the temple/cave. He also claimed that the girl attributed farcical
statements to the Blessed Mother and returned from her alleged conferences
with the Virgin lacking the appropriate emotional agitation expected of true
seers. Furthermore, she had failed to secure cures for three individuals whom
he had selected to test her. Canseco only considered male visionaries seriously,
and he treated these women as troublemakers. In fact, instead of carefully analyzing Nicha's visions, Canseco focused most of his attentions on a single
Spanish-speaking merchant from the Central Valley who described an especially fantastical and disturbing vision.

It is unclear what happened at the apparition site after January 1929, but it
is apparent that the Virgin of Ixpantepec's devotees and critics were locked in
a stalemate. Canseco communicated to his parishioners the archdiocesan ban
on visits and rituals before the cave and withheld the sacraments from Narváez,
and someone burned the vending booths and food stalls that had sprung up
near the grotto.[42] Nonetheless, Nicha continued to consult the Virgin at the
apparition site and attend to pilgrims. As noted previously, Narváez made her
sojourn to Oaxaca City in April 1930 and penned her account of the apparitions in April 1932. After this point the fortunes of the Virgin of Ixpantepec
movement and popular interest in the seer and her visions appear to have declined. Canseco died in 1933 after being swept off his horse trying to ford a
flood-swollen river during one of his pastoral trips to an outlying community.
Narváez wrote a final frantic letter to Archbishop José Othón Núñez in 1934
pleading to be allowed to take the sacraments again and consult the Virgin
with Nicha's aid. This document is particularly touching as it conveys the intertwining of Doña Matildita's personal faith, her experience in difficult times,
and a heightened sense of foreboding. Narváez, the church stalwart and religious intellectual, bemoaned local poverty, Canseco's untimely death, unre-
lenting natural disasters, and her personal economic woes. She rhetorically
threw herself at the prelate's feet, begging him to postpone her debt payment
and rescind her spiritual banishment. Narváez abandoned efforts to convince
the archbishop of the apparitions' validity, but she sought consideration for her

personal faith in the visions. In a passage that still oozes a sense of desperate, quasi–millenarian anguish, she asked for permission

> to speak with the Virgin of the grotto of Ixpantepec to see if we can communicate with His Majesty, and I will inform him. In this region there is sickness, and we are threatened by earthquakes and other calamities; for these reasons I would like to go with the girl that speaks to her so she can tell us what to do. . . . I have faith in the Queen of the heavens, the one who has come down there. . . . The calamities are approaching, and what greater blessing than that the Holy Mother calms our situation?[43]

The archdiocese refused to address Narváez's entreaties directly and instead wrote to Juquila's new pastor, instructing him to inform her that all of her quandaries should be addressed to him.[44] After Narváez's eleventh-hour effort to make peace with the church and gain the archdiocese's tolerance of her beliefs, the Virgin of Ixpantepec disappeared from archdiocesan documentary evidence and began her long fade into oblivion.

MATILDE AND MATIANA

Matilde Narváez paid a high price for her independent initiative. The church expected varying degrees of anticlericalism, but Narváez, Nicha, the seer's mother, and their supporters represented a challenge from within the flock. Their heterodox beliefs and female-led movement undermined the clergy's religious and patriarchal authority; it is no surprise that the archdiocesan clergy closed ranks and blocked the new devotion's advance. In addition, a new Marian shrine so close to Juquila threatened to overshadow the older devotion and undermine its pilgrimage festival. Of course a more intimate rancor also accompanied the dramatic falling-out of two individuals who had been friends and cohorts for over twenty years. The personal nature of the Ixpantepec standoff would have been apparent among local church supporters. Present-day oral testimony suggests that Juquila residents had to choose sides; either they backed their curate or Narváez and Nicha. As prophecies did not materialize and the Virgin of Ixpantepec failed to develop a reputation for miraculous cures that might have sustained devotion, many individuals sided with Canseco.

In the 1940s the formidable apparition-movement leader died impoverished and disgraced. Some relatives took pity on her, brought her food, and lamented that she had been duped by the devil's tricks at the grotto.[45] Others surmised that Narváez's fervently devout aspirations had driven the venerable educator to madness.[46] Still others probably embraced Cortés's theory that Nicha duped scores of believers, including the elderly local Catholic intellectual and activist. Doña Matildita remained defiant. Despite dishonor and ridicule she died convinced that the Virgin had indeed appeared in Ixpantepec and spoken to the faithful through the Chatina seer. Nicha, "the Second Juan Diego," remained in Ixpantepec and raised a family. She died in 1999, and most of her neighbors claim to have no knowledge of her visionary past.

What does Matilde Narváez's story reveal about women and the church's modern resurgence? Thomas Kselman suggests the key to broadening our understanding of religion is to examine the role of "belief in history," that is, how religious belief influences the action of individual historical actors.[47] Matilde Narváez was a church activist who for much of her life was an important agent of Catholic action in rural Oaxaca. Women like her taught catechism, administered parochial schools, led new Catholic associations, and marshaled the laity throughout Mexico. In some cases *beata* figures like Narváez were important local religious intellectuals too. Her relationship with Canseco suffered from their financial dispute, and Father Canseco may have brought this issue to the attention of archdiocesan authorities in the early 1930s to undercut Narváez's reputation.[48] It is doubtful, however, that Narváez embraced the Virgin of Ixpantepec's cause out of spite. Nor is it likely that she succumbed to pious hysteria. Most of the evidence suggests that the able spinster was anything but unbalanced. Even Father Canseco avoided such facile explanations.

Doña Matildita clearly believed that Nicha's visions were legitimate divine miracles. The foundations of this faith and her subsequent movement-leading gambit make even more sense if one factors in the apocalyptic feminism of Madre Matiana's prophecies. We lack evidence of Narváez specifically invoking Matiana, although Hilario Cortés stressed the prophecies' pivotal role in the broad positive response to Nicha's visions. Given the Matiana narratives' wide popular dissemination, their late nineteenth-century republication and militant interpretation, and the Oaxacan curia's efforts to promote them, Narváez certainly knew of Matiana's visions. In fact, heeding the colonial seer's warnings, finding evidence of their veracity in contemporary life, and practicing fervent expiatory devotion were precisely what the archdiocese encouraged.

A personal conviction that the Virgin spoke through Nicha, along with a sense that she had an important role to play in God's plan, is the only logical explanation for Narváez's actions. Of particular import in this case is the militant discourse within Matiana's prophecies that portrayed devout women as the saviors of a society suffering the consequences of modern error and religious indifference forced upon it by impious men. This interpretation of the nation's history lards late nineteenth- and early twentieth-century Catholic newspapers and popular devotional literature, and it found a receptive audience among the Catholic women in rural Oaxaca, and presumably in much of Mexico. Narváez's contemporaries in other towns reproduced this gendered militance in conflicts with local "disciples of Voltaire." They professed: "Communities that believe themselves to be enlightened . . . worship reason, and pursue progress without the charity of religious instruction. Surrounded by the darkness of materialism, these are men of the ephemeral power of the material. Many of them (without admitting it) are the footrests of the throne of the monarch of shadows."[49] Another group of women involved in the same conflict intertwined the female-exalting pious discourse and traditional notions of feminine abnegation as they sought the archbishop's support: "We women are the majority in most towns: we women suffer with humility the impieties of certain men of the day. We women nurture on our laps the future men of society. We suffering and self-effacing women sweeten the home. We women, however, are the weak part of the world. We women on our knees before God, amidst our sorrows, weeping we beg you."[50] Like these women, Narváez practiced her faith in an environment steeped in the notion that women were the primary protectors of the faith from male malevolence and folly, as well as a deserving and enlightened constituency within the church.

The Catholic newspapers, as well as the Matiana texts that Narváez knew, are replete with references to women as the Virgin's preferred agents. The oft-repeated trope is that God chooses the lowly to forward his great designs. Matiana's prophecies invoked this tradition, and in doing so sought to convince readers to suspend social prejudices against lower-class female servants and women in general. The Duarte interpretation of the prophecies introduced a long list of humble female seers and religious women leading the global fight against impiety and error. In these texts male clerics appear as the facilitators of female revelation and pious fortitude. The Matiana prophecies even asserted that stalwart, devout women would revitalize "lukewarm ecclesiastics," as well as other men.

This superheated reactionary feminism was probably tremendously empowering for women like Matilde Narváez. In Juquila's tumultuous 1920s, amidst news of national anticlericalism and religious rebellion, local conflict, natural disasters, and rumors of local schism, Matilde Narváez probably saw her own experience as part of the grand struggle described in Matiana's visions and elaborated by Duarte. It is possible that the echoes of Matiana in the visions at Ixpantepec are a product of Narváez's narrative interpretation of the Chatina girl's experience. For Narváez, when Nicha's visions came to light it was but a short step to view the Chatina seer and herself as the Blessed Mother's humble instruments. When she took up the Virgin of Ixpantepec's cause the Juquila *beata* essentially stepped into the Matiana legend and its ethos of gender reversal. Nicha spoke for the Virgin and warned the people to repent and thus avert disaster. Canseco played the part of the tepid cleric. Narváez became Nicha's spokeswoman, interpreting the visions, leading the faithful in expiatory ritual, and promoting the Virgin's message. In short, the coming together of Matiana's prophesies, gendered militance, and Nicha's local visions allowed Doña Matildita to perceive a divinely ordained role for herself in the larger struggle. In this context, curate opposition, archdiocesan sanction, and patriarchal social pressures failed to deter the resolute local Catholic leader. The Virgin of Ixpantepec offered this redoubtable devout woman a more personal connection to the ultimate paternal figure of God through the mediation of an Indian girl. In essence, she answered the call to lead the devotional activities that could forestall divine retribution, revive the church, and right society. As we endeavor to understand Catholicism's resurgence, Doña Matildita's decision suggests that the sense of a world-saving mission reserved for Catholic women served as a powerful mobilizing ideology for individuals like the remarkable Narváez. It could inspire devout individuals like her to dedicate their lives to the Catholic cause, but it could also empower them to lead the faithful where the church was unwilling to follow.

NOTES

Chapter opening image source: personal collection of Edward Wright-Rios.

1. Literally "devout woman" and "church mouse," respectively, these terms are not usually compliments. They are usually used to deprecate women seen as overbearingly sanctimonious and fawningly devoted to priests. One Oaxaca centenarian describing Narváez echoed this gendered contempt: "She, like a lot of women, was always involved with priests"; Guillermo Rojas, interview with the author, Oaxaca City, January 26, 2002.

2. Rafael León, interview with the author, Juquila, Oaxaca, February 13, 2002; Teresa Narváez, interview with author, Juquila, Oaxaca, March 10, 2002; and Justina Vásquez, interview with the author, Juquila, Oaxaca, March 11, 2002.

3. For a detailed discussion of this dynamic see Robert Orsi, *Thank You, St. Jude: Women's Devotion to the Patron Saint of Hopeless Causes* (New Haven, CT: Yale University Press, 1996).

4. For a late nineteenth- and early twentieth-century example of the broad socioeconomic role of village priests see Luis González y González, *San José de Gracia: Mexican Village in Transition*, trans. John Upton (Austin: University of Texas Press, 1972).

5. Juquila's shrine festival long served as an annual gathering of traders from Oaxaca's Central Valley and Pacific Coast. Residents of the interior associated the festival with the exoticness of tropical climes, peoples, and products; they often commented

on the presence of black *tierra caliente* dwellers and the sale of parrots and fruit at the feria: see the numerous narratives on the feria, such as José Manuel Ruiz y Cervantes, *Memorias de la portentosa imagen de Juquila* (Oaxaca: Imprenta de L. San-German, 1878); Un peregrino [an anonymous pilgrim], "Hermoso ejemplo de fe y devoción," *La voz de la verdad*, December 17, 1899; José María Bradomín, *Oaxaca en la tradición*, 2nd ed. (Mexico City: Ediciones del Autor, 1968); and Antonio Morales Sánchez, *Romería de Juquila* (Oaxaca: Sedetur, 1997). In the early twentieth century the December gathering also served as an annual horse trading fair: Guillermo Rojas, interview with the author, Oaxaca City, January 26, 2002; and Rafael León, interview with the author, Juquila, Oaxaca, February 13, 2002. Such was the economic importance of the festival in the 1920s that Oaxaca City's liberal, progovernment newspaper covered the yearly exodus of urban merchants heading to the shrine and the state's efforts to secure the pilgrimage/trade route due to rural unrest; see *El mercurio*, December 2 and 13, 1921. In the fall of 1928, amidst fears of Cristero-related social unrest and the height of interest in Nicha's visions, government authorities temporarily waived some taxes and cut livestock sales tax in half in order to encourage people to risk the trip. They also promised to post federal and state troops along the region's trails to prevent rebels and bandits from waylaying devotees, traders, and peddlers. Today the shrine's regional economic importance may be even greater; however, it is no longer due to the festival's dual nature as a trade fair. Juquila is now a center of year-round devotional tourism by charter bus.

6. Female activism was a crucial component of the church's resurgence throughout Europe. In fact, women greatly outnumbered men as participants in the process: see David Blackbourn, "The Catholic Church in Europe since the French Revolution," *Comparative Studies in Society and History* 33 (1991); David Blackbourn, *Marpingen: Apparitions of the Virgin Mary in Nineteenth-Century Germany* (New York: Alfred A. Knopf, 1994); William A. Christian Jr., *Moving Crucifixes in Modern Spain* (Princeton, NJ: Princeton University Press, 1992); William A. Christian Jr., *Visionaries: The Spanish Republic and the Reign of Christ* (Berkeley: University of California Press, 1996); Ralph Gibson, *A Social History of French Catholicism, 1789–1914* (New York: Routledge, 1989); Thomas Kselman, *Miracles and Prophecies in Nineteenth-Century France* (New Brunswick, NJ: Rutgers University Press, 1983); and Frances Lannon, *Privilege, Persecution, and Prophecy: The Catholic Church in Spain, 1875–1975* (Oxford: Clarendon Press, 1987).

7. See *Boletín oficial y revista ecclesiástica de la provincia de Antequera* (hereafter referred to as *Boletín oficial*), "*Sobre todo orar y hacer orar*," July 15, 1902.

8. See Edward Wright-Rios, "Piety and Progress: Vision, Shrine, and Society in Oaxaca, 1887–1934" (Ph.D. diss., University of California, San Diego, 2004), particularly chap. 5.

9. For a discussion of colonial patriarchy in Mexico, see Silvia Marina Arrom, *The Women of Mexico City, 1790–1857* (Stanford, CA: Stanford University Press, 1985); and Steve J. Stern, *The Secret History of Gender: Women, Men, and Power in Late Colonial Mexico* (Chapel Hill: University of North Carolina Press, 1995). Arrom also discusses the transition to the national period. I have also drawn on Carmen Ramos Escandón, "State, Gender, and Power in Nineteenth-Century Mexico," paper given at the Center for U.S.-Mexican Studies, October 22, 2003. Excellent relevant studies on other

regions in Latin America are Sueann Caulfield, *In Defense of Honor: Sexual Morality, Modernity, and Nation in Early-Twentieth Century Brazil* (Durham, NC: Duke University Press, 2000); Sarah C. Chambers, *From Subjects to Citizens: Honor, Gender, and Politics in Arequipa, Peru, 1780–1854* (University Park: Pennsylvania State University Press, 1999); and Christine Hunefeldt, *Liberalism in the Bedroom: Quarreling Spouses in Nineteenth-Century Lima* (University Park: Pennsylvania State University Press, 2000).

10. Details on the life of Hilario Cortés emerge from interviews with Ausencio Canseco's centenarian nephew who still resides in town, Cortés's niece, and another town resident: Rafael León, interview; Amparo García, interview with the author, March 10, 2002; and Felipe Neri Cuevas, interviews with the author, February 14 and March 9, 2002. Cortés's *Historia de Juquila* (unpublished manuscript, circa 1975–80) and a brief diary are in a private collection in Juquila.

11. Cortés, *Historia*.

12. "La doctrina de Madre Matiana," Bancroft Library, University of California, Berkeley.

13. María Josefa de la Pasión de Jesús, *Profecías de Matiana* (Mexico City: Imprenta de la Calle del Cuadrante de Santa Catarina, 1861); Luis G. Duarte and Antonio Martínez del Cañizo, *Profecías de Matiana acerca del triunfo de la iglesia* (Mexico City: Imprenta del Círculo Católico, 1889); and "Las profecías de Matiana," *Boletín oficial*, April 1, 1910.

14. Since the initial publication of the *Boletín* in 1901, all curates in Oaxaca had been required to keep a complete set of the archdiocese's official organ. Pastoral visit reports attest to Father Canseco's zealous compliance with archdiocesan dictates; see Libro de visitas pastorales, Archivo Parroquial de Santa Catarina Juquila. Narváez, as Juquila's parochial school principal, had access to the parish's collection of books and publications.

15. Another source on Matiana's life and prophecies is Josefina Muriel, *Conventos de monjas en la Nueva España* (Mexico City: Editorial Santiago, 1946). Muriel's book cites only one source: an anonymous 1858 document in volume 348 of the *miscelánea* collection of the National Library of Mexico. This date suggests the document in question is a printing of prophecies from this high-water mark of church-state tension like the text used by Duarte and the 1861 text cited herein.

16. De la Pasión de Jesús, *Profecías de Matiana*, 2–3.

17. De la Pasión de Jesús, *Profecías de Matiana*, 5.

18. This is the exact wording used in discussion of Matiana's visions in Oaxaca's official archdiocesan organ; See "Las profecías de Matiana," *Boletín oficial*, April 1, 1910.

19. Duarte and Martínez del Cañizo, *Profecías de Matiana acerca del triunfo de la iglesia*.

20. On the Sacred Heart devotion in Mexico see Leonora Correa Etchegaray, "El rescate de una devoción jesuítica: El Sagrado Corazón de Jesús en la primera mitad del siglo XIX," in *Historia de la iglesia en el siglo XIX*, ed. Ramón Ramos Medina (Mexico City: Condumex, 1998). For a discussion of its prominence in militant conservative politics in Europe see Christian Jr., *Visionaries*; and Raymond Anthony Jonas, *France and the Cult of the Sacred Heart: An Epic Tale for Modern Times* (Berkeley: University of California Press, 2000).

21. Duarte and Martínez del Cañizo, *Profecías de Matiana acerca del triunfo de la iglesia*, 138.

22. *Boletín oficial*, April 1, 1910.

23. On Oaxaca's complex history during and after the Revolution see Paul H. Garner, "Federalism and Caudillismo in the Mexican Revolution: The Genesis of the Oaxaca Sovereignty Movement (1915–20)," *Journal of Latin American Studies* 17, no. 1 (1985) and *La Revolución en la provincia: Soberanía estatal y caudillismo en las montañas de Oaxaca (1910–1920)* (Mexico City: Fondo de Cultura Económica, 1988); Víctor Raul Martínez Vázquez, ed., *La revolución en Oaxaca* (Oaxaca: Instituto de Administración Pública, 1985); María de los Ángeles Romero Frizzi, *Lecturas históricas del estado de Oaxaca, 1877–1930*, vol. 4 (Mexico City: INAH, 1990); and Carlos Sánchez Silva, *Crisis política y contrarrevolución en Oaxaca, 1912–1915* (Mexico City: INEHRM, 1991).

24. Luis Castañeda Guzmán, interview with the author, January 12, 2002.

25. Father Jacobo Martínez to Carlos Gracida, Archivo Histórico de la Arquidiócesis de Oaxaca (hereafter referred to as AHAO) 1927–1928, September 15, 1928.

26. The mountains around Tututepec, Juquila, Sola de Vega, Miahuatlán, and Pochutla were home to several *cristero* bands: see *El mercurio*, September 12 and 28, November 6, and December 23, 1928; and February 20, 1929. The paper also recorded a daring assault on Miahuatlan on October 3, 1928: see *El mercurio*, October 6, 1928. In subsequent months the newspaper followed federal efforts to capture or exterminate bands of *fanáticos*: see *El mercurio*, October 27, 1928. In 1929 the paper noted the surrender of several rebel bands and their leaders in these areas: see *El mercurio*, January 11; July 7, 18, and 26; and August 3, 8, and 14, 1929.

27. See *El Mercurio*, September 12, 1928, and later, in greater detail, September 28, 1928.

28. The protagonist/informant of James Greenberg, *Blood Ties: Life and Violence in Rural Mexico* (Tucson: University of Arizona Press, 1989) was taken in by his godfather Father Canseco as a young boy and raised in Juquila's church. He commented on townspeople taking advantage of the Cristiada to pillage the shrine. Canseco wrote several letters detailing his struggles during this period: see Canseco to Espinoza AHAO DGC 1926, letters dated August 31, October 6, and October 16, 1926, as well as one letter written on the 28th of an illegible month.

29. Anonymous, Teotepec to Apolinar Palacios, Oaxaca, AHAO DGP 1925–1929, November 1, 1927. The copies of the documents show that in July 1927 Father Aureo Castellanos approached municipal authorities and expressed his willingness to abide by the national, state, and local laws relating to religious observance if he could continue his ministry. Villagers also produced a document asserting that Castellanos swore to obey the Reform Laws, the Federal Constitution, and all other laws on religious matters; see AHAO, DGA 1928–1931. See Canseco to Gracida, AHAO DGC 1927–1928, January 1, 1928; and Castellanos to Espinoza, AHAO DGC 1928, April 4, 1928. After a contentious meeting Canseco convinced Castellanos to desist from his dalliance with the government. Fear of schism was a real concern among the Oaxacan clergy and the laity in many communities during this period: see Unknown priest to Carlos Gracida, Santa María Ozolotepec, AHAO DGC 1929, April 8, 1929; and Father Diego Hernández, Santa Catalina Quieri, to Carlos Gracida, AHAO DGC 1927–1928, March 5, 1928.

30. Canseco did not write to his superiors about his financial dispute with Narváez until 1931, but he specifically linked it to his efforts to retile the sanctuary floor in 1926: see Canseco to Francisco Campos, AHAO DGC 1931, May 14 and 29, 1931. See also Canseco to Agustín Espinoza AHAO DGC 1931, August 12, September 28, and November 13, 1931. Matilde Narváez addressed the issue as well: see Narváez to Francisco Campos, AHAO DGC 1931, May 17 and 26, 1931. The archdiocese brought up the issue with Narváez's brothers and made a vague reference to their sister's "spiritual anguishes"; see Francisco Campos to Samuel and Efrén Narváez, Tututepec, AHAO DGC 1931, May 21, 1931.

31. For recent works discussing the impact of coffee production on Chatino communities see Greenberg, *Blood Ties*; Jorge Hernández-Díaz, *El café amargo: Diferenciación y cambio social entre los chatinos* (Oaxaca: UABJO; Instituto de Investigaciones Sociológicas, 1987); and Gonzalo Piñón Jiménez and Jorge Hernández-Díaz, *El café: Crisis y organización: Los pequeños productores en Oaxaca* (Oaxaca: UABJO; Instituto de Investigaciones Sociológicas, 1998).

32. Cortés, *Historia*, 13.

33. Matilde Narváez, *Algunos datos proporicionados por la Señorita Matilde Narváez*, AHAO DGP 1930–1943, April 5, 1932; and Matilde Narváez to José Othón Núñez, AHAO DGC 1934–1939, February 8, 1934.

34. *El Mercurio*, August 8, 1928. A pair of smaller tremors also rocked the region in September amidst surging devotion in Ixpantepec; see *El Mercurio*, September 8 and 23, 1928. According to oral history Nicha predicted the massive January 14, 1931, earthquake that left Oaxaca City and much of the state in ruins; Justina Vásquez, interview.

35. This source preferred to remain anonymous; Ixpantepec, interviews with author, February 14, 2002.

36. In addition to Narváez, *Algunos datos*, AHAO DGP 1930–1943, April 5, 1932; see also *El mercurio*, February 7, 1929.

37. Canseco wrote at least three letters describing the apparitions in January 1929: Canseco to Gracida, AHAO DGC 1928–1929, January 12, 1929; and Canseco to Rafael Torres, AHAO DGC 1928–1929, January 16, 1929. He mentions an earlier letter written to Torres on January 9, but I was unable to locate it in the archive.

38. In this case *interesado* is not a neutral term applied simply to those who support the apparitions. It describes someone or a group with excessive and untoward interest in a matter: see *Diccionario de uso del español* (Madrid: Editorial Gredos, 1982).

39. Canseco to Gracida, AHAO DGC 1928–1929, January 12, 1929.

40. Justina Vásquez, interview. Vásquez's father, mother, and sister visited the apparition site and were very close to Narváez, both as relatives and in their sympathy for the church. However, they ultimately agreed with Canseco that the visions were demonic. Vásquez claimed that Canseco sprinkled holy water on a boulder at the site and it immediately split in two.

41. Canseco to Espinoza, AHAO DGC 1930, May 27, 1930.

42. Cortés stated that after the archdiocese ruled against the devotion the improvised shrine market was burned. However, church authorities could not have accomplished this without the support of secular authorities. Canseco enjoyed a good relationship with civil officials in Ixpantepec, in contrast to the bitter conflicts he

experienced with municipal authorities in Juquila. Hence, I suspect local officials backed the curate and ordered this action.

43. Narváez to José Othón Núñez y Zárate, AHAO DGC 1934–1939, February 8, 1934.

44. Carlos Gracida to Tereso Frías, AHAO DGP 1930–1934, Februrary 23, 1934.

45. Justina Vásquez, interview.

46. Rafael León, interview.

47. Thomas Kselman, "Introduction," *Belief in History: Innovative Approaches to European and American Religion*, ed. Thomas Kselman (Notre Dame, IN: University of Notre Dame Press, 1991).

48. Canseco's predecessor and a one-time close associate of Narváez in Juquila, Manuel Ramírez, had since risen to the rank of canon in Oaxaca City and he could have vouched for her character. In addition, Oaxaca's prelates who visited the famous shrine community, and the urban priests that led annual missions in Juquila, undoubtedly knew Narváez as well.

49. AHAO DGC 1897, Hermandad del Santísimo, Teotitlan del Valle, to Gillow, January 15, 1897.

50. AHAO DGC 1897, Hermandad de las Ánimas, Teotitlan del Camino, to Gillow, January 17, 1897.

10
Juan Soldado: The Popular Canonization of a Confessed Rapist-Murderer

Juan Soldado, as Fashioned by His Devotees. Photo by Paul J. Vanderwood.

Paul J. Vanderwood

In February 1938, an eight-year-old girl was raped and murdered in Tijuana, Mexico. A twenty-four-year-old Mexican soldier confessed to the crime. Within four days authorities had court-martialed and executed him. Soon after, curious visitors reported "signs" at the grave of the soldier. Blood seeped up from the site; the soldier's *ánima*, his spirit, cried out for revenge. Devotion began, miracles occurred, and the faithful erected a shrine at the place of burial. The devotion continues to this day. Juan Soldado is said to be *muy milagroso* (very miraculous). Illegal immigrants call him their patron saint. Hundreds visit his chapel every week to ask favors and pray for Juanito's well-being. How is this possible? How does a convicted rapist-murderer come to be worshiped as a saint?[1]

THE CRIME

Late on the Sunday afternoon of February 13, 1938, eight-year-old Olga Camacho went to the neighborhood grocery in the little border town of Tijuana to buy some meat for dinner. When she did not promptly return, her mother, Feliza, became anxious and went to the store to check on her daughter's whereabouts. Yes, the little girl had been there, said the proprietor, and bought some meat. He had last seen her bounding across the street toward home, only a block away. But now Olga had disappeared.

Feliza thought the child might have tarried at a friend's house, but a check of nearby residences produced no clues. Perhaps she had been hit by a car and taken to the hospital, but doctors there confirmed that no such patient had arrived. Menacing and dark speculations crept into the mother's mind. In the past few years San Diego and vicinity, just north of the nearby boundary with the United States, had experienced a number of child kidnap-murders, several still unsolved. Also, the Lindbergh case still echoed in people's minds. Now the mother's fear grew into panic. She phoned her husband, who managed a local cantina, to the scene, and for an hour or so they searched the neighborhood. Then they called the police.

All night long and well into the next day, police, soldiers from the local military post, and friends of the family searched for Olga to no avail. About noon a neighbor probed an abandoned garage just across the street from the Camacho residence and shrieked, "I have found her! I have found her!" There authorities found the little girl, dead, nearly decapitated by a slash across her throat; and the search for evidence began. Some hair was discovered beneath the fingernails of the victim, indicating she had put up a fight for her life. Blood splattered her clothing and the site, but was it hers or that of her assailant? A distinctive heelprint, which carried a diamond imprint, that of a boot, was found beside the body, and on the roof of a nearby building the package of meat that Olga had bought. The wrapping paper carried a clear, bloody thumbprint.

General Manuel Contreras, commander of the army garrison, took control of the investigation. By early afternoon five young men—two soldiers and three civilians—were in custody at police headquarters for questioning. The three civilians had slept the night in a horse stable near the scene of the crime and convinced the authorities that they had only huddled there as refuge against the night's chill. They were released. So was one of the soldiers, whose mother swore he was with her at home when the rape and murder had occurred. That left only one possible suspect: Juan Castillo Morales, a twenty-four-year-old private from the state of Oaxaca. Authorities questioned Castillo Morales relentlessly. He admitted that he had been hanging around the grocery store and across the street at the old military garrison commonly called the Fort, which had recently been converted into police headquarters. He said he had seen the victim but had not spoken to her and steadfastly maintained his innocence of any wrongdoing.

Meanwhile, a buzzing crowd of local citizens numbering into the hundreds gathered outside the Fort demanding that the soldier be released to their justice. They wanted to lynch him from the nearest tree. As the hours and interrogation wore on, the gathering outside turned ugly. They threw anything they could get their hands on—stones, trash cans, jars, tin cans—at the stone fort. Then someone tossed a firebomb at the building. Wooden window frames, inside paneling, beams, and furniture caught fire. Members of the mob used wooden benches as battering rams to force entry through the main gate. Soldiers inside repelled them at bayonet point but fired no shots. Firemen struggled to douse the flames even as enraged rioters cut their hoses with hatchets. These were anxious moments; the town was in anarchy. General Contreras pleaded for calm and promised there would soon be a break in the case. But he would not release the soldier to their clutches.

Inside the *comandancia* the interrogation continued. Juan Castillo Morales denied any blame in the girl's death. Then shortly before 10 p.m. authorities played their trump card; they confronted the soldier with his common-law wife, who carried the suspect's blood-stained clothes in her hands. She said that Juan had returned home late the previous night, told her that he had been bloodied in a fight, and ordered her to wash the stains from his apparel. The clothing was soaking in a washbin when police arrived to investigate the soldier's modest dwelling. At the sight of his wife and the clothing, Juan broke down. He bowed his head for a moment, then raised it and admitted: "I did it. I did it." Contreras told the crowd outside that authorities had their confession, a statement that further enraged the mob being held at bay by a cordon of soldiers and police with guns drawn and pointed. They wanted immediate revenge for Olga. The military spirited Juan Castillo Morales out a rear entrance to the Fort and hustled him to the relative safety of the army's new headquarters, which lay a mile south on the outskirts of town.

Townspeople maintained pressure on the Fort all night long and in the morning headed for the town hall, which they sacked and burned before soldiers could enforce a semblance of order. For a suspenseful hour the two forces glared and hurled insults at one another. Then the mob of more than one thousand men, women, and teenagers began a slow advance toward the military units protecting the administration building. The soldiers lowered their rifles and fired; wounded demonstrators crumpled to the pavement. The mob broke and ran for safety. Soldiers pursued them cracking heads with rifle butts, and by noon a nervous peace had been restored. Assessing casualties proved to be difficult; newspapers counted as many as twelve dead and hundreds wounded, but the official government report found none dead and six wounded. The truth lay in between. Meanwhile, authorities pondered their options of what to do with Juan Castillo Morales.

Actually, the decision of how to proceed against the confessed murderer lay in the hands of the country's highest authorities, up to the president, Lázaro Cárdenas. Telegrams flew back and forth between General Contreras, the district's governor, and governmental ministries in Mexico City where the decisions were to be made. We are not privy to the deliberations that took place in this case, but we know the result: there was an immediate court-martial of Juan Castillo Morales, which declared him guilty of rape and murder and condemned him to execution. No doubt, proceedings in this case were hurried, evidence not carefully weighed, identification of the suspect flawed, and alternatives unconsidered, but once authorities had a confession in hand (regardless of how they got it), they rushed to judgment and a denouement. Confessions frequently encourage prosecutors to shortcut justice.

It is the execution itself that deserves our attention. First of all, authorities (in Mexico City?) decreed that it be public. This made it extraordinary. Mexico had not had a public execution since late in the nineteenth century. As did most countries in the Western world, by the twentieth century Mexico had declared public executions brutal and uncivilized and moved them inside prisons and other places shielded from public view. Regardless, the execution of Juan Castillo Morales was orchestrated and made public. It was held far enough into the morning of February 17 to ensure that newspaper photographers had sufficient light for their cameras and to give those in the local populace who wished to witness the affair time to do so. More than one thousand local people along with officialdom and a full contingent of the news media attended (and therefore participated in) the spectacle.

But the public aspect of the affair was not its most notable feature. It was also decreed (by Mexico City?) that the guilty soldier be executed via the infamous Ley Fuga. That is, he would be prodded to run and then shot down as a prisoner trying to escape. The Ley Fuga was (and is) not unique to Mexico; it has appeared in many countries and still does. However, the Ley Fuga is an extralegal activity. As such, it is normally committed in a remote place, or at least one outside of public view. A prisoner being transferred from a certain jurisdiction to another never arrives at the new destination. An official inquiry perfunctorily finds that the prisoner tried to escape and therefore the escort had to shoot him or her in flight. In a sense, the prisoner is simply disappeared. The Ley Fuga eliminates the need for entangling, drawn-out judicial procedures. It also is an effective terror tactic. In the case of Juan Castillo Morales the government meant to make a show of force. It needed to restore its authority in a rebellious Tijuana. Just as important, it needed to prove to the local populace that Olga Camacho would be avenged, that her assailant, a soldier, would not be protected by the military but would be brought to rapid and certain justice.

So when the prisoner was brought in a *julia* (police van) to the town's only municipal cemetery that fateful morning, a huge crowd of accusers and two firing squads composed of his fellow soldiers awaited him. The young fellow's knees buckled as guards lifted him from the van to the ground. Then they walked him to the back rim of the cemetery, gave him a cigarette that he hurriedly smoked, and ordered him to run. Juan hesitated; he knew what awaited him. Then he bolted for a freedom that he knew would never come. He leaped over a low barbed wire fence surrounding a grave, and then came the order: "Fuego!" The soldier caught the impact of the first volley squarely in his back. It knocked him down, but he staggered to his feet and ran on. An order to the second firing squad: "Fuego!" Juan pitched forward and fell. He raised his head, pushed upward with his arms, struggled to live, but a third volley of shots from a firing squad drained him of life. A military officer stepped forward to administer the coup de grâce, a final pistol shot in the head. Then soldiers carried him to his prepared grave in the middle of the cemetery—not far from the burial plot of Olga Camacho—dropped him into the hole, and covered him with a layer of dirt. An unknown person placed a wooden cross at the site as a marker: "Juan Castillo Morales died the 17th day of February 1938 at age 24. Rest in peace." Someone had thought to give Juan a traditional Christian remembrance.

What can be said of the witnesses to (or participants in) this drama? The crowd was largely silent throughout the ritualistic pageant and, once it was over, simply melted away. But what did they think of their experience? Olga Camacho was being revenged, but at the same time a young lad, a common soldier, far from home and family, alone at a terrifying moment, was made to run for liberty and then ceremonially shot down, a victim of the hated and dreaded Ley Fuga. Later that day, or the next, people visited the grave site of the fallen soldier. The curious frequently revisit the scenes of such spectacular events. Then, within days, people began to report distinctive (but not necessarily strange) happenings at the place: they said they saw blood seeping from the grave and heard the soldier's *ánima* proclaiming his innocence and crying out for revenge on the true perpetrator. While blood may seep from a grave as a body decomposes beneath a thin covering of soil, and while it is a common belief among many people that the recently departed may hover about to fulfill an unfinished task—to give a loved one a prolonged goodbye, to indicate where some money had been secluded, to remind a person of an obligation, and less frequently to express distaste—the devout see blood emerging from a grave and the proximity of the *ánima* as possible signs of divine presence. They know that those who die suddenly or unfairly sit close to God. If so, that person would be an especially effective intermediary between themselves and the Lord. Visitors began to cover the grave of Juan Castillo Morales with flowers and palm-sized stones to illustrate their remembrance and respect. They said Rosaries at the site. Devotion began to a being that they renamed Juan Soldado—John the Soldier, because his name was Juan and he was a soldier. In keeping with traditional practices they left written petitions asking personal favors of God through the soldier, and miracles occurred. The sick were healed, jobs were found, family feuds were settled. Those who received help left plaques giving thanks at the site. And all this occurred within six months of the crime and execution.

A newspaper reporter visited the cemetery on All Souls Day the first of November 1938 expecting to write about the ways in which Tijuanenses celebrated the Day of the Dead. There he encountered a scene that both startled and fascinated him:

> On All Souls Day the most popular place in any Latin American town is the graveyard. Last Week Tijuana was no exception. In fact, it seemed as if at least half the population of the city climbed the steep hillside just west of the Escuela Obregón [the town's secondary school] to decorate the graves of the dead and say a few prayers for the souls of the departed. This is the way it always has been and the way it was this year. But this time one thing took place that is, to say the least, extraordinary.
>
> It seemed as if fully half of the people visiting the cemetery stopped to pray at the grave of Juan [Castillo] Morales, [who] in case you don't remember, was the soldier executed last February for the murder of little Olga Camacho. He was shot while attempting to escape and was buried where he fell. The crime for which he died was the most brutal, the most horrible, that had ever occurred in the history of Tijuana. Indeed, it was exactly on a par with the more sordid deeds that have taken place in the United States since the turn of the century. Though his trial was not marked with much formality, there is little doubt that [Castillo] Morales was guilty of the deed. All the evidence was against him, and to cinch the case he made a full confession of the crime.
>
> In view of all that it seems scarcely credible that such numbers of people would pray at his grave on All Souls Day. But the cause, as nearly as we have been able to discover, is that many believe [Castillo] Morales to have become an angel. Though some offer as their reason for the prayers that the soldier's soul had greater need of them [the orations] to escape from purgatory than those of others who were buried there, many are of the firm opinion that [Castillo] Morales died innocent of any crime. Some even say that when they knelt at this grave they could hear the dead soldier talking. Those hold that the crime was committed by another, and that [Castillo] Morales, as a Christian act, decided to take the blame upon himself.[2]

A devotion had been born.

Popular devotions such as these are born of both immediate and long-term circumstances as well as traditional and contemporary belief. Circumstances and belief are always inextricably mixed in human experience; they are like scrambled eggs. Nevertheless, in order to comprehend and ponder the origins, existence, and power of the Juan Soldado devotion, it is necessary to expose the building blocks of this new religious observance—first the circumstances and then the beliefs—before they can be assembled into the edifice of faith and pragmatic necessity combined that serves the needs of so many believers in Tijuana and well beyond, on both sides of the international boundary, to this day.

CONSEQUENCES

Devotions such as that accorded to Juan Soldado often develop in small, out-of-the-way places, frequently locales with soiled reputations (typically for backwardness or bawdiness), and in areas dominated by the political brawn and economic weight of better-known, much larger, and more important neighboring cities. Such tendencies are evident at several humble nineteenth-century apparition sites that since have grown into renowned shrines, such as Lourdes and La Salete in France and during the past century at Fatima in Portugal, as well as the more recent devotion at Medjugorje in present-day Bosnia-Herzegovina. Closer to Juan Soldado, the U.S.-Mexico border is also dotted with miracle-working sites, all of which originated in tiny outpost communities: the True Cross shrine to the crucified Christ, El Señor de los Milagros, in San Antonio and the Pedro Jaramillo shrine at Falfurrias, both in Texas; and across the Rio Grande near Monterrey, Mexico, the El Niño Fidencio religious site at Espinal. When devotion to Juan Soldado began, Tijuana fit the pattern. It was small then, with hardly ten thousand inhabitants, many of them fairly new arrivals. While perhaps not remote, it sat distant from the center of national affairs and was inextricably tied to its burgeoning foreign neighbor, San Diego. The town was widely renowned for vice and corruption, and many considered it to be little more than a piquant playground for tourists. Nonetheless, factors such as remoteness, neighborly dominance, and reputation, which seem to have spawned shrines elsewhere, have only limited application here. Tijuana may have seemed remote as viewed from Mexico City or Washington, DC, but it had transport connections to other locations on the peninsula, as well as to the main part of the country to the east and south, and also telegraph lines, telephones, and radio stations for faster communication with the outside world. A steady if limited flow of merchandise arrived from the interior, and thousands of tourists reminded its inhabitants every day of their connection to a wider world. Tijuanenses understood they were a long way from Mexico City, but that was not all detrimental. They wanted to improve communication with other places for economic reasons, and the border could complicate but certainly not isolate them from their neighbor to the north. Yet there is no indication that the residents of Tijuana considered themselves remote, especially in the sense of being out of touch.

People also found good and bad in their proximity to San Diego. When juxtaposed against fast-growing San Diego's much larger population (in 1940 approaching two hundred thousand), its more diversified economy, its entertainment and culinary possibilities, and the fabulous harbor that guaranteed its
future, Tijuana certainly seemed to be overshadowed. But while the two urban
neighbors enjoyed important working relationships, each maintained its own
identity, and Tijuanenses could be quite feisty in protecting their interests,
whether at the customs post, in police investigations, the marketplace, employee
relations, or in regional politics. While they knew that they were economically
dependent, they did not feel socially, politically, or psychologically dependent.
Thus in the case of Tijuana, "overshadowed" did not mean "dominated by."

As for reputation, moralists and others considered Tijuana to be the devil's
playground, a town of vice and sin. Its reputation as seen through these eyes
was pitch black. But for the great majority of outsiders, Tijuana's hue was
more subtle, perhaps a bit off-color, fuzzy, but not unappreciated. The California dream for migrants who headed west from other parts of the United
States included a chance to kick up their heels some. Tijuana was certainly a
place to do that. Tijuanenses have long decried labels such as "vice" and "sin"
being wantonly applied to their city, mainly because there is so much more to
their town than the main tourist streets, and because those sorts of negatives
can be found in any town or city. Tijuana's Chamber of Commerce and other
agencies have over time been trying to ameliorate the community's negative
image among outsiders by stressing the cultural and entertainment diversity in
town, but at they same time they fear that too much "cleanup" will hurt
tourism—that is, sterilize a place that thrives on a bit of dirt.

Residents do not appreciate being called *provincianos* by Mexico City. The
truth is that they are hardly country rubes. They cannot hope to acquire the
political power and cultural strength of Mexico City, but they can elect opposition candidates, strive to run their own affairs, and gather economic strength
that raises eyebrows in the capital. They certainly did not feel in the 1920s and
1930s that they were living in Sin City. Although memory has a way of scrap-
ing the barnacles off former times, older Tijuanenses recall a secure, neighborly, small-town past in which people used inventiveness and fortitude to
forge a respectable community in turbulent years.

Of course there were unsettling problems in the community, where national
and international currents flowed into and shaped local issues. At the time of
the Camacho tragedy, much of the world was still feeling the economic effects
of the Great Depression, although this was less true in Southern California and
Tijuana than in many other regions. Still, the forced deportation of thousands
of Mexican workers from the United States meant that border towns like Tijuana experienced an influx of refugees who established new *colonias* and

placed enormous demands on that particular town's water, refuse, and school services. The repeal of Prohibition in the United States in 1933 meant that fewer American tourists wet their whistles in Tijuana's cantinas, some of which went out of business as did a number of liquor stores. The federal government tried to ameliorate the downturn by experimenting with the establishment of a Free Trade Zone and funding various public works, but jobs were lost, underemployment persisted, and hardships occurred. Still, a good many Tijuanenses did not think it all bad. As much as anything else, the Depression and Prohibition's demise forced Tijuana owners out of one business into another. While they put some tourist places out of business, not only the bars but also barber shops, hotels, and car garages, they spawned more gift shops, perfume and tobacco outlets, gasoline stations, two stationery stores, and a couple of small factories. And while long-range tourism declined, San Diego and Southern California continued to pour visitors into town. In 1932 alone, five million tourists visited Tijuana, a average of 13,408 daily. Mainly they came in automobiles, nearly four thousand cars each day, or one and one-half million for the year. If each tourist spent only $5 (a modest estimate) together they generated nearly $25 million in income for the town. On Labor Day in 1934, more than forty-two thousand tourists came to town and spent an estimated $80,000 (U.S.) there, and all this in the midst of the worldwide, if unevenly distributed, economic depression. Material deprivation does not seem to have characterized Tijuana in the period.[3]

But were the residents spiritually denied? Church-state conflict marked most of 1920s Mexico. The government's determination to curtail the church's power in civic life (politics, schools, community presence) ignited the Cristero movement, which roiled regions of the country, especially from 1926 to 1929. Three years later in a new burst of antichurch enthusiasm the government limited the church to only one priest per fifty thousand population. This amounted to one priest for all of northern Baja California, stationed in Mexicali. This left Tijuana without a priest, although the one in the district visited the town once a year to say mass. So it was up to Catholics to pursue their religiosity as best they could. Some held neighborly prayer meetings in their homes; such sessions were not secretive, simply people getting together to say the Rosary. A priest might come to town surreptitiously from the U.S. side to perform last rites (at a substantial fee), or authorities might just look the other way when a known priest arrived in street clothes to perform a religious rite or to visit friends. Those Tijuanenses who wished to do so could cross the line for Catholic services, and many people regularly did so. Holy images adorned the dwellings of residents, and some, like the Camachos, had home altars. None of this, however, approached remembrances of Catholic life in their former hometowns or places of birth. Tijuana did not even have a patron saint, no holy figure to celebrate and to pray to for favors and protection, no one special to intercede for its citizens before the Lord. Perhaps they felt no need for one; in any case, the town's Catholics were for all practical purposes on their own.

But did it matter? It is tempting to draw a direct line from formal religious deprivation in Tijuana to the origins of the devotion to Juan Soldado. One could say that the people needed a saint and so created their own, but this explanation is much too simplistic. Other towns experienced the same sorts of general conditions that stirred Tijuana, yet no special devotion developed in them. Tijuana's Juan Soldado seems to have been unique in this regard. Furthermore, it is one thing for latter-day onlookers to judge the town and declare it wanting, and something quite different to understand and appreciate what the populace felt about itself at the time. Just how badly did Mexican migrants miss the strong Catholic presence of previous times? Judging by their answers to interviews, not very much. Many said they were Catholics because their parents raised them in the church, and they were perfectly willing to respect those wishes. Migration, however, had loosened the family ties and allowed them to practice their faith as conditions permitted and in their own ways.[4] There is no reason to suspect that Tijuanenses (themselves largely immigrants) did not do the same. Catholicism as missed or forgotten did not create the Juan Soldado shrine but was among a series of lenses, some quite murky, through which people viewed the horrendous events of mid–February 1938. It was only one of the circumstances that defined the town, its populace, and its thinking at the time.

Calamity struck Tijuana in 1935. Lázaro Cárdenas had been elected president the previous year, and his administration launched a program of strident land, education, and labor reform. It also announced one of those periodic moralization campaigns of which Mexican administrations are so fond and closed down the country's gambling casinos. Since 1915 Tijuana had depended on so-called vice taxes—taxes on casinos, cabarets, prostitution houses, horse racing, heavy drugs—to support its economy and to finance public improvements such as schools and roads. When Cárdenas shut down casinos, particularly at the sumptuous and world-renowned Agua Caliente on the outskirts of town, he closed the town's major employer; he threw more than five hundred people out of good-paying work. Protests by labor unions representing these workers immediately began. Under the pressure, the government waffled. For the next two years rumors about reopenings raised hopes that never materialized. Unions tried to run the hotel and other nongambling facilities at Agua Caliente—the bar, spa, gift shop, dance hall, and dining rooms—but they could not turn a profit. Gambling is always the big moneymaker at these sorts of resorts. The remaining entertainment was just so much "come-on." Tourists wanted to gamble at Agua Caliente, and when they could not, they stayed away.

Starting with taxi drivers in the early 1920s, the unionization of Tijuana's workers was strong and militant. The numerous trade syndicates were grouped under the Regional Confederation of Mexican Workers (CROM), the politically powerful national organization that supported federal administrations from 1920 to the ascension of Cárdenas. Determined to break with its predecessors, the new regime supported the rising and radical Confederation of Mexican Workers (CTM), and the rival confederations were locked in fierce and frequently bloody competition throughout the nation. But the CROM remained dominant in Tijuana, and therefore anti-Cardenista. In fact, Tijuanenses in general wanted little to do with this president and his policies.

Now the caldron simmering with distaste and disgust began to bubble. CROM workers who had been discharged following an aborted attempt to reopen Agua Caliente demanded severance pay. The local labor arbitration board ruled against them. On February 9—now only five days before the death of Olga Camacho and the riots that followed it—CROM occupied the municipal palace. Families of workers, women, and children set up camp in one corner of the patio, their presence marked by the union's red and black flags, their symbol of defiance.[5] These squatters were still planted inside the *palacio* when the mutilated corpse of eight-year-old Olga Camacho was discovered in the dilapidated garage near the child's home, and when the young infantry soldier Juan Castillo Morales confessed to the crime. In the ensuing riots, CROM's presence was evident, noticed, and recorded by authorities.

These, then, were among the more obvious (and verifiable) long- and short-term circumstances that affected the ways in which Tijuanenses pondered the shocking events enveloping them in February 1938. When combined with belief, they led (for some) to the worship of Juan Soldado. Surely additional circumstances such as background and personal experience influenced individuals. We can never see what they saw, know that they knew, feel as they felt. Social science techniques can carry us only so far into their realm, but then must be abandoned to possibilities (and probabilities) and faith along with the unknown and unknowable. Nonetheless, we still have our curiosity, instincts, humanness, and (hopefully) good sense, informed by the wisdom and intelligence of ageless sages, with which to examine and ponder the transcendental.

BELIEF

Nothing strained and strengthened the web of circumstances and belief for Tijuanenses more than the execution of Juan Castillo Morales that chilly February morning in the town's public cemetery. Extraordinary events such as these invite introspection and can heighten (as well as challenge) belief. Naturally, the event itself and the violence that preceded it were on people's minds, if not their consciences. Widely discussed in planned get-togethers and chance meetings of the citizenry, the occurrences provoked reactions ranging from vociferous debate to a hushed indecisiveness approaching bewilderment. Differences of opinion surfaced, along with conclusions of varied intensity. A good many thought the soldier guilty and deserving of death. Retribution reigned in their minds. Others found Castillo Morales culpable but harbored reservations about the procedures that had brought him to justice—the rapidity of the investigation, the suddenness of the announced confession, the secretive court-martial, the staged execution. Some doubted his guilt; conspiracy theories abounded. Could Juan have been the scapegoat for a higher-up? Then, in 1938, most found him guilty. Today virtually all his devotees declare him innocent. However, Olga Camacho's relatives certainly do not, and the townspeople at large simply utter, "It is said that . . ." They pass no judgment on the case and avoid further consideration with that famous Mexican phrase of avoidance, "¿Quién sabe?"—who knows, or who cares?

In this atmosphere of uncertainty and conjecture, devotion to Juan Soldado began, so quickly in fact that people must have wanted and been ready for it, or perhaps been shocked into it. The seeds had long been sown in belief and circumstance, but an unseemly event had caused the scatterings to germinate.

While on the one hand military and civil authorities certainly never envisioned the blossoming of a strong devotion at the grave site of a confessed and convicted rapist-murderer, on the other hand, they never attempted to restrain its development (beyond laughing it off as silly superstition). One wonders whether or not religiosity in any way entered their hastily planned script for the execution, specifically the decision to openly apply the Ley Fuga on sacred ground. Did they not know the importance of sacred ground to religious sensibilities? Had they not learned a lesson about the dawns of devotion to Mexican criminals denied interment in sacred ground? Best known to them would have been the story of Jesús Malverde, the bandit who ranged through the mountains above Sinaloa's state capital of Culiacán early in the twentieth century, robbing the rich and aiding the poor, according to his worshipers. When Malverde was finally captured and hanged in 1929, the governor, in keeping with historical precedent, refused to permit any burial of the corpse at all. Within a few days passers-by began to place rocks and stones on the decayed body. A few rocks quickly grew into a pile, then a mound; devotion began and the people canonized Jesús Malverde as *their* saint.[6]

Closer to Tijuana we recall the story of El Tiradito, billed by Tucson's Chamber of Commerce as "the only sinner to become a saint." Like all such tales, that of Tiradito is shrouded in murky memory, creative retelling, and reflections of changing times. In the latter part of the nineteenth century, so the most frequently told story goes, a young ranch hand named Juan Olivas, cowpoking outside of Tucson or in northern Mexico, became infatuated with his stepmother, his father's wife, and she with him. A sexual liaison developed, and one day the father caught them making love. As the youngster sought to escape the entanglement, his father cleaved him with an ax and had the corpse buried haphazardly where it fell. Mexican and Mexican-American Catholics thought the burial of Tiradito unholy. His remains lay in unblessed earth; therefore, his soul would suffer in purgatory forever and be denied its final glory. Pious neighbors placed candles on the grave (which tradition locates in the historic quarter of Tucson) and in their prayers commended the soul of the slain sinner to God. Devotion soon brought personal requests and miraculous rewards. A shrine now exists, "Dedicated to the soul of a sinner buried in unconsecrated ground."[7] The manner of death and place of burial carry profound religious meaning for any number of believers, meaning which is inextricably intertwined with more secular notions of justice and fairness.

We know what spectators at the execution of Juan Castillo Morales *saw*. The ritualistic public ceremony, the hated and dreaded Ley Fuga in action, the bloodied soldier who fell three times en route to death, the coup de grâce that left a pocket in the soil beneath his head. We know what they *saw*; the question is how did they *feel*? How might *you* feel? Did they liken his travail to the passion of Jesus Christ? Feelings can inaugurate devotion. Meanings that these witness-participants took from the execution of Juan Castillo Morales helped to substantiate his canonization as Juan Soldado.

We cannot be sure—we simply do not have sufficient evidence—to assert with any certainty that the spectators who witnessed the execution of the young soldier likened it to the painful sufferings of Christ. At least some must have sensed the connection—not that in any fashion they thought the soldier divine, but that here was an individual suffering a terrible injustice, if not in relation to the accusations against him, then at least in the prolonged agony and ultimate disgrace in which he died. These days, devotees of Juan Soldado certainly forge just such links. One man says, "The day they shot Juan Soldado it rained, the sky cried," a reference to the Biblical declaration that the skies darkened as Christ died (Luke 23:44–45). Another speaks of the execution as "the crucifixion" of the soldier. Others drop additional hints of association: Jesus and Juan, killed by their own people, executed to maintain political order; each fell three times on his way to a ghastly death; both were accused common criminals who had actually done nothing wrong; both were put to death by the military; both were scapegoats to satisfy the aims of authority. Unjust, unfair, inhumane, wrong-headed, undeserved—they all add up to grievance and sympathy.

Almost all of the faithful connect the story of Juan Soldado most directly to that of Christ through the concept of martyrdom—not those martyrs of the early Christian Church who died for their faith, for their refusal to renounce their belief in Christ as God, but martyrs to justice: those who suffered injustice and died unfairly at the hands of unfettered authority. The mix of circumstance and belief now thickens; the virulent strain of politics, including power, authoritarianism, and arrogance, becomes more evident along with those of social imbalance and official corruption. Spirituality, religiosity, piety, and faith are lived within this context.

Mexicans, in general, have little confidence or trust in their government or its judicial arm, the result of centuries of official corruption and abuse. In the public mind, explanation of untoward events frequently alleges government complicity or conspiracy, so it is not surprising that those who worship Juan Soldado as a saint insist that he was the victim of a military conspiracy, that Juan Castillo Morales had nothing to do with the ghastly rape and murder of Olga Camacho but that an officer in his army unit committed the crime and framed Juan to take the blame. At least, that is what his followers say today in a kaleidoscopic tale of ever-changing detail. In one common version a captain did the deed and then handed Castillo Morales a package containing the little girl's bloody clothing, telling him to get rid of it. Juan did so, but some of the blood got on his uniform, which explains how the spots found on his clothing later implicated him. This captain, often identified as Juan's commanding officer, emerges as the bête noire in many versions of the story.

All of these stories emanate from a patchwork of tradition, lore, lived experience, and personal predilection. Like all such accounts, they breathe; they change in content and emphasis. But they are not willy-nilly inventions meant to justify a devotion. Better said, they are explanations of why these devotees of Juan Soldado think and act as they do over time, how the travail of the soldier resonates with their own lives and aspirations, and how a despicable criminal can become a revered saint.

As with all explanations concerning religious practices, thoughts, and sensibilities, generalities do not notably clarify how or why criminals (or purported criminals) become saints. Most have been canonized by the people, as opposed to the church, although the latter has scrubbed clean the histories of a good many of its own saints to ensure that they meet the standards of virtue. The masses have also done their share to soak their saints in admirable human qualities, and Juan Soldado is no exception. Dissonance occurs because those who are labeled criminals by the state are often considered heroes by the people, or they are seen as criminals unjustly convicted by officialdom or wrongdoers cruelly mistreated and spitefully punished by government. Popular canonizations that stem from these sorts of circumstances seethe with political recrimination and retaliation.

Criminals thought to be guilty but repentant have also been declared saints by the populace. The blood and bodies of executed criminals often carried religious significance for spectators at public executions. Such figures were seen as different from ordinary mortals and as kinds of martyrs, closer to God. Therefore their *ánimas* carried a special import—these were souls that were most in need of prayer and that in grateful return would more fervently represent human needs to the Almighty. A special devotion to the *ánimas* of criminals who had lost their heads to the guillotine emerged several centuries ago in Palermo, Sicily, and a church on what was then the outskirts of town became a pilgrimage site dedicated to their memory. Although executed criminals who had enjoyed higher social status in life were often buried with much pomp in private cemeteries, the repentant convict unclaimed by friends or kin might well have ended up in the graveyard behind the Church of the Beheaded Ones. In life, these venerated individuals may have been brutally violent, but before execution they asked the pardon of their victims and God and renounced untoward violence in all forms. Spectators remembered and embraced the Biblical dictum "There will be more joy in heaven over one sinner who repents than over ninety-nine just persons who need no repentance" (Luke 15:7). Hence the living saw the *ánimas* of these repentant convicts as close to God and so as protectors against robbers and other dangers.[8]

Who knows whether or not Juan Castillo Morales repented at the hour of his death? Only God, for certain. Today few followers mention repentance as the reason for their devotion. Those who do, pray to Juan as an *ánima purgando*, a restlessly wandering spirit in search of the path to Heaven. If he did commit the crime (and a handful of devotees still insist that he did so), no one is in more need of prayer than Juan Soldado, and no one would be more grateful for prayers received or more willing to ask the Lord for favors on behalf of his benefactors. When asked how they know that Juan repented, these people simply reply, "How do you know that he did not?" Even if he did not openly, loudly, and clearly ask forgiveness at the execution, they note that the soldier's *ánima* (as do all such spirits) hovered about the grave site for three or four days after his death, and that repentance most likely occurred during that period.

Saints provide a connection between heaven and earth. Saints are venerated not because they are different from us, but because they are like us. They are compassionate, humorous, boisterous, forgetful, sometimes uncooperative, capable of revenge, consoling, mysterious, imperfect, and unpredictable. God is glorious, but remote, while saints are family. A saint could be a neighbor, a teacher, a derelict, or a homeless person. At heart, saints are human. That the

Almighty is omnipresent and interventionist is at the core of Christian thought, but miracles abetted by saints prove the point in concrete form.

Some still think of saints as extraordinarily virtuous people, which remains the official position of the church, but in our times human foibles are viewed as understandable, and good works are recognized despite personal shortcomings. There is no one topology that embraces all saints. Instead, saints tend to reflect the politics, social realities, and transcendent religious aspirations in which they developed and became admired. The faithful expect their otherworldly saints to respond to the needs of contemporary times.

The foundation of the devotion to Juan Soldado has emerged as a rich composite of circumstances and belief that portrays Tijuana and its populace in 1938. The gruesome manner of the public execution accorded the young soldier convicted of murder and rape, set against a background of social agitation caused by national politics, fallout from the Depression, and the stress of growth and change, pressed people to ponder their perceptions of the calamitous events surging about them. It challenged (and in some cases confirmed) their sense of justice as administered by the state, raised the specter of their own complicity (by silence or otherwise) in the horrid affair, and heightened their spiritual sensibilities pertaining to divine intervention in worldly affairs. Adoration followed, miracles occurred, a saint was born. As with most relationships between *santos* and their followers, this association had both practical and material elements mingled with abiding religiosity. Worshipers begged the grace of God for material betterment on earth but at the same time honored the supremacy of the Lord in their lives and recognized the domination of divine will over earthly power.

Devotions, such as that to Juan Soldado, are never static; they are always percolating, being reshaped and remodeled. How can it be otherwise, when the interplay between those circumstances and beliefs that led to the adoration in the first place are so different from those generating the devotion today? A thin residue of an earlier mix may remain, but the requisites and aspirations of the pious fluctuate and are transformed by the realities and fantasies of their own age. When veneration to Juan Soldado began, Tijuana was a physically cohesive town of less than fifteen thousand inhabitants, principally lodged on a small mesa. Now its population is estimated to be nearly two million; the city sprawls for miles in a crazy-quilt pattern over the abrupt hills and canyons of the surrounding countryside down to the sea.

Tijuana is a stew of people. What was in 1938 a relatively insignificant, loosely patrolled, and easily negotiated border post is now the most crossed international line in the world, tightly guarded from the U.S. side, and smothered in bureaucratic rigmarole. Today's formidable waves of migration dwarf the ripples of the 1930s. Protestantism possessed only a tiny toehold in the town sixty years ago, but now an evangelical presence is notable in the city. Consumerism, materialism, secularization—those hallmarks of bustling, modern cities—have created opportunities, raised expectations, and torn at family ties as well as community relations and comradeships; they have strained public services, frustrated bureaucrats, worried spiritual leaders, forced individualism on many who fear it, encouraged artistic creation, and made Tijuana both a beacon of possibility and siren of disaster. Much of this effervescence is reflected at the shrine of Juan Soldado. It can be seen in the petitions that the pious address to their *santo*:

Please allow our family a good personal relationship so that our parents do not suffer. In return, I PROMISE not to fight with my brothers and sisters. Help my mother through her operation. I promise to bring her here [to the shrine] personally to see you.

Good soldier: I ask you with all my heart and all my faith that Benny has his child with him forever. Good soldier: help me as I am a mother, and like your mother, I suffer for my children. I promise to come with Benny and his son, and each will light three candles to you.

[A business card] Larry McClements, Oakwood Multi-Media Services, Woodland Hills, California. [When contacted, he said he does not venerate Juan Soldado, but that four years ago he left a card at the shrine, "just in case." And how has business fared since then? "I have had very good luck."]

Care for my mother, as I am going to the other side [the United States] to work for awhile.

Thank you for helping my son to graduate from Redlands High School [in southern California]. [As she promised to do, she has left a photocopy of her son's diploma leaning against a bust of Juan Soldado.]

My love, a helicopter pilot, was killed in a crash of his helicopter. Bring me more information about the accident. Bring him back to me. Help that my sweetheart [male] never deceives me.

Unite me with this woman. If so, I promise . . . I really do not know what to promise, but I will promise something.

[On the picture of a 1980s station wagon] Gracias.

Make me a good soldier like you. The best. Strong and valiant.

Thank you for the miracle of caring for my brother. I did not believe in your miracles. I ask you to pardon me for not believing in your miracles. Today I believe in you.

I am from Tijuana. One day let me pass to the U.S.A. through the great door [customs and immigration] without hiding from anyone.

Juan Soldado, I ask you to care for my family, and I give you thanks, although I am not a Catholic.

Thanks for the miracles. You know that powerful people work with the devil [to torment me].

Juan Soldado, I thank you for all that you have granted me. Give me strength so that I can solve my problems. I am a very lonely woman. I have my husband and daughter, but you know that I love another man, because we have come here together [to see you]. Please make sure he never abandons me.

[A police wanted poster from the Fresno, California, sheriff's office is on the wall.] Here is the man who killed my daughter [who was married to the suspect]. I ask that you help me by bringing him to justice. Thank you. [A Fresno detective confirmed the man's capture, trial, conviction, and sentence to life imprisonment. The suspect had fled to Tijuana, where a friend convinced him to turn himself over to authorities who delivered him to Fresno authorities. The detective in charge said that it would have been difficult to apprehend the defendant had it not been for the lucky break in Tijuana. He said he knew nothing of Juan Soldado's miracles, but . . .]

Fulfill my greatest dream. Let me win the lottery.[9]

Petitioners at the Juan Soldado shrine seek divine energy to solve problems familiar to us all. Individual needs surpass superficial similarities on the petitions. Their words are intensely personal and frequently moving. They make compassionate observers want to help, but the matter is in other hands.

So was Juan Castillo Morales guilty or innocent? Followers of Juan Soldado have already decided, based not so much on material evidence, but on their convictions about earthly justice and heavenly grace. God sent signs to these people, who have a lively attachment to the unseen and spiritual, and then worked through the soldier to perform miracles and is continuing to do so. Faith is their touchstone, and when they tell you that their veneration of Juan Soldado is a matter of faith, it probably means "You really do not understand"—or it could be a polite slap in the face: "I believe and you do not." "I have faith" can also be a defensive mechanism against the attacks of others: "This belief is mine, not yours." Faith, normally larded with doubt, exists in various forms and intensities that can be neither measured or weighed. Under the circumstances, the devotion to Juan Soldado is best seen as simply something that the faithful *need* to do.

NOTES

Unless otherwise noted, translations are by the author.

1. This essay contains summaries and excerpts from the author's book, *Juan Soldado: Rapist, Murderer, Martyr, Saint* (Durham, NC: Duke University Press, 2004).

2. The newspaper quotation is from the *San Isidro Border Press*, November 11, 1938, 1. This section, "The Crime," has been reconstructed through newspaper accounts of the events from February 14 to February 17, 1938. Newspapers consulted include *La Época* (Tijuana), *El Excelsior* (Mexico City), *Los Angeles Examiner, Los Angeles Times, La Opinión* (Los Angeles), *San Diego Evening Tribune, San Diego Sun, San Diego Union, San Francisco Chronicle, St. Louis Post Dispatch, El Universal* (Mexico City), and *El Universal gráfico* (Mexico City). Interviews with participants such as Feliza Camacho, Olga's mother, and José Camareño Iñíquez, secretary to the town's *delegado* (mayor), provided additional details. The interviews were conducted in their respective homes in Tijuana in 2000. I am extremely grateful to Feliza Camacho and José Camareño Iñíquez for their friendly willingness to recall these tragic days for my benefit.

3. David Piñera Ramírez and Jesús Ortiz Figueroa, *Historia de Tijuana, 1889–1989: Edición conmemorativa del centenario de su fundación*, 2 vols. (Tijuana: n.p., 1989), 1:129–34; Vincent Z. C. de Baca, "Moral Renovation of the Californias: Tijuana's Political and Economic Role in American-Mexican Relations, 1920–1935" (Ph.D. diss., University of California, San Diego, 1991), 137; and Universidad Autónoma de Baja California, Instituto de Estúdios Históricos, Fondo Abelardo Rodríguez, Leg. 7.50, Exp. Tourist Guide, 1933. U.S. Consul Reports from Mexicali and Ensenada, 1931–1936 (U.S. National Archives, Record Group 59) also detail the impact of these events and their aftermath.

4. Manuel Gamio, orally and with questionnaires, interviewed Mexican migrants to the United States in the late 1920s. Although scholars have challenged his analysis and conclusions, the testimony of those interviewed remains invaluable. See Gamio's *The Life Story of the Mexican Migrant* (New York: Dover, 1971) and *Mexican Immigration to the United States. A Study of Human Migration and Adjustment* (Chicago: University of Chicago Press, 1930).

5. The *San Diego Sun* colorfully elaborates these events in its January 3–6, 1938, editions.

6. There are many journalistic accounts concerning Jesús Malverde. Among the most recent and informative are Daniel Sada, "Cada piedra es un deseo," *Letras libres* 15 (2000); *La Jornada* (Mexico City), August 10 and 11, 2000; and Sam Quiñones, *True Tales from Another Mexico: The Lynch Mob, The Popsicle Kings, Chalino, and the Bronx* (Albuquerque: University of New Mexico Press, 2001), 225–32.

7. A full file of newspaper clippings and other materials about the Tiradito story and shrine exists in the archives of the Arizona Historical Society, Tucson, Arizona. See, especially, ephemeral files "Tucson," "Neighborhoods," and "Barrio Libre," and place folders "Tucson" and "Wishing Shrine." Also see Gamio, *Mexican Migration*, 127–47. Juan Soldado is considered along with Tiradito in James S. Griffith, "El Tiradito and Juan Soldado," *International Folklore Review* (1987).

8. The fascinating cult of the Decollati (beheaded ones) is discussed in E. Sidney Hartland, "The Cult of Executed Criminals at Palermo," *Folk-Lore* 21 (1910); M. P. Carroll, *Veiled Threats: The Logic of Popular Catholicism in Italy* (Baltimore: Johns Hopkins University Press, 1996), 142–45; and Lucia Franzonello, "Il Culto delle anime decollate in Sicilia" (Tesi di Laurea, Università da Palermo, 1946).

9. The author has visited the shrine on numerous occasions over the past decade. He has been there several times on San Juan Day (June 24) when Juan Soldado's birthday is celebrated by the faithful. With the needed and thoroughly appreciated assistance of Mexican and Mexican-American colleagues, he conducted a survey of devotees in June 2000, which resulted in a composite portrait of visitors to the shrine that appears in the book.

11
Religion and the Mexican Revolution: Toward a New Historiography

Adrian Bantjes

V. R. DE LA MILAGROSA IMAGEN DE JESUS NAZARENO.

Shrine Souvenir of the Señor de las Peñas of San Pedro Etla, Oaxaca, 1889. Established in the colonial period and very popular in the late nineteenth and early twentieth century, devotion to this pilgrimage image was viewed by ecclesiastical officials as a model of well-ordered popular piety. According to oral history sources, indigenous pilgrims from distant communities thronged the Lord's official feast each fifth Friday of Lent, and the following Sunday specially chartered trains ferried devotees and revelers from Oaxaca City to the shrine.

There are more things in heaven and earth, Horatio,
Than are dreamt of in your philosophy.

—Shakespeare, *Hamlet*, Act 1, Scene 5.

Judging from the recent political and moral assertiveness of the Mexican Roman Catholic Church and laity, and the shrill responses of clerophobes, Catholicism is alive and well in post-*priista* Mexico.[1] During his momentous and ultimately successful bid for the presidency in 2000, PAN candidate Vicente Fox unfurled the banner of the Virgin of Guadalupe, Mexico's most powerful symbol of national identity.[2] Soon after Fox's inauguration, *panistas* in various states, including Fox's home state of Guanajauto, launched moralistic campaigns that attacked the wearing of miniskirts and table dances and passed legislation penalizing women seeking abortion after being raped. Catholic laymen and clergy, including the ultraconservative lay organization Pro-Vida, sought to stop the screening of Carlos Carrera's allegedly sacrilegious film *El crimen del Padre Amaro*, while recently Catholics decried the Mexican government's intriguing decision to give Mel Gibson's movie *The Passion of the Christ* an X rating.[3] The outspoken Mexican cardinal Norberto Rivera Carrera is still seriously considered *papabile*.[4] And on July 31, 2002, Pope John Paul II canonized Juan Diego at the Basilica of the Virgin of Guadalupe in Mexico City, bolstering Guadalupanismo as an alternative Catholic source of Mexican nationalism. The Virgin's shrine at Tepeyac is now the center of the world's largest Christian pilgrimage, attracting 14.8 million pilgrims in 1999.[5]

The newly galvanized Catholic Church has also reveled in revisiting the nation's violent past, especially the profound religious conflict that nearly sundered the country during the Mexican Revolution. In March 2000, the Mexican Bishops' Conference issued a *carta pastoral*, titled "Del encuentro con Jesucristo a la solidaridad con todos . . . ," which reminded Mexicans that "During the religious persecution, the Church witnessed the martyrdom of many of its members, who offered their lives for the right to religious freedom by dying for their faith in Christ King and the Virgin of Guadalupe and for their love of Church and Fatherland."[6] To the elation of Mexican Catholics, the Vatican responded two months later, on May 21, 2000, by canonizing twenty-five Mexicans, mainly clergymen and laypersons martyred during the 1920s Catholic Cristero rebellion against the revolutionary state. The *carta pastoral* goes further than acknowledging the era of religious persecution as a seminal moment for Mexican Catholics. According to church historian Roberto Blancarte, it actually "proposes a new national project, based . . . on a Catholic-Guadalupan identity. . . . The future of the nation and of the social and political institutions that we have shaped could to a large extent depend on whether Mexicans accept or reject it as an interpretive model of history. *No es poca cosa*."[7]

Many Mexicans greeted this Catholic resurgence with scorn and fear. Threatened by the *panista* insurgence, old-time PRI politicians, as well as other critics of the church, warned of "the continuity of an old project, the last crusade that could, as spokesmen of the Catholic clergy and the extreme Right suggest, culminate in the electoral . . . victory of the Fox campaign."[8] Once again, during the 2003 electoral campaign, politicians vociferously condemned the *Instrucción pastoral* of the Bishop of Querétaro, titled "Un católico vota así," as an example of unwarranted clerical meddling in national politics.[9]

Today's acrimonious debates clearly demonstrate that Mexicans still consider religion a relevant factor in national life and the Catholic Church either a welcome or a dangerous political and social player in contemporary Mexican society. They also remind us of an earlier epoch, the days of the Mexican Revolution, when a Jacobin revolutionary elite attacked not just the privileges of the powerful Catholic hierarchy but Catholic religiosity and identity as well. In many ways, today's controversies take up the thread where it left off in the 1940s, when church and state reached a tenuous modus vivendi that relegated a battered Catholic clergy and laity to a state of compliant submission. Thus, current political and cultural developments offer an excellent vantage point from which to search for the origins of the religious conflict. While in postrevolutionary historiography church and religion were almost taboo topics for many years, the time is now ripe for a critical reevaluation of the role of religiosity during the Mexican Revolution.

In this admittedly impressionistic historiographical essay, I examine a range of theoretical approaches to the Mexican *Kulturkampf*. I argue that ideological, political, and cultural biases have tainted our understanding of the cultural history of the revolution, producing a skewed historiography that largely ignores religiosity, especially *popular* religiosity, instead interpreting religiously inspired acts as derivative of "deeper" socioeconomic and political factors. This is particularly odd in light of the analytical centrality accorded to religion in the work of anthropologists and historians of the colonial era. Historians of the revolution are fortunate to be able to draw on a rich historiographical foundation that, with the recent work of William Taylor, Eric Van Young, and David Brading, carries through the Wars of Independence.[10] Historians of the nineteenth century are also rapidly closing this historiographical lacuna.[11] In their analysis of twentieth-century Mexican society, pioneering Mexican and United States ethnographers who conducted fieldwork in rural Mexico starting in the 1920s and 1930s certainly reserved a central place for the rich and diverse forms of local religion.[12] For all their biases and methodological shortcomings—they tended to privilege the "closed corporate community" and often neglected linkages with the broader revolutionary cultural and political project—vintage anthropological studies remain a rich source for the historian. Despite this wealth of historical and ethnographic evidence, historians of the Mexican Revolution have, with a few very important exceptions that I examine below, neglected religiosity, or reduced it to an epiphenomenal manifestation of agrarian struggle or a reflection of the church-state political conflict.

A useful starting point for this discussion can be found in Eric Van Young's magnum opus, *The Other Rebellion*, which analyzes popular insurgency during the Wars of Independence. Van Young argues that popular insurgency between 1810 and 1821, far from being rooted in material deprivation, instead reflected an atavistic, culturally defensive movement of rural, mostly indigenous, peasants motivated by factors of ethnicity, community ("localocentrism"), and group identity. Variables such as class, protonationalism, and material (agrarian) conflict ultimately fail to explain popular participation. Instead, local religion was the primary discursive and practical matrix through which rural folk expressed themselves and made sense of the world.[13] In his final chapter, Van Young speculates on the similarities between the revolutionary movements of 1810 and 1910 and asserts that "the intertwining discourses of citizenship, liberalism, *mexicanidad*, and class confrontation seem to have replaced religious thought and its relationship to ethnicity and locality by 1910."[14] Industrialization and rising capitalism forged a new, urban, modern Mexico, in which religiosity and, certainly, messianism dwindled or disappeared entirely as motivating factors in Mexico's rich panoply of social movements. This interesting hypothesis is in many ways persuasive, but, as Van Young admits, little can be said "about the relationship of political thinking to religious discourse within popular rebellion in the decade 1910–20, primarily because the issue has not yet received much scholarly attention, and less still about popular forms of messianic expectation."[15]

It is this historiographical lacuna identified by Van Young that interests me here. Though modernity had certainly left its mark on Mexican culture by 1910, it is easy to overlook the continuity of profoundly religious local cultures in many regions of revolutionary Mexico. Historians have largely ignored religiosity, despite the fact that the revolutionary years witnessed constant and widespread acts of religiously inspired dissidence and conflict. While the short-lived and geographically circumscribed Cristiada of 1926–29 has received considerable scholarly attention, innumerable religiously motivated, local-level *tumultos* still await the historian's close scrutiny, and they have the potential of providing new perspectives on Mexican revolutionary culture.[16] Though I would be reluctant to assert that the Mexican Revolution was, like events a century earlier, largely driven by religiously inspired and culturally defensive communities, a good case can be made for the incorporation of religiosity as a factor in the analysis of local-level disorder and violence during the revolution.

Luckily, historians now have at their disposal a range of theoretical tools that make the interpretive task somewhat easier. The rise in the 1980s of the so-called New Cultural History opened up a new realm of interdisciplinary research, allowing for fruitful cross-fertilization. Borrowing heavily from anthropology and religious studies, historians are beginning to take a fresh look at religiosity and religiously motivated resistance during the Mexican Revolution. This approach tends to decenter the church and orthodoxy and instead focuses on local, "popular," or "traditional" forms of religiosity and the ways in which these forms informed and empowered subaltern groups in their struggle to shape their destiny in an age of revolution.

Before embarking on a review of the literature, some discussion of the concepts "popular religion" and "local religion" is required. Like the term "popular culture," the concept "popular religion" is both convenient and theoretically problematic, suggesting a rigid dichotomy between popular and elite forms of piety. As Peter Brown has persuasively argued, a two-tiered interpretive model reflects ancient prejudices that contrast elite, rational, "true" religious thought with a vulgar, unchanging, superstitious, often feminine popular religion.[17] More useful is William Christian Jr.'s term "local religion," developed for sixteenth-century Spain, but successfully applied to the case of Mexico.[18] According to Christian, "there were two levels of Catholicism— that of the Church Universal, based on the sacraments, the Roman liturgy, and the Roman calendar; and a local one based on particular sacred places, images, and relics, locally chosen patron saints, idiosyncratic ceremonies, and a unique calendar built up from the settlement's own sacred history."[19] Far from constituting two hermetically closed, autonomous realms, "[l]ocal places, saints, and times differed from, but only occasionally conflicted with, the set proposed by Rome and the diocese . . . the two cycles, pantheons, and sacred geographies could be easily melded."[20] Local religion is remarkably resilient, and "has in Catholic countries largely survived to the present day."[21] This does not mean that local religion is by nature primordial and static. In his seminal work on early modern English religiosity, Eamon Duffy clarifies this problem when he defines *traditional religion* as "a religious culture which was rooted in a repertoire of inherited and shared beliefs and symbols, while remaining capable of enormous flexibility and variety." Duffy argues that, in England, Catholic liturgical orthodoxy was fully integrated into local religion.[22] Duffy's insights help define Mexican local religion as a belief system based on and constantly influenced by Catholic orthodoxy—a good example would be the dramatic rise of ultramontane Marian cults during the nineteenth century—yet centered on a web of locally significant sacred images, sites, rituals, practices, and temporal cycles. This local religious matrix provides communities and individuals with ontological and practical security, identity, community, and historical memory, often through the intervention of saints and other sacred entities. Within this cultural continuum there is considerable room for the survival and development of indigenous forms of religious practice, such as shamanism, fertility rites, ancestor worship, and cyclical calendars.[23] The term "syncretism" may well have outlived its utility as a definer of the type of indigenous Catholicism that emerged in colonial Mexico. As William Taylor points out, "people may operate comfortably in more than one religious tradition at a time, enlarging their cosmovision and repertoire of world renewing."[24]

Before examining the main historiographical currents, a brief overview of the history of church, state, and religion during the revolution is called for.

CHURCH, STATE, AND RELIGION
IN REVOLUTIONARY MEXICO

Church-state relations in Mexico moved from a close symbiotic relationship throughout much of the colonial era toward increasing confrontation during the years of the Bourbon reforms. This trend deepened during the nineteenth century, culminating in the liberal *Reforma*, which dealt a serious blow to the economic, political, and cultural influence of the Catholic Church. Though a temporary détente emerged during the dictatorship of Porfirio Díaz, radical liberals rejected this rapprochement and lambasted Díaz's lax enforcement of the anticlerical articles of the Constitution of 1857.

The fate of local religion did not necessarily follow the ebb and flow of church-state relations. Efforts to suppress or modify local forms of religion perceived as "superstitious" have their origins not in the secularizing drive of modernity but in modernizing developments within orthodoxy itself. In sixteenth-century Mexico, Franciscans influenced by the Old Testament and Erasmianism launched massive anti-idolatry campaigns in an effort to eradicate indigenous modes of devotion.[25] By the seventeenth century these campaigns subsided, allowing for the development of indigenous forms of Christianity. In baroque Catholicism, elements of pre-Conquest indigenous belief systems and local practices coexisted comfortably with Tridentine orthodoxy, in part due to the renewed doctrinal emphasis on the veneration of saints' images, the miraculous, and supernatural apparitions.[26] During the dynamic late colonial years, both the Enlightened Catholic Church and the Bourbon state renewed their attacks on popular culture and religiosity in favor of a more decorous, internalized, rational form of piety, but these efforts undoubtedly subsided during the Wars of Independence and the chaotic years of the early republic.[27] Only gradually did liberal anticlericalism and antireligiosity combine during the second half of the nineteenth century. The ultramontane church successfully introduced new forms of Catholic devotion, especially Marian cults, without necessarily attempting to root out existing forms of local piety. As Edward Wright-Rios has demonstrated for the case of Oaxaca, both strands of religiosity could combine to create new and vibrant hybrid cults, but cults in which traditional indigenous religious matrixes maintained a dominant presence.

The outbreak of the Mexican Revolution in 1910 would lead to a resurgence of traditional liberal anticlericalism, now in the guise of Constitutionalism, as evidenced by sporadic iconoclasm, the persecution of priests, and anticlerical legislation. The revolutionary Constitution of 1917 incorporated a set of strongly anticlerical laws. Key articles denied the church legal personality and priests political rights (Article 130), outlawed clerical primary education (Article 3), banned religious orders (Article 5), nationalized real property of the church (Article 27), and granted the nation-state the right to intervene in religious affairs, and individual states the right to limit the number of priests in their jurisdiction (Article 130). As was the case with many other constitutional provisions, these articles were not implemented immediately but set the stage for the local and national religious conflicts of the '20s and '30s.[28]

From the mid-teens on, Jacobins in regional laboratories of the revolution, such as Yucatán and Jalisco, and, later, during the 1920s and 1930s, Tabasco, Sonora, Veracruz, Michoacán, Chiapas, and other states went beyond anticlericalism and experimented with antireligious cultural campaigns (*campañas desfanatizadoras*), aimed at eradicating what revolutionaries referred to as "fanaticism" and "superstition."[29] The central government directly supported these campaigns during the presidency of Plutarco Elías Calles (1924–28), the Maximato (1929–35), and the early years of the presidency of Lázaro Cárdenas.[30] Given the diversity of opinion within the revolutionary ranks, I would hesitate to define "the revolution" as uniformly antireligious. But local defanaticization campaigns often went well beyond the realm of anticlericalism and exhibited a marked *antireligious* character. Thus, antireligiosity must be considered a central point on the agenda of some, primarily Carranicista and, later, Callista, revolutionaries, such as Salvador Alvarado, Adalberto Tejeda, Tomás Garrido Canabal, Rodolfo Elías Calles, and others.

Early Catholic resistance ranged from the intensification of Social Catholicism and Catholic party politics to clerical support for the counterrevolutionary regime of General Victoriano Huerta.[31] Frequently, Catholics responded to anticlerical and antireligious actions with local riots, in which women played a prominent role. As religious persecution deepened during the 1920s, however, many rural Catholics found no other way out than taking up arms against the revolutionary state. The result was one of the bloodiest episodes in Mexican history, the Cristero Rebellion, which erupted in 1926. The rebellion pitted as many as thirty-five thousand Catholic guerrilla fighters, most from the Bajío and central-northern Mexico, against the federal army.[32] The violence only came to an end in 1929, when the Catholic Church accepted the so-called *arreglos* with the Mexican government, which, however, failed to settle the issue. Disgruntled Catholics and some clergy found it difficult to accept the political machinations of the church hierarchy, and religious persecution and resistance resumed by the 1930s, as state and national governments renewed their efforts to establish antireligious education, limit clerical influence, suppress expressions of religiosity, and implement a new wave of defanaticiza-tion campaigns. Catholics responded once again with school boycotts, church takeovers, demonstrations, and widespread acts of violence, collectively known as the Segunda Cristiada. It wasn't until the late 1930s that vigorous Catholic opposition convinced the Cárdenas government of the necessity of gradually phasing out the antireligious aspects of its cultural campaign. By 1938, a pre-carious modus vivendi between church and state emerged that solidified un-der President Manuel Ávila Camacho and would last until 1992, when Presi-dent Carlos Salinas de Gortari finally normalized relations with the Vatican and reformed the constitutional framework for church-state relations.[33]

Revolutionary attitudes toward religion exhibited a great diversity. States such as San Luis Potosí and Morelos never experienced concerted defanati-cization campaigns. In San Luis Potosí, a tactical tolerance toward the clergy and local religion reflected Saturnino Cedillo's growing defiance in the face of political centralization.[34] In some cases, anticlericalism did not necessarily in-volve an attack on popular religiosity. Yet in the minds of many influential rev-olutionary cultural reformers, anticlericalism meshed with a contempt for or rabid hatred of religiosity. This volatile combination sparked serious religious conflicts in many "laboratories" of the revolution, starting in the teens, but es-pecially during the '20s and '30s.

Even after the revolution examples abound of renewed, now clerical, attacks on local religiosity. During the 1960s, the bishop of Cuernavaca, Sergio Mén-dez Arceo, launched a Vatican II–inspired assault on popular religious images, which were purged from many churches, including the Cathedral of Cuer-navaca, sparking unrest among Catholics. In towns such as Tlayacapan and Cuernavaca, modernizing priests led by the bishop cracked down on tradi-tional religious practices and institutions, such as *mayordomías*, festivals, *posadas*, All Souls Day gatherings in the cemeteries, and bell ringing; eliminated side altars and images of the Virgin Mary and the saints; and introduced mariachis in the church. One priest made himself enormously unpopular by comparing an image of the Christ of the Resurrection with a "red grasshopper," a refer-ence to the television character for children, "el Chapulín Colorado," played by Chespirito. Morelos Catholics began to compare the radical clergy with the irreligious Carrancistas of revolutionary days.[35]

Clerical iconoclasm and hostility toward local, especially indigenous, forms of piety seem to have waned for the moment. During Pope John Paul II's sum-mer 2002 visit to Mexico, the Vatican master of ceremonies, Bishop Piero Martini, permitted indigenous shamanistic practices during the liturgy: "one liturgy featured a *limpia*, or purification, ceremony. The Indian blessing is be-lieved to cure spiritual and physical ailments by driving off evil spirits. Indian women bearing smoking pots of incense brushed herbs on the pontiff, Mexico City Cardinal Norberto Rivera Carrera and other prelates." According to Bishop Martini,

> We discussed it a great deal . . . with the responsible parties from the local church. . . . At the beginning, I have to say I was against using this rite, which not even they seemed to understand very well. Obviously our penitential act is one thing, their expression is another. But we continued talking, and in the end this was not during the Eucharistic celebration, and the bishop wanted the rite at any cost. It was important as a sign of respect for the indigenous, but it's also a matter of liturgical history. Often rites that were not originally Christian have been "Christianized." If the indigenous have this rite, it can with time take on a Christian meaning concerning the purification of sins. Just as we use holy water, which for us recalls the waters of baptism, forgiveness of sins and the resurrection, so for them this element of smoke can have a sense of liberation and forgiveness. This is the reason for which we at the end agreed to insert this element.[36]

Thus, both waves of anticlericalism and related but not necessarily concurrent attempts to suppress local forms of religion have characterized the history of Mexico since the sixteenth century. These attempts have had a variety of sources, popular, statist, and clerical, and have tended to coincide with wider efforts to establish modernity in local Mexican societies.

PARTISAN APPROACHES: CATHOLIC HAGIOGRAPHY AND OFFICIAL HISTORY

Revolutionary-era clerical and statist literature on church-state relations and religion was largely of a propagandistic and hagiographic nature and tended to glorify or demonize church, clergy, and believers. Catholics lambasted the government as atheistic, communist, and Godless, while government authors, such as Attorney General and later President Emilio Portes Gil, defended official anticlericalism—though not necessarily antireligiosity—from a classic radical liberal position. Portes Gil used legal, historical, and cultural arguments to justify cracking down on a seditious, rebellious clergy, but in the process he developed a cultural critique of popular religious "superstition":

> The men of the Revolution cannot allow the people to sink into stupidity and sloth; the first because it makes of man just another animal in the herd, because it sacrifices all scientific knowledge. . . . Into sloth, because the accumulation of capital in the hands of the clergy extracts it from the country to sustain a foreign sovereign with ruinous effects, while the convents, seminaries, and other associations are centers of indolence, idleness, and of the repetition of useless acts, and

places where superstition and lies are propagated that darken the souls of children, the teaching of youth and the judgment of free men.[37]

Alfonso Toro's virulent indictment of clerical domination, *La Iglesia y el estado en México*, published by the Mexican government in 1927 at the height of the Cristero Rebellion, was even more explicit in its attack on popular religiosity. Toro argued that Mexican religion was a deeply engrained blend of indigenous and Spanish fanaticism. "Christianity, in whatever form it assumes in the civilized nations that lead in the world, is almost completely unknown in Mexico; the majority of its inhabitants are either fanatics, who, under the guise of Catholicism, maintain ancient traditional superstitions, whether Indian or Spanish, or are skeptics or indifferent in religious matters."[38] Citing both "scientific" anthropological data and, tellingly, clerical reports, Toro ridiculed the inane "idolatrous" practices of the Mexican masses, including immoral popular festivals and dances (such as *huehuenches* and *matachines*); the veneration of saints, the Virgin Mary, and Christ; "false miracles"; and indigenous notions of the afterworld and limbo ("the confused memory of primordial Indian religious traditions"). Thus, the source of Mexico's underdevelopment was twofold: the clergy and the superstitious Indian masses.[39]

Foreigners also joined in the debate. Graham Greene, the British author of the novel *The Power and the Glory* (1940), characterized Mexico's anticlerical policy as "the fiercest persecution of religion anywhere since the reign of Elizabeth."[40] In the United States, the Catholic Church paid close attention to the rise of Mexican anticlericalism and launched a vigorous propaganda campaign, including active lobbying before Congress, to draw attention to the plight of Mexican Catholics.[41] In his *Blood-Drenched Altars* (1935), Bishop Francis Clement Kelley of Oklahoma warned that Mexico's religious persecution was not "an exclusively Catholic problem. [Conditions in Mexico] are first and foremost a challenge to justice and the moral law of nature. They are, secondly, a challenge to all Christian civilization."[42] In *Mexican Martyrdom* (1936), the Jesuit Wilfrid Parsons, who at one time contemplated joining the *cristeros*, concluded that "the radicals under Calles . . . have been forced into the recognized position of attempting the destruction of the Catholic Church, which in Mexico means the destruction of religion."[43]

Though after 1940 efforts to maintain a precarious church-state détente resulted in an official Catholic historiographical tendency to downplay the depth of the conflict, partisan Catholic hagiography continued. A good example is the work of Antonio Ríus Facius, who eulogized the heroic resistance of the Asociación Católica de la Juventud Mexicana (ACJM) and the cristeros against a "Revolutionary-Masonic-Protestant conspiracy."[44] Likewise, historiography supportive of the postrevolutionary state described the religious conflict as a clash between the nation-state and a powerful and retrograde Catholic Church allied with large landowners and other counterrevolutionary forces. Mexican and foreign Marxist historians reflected this position in generally simplistic historical accounts.[45]

While partisan narratives are informative sources for the period, they obviously fail in terms of historical analysis. Only in the 1960s, several decades after the end of the religious conflict, would serious scholarship slowly begin to emerge.

EARLY SCHOLARLY ANALYSIS: 1960S AND 1970S

For many years after the Revolution, the religious conflict was essentially a taboo in academic scholarship.[46] It wasn't until the 1960s and 1970s that scholarly interest, both in Mexico and the United States, led to the rise of an important new historiography on church-state relations, and, especially, the Cristero War (1926–29). Nonpartisan scholars, such as Alicia Olivera Sedano, Robert E. Quirk, and David C. Bailey, began to develop a more refined analysis of the religious conflict and the Cristiada, basing their conclusions on archival research and scholarly rigor.[47] The use of valuable archival collections, such as the Miguel Palomar y Vizcarra papers, the archives of the Liga Nacional Defensora de la Libertad Religiosa (LNDLR), and United States, British, and French diplomatic records, contributed to the quality of these studies. Quirk and Bailey concentrated on the actions and motivations of elite actors, such as revolutionary leaders, the church hierarchy, and the middle-class leadership of the ACJM and the LNDLR. Both emphasized the ideological and political clash between church and state as the crux of the conflict. Local religion, on the other hand, seldom figured in their analysis. However, Olivera Sedano did examine popular motivations and hinted that agrarian issues may have inspired some Cristero peasants.[48] Quirk, on the other hand, dismissed popular Catholicism offhand and argued that the church had failed in its efforts to use spirituality to mobilize Catholics against the government:

> The villagers call themselves Catholics, but they know nothing of the Church Universal and probably very little of Christian theology. An attack upon a bishop or the persecution of the clergy in the faraway capital means little, so long as the village saint is not molested. They are illiterate, most of them, and have never read the Bible or had it read to them. They remain ignorant even of the most basic catechismal teachings of the Church. . . . [The priests] shared the ignorance,

the prejudices, and even the vices of their charges. . . .The Church was weakest where it should have found its greatest strength, among the conservative Indian peasants and peons. When it came under attack, it could not count on the strong and united support of the rural majority.[49]

Here Quirk exhibits a profound incomprehension of and condescension toward Mexican Catholics and popular religiosity, comparable to that of many revolutionaries, that strongly color his conclusions.

RELIGIOUS REBELLION WITHOUT RELIGION: REDUCTIONIST INTERPRETATIONS OF THE CRISTIADA

During the 1970s and 1980s, Marxist and liberal historians in both Mexico and the United States continued to ignore religiosity per se and barely deemed it an historical factor of interest. While many U.S. historians were reluctant to consider religion a key historical variable, Mexican Marxists viewed it merely as a superstructural epiphenomenon. By focusing on the Cristiada, scholars limited themselves temporally to a relatively short period of the Mexican Revolution and geographically to the hardly typical Central Plateau. Much of their analysis centered on land conflicts. José Díaz and Román Rodríguez, for example, argued that the Cristero Rebellion in Los Altos de Jalisco was essentially the result of an "ecological crisis" caused by demographic growth and the concentration of land in the hands of a regional oligarchy. Peasant frustration with the shortage of land, long kept in check by outmigration and the hegemony of an orthodox religiosity that legitimized local power relations and the status quo, finally found an outlet in religious revolt. According to this interpretation, church and religion were essentially factors favoring societal continuity and stability. The cristeros were largely *medieros* and *peones*, but led by smallholding families and priests defending "the status quo, that is, the assurance of survival in a society characterized by private property relations sanctioned by natural law." Though they expressed themselves in religious terms, the cristeros were essentially fighting the same battle as Emiliano Zapata: "There was no call for land and liberty as in the case of the Zapatistas, as in Jalisco the war cry was '¡Viva Cristo Rey y Santa María de Guadalupe!' But who can deny that implicit in these exclamations is the desire for land?"[50]

Andrés Fabregas, in his introduction to the abovementioned study, is even more explicit. The peasants of Los Altos clearly exhibited false consciousness. They were manipulated by the clergy and the regional landed oligarchy, which used religious arguments to maintain their position of privilege during a time of socioeconomic crisis. The conservative peasantry took up arms against the *agrarista* forces, Catholics just like them, and against the revolutionary government and its project of land reform. In the process, "[t]he campesinos channeled the handling of their own objective crisis toward support for the oligarchy."[51] "One should interpret the peasant mobilization achieved by the Jalisco oligarchy, not as a religious conflict, but as the clash between a regional elite and an elite linked to the nation state."[52] Fabregas thus attacks Jean Meyer's depiction of the Cristiada as a holy war: "An interpretation along the lines offered by Meyer is ideological, and, thus, unacceptable."[53] Following a related, though more nuanced, approach, Ramón Jrade argues that "the Cristero phenomenon cannot be explained solely in terms of religiosity. . . . In areas of the countryside that were relatively shielded from market forces, the centralizing efforts of revolutionary authorities crystallized class divisions between cultivators in de facto control of the land and cultivators seeking the benefits of land reform. . . . [T]he Cristero uprisings were outcomes of class divisions and power struggles that developed in sections of the countryside following the revolution."[54] Once again, these works largely neglected popular religion and explained religious resistance as a superficial reflection of deeper, class-based, material conflicts.

REVISIONIST TRENDS:
RELIGIOSITY AND THE CRISTERO REBELLION

Some historians bucked the prevailing historiographical trend. More attuned to the importance of Catholicism, scholars such as Luis González y González and his followers attempted to incorporate religion into their accounts of the Cristiada and the revolution. Though in his classic microhistory of San José de Gracia, Michoacán (1972), González offered a subtle assessment of the motivations that led the villagers to take up arms against the Calles government and acknowledged that the search for fame, money, power, excitement, and criminal opportunity all played a role, yet he concluded that "the basic sources [of the conflict] were wounded religiosity, a feeling of humiliation, . . . the protection of threatened smallholdings, and . . . hatred of the government."[55]

Not surprisingly, French historians, always eager to see parallels between their own past and that of Mexico, also took up the study of religiosity in modern Mexico. Jean Meyer's monumental *La Cristiada*, published in 1973, well before religion had become a fashionable topic, remains even today an astonishingly rich starting point for research in the field, though it is somewhat marred by the zeal of the convert. Armed with a personal attitude hostile to the cristeros, Meyer set out to study the Cristiada from a conventional

sociohistorical perspective, only to write a sweeping and passionate vindication of traditional folk Catholicism as a source of heroic antimodernist resistance.[56] "Not only is a purely economic study incapable of explaining . . . the
simple appearance of such an important phenomenon as the war of the cristeros, this kind of analysis poses the risk of dissolving the most profound contents of this human history in full effervescence and robbing it of its original
character by reducing it to pure ideology."[57] What was at the time novel about
Meyer's study was that he took religiosity seriously as a motivating factor in
human behavior, contradicting the reductionist approach of most contemporary analysis.

For Meyer, who considered Luis González a mentor, the Cristiada was an
independent grassroots movement of Catholic peasants motivated by a profound and traditional religious orthodoxy: "The great war of the Cristiada was
the clash of two worlds, that of the pilgrims of Peter the Hermit and that of
the Jacobins of the Third Age. . . . In the face of a radical, sudden, and brutal anticlericalism, the Catholic country people rise up, taking up arms to defend their faith."[58] The Cristiada was never led or inspired by the church; instead, the Mexican church hierarchy and the Vatican did their best to avert
violence, and once they had reached an agreement with the revolutionary government in 1929, the glorious cristero martyrs were abandoned to their
bloody fate.[59] The Cristiada was in essence all about popular religion.

Meyer's work was well received among historians and the broader Catholic
public and became a best-seller. Nevertheless, questions soon arose about the
accuracy of his historical data and methodology, unfortunately casting doubt
on the general validity of his thesis. Jrade, for example, argues that Meyer's interviews and questionnaires "inevitably yielded testimonies that lent support to
[his] apocalyptic vision of the rebellion."[60] In addition, Meyer, not unlike
Quirk, underestimates the significance of ties between the clergy and the laity.
Most recent studies correctly emphasize the profound impact clerical policy
had on local actions. We now have a much better appreciation of the complex
interaction between "official" and "popular" cultures that belies his dichotomous approach.

In Mexico the work of Meyer and González inspired other historians and
anthropologists, especially those studying the history, society, and culture of
the Bajío, to incorporate religiosity as a factor for historical analysis in their
work, while it also opened up broader areas of research.[61] Yet the majority—
Marxists and U.S. historians in particular—continued to neglect the topic, and
reductionist approaches dominated studies of church-state relations and the
Cristiada as well as many general histories of Mexico and the revolution.[62] Reflecting this neglect, in his classic study of the Mexican Revolution, *The Great
Rebellion* (1980), Ramón Eduardo Ruíz stated that "the issue of the Church,

while significant, may be essentially irrelevant to a discussion whether Mexico had a revolution or not."[63]

RECENT SCHOLARSHIP

Unfortunately, current studies of revolutionary Mexico have not advanced much in terms of incorporating the variable of religiosity into their analysis. Most continue to either emphasize the church-state struggle for power or offer reductionist views of popular religion. Still, some progress has been made. The wave of regional histories that started in the 1970s and still flourishes today, written by Mexicans and foreigners alike, has shaped our understanding of the importance, even the centrality, of religion during the revolution.[64] Delving into local and regional histories, we come to realize that the grand politics of church-state conflict was but one aspect of a broader cultural conflict that influenced the lives of millions of Mexicans.

New studies of *agrarismo*, especially in the state of Michoacán, are sensitive to the issue of religion, and some introduce a novel analytical factor: *identity*. In her study of Michoacán peasant movements during the 1920s, political scientist Jennie Purnell acknowledges the importance of popular culture, stating that "most scholars of the revolution treat the *Cristiada* as an instance of church-state conflict, ignoring its popular character altogether, or attributing popular support for the Church to fanaticism and false consciousness."[65] Purnell claims not to share the essentially structuralist approach of theorists such as James C. Scott, Samuel L. Popkin, and Jeffrey M. Paige, who consider peasant political behavior as parochial, limited, and ultimately materialist. She seeks to explain this important question: why did some Michoacán peasants become anticlerical *agraristas*, while others decided to identify themselves as anti-agrarista *cristeros*?

Purnell argues that the agraristas and cristeros shared a common religiosity but had adopted sharply differing *political identities*. She focuses on the local history and culture of individual communities in an effort to understand the process by which these identities were forged. Local histories determined how peasants perceived the interaction of revolutionary anticlericalism and *agrarismo* with "popular understandings of property, citizenship, and legitimate authority."[66] Essentially, Purnell argues that the Cristiada's regional character can be explained by "the survival [in the cases of the Pacific Coast, and the central, northwestern, and southwestern highlands] of a significant number of communities with their landed bases and traditional institutions at least partially intact" and by "the existence of a dense network of lay grassroots organizations

loosely affiliated with the Catholic Church."[67] Elsewhere, in the areas of Za-
capu, Lake Pátzcuaro, and the Northeast, loss of land, local political authority,
and traditional religious structures during the nineteenth century created conditions in which revolutionary *agrarismo* could later flourish.[68] Purnell ultimately discards religiosity, as well as class and ethnicity, as variables determining peasant behavior during the Cristiada in Michoacán. "Explanations of
partisanship based on religiosity . . . are often simply tautological: the *cristero*
peasants rebelled because they were more religious, and the proof of their
greater religiosity lies in the fact of their having rebelled."[69] Though Purnell's
innovative analysis brings us a step closer to understanding the role of peasant
religious attitudes during the Revolution, it still stops short of considering religion as an independent factor, and it fails to delve into the meanings and
manifestations of local religion and religious identity in Michoacán.

The case of Michoacán has also been closely scrutinized by Marjorie
Becker, who has examined the Cárdenas years. According to Becker, Cardenismo in Michoacán was the result of the interaction of an often anticlerical, top-down revolutionary cultural project with peasant culture and piety.[70]
She characterizes Cardenismo as markedly anticlerical and Michoacán peasant
culture as a culture of "purity and redemption" but also a "marriage of piety
and property."[71] Most interestingly, whereas others stress class, ethnicity, re-
gionalism, or politics, Becker centers on the relationship between gender and
religion. While the revolution offered men political alternatives and land, it
had less to offer women, who consequently clung to their rosaries.[72] Yet while
Becker at least takes religiosity seriously, she once again fails to fathom its intricate meanings at the local level.

Christopher Boyer develops the concepts of agrarista and Catholic identities beyond Purnell's observations. He argues that the revolutionary project in
Michoacán was not just a top-down attempt to reshape traditional rural culture, including popular religion, but actually reflected popular agrarista sentiments and identities. Landless peasants developed a new agrarista *identity* that
incorporated anticlericalism. When the Cristiada broke out, agraristas battled
cristeros and burned saints in an effort to show their allegiance to the revolutionary government and to defend their newfound identity.[73] In return, the
new political configuration allowed them access to land and political opportunity. However, popular agrarista anticlericalism focused primarily on linkages
between the Roman Catholic Church and the large landowners and eschewed
a broader official discourse linking religion with the backwardness of peasant
culture. While *agrarismo* declined by the 1940s, a *campesino* cultural identity,
which was forged through the interaction of revolutionary official culture and
popular militancy and stressed the commonality and political unity of rural
folk, survives to this day.[74] This new campesino identity purged unpopular el-

ements such as anticlericalism, thus becoming attractive for Catholic and agrarista peasants alike, and coincided with Cárdenas's efforts to incorporate both into his regime.[75] While Boyer's explanation of agrarista and campesino identities is convincing, it is less successful at defining and explaining Catholic identities in Michoacán, instead focusing on the project of Catholic nationalism, which, as Boyer admits, had little popular appeal.[76] The two are, of course, related, but not the same thing.

Building on these innovative works, Matthew Butler's recently published study of the Cristero Rebellion in eastern Michoacán makes a significant contribution to this inquiry, namely the deceptively simple observation that *religion matters*.[77] Butler argues that material factors per se are insufficient to explain the intense polarization and violence that Michoacán experienced during the 1920s. Actually, religion and culture frequently were the principal determinants of historical outcomes. This is not a mere restating of Meyer's argument. Butler is critical of Meyer's romantic, essentializing portrayal of the cristeros as a monolithically pious peasantry heroically defending its religion and traditional way of life against a brutal, secularizing revolutionary state. In fact, the region displayed a remarkable diversity of religious beliefs and practices, ranging from a highly sacramentalized, orthodox Catholicism to indigenous Christianity and Presbyterianism. Butler avoids viewing local religion in Michoacán as an autonomous realm separate from clerical influence and orthodoxy. Eschewing misleading dichotomies (tradition/modernity, elite/popular), he develops an intricate, *longue durée* analysis of material, political, ethnic, and cultural/religious factors that forged the widely divergent local cultures that ultimately generated either cristero resistance or agrarista militancy.

Butler's study consists of a detailed comparison of the histories and cultures of two regions of eastern Michoacán. The wide range of local identities within this relatively small area has its origin in factors such as distinct land tenure patterns and the cultural and political fragmentation caused by the nineteenth-century liberal Reform. These fault lines resurfaced during the 1920s. In the northeastern highlands of the Zinapécuaro and Maravatío districts, an agrarian regime based on smallholdings and modest haciendas emerged during the eighteenth century as indigenous villages lost their communal lands and autonomy. During the nineteenth century, an activist Catholic Church developed an extensive parochial infrastructure and established new forms of clericalized worship. A deeply rooted, conservative Catholic culture came to define local identity, and it proved highly resistant to liberal and revolutionary reform. Many peasants considered applying for *ejidos* sinful. Not surprisingly, the northern areas contributed heavily to the conservative and cristero causes. On the other hand, in the southern lowlands of Zitácuaro, large haciendas and church estates coexisted uneasily with defiant Mazahua and Otomí Indian communities well into the nineteenth century. The liberal attack on church and communal lands was a late and highly contentious phenomenon. After the secularization of regular parishes in the eighteenth century, Indian villages jealous of their autonomous baroque spirituality kept the diocesan clergy at arm's length, and the church's hold on the region remained weak. Heterodoxy, religious indifference, and popular anticlericalism characterized the local mentality, and Protestantism and secularization spread rapidly during the nineteenth century. The liberal-conservative conflict fostered the rise of a liberal, anticlerical, and frequently Protestant political culture. During the revolution, the southern areas embraced state-sponsored *agrarismo*, cultural reform, and religious persecution and developed a distinct revolutionary identity. After 1926, the region's revolutionaries pushed the church underground and agrarian reserves easily suppressed weak attempts to launch a Cristiada. Thus, local patterns of religion and culture, which developed in continuous interaction with material and political factors, essentially determined the regional strength and success of the revolt. Butler demonstrates that it is possible to integrate religion as an independent variable into the broader analysis of phenomena such as the Cristero Rebellion.

A subtle, and sometimes persuasive, revisionism can be found in the work of historians probing the day-to-day workings of Social Catholicism, as expressed in Catholic lay organizations, unions, schools, and other grassroots venues, thus demonstrating how progressive Catholicism permeated many basic aspects of Mexican society and, in some cases, paralleled revolutionary social activism. Pioneering work in this area, especially on the impact of the papal encyclical *Rerum Novarum*, was conducted by Manuel Ceballos Ramírez and Jorge Adame and recently developed by Randall Hanson and others.[78] Kristina Boylan, for example, argues that the activity of the Unión Femenina Católica Mexicana (UFCM), established in 1929 as the women's arm of Acción Católica, contributed "to the gradual cessation of government attacks on the church, the maintenance of the Catholic Church as a cultural presence in Mexico, and the reinvention of Catholicism as a valid part of Mexican postrevolutionary culture."[79] The UFCM's realm was the household, the catechism class, the home school, the parochial group. Its 115,000 members, mostly upper- and middle-class women, "defended their value system against the Revolutionary State's call for women to reject their heritage, which it condemned as anachronistic and superstitious. These women created an influential niche for themselves in the church and in their communities. Mexican Catholic women activists used their mobilizations to circumvent prescribed behavior for Mexican women to realize their personal and-defined broadly-political goals."[80] Likewise, Patience A. Schell has recently examined the progressive role of the social action wing of the Roman Catholic Church in education. Her findings indicate that church and state found common reformist ground between 1917 and the breakdown of relations in 1926, after which a more conservative, church-controlled Catholic Action movement replaced Social Catholicism.[81]

Less convincing is the blatantly revisionist work of Peter Lester Reich, which goes so far as to deny the existence of a profound church-state conflict after 1929. Instead, Reich claims that Catholic lay organizations mitigated ideological polarization, while anticlerical provisions of the revolutionary Constitution of 1917 were seldom enforced. Reich's study supposedly "demonstrates that beneath the formal anticlericalism of the 'official' Revolution, a quiet network of ecclesiastical-secular conciliation, or 'hidden revolution,' highlights the superficiality of the traditional scholarly interpretation and helps explain the collaboration of today."[82]

Unfortunately, Reich's study suffers from revisionism for revisionism's sake. His point is well taken that the religious conflict was mitigated by a variety of high- and low-level contacts between government officials, clergymen, believers, and other players. But Reich has a tendency to view Mexican history in teleological terms: the religious conflict of the 1930s was essentially superficial because it masked the church-state modus vivendi that emerged in the 1940s. However, just because the conflict of the 1930s was, with hindsight, short-lived doesn't mean that Catholics, revolutionaries, the Vatican, and international observers did not consider it an extremely ominous historical development. Using a counterfactual approach, one might even envision an alternative scenario in which Mexico might have headed down the Spanish road of civil war instead of that of conciliation. Reich downplays the despair of the Mexican Catholic hierarchy, evident, for example, in the bleak and depressing correspondence of the apostolic delegate, Monsignor Leopoldo Ruiz y Flores.[83] Moreover, he tends to overlook archival evidence for widespread Catholic resistance in the form of school boycotts, the violent reopening of closed churches, street riots, and rural violence. Reich makes another common mistake: by concentrating on a relatively short period, essentially the decade of the 1930s, he ignores the rise and fall of powerful anticlerical and antireligious regimes in many states during the 1910s and 1920s. While Jacobin radicalism led to profound divisions in Sonora during the 1930s, one has to go back to the teens to find a similar movement in, say, Yucatán (the socialist experimentation under Salvador Alvarado and Felipe Carrillo Puerto), which Franco Savarino has described as a near-totalitarian experience.[84] Thus, the impact of Jacobin radicalism was much more widespread than Reich's narrow focus on the 1930s might indicate, affecting numerous states, such as Sonora, Michoacán, Chiapas, Jalisco, Veracruz, Tabasco, Hidalgo, Colima, and Sinaloa. Of course, religious conflict was centered not just in the mestizo, ultraconservative, and Catholic central-northern region of the country, an impression that research on the Cristiada might convey, but also in southern states with a large indigenous population.[85] Basing my argument on a wide sampling of regional conditions, I have tried to depict Mexican iconoclasm and anticlericalism as an integral aspect of a *nationwide* cultural project.[86] Only a national perspective that transcends temporal limitations and generalizations based on the rather exceptional case of the Bajío can lead us to a general understanding of the problem.

Meanwhile, Mexican scholars continue to publish high-quality empirical studies on various aspects of the religious conflict, including the ancient themes of church-state conflict and the Cristiada but also, increasingly, novel topics that flesh out popular and local perspectives, such as Sinarquismo, the lower clergy, local religion, religious identity, and Masonry.[87] Pablo Serrano Álvarez, for example, depicts Sinarquismo as a movement created by the church hierarchy, the Jesuits, and the Catholic elite, yet one that rapidly evolved into a *popular* sociocultural movement, conservative, authoritarian, anticommunist, hispanicist, counterrevolutionary, reformist, and nationalist.[88]

TOWARD A NEW HISTORY OF RELIGION DURING THE MEXICAN REVOLUTION

In Mexico, the political space that has recently emerged for Catholics and the Roman Catholic hierarchy has led to a new wave of hagiography and apologetic publications quite similar to those of earlier days.[89] But the real opening has been in the realm of theory. It wasn't until the "cultural turn" made its impact in Mexican studies during the late 1980s that historians of modern Mexico began to show serious interest in culture as a historical factor in its own right. In the United States, the rise of the so-called New Cultural History, influenced by a diverse range of disciplines and approaches, such as Geertzean cultural anthropology, the French *Annaliste "histoire des mentalités,"* postmodern theory, and discourse analysis, resulted in a renewed interest in the value of symbols and ritual and spawned a spate of studies on popular culture. Yet North American historians have been more reluctant than their Mexican colleagues to move into the realm of religiosity. Two seminal collections on revolutionary and postrevolutionary Mexican popular culture fail to address the issue of religiosity and instead focus on topics such as cinema, television, comics, and rock music.[90]

Nevertheless, even in the United States research is under way, but it is only slowly emerging in published form.[91] Leading scholars of modern Mexico and the revolution, such as Paul Vanderwood and Linda Hall, are now turning to research topics such as folk saints (Santa Teresa de Cabora, Juan Soldado) and the Virgin Mary. In *The Power of God against the Guns of Government*, Vanderwood characterizes the 1891–92 Tomóchic rebellion in Chihuahua as an essentially millenarian movement, though he does pay considerable attention to structural factors.[92] Particularly promising is the new, quasi-anthropological work being conducted on the basic elements of local religion, namely saints' cults, pilgrimages, *cofradías* and other religious associations, women's religiosity, visions and apparitions, and ethnic historical memory, especially when related to the analysis of the wider political and socioeconomic context.[93]

What might a future history of local religiosity during the Mexican Revolution look like? If we are to fathom the *mentalités* of diverse subaltern groups, such as peasants, women, and indigenous peoples, we have to examine how they understood local religion. Here all I can do is identify some of the main points of a future research agenda. First and foremost, we need to understand the ontological nature of local religion, namely its function as a cultural matrix through which many Mexicans tried to make sense of a chaotic revolutionary world. The poorly understood secularization process, along with its relationship to revolutionary and local cultures, the media, and socioeconomic development, is another area of research in dire need of attention, especially in light of the facile tendency of an earlier generation of sociologists automatically to link the phenomenon to socioeconomic modernization. Despite widespread secularizing trends, local religiosity remains crucial in contemporary Mexico. Instead of disappearing, as sociologists predicted, local religion has undergone a process of constant change, most recently manifesting itself in novel forms, such as evangelical Christianity, Protestantism, and liberation theology.[94] We also need a clearer sense of the relationship between local religious factors such as identity, community, gender, ethnicity, local politics, and economics. For example, the interface between revolutionary politics and culture and the cargo or *mayordomía* system, pilgrimages, and fiesta cycles is an important topic that sheds light on ethnic identity and autonomy and the fate of local political systems in postrevolutionary Mexico.[95] The central role of women in a highly feminized local religion highlights the masculine nature of the Revolution and possibly explains the prevalence of women in the resistance against defanaticization campaigns. Feminine religion has been interpreted as a realm of empowerment or even protofeminism. However, care must be paid not to fall into the trap of reifying the feminine, as Caroline Ford stresses.[96]

The intense nature of revolutionary anticlericalism and antireligiosity in many laboratories of the Revolution can be explained only by fathoming the meaning of local religion to both believers and unbelievers. Clearly, revolutionaries considered religion of sufficient importance to engage in acts of iconoclasm and violence that would jeopardize other aspects of the Revolution that today we tend to consider more central, such as agrarian reform. In short, only by admitting that religion was a key aspect of local societies as well as a principal target of the revolutionary cultural project can we begin to understand the impact of local belief systems on revolutionary-era cultures.

RELIGION, NATION, AND CULTURE: WIDER THEORETICAL CONSIDERATIONS

As can be expected, this shift toward the reenchantment of Mexican revolutionary studies has not gone unnoticed and has sparked some lively debates.[97] Two distinct historiographical camps on religion are visible, which I shall call, somewhat facetiously, "Millenarians" and "Children of the Enlightenment," and which reflect wider debates on religion and rationality.[98]

The Millenarians are basically Lévy-Bruhlian or Geertzean relativists, idealists, or splitters, who are willing to accept the existence of plural rationalities and who, in the case of modern Mexico, consider local forms of religiosity, including millenarianism, crucial and independent motivation for popular resistance. They essentially follow anthropologist Marshall Sahlins's approach of "different cultures, different rationalities."[99] Millenarians argue that one should consider the sacred and the profane as intimately intertwined, if we are to understand the popular *mentalité*. They believe "there are more things in heaven and earth . . . "

Children of the Enlightenment, on the other hand, are wary of the inclusion of religion as an independent variable and might be considered Comtean or Lévi-Straussian universalists, or lumpers, who, deep down inside, consider humankind as one and ultimately view their subjects, whether primitives, "the Other," or peasants, as rational, practical beings. In a way they echo anthropologist Gananath Obeyesekere's argument in favor of a universal "practical rationality," "the process whereby human beings reflectively assess the implications of a problem in terms of practical criteria."[100] "Irrational" religious behavior should thus be explained in relationship to other, political, socioeconomic, and material factors, such as community, land tenure, local factionalism, political centralization, class, and deprivation. Children of the Enlightenment are suspicious of explanations in terms of religiosity, spirituality, or, especially, millenarianism.

Thus, historians are still grappling with an age-old problem: how does one evaluate religious behavior? As an independent variable, or merely as an epiphenomenal factor that can be reduced to economics, politics, class, or psychology? Is "religion" merely a cultural construct, a Western discursive invention? Is religion, as Hume states, maybe even just a function of "the anxious concern for happiness, the dread of future misery, the terror of death, the thirst for revenge, the appetite for food and other necessities"?[101] Such questions are bound to make many historians slightly queasy. As William Taylor reminds us, speaking of the colonial era, the believers' "lived allegiance to a cosmic order that transcended human power . . . is a barely accessible subject—thinly documented, remote from the experience of most . . . twentieth century observers, and complicated by changes . . . that are as yet poorly understood."[102]

Clearly, some combination of idealist and reductionist positions is called for, as Alan Knight has recently suggested.[103] Unfortunately, most historians are woefully unprepared to tackle the theme of popular religion effectively.[104] What is now needed is a serious attempt to combine the historian's understanding of revolutionary politics, agrarianism, and culture with the insights afforded by the sociology and anthropology of religion and postmodern religious studies, and engage in debates on the broader significance of popular religion to Latin American culture.

The insights of sociologists of religion are quite pertinent to our discussion and provide useful models worth testing or critiquing. An influential school of Catholic thought, represented by sociologists such as Alberto Methol Ferré, Juan Carlos Scannone, Pedro Morandé, and Cristián Parker, argues that the *true* past and future identity of Latin America lies in its mestizo baroque Catholicism, with its emphasis on representation, liturgy, and theatricality, which is most clearly expressed in Latin American popular religion. This culture is an alternative to the Latin American elite's failed Enlightenment-based instrumental rationalism and the source of a distinct Latin American modernity, an "*otra lógica*," as Parker puts it. Parker even argues that popular religion may well form the basis for a future Latin American culture of solidarity.[105] Roberto Blancarte, Jorge Larrain, and others have recently criticized these thinkers as "*esencialistas*" who, they argue, posit the existence of an authentic and deep-rooted Latin American baroque (or symbolic-dramatic) culture based on Catholicism and especially, popular religiosity, while at the same time criticizing a narrowly defined, authoritarian, Enlightenment rationalism and modernity. In the Mexican context, Blancarte criticizes attempts to portray Mexican history "as a state of schizophrenia (a Catholic people with a liberal and anticlerical regime). . . . To say that Mexican liberalism was foreign to the cultural reality of the nation is to want to present it as something alien to our history and Catholicism as something intrinsic to our culture."[106]

One way out of the theoretical dead end might be to discard the dichotomies of reductionism/idealism and universalism/relativism as well as many others that inform research on religion and revolution, i.e., secular/sacred, modernity/tradition, and religion/nation. As Peter van der Veer and Hartmut Lehmann point out, it may be time to disabuse ourselves of the notion that the rise of modernity, nationalism, capitalism, individualism, and secularism necessarily leads to a clash with "traditional" religious society. Indeed, nationalism may well be considered a novel form of religion. While the nineteenth and twentieth centuries witnessed the modernization of religion, the rising nation-state drew heavily on religious discourse and symbolism.[107] Thus, as Talal Asad points out, "The concept of the secular cannot do without the idea of religion."[108] By taking religion and its linkages with modernity and the nation-state seriously, we might better understand how religion informed Mexican local cultures during the revolution, what local religion meant to the revolutionary state, and whether religion made its mark on Latin America's greatest social movement. In any case, these are fascinating and most timely debates, and historians have much to contribute.

NOTES

Chapter opening image source: AHAO, impresos religiosos, 1880–89.

An earlier version of this article appeared under the title "Iglesia, estado y religión en el México revolucionario: Una visión historiográfica de conjunto," in *Revista Prohistoria* 6:6 (2002). I thank the editor, Darío Barriera, for his gracious permission to reproduce parts of that article in this volume.

1. On the role of the Mexican Catholic Church in the democratic transition and today, see, for example, Carlos Martínez Assad, ed., *Religiosidad y política en México* (Mexico City: Universidad Iberoamericana, 1992); Rodolfo Soriano Núñez, *En el nombre de Dios. Religión y democracia en México* (Mexico City: Instituto Mexicano de Doctrina Social Cristiano; Instituto de Investigaciones Dr. José María Luis Mora, 1999); Roberto Blancarte, ed., *Religión, iglesias y democracia* (Mexico City: La Jornada Ediciones; Centro de Investigaciones Interdisciplinarias en Humanidades, UNAM, 1995); David Alejandro Delgado Arroyo, *Hacia la modernización de las relaciones iglesia-estado. Génesis de la administración pública de los asuntos religiosos* (Mexico City: Editorial Porrúa, 1997); Roderic Ai Camp, *Crossing Swords: Politics and Religion in Mexico* (New York: Oxford University Press, 1997); and José Legorreta Zepeda and José de Jesús, eds., *La iglesia católica y la política en el México de hoy* (Mexico City: Universidad Iberoamericana, 2000).

2. Édgar González Ruiz, *La última cruzada. De los cristeros a Fox* (Mexico City: Grijalbo, 2000), 216.

3. González Ruiz, *La última cruzada*, 214; *El Observador*, March 28, 2004.

4. *New York Times*, May 30, 2000; *National Catholic Reporter*, November 21, 2003; Reforma.com, January 13, 2003.

5. zenit.org, November 17, 2000.

6. Cited in González Ruiz, *La última cruzada*, 1.

7. Roberto Blancarte, "Iglesia y estado: Las dos espadas," *Nexos* 282 (2001). For the complete text of the *carta pastoral* see http://www.iglesiatijuana.org/enc_jesus.html.

8. González Ruiz, *La última cruzada*, xiii.

9. See http://www.cem.org.mx/news/comunicado/queretaro.htm and http://www .cem.org.mex/Noticias/elecciones/ReflexionesQueretaro.htm.

10. Eric Van Young, *The Other Rebellion: Popular Violence, Ideology, and the Mexican Struggle for Independence, 1810–1821* (Stanford, CA: Stanford University Press, 2001); William B. Taylor, *Magistrates of the Sacred: Priests and Parishioners in Eighteenth-Century Mexico* (Stanford, CA: Stanford University Press, 1996); and D. A. Brading, *Church and State in Bourbon Mexico: The Diocese of Michoacán 1749–1810* (Cambridge: Cambridge University Press, 1994). For recent examples of the analysis of religiosity in colonial Mexico, see Clara García Ayluardo and Manuel Ramos Medina, eds., *Manifestaciones religiosas en el mundo colonial Americano* (Mexico City: INAH, Universidad Iberoameri- cana; Centro de Estudios de Historia de México CONDUMEX, 1997). The most im- portant work in this field is that of Serge Gruzinski, in particular his *La colonisation de l'imaginaire* (Paris: Gallimard, 1988). On religion and modernity in late colonial Mex- ico, see the revisionist work of Pamela Voekel, *Alone before God. The Religious Origins of Modernity in Mexico* (Durham, NC: Duke University Press, 2003).

11. See, for example, Terry Rugeley, *Of Wonders and Wise Men: Religion and Popular Cultures in Southeast Mexico* (Austin: University of Texas Press, 2001); Álvaro Matute, Evelia Trejo, and Brian Connaughton, eds., *Estado, iglesia y sociedad en México, siglo XIX* (Mexico City: Facultad de Filosofía y Letras, UNAM, Grupo Editorial M.A. Porrúa, 1995); and Brian Connaughton, *Clerical Ideology in a Revolutionary Age: The Guadalajara Church and the Idea of the Mexican Nation* (1788–1853) (Boulder; Calgary: University Press of Colorado; University of Calgary Press, 2003). An important study with a *longue durée* perspective is D. A. Brading's *Mexican Phoenix. Our Lady of Guadalupe: Im- age and Tradition across Five Centuries* (Cambridge: Cambridge University Press, 2001).

12. Classic anthropological accounts include Pedro Carrasco, *El catolicismo popular de los Tarascos* (Mexico City: SEP, 1976); George M. Foster, *Tzintzuntzan: Mexican Peas- ants in a Changing World* (Boston: Little, Brown and Company, 1967); Robert Redfield and Alfonso Villa Rojas, *Chan Kom: A Maya Village* (Washington, DC: Carnegie Insti- tute, 1934); Robert Redfield, *Tepoztlán: A Mexican Village* (Chicago: University of Chicago Press, 1930) and *A Village that Chose Progress: Chan Kom Revisited* (Chicago: University of Chicago Press, 1950); and Oscar Lewis, *Life in a Mexican Village: Tepoztlán Revisited* (Urbana: University of Illinois Press, 1963).

13. Van Young, *The Other Rebellion*, 496–97, 512.

14. Van Young, *The Other Rebellion*, 523.

15. Van Young, *The Other Rebellion*, 522.

16. Compare Van Young, *The Other Rebellion*, 501–2.

17. Peter Brown, *The Cult of the Saints: Its Rise and Function in Latin Christianity* (Chicago: University of Chicago Press, 1981).

18. Taylor, *Magistrates of the Sacred*.

19. William Christian Jr., *Local Religion in Sixteenth-Century Spain* (Princeton, NJ: Princeton University Press, 1981), 3. Taylor follows this approach in his *Magistrates of the Sacred*.

20. Christian, *Local Religion*, 177.

21. Christian, *Local Religion*, 177.

22. See *The Stripping of the Altars: Traditional Religion in England 1400–1580* (New Haven, CT: Yale University Press, 1992), 2–4.

23. Taylor, *Magistrates of the Sacred*, 49–50.

24. Taylor, *Magistrates of the Sacred*, 73. For the case of Yucatán, see Rugeley, *Of Wonders*, chap. 1.

25. Serge Gruzinski, *La guerre des images de Christophe Colomb à Bladerunner (1492–2019)* (Paris: Fayard, 1990), 105–6.

26. Taylor, *Magistrates of the Sacred*, 49–50, 67–68; and Gruzinski, *La guerre*, 150–51, 156, 162–63, 169–70.

27. Juan Pedro Viqueira Albán, *¿Relajados o reprimidos? Diversiones públicas y vida social en la ciudad de México durante el Siglo de las Luces* (Mexico City: Fondo de Cultura Económica, 1987), 152–53. Also see Voekel, *Alone before God*. Compare Van Young, *The Other Rebellion*, 412.

28. Jean Meyer, *La cristiada*, vol. 2, *El conflicto entre la iglesia y el estado, 1926–1929* (Mexico City: Siglo Veintiuno, 1973), 69–70. For a detailed discussion, see E. V. Niemeyer Jr., *Revolution at Querétaro: The Mexican Constitutional Convention of 1916–1917* (Austin: University of Texas Press, 1974), chap. 3.

29. See my "Idolatry and Iconoclasm in Revolutionary Mexico: The De-Christianization Campaigns, 1929–1940," *Mexican Studies/Estudios Mexicanos* 13 (1997). On the role of local religion, see my "Saints, Sinners and State Formation: Local Religion and Cultural Revolution in Mexico," in Stephen Lewis and Mary Kay Vaughan, eds., *The Eagle and the Virgin: National Identity, Memory and Utopia in Mexico, 1920–1940* (Durham, NC: Duke University Press, 2006), and, on iconoclasm, my "Iconoclasm and the Mexican Revolution," in Anne L. McClanan and Jeffrey Johnson, eds., *Negating the Image: Case Studies in Iconoclasm* (Aldershot, UK and Burlington, VT: Ashgate, 2005).

30. On Cárdenas's anticlericalism, see Roberto Blancarte, "Aspectos internacionales del conflicto religioso mexicano en la década de los treinta," in Roberto Blancarte, ed., *Cultura e identidad nacional* (Mexico City: Fondo de Cultura Económica; Consejo Nacional para la Cultura y las Artes, 1994), 244, 258.

31. See Eduardo J. Correa, *El Partido Católico Nacional y sus directores. Explicación de su fracaso y deslinde de responsabilidades* (Mexico City: Fondo de Cultura Económica, 1991); and Alan Knight, *The Mexican Revolution. Vol. 2, Counter-Revolution and Reconstruction* (Cambridge: Cambridge University Press, 1986), 203.

32. The figure is from Jean Meyer, "Revolution and Reconstruction in the 1920s," in *Mexico since Independence*, ed. Leslie Bethell (Cambridge: Cambridge University Press, 1991), 214.

33. Blancarte, "Aspectos internacionales," 259. For a more detailed overview, see Roberto Blancarte, *Historia de la iglesia católica en México* (Mexico City: Fondo de Cultura Económica; El Colegio Mexiquense, 1992), chap. 1. For a revisionist approach, see Daniel Newcomer, *Reconciling Modernity: Urban State Formation in 1940s León, Mexico* (Lincoln: University of Nebraska Press, 2004).

34. Dudley Ankerson, *Agrarian Warlord: Saturnino Cedillo and the Mexican Revolution in San Luis Potosí* (DeKalb: University of Northern Illinois Press, 1984), 152.

35. John M. Ingham, *Mary, Michael, and Lucifer: Folk Catholicism in Central Mexico* (Austin: University of Texas Press, 1986), 48–49, 52; and Michael Tangeman, *Mexico at the Crossroads: Politics, the Church, and the Poor* (Maryknoll, NY: Orbis Books, 1995), 47.

36. *National Catholic Reporter*, June 20, 2003.

37. *La lucha entre el poder civil y el clero* (Mexico City: n.p., 1934), 8–9; also see, for example, J. M. Puig Casauranc, *La cuestión religiosa en relación con la educación pública en México* (Mexico City: Talleres Gráficos de la Nación, 1928).

38. Alfonso Toro, *La iglesia y el estado en México* (Mexico City: Talleres Gráficas de la Nación, 1927), 361.

39. Toro, *La Iglesia*, 5, 361–66.

40. Graham Greene, *The Lawless Roads* (London: Heinemann, 1960 [1939]), 11, and *The Power and the Glory* (London: Heinemann, 1940). Also see, for example, Evelyn Waugh, *Robbery under Law: The Mexican Object Lesson* (London: Chapman and Hall, 1939).

41. For a Mexican perspective on the role of the United States and France, see Blancarte, "Aspectos internacionales."

42. Francis Clement Kelley, *Blood-Drenched Altars. Mexican Study and Comment* (Milwaukee, WI: The Bruse Publishing Company, 1935), 394. Also see William F. Montavon, *Religious Crisis in Mexico* (Washington, DC: National Catholic Welfare Conference, 1926).

43. Wilfrid Parsons, *Mexican Martyrdom* (New York: The Macmillan Company, 1936), 295. On Parsons, see Jim Tuck, *The Holy War in Los Altos: A Regional Analysis of Mexico's Cristero Rebellion* (Tucson: University of Arizona Press, 1982), 217.

44. Ramón Jrade, "Inquiries into the Cristero Insurrection against the Mexican Revolution," *Latin American Research Review* 20 (1985): 55; and Antonio Ríus Facius, *La juventud católica y la revolución mejicana, 1910–1925* (Mexico City: Editorial Jus, 1963) and *Méjico cristero: Historia de la ACJM, 1925 a 1931* (Mexico City: Editorial Patria, 1966). For partisan regional accounts, see, for example, José Ignacio Gallegos C., *Apuntes para la historia de la persecución religiosa en Durango de 1926 a 1929* (Mexico City: Editorial Jus, 1965) and Enrique de Jesús Ochoa, *Los Cristeros del volcán de Colima*, 2 vols. (Mexico City: Editorial Jus, 1961).

45. For example, Nicolás Larín, *La rebelión de los cristeros (1926–1929)* (Mexico City: Era, 1968).

46. Jean Meyer, *La Cristiada*. Vol. 1, *La guerra de los cristeros* (Mexico City: Siglo Veintiuno, 1974), 399.

47. Jrade, "Inquiries," 55–58; Alicia Olivera Sedano de Bonfil, *Aspectos del conflicto religioso de 1926 a 1929: Sus antecedentes y consecuencias* (Mexico City: Instituto Nacional de Antropología e Historia, 1966); Robert E. Quirk, *The Mexican Revolution and the Catholic Church, 1910–1929* (Bloomington: Indiana University Press, 1973); and David C. Bailey, *¡Viva Cristo Rey! The Cristero Rebellion and the Church-State Conflict in Mexico* (Austin: University of Texas Press, 1974). Also see James W. Wilkie, "The Meaning of

the Cristero Religious War against the Mexican Revolution," *Journal of Church and State* 8 (1966). Servando Ortoll followed in the footsteps of these authors by examining the role of Catholic organizations such as the Caballeros de Colón, Acción Católica, and Sinarquismo in the church-state conflict and international politics. Ortoll examines these organizations from a top-down perspective as creations of the Mexican bishops, the Jesuits, or other members of the Catholic elite. See Servando Ortoll, "Catholic Organizations in Mexico's National Politics and International Diplomacy (1926–1942)" (Ph.D. diss., Columbia University, 1987). Some historians tried to move beyond the temporal confines of the Cristiada. Lyle C. Brown, for example, pointed out that the religious conflict did not end in 1929 but continued during the Maximato and even into the years of Lázaro Cárdenas, coming to an end only in 1938. Thus, an argument could be made that the "religious conflict" actually lasted for most of the revolutionary years, say, from 1914 to 1938 or 1940. Lyle C. Brown, "Mexican Church-State Relations, 1933–1940," *A Journal of Church and State* VI (1964).

48. Olivera Sedano, *Aspectos*, 253–54.

49. Quirk, *The Mexican Revolution*, 6.

50. *El movimiento cristero: Sociedad y conflicto en Los Altos de Jalisco* (Mexico City: Editorial Nueva Imagen, 1979), 223–32.

51. Andrés Fabregas, "Los Altos de Jalisco: Características generales," in Díaz y Rodríguez, *El movimiento cristero*, 66.

52. Fabregas, "Los Altos de Jalisco," 50, 53.

53. Fabregas, "Los Altos de Jalisco," 62.

54. Jrade, "Inquiries," 66. See also, by the same author, "Counterrevolution in Mexico: The Cristero Movement in Sociological and Historical Perspective" (Ph.D. diss., Brown University, 1980).

55. Luis González y González, *Pueblo en vilo: Microhistoria de San José de Gracia* (Mexico City: Fondo de Cultura Económica; SEP, 1984), 150.

56. Meyer, *La Cristiada*, vol. 1: 391.

57. Meyer, *La Cristiada*. Vol. 3, *Los cristeros* (Mexico City: Siglo Veintiuno, 1974), 322.

58. Meyer, *La Cristiada*, vol. 3: 387.

59. Meyer, *La Cristiada*, vol. 1: 385–86, 391; vol. 3: 321–22.

60. Jrade, "Inquiries," 62.

61. For example, Jesús Tapia Santamaría, *Campo religioso y evolución política en el Bajío zamorano* (Zamora: El Colegio de Michoacán, 1986); Guillermo Zermeño Padilla and Rubén V. Aguilar, eds., *Hacia una reinterpretación del sinarquismo actual: Notas y materiales para su estudio* (Mexico City: Universidad Iberoamericana, 1988); and Rubén Aguilar and Guillermo Zermeño Padilla, eds., *Religión, política, y sociedad: El sinarquismo y la iglesia en México* (Mexico City: Universidad Iberoamericana, 1992). Another French historian has followed in Meyer's footsteps, with important results for the study of Mexican Protestantism and Jacobinism. See Jean-Pierre Bastian, *Los disidentes: Sociedades protestantes y revolución en México 1872–1911* (Mexico City: Fondo de Cultura Económica, El Colegio de México, 1989) and "Jacobinismo y ruptura revolucionaria durante el porfiriato," *Mexican Studies/Estudios Mexicanos* 7 (1991).

62. Jim Tuck, in *The Holy War in Los Altos*, x, does follow Meyer's view of the Cristiada as a popular holy war, but only in Los Altos de Jalisco.

63. *The Great Rebellion: Mexico 1905–1924* (New York: W. W. Norton, 1980), 413.

64. See, for example, my *As if Jesus Walked on Earth. Cardenismo, Sonora, and the Mexican Revolution* (Wilmington, DE: Scholarly Resources, 1998); Jean Meyer, *La Cristiada en Colima* (Colima: Gobierno del Estado de Colima; Universidad de Colima; Consejo Nacional para la Cultura y las Artes, 1993); Yolanda Padilla Rangel, *El Catolicismo social y el movimiento Cristero en Aguascalientes* (Aguascalientes: Instituto Cultural de Aguascalientes, 1992); and Martelena Negrete, *Relaciones entre la iglesia y el estado en México 1930–1940* (Mexico City: El Colegio de México; Universidad Iberoamericana, 1988). Religiosity clearly fails to explain everything. On nonreligious motivations of the Cristiada in Michoacán, see the revisionist work of Matthew Butler, "The 'Liberal' Cristero: Ladislao Molina and the Cristero Rebellion in Michoacán, 1927–1929," *Journal of Latin American Studies* 31 (1999).

65. Jennie Purnell, *Popular Movements and State Formation in Revolutionary Mexico: The Agraristas and Cristeros of Michoacán* (Durham, NC: Duke University Press, 1999), 4.

66. Purnell, *Popular Movements*, 12.

67. Purnell, *Popular Movements*, 19.

68. Purnell, *Popular Movements*, 183.

69. Purnell, *Popular Movements*, 8.

70. Compare my *As if Jesus Walked on Earth*.

71. Marjorie Becker, *Setting the Virgin on Fire: Lázaro Cárdenas, Michoacán Peasants, and the Redemption of the Mexican Revolution* (Berkeley: University of California Press, 1995), 19.

72. Becker, *Setting the Virgin on Fire*, 160.

73. Christopher R. Boyer, "Old Loves, New Loyalties: Agrarismo in Michoacán, 1920–1928," *Hispanic American Historical Review* 78 (1998).

74. Christopher Boyer, *Becoming Campesinos: Politics, Identity, and Agrarian Struggle in Postrevolutionary Michoacán, 1920–1935* (Stanford, CA: Stanford University Press, 2002), 25.

75. Boyer, *Becoming Campesinos*, 234–35, 239.

76. Boyer, *Becoming Campesinos*, 161–66.

77. *Popular Piety and Political Identity in Mexico's Cristero Rebellion: Michoacán, 1927–29* (Oxford: Oxford University Press, 2004).

78. Manuel Ceballos Ramírez, *El Catolicismo social: Un tercero en discordia. Rerum Novarum, la cuestión social, y la movilización de los católicos mexicanos, 1891–1911* (Mexico City: El Colegio de México, 1991); Jorge Adame Goddard, *El pensamiento político de los católicos mexicanos 1867–1914* (Mexico City: UNAM, 1981); Randall D. Hanson, "The Day of Ideals: Catholic Social Action in the Age of the Mexican Revolution" (Ph.D. diss, Indiana University, 1994); and Roberto J. Blancarte, ed., *El pensamiento social de los católicos mexicanos* (Mexico City: Fondo de Cultura Económica, 1996).

79. Kristina Boylan, "They Were Always Doing Something: Catholic Women's Mobilization in Mexico in the 1930s," Paper presented at St. Antony's College, Oxford University, May 18, 1998. Also see her "Mexican Catholic Women's Activism,

1929–1940" (D. Phil. thesis, Oxford University, 2001) and "The Feminine 'Apostolate in Society' versus the Mexican State: The Unión Femenina Católica Mexicana, 1929–1940," in Margaret Power and Paola Bacchetta, eds., *Right Wing Women: From Conservatives to Extremists around the Globe* (New York: Routledge, 2002).

80. Boylan, "They Were Always Doing Something," 17, 26, 29.

81. *Teaching the Children of the Revolution: Church and State Education in Mexico City, 1917–1926* (Tucson: University of Arizona Press, 2003), xx, 194–95. Similarly, María Teresa Fernández Aceves has examined the activities of lay Catholic schoolteachers in Guadalajara. See her "'Science, Work, and Virtue': Lay Catholic Women Schoolteachers in Revolutionary Guadalajara, 1934–1942," paper presented at the Meeting of the Latin American Studies Association, Miami, 2000.

82. Peter Lester Reich, *Mexico's Hidden Revolution: The Catholic Church in Law and Politics since 1929* (Notre Dame, IN: University of Notre Dame Press, 1995), 1–2.

83. Adrian A. Bantjes Aróstegui, "Religión y revolución en México, 1929–1940," *Boletín. Fideicomiso Plutarco Elías Calles y Fernando Torreblanca* 15 (1994).

84. Franco Savarino, *Pueblos y nacionalismo, del régimen oligárquico a la sociedad de masas en Yucatán, 1894–1925* (Mexico City: Instituto Nacional de Estudios Históricos de la Revolución Mexicana, 1997). Also see Ben Fallaw, "Accomodation or Acrimony?: Church and State in Revolutionary and Postrevolutionary Yucatán, 1926–1940," paper prepared for the Congreso Internacional Iglesia y Estado en América Latina, Mérida, April 11–13, 2000.

85. For example, see Savarino, *Pueblos*, Carlos Martínez Assad, *El laboratorio de la revolución. El Tabasco garridista* (Mexico City: Siglo Veintiuno, 1979); Bantjes, *As If Jesus Walked on Earth*; Stephen E. Lewis, "Negotiating State and Nation: Local Responses to Federal Education in Chiapas, Mexico, since 1929" (Ph.D. diss. University of California at San Diego, 1998); John B. Williman, *La iglesia y el estado en Veracruz, 1840–1940* (Mexico City: SEP, 1976); and Julio Ríos, *Persecución religiosa y construcción de estado en Chiapas, 1930–1938* (Mexico City: CIDE, Documento de trabajo H-8, 2001).

86. Bantjes, "Idolatry and Iconoclasm."

87. See, for example, Zermeño P. and Aguilar, *Hacia una interpretación del Sinarquismo actual*, Rodolfo Morán Quiroz, ed., *La política y el cielo. Movimientos religiosos en el México contemporáneo* (Guadalajara: Editorial Universidad de Guadalajara, 1990); Assad, ed., *Religiosidad y política en México*; and Carlos Martínez Assad, ed., *A Dios lo que es de Dios* (Mexico City: Aguilar, 1995). On church-state relations during the '30s, see Negrete, *Relaciones*, and for the post-1929 period, Blancarte, *Historia de la iglesia*, and Martín de la Rosa and Charles A. Reilly, eds., *Religión y política en México* (Mexico City: Siglo XXI, 1985).

88. *La batalla por el espíritu. El movimiento sinarquista en el Bajío (1932–1951)* (Mexico City: Consejo Nacional para la Cultura y las Artes, 1992), 2:314, 321; and María Alicia Puente de Guzmán, "Entre la sujeción y la autonomía: La iglesia en el movimiento cristero," in María Alicia Puente Lutteroth, ed., *Historia mínima de la iglesia en México* (Mexico City: Jus, CEHILA, 1993). Unfortunately, I was unable to consult her "Movimiento cristero: Afirmación y fisura de identidades. Un acercamiento panorámico al conflicto sociorreligioso en México de 1926–1929" (Ph.D. diss.,

CIESAS, Mexico, 1993). Moisés González Navarro has collected a wealth of fascinating (yet often chaotically organized) information on a poorly understood revolutionary group, the Masons. See his *Cristeros y agraristas en Jalisco*, 5 vols. (Mexico City: El Colegio de México, 2000–2003). On Sinarquismo, compare Newcomer, *Reconciling Modernity*.

89. A recent example of the continued Catholic fascination with the religious conflict, and especially the Cristiada, is Consuelo Reguer's massive *Dios y mi derecho*, 4 vols. (Mexico City: Editorial Jus, 1997). However, critical studies of the role of clergy and believers in the Cristiada are now being published. See, for example, Fernando M. González, *Matar y morir por Cristo rey. Aspectos de la Cristiada* (Mexico City: Plaza y Valdés; Instituto de Investigaciones Sociales, UNAM, 2001).

90. Gilbert M. Joseph and Daniel Nugent, eds., *Everyday Forms of State Formation: Revolution and the Negotiation of Rule in Modern Mexico* (Durham, NC: Duke University Press, 1994); and Gilbert M. Joseph, Anne Rubinstein, and Eric Zolov, eds., *Fragments of a Golden Age: The Politics of Culture in Mexico since 1940* (Durham, NC: Duke University Press, 2001).

91. See, for example, Luis Enrique Murillo, "The Politics of the Miraculous: Popular Religious Practice in Porfirian Michoacán, 1876–1910" (Ph.D. diss., University of California, San Diego, 2002); and Eddie Wright-Rios, "Piety and Progress: Vision, Shrine, and Society in Oaxaca, 1887–1934 (Ph.D. diss., University of California, San Diego, 2004).

92. See Paul J. Vanderwood, *The Power of God against the Guns of Government: Religious Upheaval in Mexico at the Turn of the Nineteenth Century* (Stanford, CA: Stanford University Press, 1998) as well as his recent *Juan Soldado: Rapist, Murderer, Martyr, Saint* (Durham, NC: Duke University Press, 2004), which I was unable to consult for this review, and Linda Hall, *Mary, Mother and Warrior: The Virgin in Spain and the Americas* (Austin: University of Texas Press, 2004).

93. See notes 79, 91, and 92. See in particular Matthew Butler, *Popular Piety and Political Identity in Mexico's Cristero Rebellion: Michoacán, 1927–1929* (Oxford and New York: Published for the British Academy by Oxford University Press, 2004), especially chap. 4. A Mexican example is José Velasco Toro, *De la historia al mito: Mentalidad y culto en el Santuario de Otatitlán* (Xalapa: Instituto Veracruzano de Cultura, 2000).

94. See, for example, Peter S. Cahn, *All Religions are Good in Tzintzuntzan: Evangelicals in Catholic Mexico* (Austin: University of Texas Press, 2003); and, for a general overview, Cristián Parker, *Otra lógica en América Latina: Religión popular y modernización capitalista* (Santiago: Fondo de Cultura Económica, 1993).

95. See Lynn Stephen and James Dow, eds., *Class, Politics, and Popular Religion in Mexico and Central America* (Washington, DC: Society for Latin American Anthropology, 1990).

96. Caroline Ford, "Religion and Popular Culture in Modern Europe," *Journal of Modern History* 65 (1993).

97. For example at the 1999 conference of the American Historical Association during a session on Vanderwood's *The Power of God*.

98. Paul Stoller, "Rationality," in Mark C. Taylor, ed., *Critical Terms for Religious Studies* (Chicago: University of Chicago Press, 1998).

99. *How Natives Think. About Captain Cook, For Example* (Chicago: University of Chicago Press, 1995), 14.

100. *The Apotheosis of Captain Cook: European Mythmaking in the Pacific* (Princeton, NJ: Princeton University Press, 1992), 19.

101. Cited in Mark C. Taylor, "Introduction," in Taylor, ed., *Critical Terms for Religious Studies*, 9.

102. Taylor, *Magistrates of the Sacred*, 47.

103. Alan Knight, "Rethinking the Tomóchic Rebellion," *Mexican Studies/Estudios Mexicanos* 15 (1999).

104. For a critique of the analysis of religion in recent historiography, see Paul Vanderwood, "Religion: Official, Popular, and Otherwise," *Mexican Studies/Estudios Mexicanos* 16 (2000).

105. For a critical discussion, see Jorge Larrain, *Identity and Modernity in Latin America* (Cambridge: Polity Press, 2000), 150–65; and Parker, *Otra lógica*. A related, and markedly progressive, position is held by Enrique Dussel, who argues that a deep-rooted, autonomous popular religion is a key source of liberation for Latin America's masses. See his "Popular Religion as Oppression and Liberation: Hypotheses on its Past and Present in Latin America," in Norbert Grienacher and Norbert Mette, eds., *Popular Religion* (Edinburgh: T. & T. Clark Ltd., 1986).

106. Blancarte, "Iglesia y Estado," 49, 53; and Larrain, *Identity*, 158–65.

107. Peter van der Veer and Hartmut Lehmann, "Introduction," in Peter van der Veer and Hartmut Lehmann, eds., *Nation and Religion. Perspectives on Europe and Asia* (Princeton, NJ: Princeton University Press, 1999).

108. Talal Asad, "Religion, Nation-State, Secularism," in van der Veer and Lehmann, eds., *Nation and Religion*, 192. For a related argument on Mexico, see Voekel, *Alone before God*.

Suggested Further Reading

Adame Goddard, Jorge. *El pensamiento político y social de los católicos mexicanos, 1867–1914*. Mexico: UNAM, 1981.

Altamirano, Ignacio Manuel. *Zarco; y La Navidad en las montañas*. Intro. María del Carmen Millán. Mexico: Ed. Porrúa, 1986.

Arrom, Silvia Marina. *Women of Mexico City, 1790–1857*. Stanford, CA: Stanford University Press, 1985.

Asad, Talal. *Formations of the Secular: Christianity, Islam, Modernity*. Stanford, CA: Stanford University Press, 2003.

Bailey, David C. *¡Viva Cristo Rey! The Cristero Rebellion and the Church-State Conflict in Mexico*. Austin: University of Texas Press, 1974.

Bantjes, Adrian. *As if Jesus Walked on Earth. Cardenismo, Sonora, and the Mexican Revolution*. Wilmington, DE: Scholarly Resources, 1998.

———. "Idolatry and Iconoclasm in Revolutionary Mexico: The De-Christianization Campaigns, 1929–1940." *Mexican Studies/Estudios Mexicanos* 13 (1997).

Becker, Marjorie. *Setting the Virgin on Fire. Lázaro Cárdenas, Michoacán Peasants, and the Redemption of the Mexican Revolution*. Berkeley: University of California Press, 1995.

Beezley, William H. *Judas at the Jockey Club and Other Episodes of Porfirian Mexico*. 2nd edition. Lincoln: University of Nebraska Press, 2004.

Blancarte, Roberto, ed. *Cultura e identidad nacional*. Mexico: Fondo de Cultura Económica; Consejo Nacional para la Cultura y las Artes, 1994.

Brading, D. A. *Mexican Phoenix. Our Lady of Guadalupe: Image and Tradition across Five Centuries*. Cambridge: Cambridge University Press, 2001.

Butler, Matthew. *Popular Piety and Political Identity in Mexico's Cristero Rebellion: Michoacán, 1927–29*. Oxford: Oxford University Press, 2004.

Cahn, Peter S. *All Religions are Good in Tzintzuntzan: Evangelicals in Catholic Mexico*. Austin: University of Texas Press, 2003.

Calderón de la Barca, Fanny. *Life in Mexico*. Berkeley: University of California Press, 1982.

Camp, Roderic Ai. *Crossing Swords: Politics and Religion in Mexico*. New York: Oxford University Press, 1997.

Cash, Marie Romero. *Santos: Enduring Images of Northern New Mexican Village Churches.* Boulder: University of Colorado Press, 2003.

Castañeda, Jorge. *Perpetuating Power: How Mexican Presidents Were Chosen.* Trans. Padraic Arthur Smithies. New York: The New Press, 2001.

Ceballos Ramírez, Manuel. *El catolicismo social: Un tercero en discordia:* Rerum Novarum, *la "cuestión social" y la movilización de los católicos mexicanos (1891–1911).* Mexico: El Colegio de México, 1991.

Chassen-López, Francie R. *From Liberal to Revolutionary Oaxaca: The View from the South, Mexico, 1867–1911.* State College, PA: Pennsylvania State University Press, 2005.

Chowning, Margaret. *Rebellious Nuns: The Troubled History of a Mexican Convent, 1752–1863.* Oxford: Oxford University Press, 2005.

Christian, William A., Jr. *Local Religion in Sixteenth-Century Spain.* Princeton, NJ: Princeton University Press, 1981.

———. *Visionaries: The Spanish Republic and the Reign of Christ.* Berkeley: University of California Press, 1999.

Connaughton, Brian. *Clerical Ideology in a Revolutionary Age: The Guadalajara Church and the Idea of the Mexican Nation (1788–1853).* Trans. Mark Alan Healey. Calgary: University of Calgary Press, 2003.

Cortazar, Alejandro. *Reforma, novela y nación: México en el siglo XIX.* Puebla: Benemérita Universidad Autónoma de Puebla, 2006.

Cosío Villegas, Daniel. *Historia moderna de México.* 9 vols. Mexico: Editorial Hermes [c. 1955–1972].

Cuevas, Mariano. *Historia de la iglesia en México.* 5 vols. El Paso: Ed. "Revista Católica," 1928.

Díaz Covarrubias, Juan. *El diablo en México: Novela de costumbres.* Mexico: Ed. Castro, 1858.

Fuentes, Carlos. *The Death of Artemio Cruz.* Trans. Alfred Mac Adam. New York: Farrar, Straus and Giroux, 1991.

González, Fernando M. *Matar y morir por Cristo Rey: Aspectos de la cristiada.* Mexico: Plaza y Valdés; UNAM; Instituto de Investigaciones Sociales, 2001.

González Navarro, Moisés. *Cristeros y agraristas en Jalisco.* 5 vols. Mexico: El Colegio de México, 2000–2003.

González y González, Luis. *San José de Gracia: Mexican Village in Transition.* Trans. John Upton. Austin: University of Texas Press, 1972.

Greenberg, James. *Blood Ties: Life and Violence in Rural Mexico.* Tucson: University of Arizona Press, 1989.

Greene, Graham. *The Power and the Glory.* London: Heinemann, 1940.

Hale, Charles A. *Mexican Liberalism in the Age of Mora, 1821–1853.* New Haven, CT: Yale University Press, 1968.

Hamill, Hugh M. *The Hidalgo Revolt: Prelude to Mexican Independence.* Gainesville: University of Florida Press, 1966.

Hamnett, Brian. *Juárez.* New York: Longman, 1994.

Ingham, John M. *Mary, Michael, and Lucifer: Folk Catholicism in Central Mexico.* Austin: University of Texas Press, 1986.

Ivereigh, Austen, ed. *The Politics of Religion in an Age of Revival: Studies in Nineteenth-Century Europe and Latin America.* London: Institute of Latin American Studies, 2000.

Joseph, Gilbert, and Timothy J. Henderson, eds. *The Mexico Reader: History, Culture, Politics.* Durham, NC: Duke University Press, 2003.

———, and Daniel Nugent, eds. *Everyday Forms of State Formation: Revolution and the Negotiation of Rule in Modern Mexico.* Durham, NC: Duke University Press, 1994.

Knab, Timothy J. *Mad Jesus: The Final Testament of a Huichol Messiah from Northwest Mexico.* Albuquerque: University of New Mexico Press, 2004.

Knight, Alan. *The Mexican Revolution.* 2 vols. Cambridge: Cambridge University Press, 1986.

Knowlton, Robert J. *Church Property and the Mexican Reform, 1856–1910.* De Kalb: Northern Illinois University Press, 1976.

Krauze, Enrique. *Mexico: Biography of Power. A History of Modern Mexico, 1810–1996.* Trans. Hank Heifetz. New York: Harper Collins, 1997.

Lafaye, Jacques. *Quetzalcoatl and Guadalupe: The Formation of Mexican National Consciousness, 1531–1813.* Chicago: University of Chicago Press, 1976.

Lewis, Stephen, and Mary Kay Vaughan, eds. *The Eagle and the Virgin: National Identity, Memory and Utopia in Mexico, 1920–1940.* Durham, NC: Duke University Press, 2005.

Lomnitz-Alder, Claudio. *Death and the Idea of Mexico.* New York: Zone Books; distributed by MIT Press, 2005.

———. *Deep Mexico, Silent Mexico: An Anthropology of Nationalism.* Minneapolis: University of Minnesota Press, 2001.

Martínez Assad, Carlos. *El laboratorio de la revolución. El Tabasco garridista.* Mexico: Siglo Veintiuno, 1979.

———, ed. *Religiosidad y política en México.* Mexico: Universidad Iberoamericana, 1992.

Matute, Álvaro, Evelia Trejo, and Brian Connaughton, eds. *Estado, iglesia y sociedad en México, siglo XIX.* Mexico: Facultad de Filosofía y Letras, UNAM; Editorial Porrúa, 1995.

Meyer, Jean A. *The Cristero Rebellion: The Mexican People between Church and State, 1926–1929.* Trans. Richard Southern. Cambridge: Cambridge University Press, 1976.

Monsiváis, Carlos. *Mexican Postcards.* Ed., trans., and intro. by John Kraniauskas. New York: Verso, 1997.

Niemeyer, E. V., Jr. *Revolution at Querétaro. The Mexican Constitutional Convention of 1916–1917.* Austin: University of Texas Press, 1974.

O'Dougherty Madrazo, Laura. *De urnas y sotanas: El Partido Católico Nacional en Jalisco.* Mexico: CONACULTA, 2001.

Orsi, Robert. *Thank You, St. Jude: Women's Devotion to the Patron Saint of Hopeless Causes.* New Haven, CT: Yale University Press, 1996.

Overmyer-Velázquez, Mark. *Visions of the Emerald City: Modernity, Tradition, and the Formation of Porfirian Oaxaca, Mexico.* Durham, NC: Duke University Press, 2006.

Paz, Octavio. *Labyrinth of Solitude: Life and Thought in Mexico.* Trans. Lysander Kemp. New York: Grove Press, 1962.

Poole, Stafford. *Our Lady of Guadalupe: The Origins and Sources of a Mexican National Symbol, 1531–1797*. Tucson: University of Arizona Press, 1996.

Purnell, Jennie. *Popular Movements and State Formation in Revolutionary Mexico. The Agraristas and Cristeros of Michoacán*. Durham, NC: Duke University Press, 1999.

Quiñones, Sam. *True Tales from Another Mexico: The Lynch Mob, the Popsicle Kings, Chalino, and the Bronx*. Albuquerque: University of New Mexico Press, 2001.

Quirk, Robert E. *The Mexican Revolution and the Catholic Church, 1910–1929*. Bloomington: Indiana University Press, 1973.

Reardon, Bernard M. G. *Religion in the Age of Romanticism. Studies in the Early Nineteenth Century Thought*. Cambridge: Cambridge University Press, 1985.

Redfield, Robert. *Tepoztlán: A Mexican Village*. Chicago: University of Chicago Press, 1930.

Reich, Peter Lester. *Mexico's Hidden Revolution: The Catholic Church in Law and Politics since 1929*. Notre Dame, IN: University of Notre Dame Press, 1995.

Rugeley, Terry. *Of Wonders and Wise Men: Religion and Popular Cultures in Southeast Mexico*. Austin: University of Texas Press, 2001.

Rulfo, Juan. *Pedro Páramo*. Trans. Margaret Sayers Peden. Foreword by Susan Sontag. New York: Grove Press, 1994.

Sawatzky, Harry Leonard. *They Sought a Country: Mennonite Colonization in Mexico*. Berkeley: University of California Press, 1971.

Schaefer, Stacy B., and Peter T. Furst, eds. *People of the Peyote: Huichol Indian History, Religion, and Survival*. Albuquerque: University of New Mexico Press, 1996.

Shorris, Earl. *The Life and Times of Mexico*. New York: W. W. Norton, 2004.

Sierra, Justo. *Mexico, Its Social Evolution . . .* Trans. G. Sentiñón. 2 vols. Mexico: J. Ballescá and Co., 1900–4.

Sinkin, Richard N. *The Mexican Reformation: 1855–1876: A Study in Liberal Nation-Building*. Austin: Institute of Latin American Studies, University of Texas at Austin; distributed by University of Texas Press, c. 1979.

Taylor, Mark C., ed. *Critical Terms for Religious Studies*. Chicago: University of Chicago Press, 1998.

Traffano, Daniela. *Indios, curas y nación. La sociedad indígena frente a un proceso de secularización. Oaxaca, siglo XIX*. Torino: Otto Editores, 2001.

Tuck, Jim. *The Holy War in Los Altos. A Regional Analysis of Mexico's Cristero Rebellion*. Tucson: University of Arizona Press, 1982.

Vanderwood, Paul J. *Juan Soldado: Rapist, Murderer, Martyr, Saint*. Durham, NC: Duke University Press, 2004.

———. *The Power of God against the Guns of Government: Religious Upheaval in Mexico at the Turn of the Nineteenth Century*. Stanford, CA: Stanford University Press, 1998.

———. "Religion: Official, Popular, and Otherwise." *Mexican Studies/Estudios Mexicanos* 16 (2000).

Van Young, Eric. *The Other Rebellion: Popular Violence, Ideology, and the Mexican Struggle for Independence, 1810–1821*. Stanford, CA: Stanford University Press, 2001.

Voekel, Pamela. *Alone before God. The Religious Origins of Modernity in Mexico*. Durham, NC: Duke University Press, 2003.

Yáñez, Agustín. *The Edge of the Storm*. Trans. Ethel Brinton. Illustrated by Julio Prieto. Austin: University of Texas Press, 1963.

Zarur, Elizabeth Netto Calil, and Charles Muir Lovell, eds. *Art and Faith in Mexico: The Nineteenth-Century Retablo Tradition*. Albuquerque: University of New Mexico Press, 2001.

Index

About the Contributors

Silvia Marina Arrom (Ph.D., Stanford University) is Jane's Professor of Latin American studies at Brandeis University. Her publications include *The Women of Mexico City, 1790–1857* (1985), *Containing the Poor: The Mexico City Poor House, 1774–1871* (2000), and *Riots in the Cities: Popular Politics and the Urban Poor in Latin America, 1765–1910* (edited with Servando Ortoll, 1996).

Adrian Bantjes (Ph.D., University of Texas, Austin) is associate professor of Latin American history at the University of Wyoming. He is author of *As if Jesus Walked on Earth: Cardenismo, Sonora, and the Mexican Revolution* (1998) and has published a series of articles on Mexican politics, religion, and cultural revolution, including, most recently, "The War against the Idols: The Meanings of Iconoclasm in Post-Revolutionary Mexico, 1910–40," in Anne McClennan and Jeffrey Johnson, eds., *Negating the Image: Case Studies in Iconoclasm* (2005), and "Saints, Sinners and State Formation: Local Religion and Cultural Revolution in Mexico," in Stephen Lewis and Mary Kay Vaughan, eds., *The Eagle and the Virgin: Nation and Cultural Revolution in Mexico, 1920–1940* (2006). He is currently completing a monograph on de-Christianization campaigns and iconoclasm in revolutionary Mexico.

Alejandro Cortazar (Ph.D., University of Iowa) is associate professor of Spanish at Louisiana State University. He teaches nineteenth- and twentieth-century Latin American literature, civilization, and culture and focuses his research on nation-state building and cultural identity formations. His book *Reforma, novela y nación: México en el siglo XIX* was published in 2006.

Jason Dormady (Ph.D. candidate, University of California, Santa Barbara) is a former farmer, journalist, and graphic artist. He is currently a Regents Fellow at the University of California at Santa Barbara. His dissertation research investigates intentional religious communities (Pentecostal, Mormon, and Catholic) in Mexico between 1920 and 1964.

Martin Austin Nesvig (Ph.D., Yale University) is assistant professor of history at the University of Miami. He is editor of *Local Religion in Colonial Mexico* (2006) and author of numerous scholarly articles in journals, including the *Hispanic American Historical Review*, *Mexican Studies/Estudios Mexicanos*, *Tzintzun*, *Boletín del Archivo General de la Nación*, and *Church History*. His current research focuses on the Mexican Inquisition and processes of censorship, the Atlantic book trade, and early modern theology. He is at work on a monograph, *The World of the Censors in Early Mexico*.

Matthew D. O'Hara (Ph.D., University of California, San Diego) is assistant professor of history at the University of California, Santa Cruz. His research has been funded by the National Endowment for the Humanities, the Rockefeller Foundation, the Andrew W. Mellon Foundation, Spain's Ministry of Culture, and the Tinker Foundation. O'Hara is completing a book manuscript titled *A Flock Divided: Race, Religion and Politics in Mexico (1749–1857)*. He is also coeditor (with Andrew Fisher) of a forthcoming collection of essays titled *Imperial Subjects: Race and Identity in Colonial Latin America*.

Mark Overmyer-Velázquez (Ph.D., Yale University) is assistant professor of history at the University of Connecticut and author of *Visions of the Emerald City: Modernity, Tradition and the Formation of Porfirian Oaxaca, Mexico* (2006). The book and related articles analyze how elites (city officials and church leaders) and commoners (city artisans and female sex workers) mobilized visual cultures to construct and experience the mutually defining processes of modernity and tradition in late nineteenth- and early twentieth-century Mexico. Supported by an SSRC International Migration Studies Grant, he has initiated research on a second book project, "'Bleeding Mexico White': Race, Nation, and the History of Mexico-U.S. Migration," which examines the binational twentieth-century history of Mexican migration.

Daniela Traffano (Ph.D., El Colegio de México) is a research fellow at CIESAS in Oaxaca, Mexico. She is author of *Indios, curas y nación. La sociedad indígena frente a un proceso de secularización. Oaxaca, siglo XIX* (2001).

Paul J. Vanderwood (Ph.D., University of Texas, Austin) is emeritus professor of Mexican history at San Diego State University. He has written ten books and numerous articles mainly on late nineteenth- and early twentieth-century Mexico. His latest books are the award-winning *The Power of God* *against the Guns of Government: Religious Upheaval in Mexico at the Turn of the Nineteenth Century* (1998) and *Juan Soldado: Rapist, Murderer, Martyr, Saint* (2004). He is currently working on the world-renowned casino/horse racing/gaming resort called Agua Caliente, which flourished in Tijuana around 1930, attracting kings, maharajahs, ambassadors, financiers, movie stars, and the Mob.

Pamela Voekel (Ph.D., University of Texas, Austin) teaches at the University of Georgia in Athens. She is the author of *Alone before God: The Religious Origins of Modernity in Mexico* and is currently at work on a second book on piety, liberalism, gender, and peasant protest in nineteenth-century Mexico. She and her friend Elliott Young are the cofounders of the Tepoztlan Institute for the Transnational History of the Americas, an annual weeklong seminar held in Tepoztlan, Morelos, Mexico.

Edward Wright-Rios (Ph.D., University of California, San Diego) is assistant professor of history at Vanderbilt University. Recent publications include "Indian Saints and Nation-States," in *Mexican Studies/Estudios Mexicanos*, and a forthcoming article, "Envisioning Mexico's Catholic Resurgence," in *Past and Present*. He is currently working on a book under the working title "Revolutions in Mexican Catholicism."